Power BI Data Modeling

Build Interactive Visualizations, Learn DAX, Power Query, and Develop BI Models

Nisal Mihiranga

bpb

www.bpbonline.com

FIRST EDITION 2022
Copyright © BPB Publications, India
ISBN: 978-93-89328-837

All Rights Reserved. No part of this publication may be reproduced, distributed or transmitted in any form or by any means or stored in a database or retrieval system, without the prior written permission of the publisher with the exception to the program listings which may be entered, stored and executed in a computer system, but they can not be reproduced by the means of publication, photocopy, recording, or by any electronic and mechanical means.

LIMITS OF LIABILITY AND DISCLAIMER OF WARRANTY

The information contained in this book is true to correct and the best of author's and publisher's knowledge. The author has made every effort to ensure the accuracy of these publications, but publisher cannot be held responsible for any loss or damage arising from any information in this book.

All trademarks referred to in the book are acknowledged as properties of their respective owners but BPB Publications cannot guarantee the accuracy of this information.

To View Complete
BPB Publications Catalogue
Scan the QR Code:

www.bpbonline.com

Dedicated to

Ruwanthi Abeywickrama

My wife, who supports every possible way throughout my journey

About the Author

Nisal Mihiranga is a seasoned technical consultant who has spent the last ten years designing and implementing business intelligence solutions for customers and partners. Nisal has given talks at major IT conferences such as SQL Saturday, Singapore Datacamp, and user group meetings throughout his career. He has also worked at ZoneTwentyFourSeven, Virtusa, and Fortude as an engineering consultant and in training and mentoring roles.

It was back in 2017 that Nisal got his taste for writing when he was started writing blog posts and technical articles. This combining with his passion for the Power BI .tool led him to write this book.

Outside work, Nisal volunteers his spare time as a tech community contributor, helping, organizing events, and mentoring young people in taking up careers in technology.

About the Reviewer

Dinesh Asanka has 20+ years of experience in the areas of Data. Dinesh has experienced in the areas of Machine Learning, Data Mining, Data Warehousing and Database Administration. He has obtained MPhil in data warehousing. He is a frequent columnist in popular web sites. Currently he is a Senior Lecturer at University of Kelaniya Sri Lanka.

Acknowledgement

There are a few people I want to thank for the continued and ongoing support they have given me during the writing of this book. First and foremost, I would like to thank my wife for putting up with me while I was spending many weekends and evenings on writing—I could have never completed this book without her support.

This book wouldn't have happened if I hadn't had great support from Dinesh Asanka who did the technical review for this book. My gratitude goes to him and all who supported me to make this real.

Finally, I would like to thank BPB Publications for giving me this opportunity to write my first book for them.

Preface

When compared to the traditional distribution of business intelligence solutions, self-service business intelligence tools are a relatively new invention. In the past, data warehouses were built, and a development team developed a web-based application with an agreed-upon set of visuals to offer insights. With the latest and greatest self-service business intelligence products, the BI delivery paradigm has been revolutionized.

This move was made to solve a number of significant challenges, including how to undertake ad-hoc analysis, how to lessen reliance on the software application development team, and how the new technology adds value in terms of insight generation. There are various types of users in an organization, including top-level business users with little programming experience, middle-layer operational users, and technical users such as software engineers, data scientists, and data analysts. The difficulty here is to figure out how to provide a single tool that can help all of the users described above. This is where a product like Power BI really benefits.

The majority of us are familiar with spreadsheet programs such as Microsoft Excel, Lotus 123, Google Sheets, and Open Office. The most of the functionalities and look and feel of the Power BI software are inherited from Microsoft Excel. As a result, even the most inexperienced user can quickly learn how to use the technology.

Power BI is a product that has been on the market since mid-2014. It had swiftly grown since then, with many new features added to the broader ecosystem. There is strong community support, and the product has recently become very popular among us. There are numerous online tools for learning how to use Power BI. When compared to other tools, it is quite simple and straightforward. The true gold, though, is learning how to accurately design data models that work effectively even as data accumulates over time. This book is all about it.

The main purpose of this book is to give you the knowledge and skills you need to implement Power BI data models in your own scenarios. This book includes real-world examples that demonstrate how to install, configure, and design Power BI reports, as well as deploy and maintain Power BI solutions. You will learn the following during the course of this book's 19 chapters:

Chapter 1 introduces the Power BI to the readers. It mainly talks about the history of the Power BI and the journey so far it came as a BI product. This chapter also focused to mention the position of Power BI as a BI tool comparing other tools in the market.

Chapter 2 discusses the different products in the Power BI ecosystem and how each connects each other to provide end-to-end self-service BI solutions for all types of users.

Chapter 3 with this chapter, you have installed Power BI desktop, this chapter gives you a guided tour of how to connect into data source using Power BI desktop

Chapter 4 is a chapter that discusses, how to turn the data into quick visuals with minimum steps. The focus was to give a quick guide for reporting

Chapter 5 is also a key chapter that discusses, in-depth, dimensional modeling and why we need to create data models. This also covers some data warehousing key elements.

Chapter 6 describes how to connect Power BI with relational databases like Microsoft SQL Server. Predominantly talked about connection types and when to use it.

Chapter 7 introduces the data transformation with Power Query. This covers some key elements of data cleansing techniques and transformations. It is vital to have clean data in data projects.

Chapter 8 describes how to create data models through creating relationships.

Chapter 9 discussed DAX query language and key elements like calculated columns, calculated measures, and hierarchies.

Chapter 10 describes how to deliver the insightful report in Power BI. details about key features in data visualization you can find in Power BI.

Chapter 11 describes how to implement row-level security in Power BI.

Chapter 12 discusses how to use Calculation Groups as a feature to reduce the complexity of Power BI data models.

Chapter 13 discusses about AI features offered in Power BI and its usage.

Chapter 14 When you are having large datasets its impossible to reduce the data refresh time. In this chapter discussed about how Incremental refresh feature helps to reduce the data refresh time.

Chapter 15 Big datasets its a norm in modern era. Power BI has techniques to cater big data requirements. Discusses aggregations and composite models.

Chapter 16 Dataflows is another cool feature in Power BI. This chapter discusses how to create dataflows and collaborate.

Chapter 17 discusses how to optimize DAX queries.

Chapter 18 discusses how to collaborate the Power BI workloads in your organization.

Chapter 19 It is important to improve the performance in your models This chapter discusses how to improve performance.

Code Bundle and Coloured Images

Please follow the link to download the
Code Bundle and the *Coloured Images* of the book:

https://rebrand.ly/d05c7e

The code bundle for the book is also hosted on GitHub at **https://github.com/bpbpublications/Power-BI-Data-Modeling**. In case there's an update to the code, it will be updated on the existing GitHub repository.

We have code bundles from our rich catalogue of books and videos available at **https://github.com/bpbpublications**. Check them out!

Errata

We take immense pride in our work at BPB Publications and follow best practices to ensure the accuracy of our content to provide with an indulging reading experience to our subscribers. Our readers are our mirrors, and we use their inputs to reflect and improve upon human errors, if any, that may have occurred during the publishing processes involved. To let us maintain the quality and help us reach out to any readers who might be having difficulties due to any unforeseen errors, please write to us at :

errata@bpbonline.com

Your support, suggestions and feedbacks are highly appreciated by the BPB Publications' Family.

Did you know that BPB offers eBook versions of every book published, with PDF and ePub files available? You can upgrade to the eBook version at www.bpbonline.com and as a print book customer, you are entitled to a discount on the eBook copy. Get in touch with us at :

business@bpbonline.com for more details.

At **www.bpbonline.com**, you can also read a collection of free technical articles, sign up for a range of free newsletters, and receive exclusive discounts and offers on BPB books and eBooks.

Piracy

If you come across any illegal copies of our works in any form on the internet, we would be grateful if you would provide us with the location address or website name. Please contact us at **business@bpbonline.com** with a link to the material.

If you are interested in becoming an author

If there is a topic that you have expertise in, and you are interested in either writing or contributing to a book, please visit **www.bpbonline.com**. We have worked with thousands of developers and tech professionals, just like you, to help them share their insights with the global tech community. You can make a general application, apply for a specific hot topic that we are recruiting an author for, or submit your own idea.

Reviews

Please leave a review. Once you have read and used this book, why not leave a review on the site that you purchased it from? Potential readers can then see and use your unbiased opinion to make purchase decisions. We at BPB can understand what you think about our products, and our authors can see your feedback on their book. Thank you!

For more information about BPB, please visit **www.bpbonline.com**.

Table of Contents

1. **Introducing Microsoft Power BI** 1
   Structure 1
   Objective 2
   Business intelligence 2
       History of Business Intelligence 4
           Business Intelligence process 4
           Self-service BI 5
   Introducing Power BI 6
       Components in Power BI 7
       Why does Power BI stand out from other BI tools in the market? 9
   Conclusion 11
   Questions 12
       Answers 12

2. **Power BI Ecosystem** 13
   Structure 13
   Objectives 13
   Power BI ecosystem 14
       Power BI desktop 14
       Power BI service 25
       Power BI mobile 27
   Conclusion 29
   Questions 29
       Answers 30

3. **Getting Started with Power BI and Connect with Data** 31
   Structure 31
   Objective 31
   Get data 32
   Power BI connectors 32

Connection types	*33*
Conclusion	41
Questions	42
Answers	*42*

4. My First Power BI Report 43
Structure	43
Objective	43
Download the demo materials	*44*
Load data into Power BI	44
Data cleansing and blending	*49*
Create product hierarchy	54
Create calculations	*56*
Data visualizing	56
Add a map visual	61
Add a clustered column chart	61
Add a matrix visual	62
Cross filtering	64
Drill-down	64
Add a slicer	65
Conclusion	67
Questions	68
Answers	*68*

5. Introducing BI Building Blocks: Dimensional Modeling Concepts 69
Structure	69
Objective	69
What is data modeling, and why?	70
Classic BI approach	*70*
Modern self-service BI approach	72
End-to-end BI with Microsoft Power BI	72
Data warehouse	73
Bus matrix architecture	*74*

  Fact tables 75
  Dimension tables 75
  Granularities 76
   Star schema 76
   Snowflake schema 77
 Conclusion 78
 Questions 79
  Answers 79

6. Get Data from Relational Databases 81
 Structure 81
 Objective 81
 Relational database connectors 82
  Getting data with SQL Server database 83
 Conclusion 93
 Questions 93

7. Cleansing, Blending, and Transforming Data Using Power Query 95
 Structure 95
 Objective 96
 Introducing Power Query 96
  Business scenario 96
   Connect to the database and extract tables 97
 Data cleansing 97
  Work with budget data 106
 Conclusion 109
 Questions 109
  Answer 109

8. Build Relationships 111
 Structure 111
 Objective 111
 Relationships in Power BI 112

Methods of creating relationships *113*
Demystify relationships in Power BI *116*
    Select cardinality of a relationship *117*
    Select cross filter direction *119*
    Active and inactive relationships *122*
Conclusion 123
Questions 124

9. Introducing DAX, Calculated Columns, Calculated Measures, and Hierarchies 125
Structure 125
Objective 126
Calculations in Power BI 126
    Calculated columns *127*
    Calculated measures *129*
    Calculated tables *131*
Hierarchies *134*
Conclusion 135
Questions 136

10. Creating Insightful Reports Using Visualization Techniques 137
Structure 137
Objective 138
Data visualization practices 138
    Designing the report *139*
        Filtrations *140*
        Use slicers in the report *141*
        Cross-filtering *142*
        Drill-down visuals *143*
        Drill-through visuals *145*
        Theming *148*
        Mobile layout *149*
Conclusion 150

Questions 150

11. Row-Level Security in Power BI 151
Structure 151
Objective 151
Security overview 152
    Static row-level security—role-based 152
        Creating roles 154
        How to test raw-level security? 156
        Dynamic row-level security 160
Conclusion 163
Questions 163

12. Calculation Groups in Power BI 165
Structure 165
Objective 165
Calculation groups requirement 166
    Calculation groups and how it works? 167
    Creating calculation groups in Power BI 169
        Sorting the calculated items 174
    Limitations in calculation groups 174
Conclusion 175
Questions 175

13. Self-service AI Capabilities in Power BI 177
Structure 177
Objectives 178
Introducing AI capabilities in Power BI 178
    Quick insights 178
Q&A visual in Power BI 180
    Q&A visual in the Power BI desktop 181
Decomposition tree visual 186
    Key influencer 187

Smart narrative	*190*
Perform text analytics, vision, and Azure Machine Learning	*191*
R and Python integration	*191*
Conclusion	193
Questions	193

14. Incremental Refresh for Data Models 195
Structure 195
Objective 195
Data refresh requirement 196
    Incremental data refresh requirement *197*
    Configuring incremental refresh *198*
    Defining the filter parameters *198*
    Applying filter using parameters *201*
    Defining incremental refresh policy *204*
Conclusion 207
Questions 207

15. Composite Models and Perform Aggregations to Improve Query Performance 209
Structure 209
Objective 209
Prerequisites 210
Connection types—recap 210
    Import *210*
    DirectQuery *211*
        Demo database *211*
        Let us consume the demo database using Power BI *212*
    Let us build aggregations *217*
        Add newly created aggregated table into model *218*
        How to determine whether the aggregation table is used by the Power BI engine or not? *219*
        Power BI performance analyzer *219*

　　　　How to configure aggregations? *221*
　　　　Let us try some advanced aggregations *226*
　　　　Composite models *232*
　　　　Composite models explained *233*
　　　　Configure storage mode *234*
　　　　Force engine to select right aggregation table *239*
　　　　Composite models allow to achieve balanced architecture *240*
　　Conclusion 241
　　Questions 241

16. Self-service Data Preparation for Any Data **243**
　　Structure 243
　　Objective 244
　　Introducing citizen ETLing 244
　　Why self-service data preparation? 245
　　　　Creating dataflows in Power BI *246*
　　　　　　ETL for large data sets *255*
　　Conclusion 255
　　Questions 255

17. Optimize DAX **257**
　　Structure 257
　　Objective 257
　　Basic optimization and techniques 258
　　　　Clear cache *258*
　　　　　　Measure the performance *259*
　　　　　　Optimize DAX syntax *261*
　　　　DAX functions optimization *263*
　　Conclusion 264
　　Questions 264

18. Collaborating Your Power BI Workload **265**
　　Structure 265

Objective	266
Power BI Workspace 101	266
Creating a workspace	267
Data gateway configurations	*271*
Sharing Power BI content	*272*
Share with a website or portal	*273*
Share dashboards	*274*
Power BI app	*274*
Conclusion	277
Questions	277

19. Performance Tuning via Optimizing Storage and Memory 279

Structure	279
Objective	280
Introducing VertiPaq engine	280
Single table versus star schema model	*282*
Filter only required data for analysis	*282*
Applying correct data types	*283*
Creating custom columns in Power Query	*284*
Using subset of data	*284*
Disabling the Power Query load	*285*
Limiting distinct columns as much as possible	*286*
Conclusion	287
Question	287

Index **289-294**

CHAPTER 1
Introducing Microsoft Power BI

In the first chapter of this book, you will learn about **Business Intelligence (BI)**, the process of BI, self-service BI, and its journey. Later in this chapter, you will be introduced to Microsoft Power BI and its components. The latter part of this chapter will discuss *why Power BI stands out in the BI market* and *why you should start to learn Power BI?*

Structure

The following topics will be covered in this chapter:

- *What is Business Intelligence?*
- History of BI
- Business Intelligence process
- Self-service BI
- Introduction to Power BI
- *Why is Power BI stand out from other BI tools in the market?*

Objective

The objective of this chapter is to get an introductory understanding of self-service Business Intelligence and its history. *How Microsoft Power BI came into play*, and finally, *why Power BI is so popular among other BI tools in the market*, and *why you should learn Power BI?*

Business intelligence

Before you deep dive into self-service Business Intelligence and Microsoft Power BI, it is better to brush up on your understanding of the term **Business Intelligence**. There may be various definitions for Business Intelligence out there, in which if one can simplify and put it in the way, basically by the name itself, **Business Intelligence** is the process of transforming the data in your organization in a way the business users can understand and take decisions by looking at it for the better outcome at present and future.

A Business Intelligence solution can be used by any kind of user in the organization. These BI solutions can help to understand the status of the business, *what is exactly going on in each department, which account has spent more money than the budgeted amount*, and *when* and *how they are spent*. You will be able to resolve these queries much faster than earlier. Further, once you have placed the proper foundation, you may also be able to get answers for *what will happen in the future* and *how the company revenue will be in the next quarter*. So, you can better understand how to improve each for a better outcome. Nowadays, computer hardware is becoming relatively cheaper than earlier. Therefore, we have more analytics potential, especially with cloud computing. With the emergence of **Big Data** analytics, nowadays, real-time data processing is also an adequate component in a Business Intelligence solution. So, it is fair to say in a modern BI solution, which will not stick to the on-premises solution, but it will be a cloud base implementation with more components such as real-time analytics, stream data analytics, and predictive analytics. Moreover, you have full potential to process text data and perform sentiment analysis in order to get an understanding of *what is the public opinion of your organization's products and services*. The right BI solution will always help them to make decisions easily within less time. However, we are not focusing on Big Data implementations in this book.

> **What differs Big Data solution from traditional DW solution is, by the name itself in a Big Data solution, able to store and process huge amounts of data which generated in different formats in different frequencies, for example, e-mail content (which does not have a pre-defined schema), stream data coming through sensors, media data images, audio, video, and of course relational data. These varieties of data cannot be catered to traditional DBMS systems. So, we need cloud-based systems to implement a Big Data solution.**

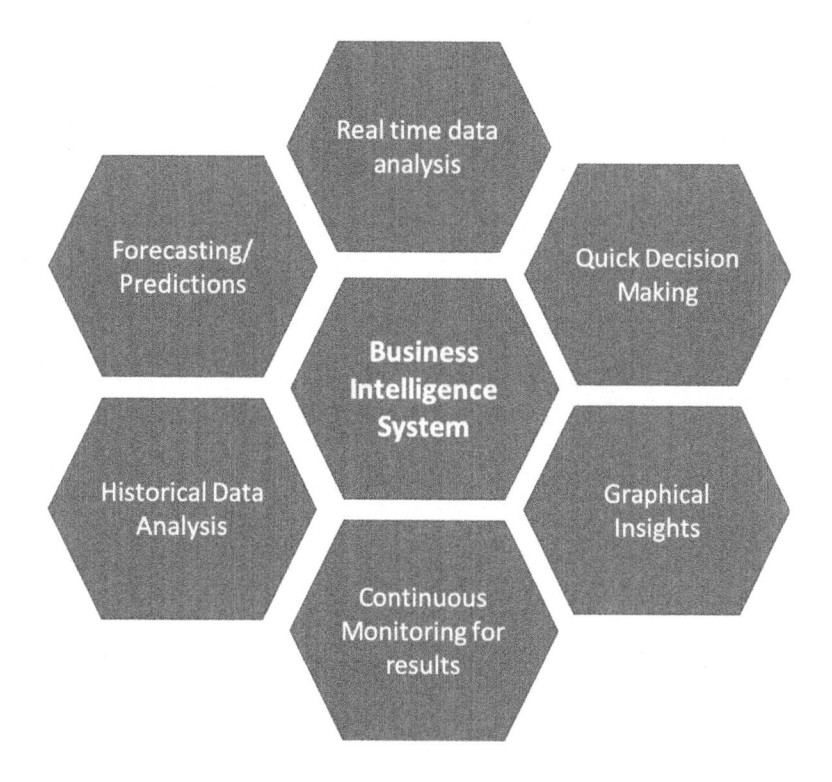

Figure 1.1: Characteristics of a Business Intelligence system

Figure 1.1 explains the fundamental components of a BI system. It has historical data collected over time that enables it to identify patterns and forecast the future. In this BI system, the data is up-to-date. The latest data comes through an ETL process that runs every night. In modern BI capable of processing real-time data such as social media data, Web clicks, and credit card transactions, which have great potential, for example, identifying fraud transactions. This enables to make quick decisions based on the insights.

If we think about Business Intelligence users, they usually do not come from IT departments most of the time. Different types of users in organizations use the BI reports in different ways. C-level users are mostly driven by dashboards; they are more likely to see numbers, **Key Performance Indicators (KPIs)**, and charts. For example, the CEO of the company is a really busy person. So, he may have limited time to pay attention to certain things if he also manages other companies. In such a scenario, the chances of him drilling into a detailed report are very low. So, most of the time, he is only interested in whether the company is profitable or not. Last month's turnover, profit margin, company performance, and so on. So, once a BI system is placed, we can build detailed reports and dashboards at a high level. Then CEO can check the health of his business even from his mobile. However, Business Intelligence systems are not only limited to business leaders and top management but also the majority of process workers who consume detailed reports and look at data in various granularity levels. They always have repetitive questions and are more familiar with row-level data. So, this means, BI system can serve any user. If the right data is collected in place, a BI system can generate actionable insights for any level of user at any time.

> **Key performance indicators (KPIs) are one of the key elements in any Business Intelligence system. It allows measuring the performance of any organization, department, or individual. Always there are two values in a KPI. The goal or target value and the actual value can measure how well performed against the target.**

History of Business Intelligence

Let us get to know a bit of a history in BI. The term of Business Intelligence was moving around for more than five decades. In *1865, Richard Miller Devens* used the term Business Intelligence term in a book he has written – *Cyclopedia of Commercial and Business Anecdotes*. After in the recent past, the year *1958 IBM* computer scientist called *Hans Peter Luhn* published an article on the subject *A Business Intelligence System*. In his article, he explains the importance use of Business Intelligence via the technology he had at that time, which is quite similar to gathering data and analyzing for insights we do in the present day. This article described an automated system, which was developed to cater to the information needs of the various sections of any industry, including scientific firms, the financial sector, and any government organization.

In 1990, the modern Business Intelligence phase began. Competitions among various vendors led to more rapid growth in the BI industry. A completely new data structure for the reporting, the data warehousing concept, came into play. It helps drastically reduce the time taken to access data.

Along with the data warehousing, other components also arrived which BI engineers are heavily using at the present day, **Extract-transform-load** (**ETL**) tools, **Online-Analytical Processing** (**OLAP**) databases, and so on. Hereafter, in order to cater to the demand of Business Intelligence queries, reporting platforms like **Reporting Services** arrived on the market. There were many third-party visual libraries also established during that period.

Business Intelligence process

Every IT-related discipline has its own unique process of doing projects. These processes have been developed gradually over the years with many trials and errors. Similarly, there is a process flow used to be in when developing Business Intelligence solutions. Please see *figure 1.2*, which describes the traditional BI approach:

Traditional BI approach

| Business identify the requirement | → | Business User submit the requirement to IT | → | IT extract, transform and load into DW/ Build Models | → | IT creates reports and dashboards based on the requirement | → | Business user approve reports or request for changes |

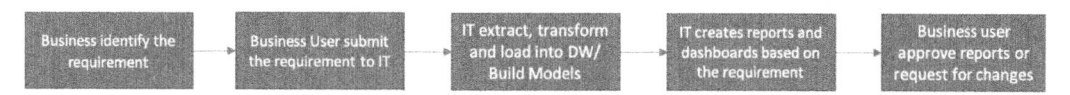

Figure 1.2: Traditional BI approach

As in *figure 1.2*, in a typical BI project, the business user submits their requirements if they are identified. Sometimes, a *Business Analyst* role with data analytics discipline comes into play. They basically sit with the clients and ask continuous questions in order to clear the exact requirements. Once the requirement is finalized, *Data Warehouse Architect* starts to design the data warehouse by creating enterprise bus matrix architecture, which follows the *Kimball* practices. Then, the data warehouse team creates the physical data warehouse database as per the design. ETL team pulls the data from sources, performs various ETL operations such as, remove unnecessary columns, changing data types, adding new derived columns, filtering data based on the business logic, and advanced transformations such as pivot, un-pivot columns, merging data sets also involved, and finally, loading the data into the data warehouse.

> **Enterprise bus matrix: It is an architectural design diagram for data warehouses, which was introduced by the *Kimball* group in *1990*. It decomposes organization Business Intelligence requirements into manageable pieces and allows us to focus on core business processes. The bus matrix consists of business processes along with dimensions linked to each process. You will learn more about the bus matrix in *Chapter 5, Dimensional Modelling Concepts*.**

Then, the software application development team or report development team develops reports and dashboards as per the requirement. The entire process cycle might take *6–12 months* to complete, which also depends on the complexity of the requirement. Very-large-scale data warehousing projects would take more than one year to complete.

Self-service BI

There were considerable limitations in the traditional BI approach. Especially in reporting and dashboard creation in the presentation layer. Typical BI projects were following the process, gathering the BI requirement, and implementing the data warehouses or data marts. Then the presentation layer, as covered in the previous section. However, when the new dashboard requirement comes, the developer has to work on that and it takes time to deliver the new requirements. Until they deliver the new dashboards, the business user has to wait for days, even months. Predominantly because of this reason, the BI end-user is always limited with analytical capacity.

They are unable to throw ad-hoc queries for their new analysis. Further, because of this reason, most of the BI projects end up with unsatisfactory or failures. Because of these limitations, it was clearly identified the requirement of a new methodology for doing BI. Then self-service BI originated.

With the arrival of self-service BI, preceding limitations were disappeared. Without going through the entire cycle of BI and always been demanding the help of the IT team, business users are able to connect to data and start their own analysis as desired. With that, not only tech-savvy people but non-technical users were also able to do their own analysis using self-service BI tools. Simply, they serve on their own using these kinds of BI tools. Please look into *figure 1.3*, which explains the self-service BI approach:

Self-service BI approach

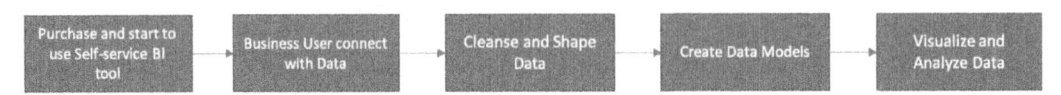

Figure 1.3: *Self-service BI approach*

During the self-service BI process, only one actor plays each role that is a Business Intelligence user. The BI user can be a *Data Analyst*, *Data Engineer*, *computer programmer*, *Business Analyst*, *Manager*, *company CEO*, or any user who works with data. As you read this book, you will fall into one of those categories. As a BI user, after you install the self-service BI tool, and then you connect to the sources on your own and extract data. Then, you can perform the data shaping tasks, or else what we called **cleansing** and **blending data**. After the do the transformation, you can connect multiple tables(queries) and build models. Finally, in this process flow, you can visualize the data and generate actionable insights. In order to make this happen, the self-service BI tools have a built-in simplified manner so anyone can understand how to use it even who are not a tech-savvy person. Because the entire process flow is performed by the BI user, it means the user serves him/herself the BI. That is why we called it a **self-service BI**.

We can consider Excel as the first self-service BI tool offered by Microsoft. We can call it as a self-service BI tool because it has characteristics of a self-service BI tool.

However, due to the limitations that you cannot store more than *1 million* rows in excel, which led to the need for a separate self-service BI tool with robust and rich characteristics such as ETL, cleanse data, modeling, and allow analytic capabilities with unlimited data volume. Then, Microsoft Power BI came into the market.

Introducing Power BI

Microsoft Power BI is a self-service BI tool filled with rich, stable, powerful capabilities to serve self-service BI requirements. There are many components in the

Power BI ecosystem. The **Power BI desktop** application, which is free to download, can connect with a spectrum of data sources, varying from simple CSV files to Apache spark Big Data sources. Then you can do data preparation and perform data discovery by building data warehouse models and creating interactive reports. It has a cloud-based solution, the **Power BI service**, in which you can publish and share the reports that you authored using the Power BI desktop. These are the two main components; you work with, even though there are other components like **Power BI Mobile**. Power BI desktop is the platform we predominantly work with for authoring reports. We will discuss each and every component in the upcoming chapter, the Power BI echo-system.

Components in Power BI

You can find the main components in the Power BI ecosystem as in the following list:

- Power BI desktop
- Power BI service
- Data gateway
- Power BI mobile
- Power BI marketplace
- Power BI report server

Figure 1.4: Power BI (**Image source**: Microsoft)

Power BI was initiated more than eight years ago by Microsoft's Business Intelligence team. The initial project was called **Project Crescent**. Later Microsoft branded that project as Power BI and released it in *2013* as Power BI for Office. In that release, the Power BI came along with the Excel with plug-ins such as **Power Query**, **PowerPivot**, **PowerView**, and so on. There were some additional features too, like **Question and Answer (Q&A)** using **Natural Language Processing (NLP)**:

Figure 1.5: Power BI with Excel

- **Power Query**: Power Query enables self-service BI experience in Excel by allowing ETL work like cleansing and blending the data from various sources.

- **Power Pivot**: Power Pivot integrated local instances of Microsoft SQL **Server Analysis Services Tabular** with Excel workbooks to store data and allow you to create data models and analyze data using Pivot tables.

- **Power View**: Power View is a data visualization technology that allows you to create a rich visual experience by offering interactive charts, graphs, map visuals, and so on.

The first release of the Power BI for the general public was on *July 24, 2015,* along with the Power BI desktop, Power BI service, and mobile app. The initial release was with a bunch of features for each platform. Since then, throughout the time while writing this book, there were many releases along with the new feature capabilities for each platform (Power BI desktop, Power BI service, and others).

Microsoft has integrated many machine learning components with Power BI. You can create a Power BI report and integrate it with **Microsoft Cortana**, the personal digital assistant. Then the user can speak using natural language and generate reports. Not only that, **Quick Insights** feature in Power BI, you can create a data set and allow Power BI to generate insights. It runs machine learning algorithms behind the scene to generate visuals along with descriptive analysis.

> *Do you know that Microsoft Excel PowerPivot, Microsoft Power BI, and SQL Server Analysis Services Tabular share the same database engine technology?* **It is an in-memory database engine called Vertipaq. It is capable of compressing data and responding to queries fast.**
>
> **You will learn about the Vertipaq engine in** *Chapter 11, Storage Architecture (Vertipaq) and Cater High Volume of Data.*

Why does Power BI stand out from other BI tools in the market?

When Power BI arrived in the BI market, there were other BI tools out there. The Power BI was able to grow faster and quite popular among the Business Intelligence community. The following are several reasons for this:

- **Design simplicity**: Power BI has built the way any non-tech user can easily grab the features. Some features, such as Power Query, have already been in MS Excel.

- **Large community support**: Power BI has huge community support. Even a user can suggest ideas to be in Power BI.

- **Monthly releases with new features**: Power BI desktop and service release every month bundle with new features.

- **Built-in AI features**: Cortana integration and ML features like **quick insights** draw the attention of new users quickly.

As a result of all these great offerings of the Power BI platform, In *February 2019, Gartner* confirmed *Microsoft* as Leader in the *2019 Gartner Magic Quadrant for Analytics and Business Intelligence Platform.*

According to Microsoft, they have been considered as a leader of analytics by *Gartner* report for consecutive past twelve years. *Figure 1.7* shows Microsoft holds a leading position as a leader and visionary. Also, you can see Microsoft has surpassed **Tableau** and **Qlik** too:

Figure 1.6: Gartner's magic quadrant for BI and analytics

Microsoft Power BI rapidly became popular in the BI market. There are many reasons why Microsoft Power BI is widely used in the market while some other self-service BI tools are out there. One of the key reasons that Power BI became quite popular is the process of working with data inside Power BI was not completely new to the users who work with data. It had the influence, look and feel of Microsoft Excel. Because people who are already familiar with Excel (as many businesses' data still maintained in Excel formats) easily pick up this new BI tool. Microsoft was making sure they did not introduce something completely new to the BI market.

Another reason for Power BI growing fast among the community, its release cycle is very attractive. They release a new update of the Power BI desktop and Power BI service every month along with the feature release note and video tutorials. This allows users to try-out new features by their own and give feedback continuously. Power BI has opened a separate portal, which you can give raise issues, give feedback for the product. This allows the wider tech community to collaboratively answer the questions, fix problems, and so on.

With all these benefits, Power BI pricing also was a factor in its popularity. It has a unique pricing model. Power BI is not the most expensive BI tool in the market. You can freely download the Power BI desktop, connect with any offered data source, and start analyzing data and generating insights. In order to share the reports, among others, you need to have a **Power BI Pro** license. If your requirement is to perform enterprise BI using Power BI, process Big Data sources along with dedicated storage, and computation power, then your choice would be **Power BI Premium**. In order to have a detailed look at licensing please visit the following link:

https://powerbi.microsoft.com/en-us/pricing/

Do you know that Power BI opened the opportunity for you to submit your own ideas need to become with their new releases? **Further, others can vote if they like that idea to see it getting implemented. Based on the number of votes and some other factors, these ideas move to the backlog and are prioritized. If you see a product feature limitation or new idea, then the first thing you can do is search in the Power BI idea portal and check whether the idea already exists. Visit https://ideas.powerbi.com/.**

- **If exists: Vote for the existing idea.**
- **Else: Do submit as your own idea.**

This is a more effective way of getting implementing the features people actually want.

Conclusion

In this chapter, you learned *what Business Intelligence is* and *how BI evolved*. Then we discussed the need for having self-service BI and how Microsoft Power BI came into the picture. Later in this chapter, we discussed how well Power BI become popular and for any user, why important to learn Power BI. In the upcoming chapter, you will learn about the Power BI ecosystem.

Questions

1. What is the initial Power BI project named?

    A. Project Catalyst

    B. Project Denali

    C. Project Crescent

    D. Project Vertipaq

2. In which year was Power BI initially released for the general public?

    A. 2015

    B. 2013

    C. 2009

    D. 2016

3. Before Power BI came into the market as a separate BI tool, Microsoft released Power BI core components as Excel plug-ins and released them along with Excel 2013. List down those plug-ins and describe each plug-in's role from BI perspective.

Answers

1. C

2. A

3. The plug-ins are as follows:

    - **Power Query**: Power Query enables self-service BI experience in Excel by allowing ETL work like cleansing and blending the data from various sources.

    - **Power Pivot**: Power Pivot integrated local instance of Microsoft SQL Server Analysis Services Tabular with Excel workbooks, to store data and allow you to create data models and analyze data using Pivot tables to store.

    - **Power View**: Power View is a data visualization technology that allows you to create a rich visual experience by offering interactive charts, graphs, map visuals, and so on.

CHAPTER 2
Power BI Ecosystem

In the first chapter of this book, you learned the terminology of self-service BI, how Power BI originates, and its evolution. Before deep-diving into Power BI, it is always a good idea to know about each component in the Power BI. So, this chapter introduces the Power BI Ecosystem and its features.

Structure

The following topics will be discussed in this chapter:

- Power BI desktop
- Power BI service
- Power BI mobile

Objectives

The objectives of this chapter are to provide a proper understanding of the Power BI products and their features before going into advanced topics in the upcoming chapters. After successfully studying this chapter, you will get to know about a high-level understanding of the features.

Power BI ecosystem

Microsoft Power BI ecosystem comprises multiple products. Each product performs a crucial role to serve the Business Intelligence needs of the users. In this chapter, you will be introduced to the features of the Power BI desktop, service, and mobile app. Readers who are already familiar with these tools can feel free to skip certain sections of this chapter.

You can see the holistic view of the Power BI ecosystem in *figure 2.1* as follows:

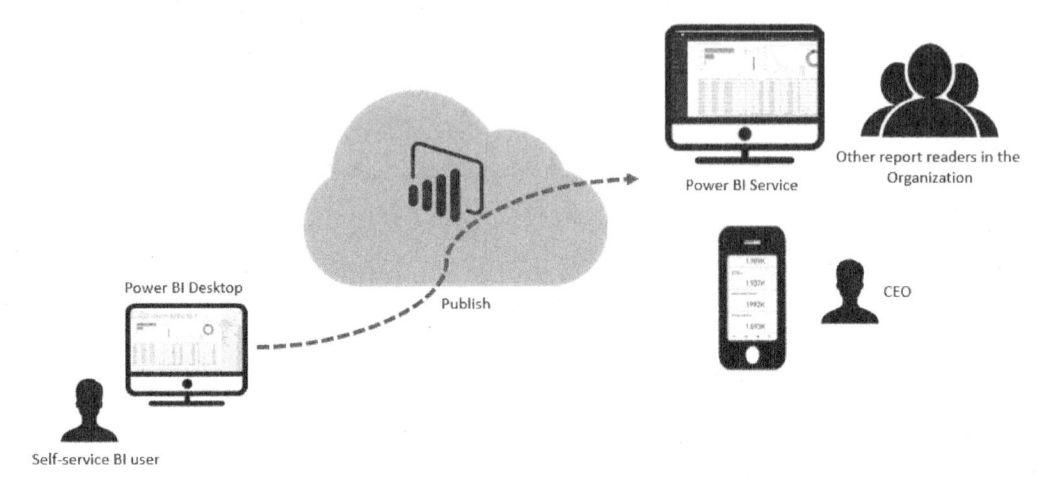

Figure 2.1: Power BI ecosystem diagram

As you can see in the preceding diagram, we face the main three components: **Power BI desktop**, **Power BI service**, and **Power BI mobile**, mostly on a daily basis.

As shown in the preceding diagram, the self-service BI user connects with different sources, gets data, and builds the reports using the **Power BI desktop**. After that, you can publish them to the **Power BI service**, where you can share your work with other members of your organization. Not only that, you can pick important widgets in the reports and *pin them into* a dashboard, which can serve to the top management in your organization. The same reports and dashboards you shared can be accessed via the **Power BI mobile** app, which brings the organization's insights to your fingertips.

Power BI desktop

Power BI desktop is a free tool you can download and install on your Windows computer. Predominantly used for developing the Power BI data models and reports. In order to download, you can prompt the following URL in your Web browser to visit and download the Power BI desktop:

https://powerbi.microsoft.com/en-us/downloads/

That is one reason anyone would love Power BI. It consists of *75+ connectors* starting from MS Excel, CSV, the list is growing till Web, Apache Spark, Azure, and so on. So, once you download the MS Power BI desktop, you can do end-to-end analytics and visualization without spending any cent. Wide community support Power BI has lifted up to this level. You can open the Power BI desktop by clicking the icon on the desktop or else types **Power BI** in the search bar to open it.

The following image is the first screen you will see whenever you open Power BI:

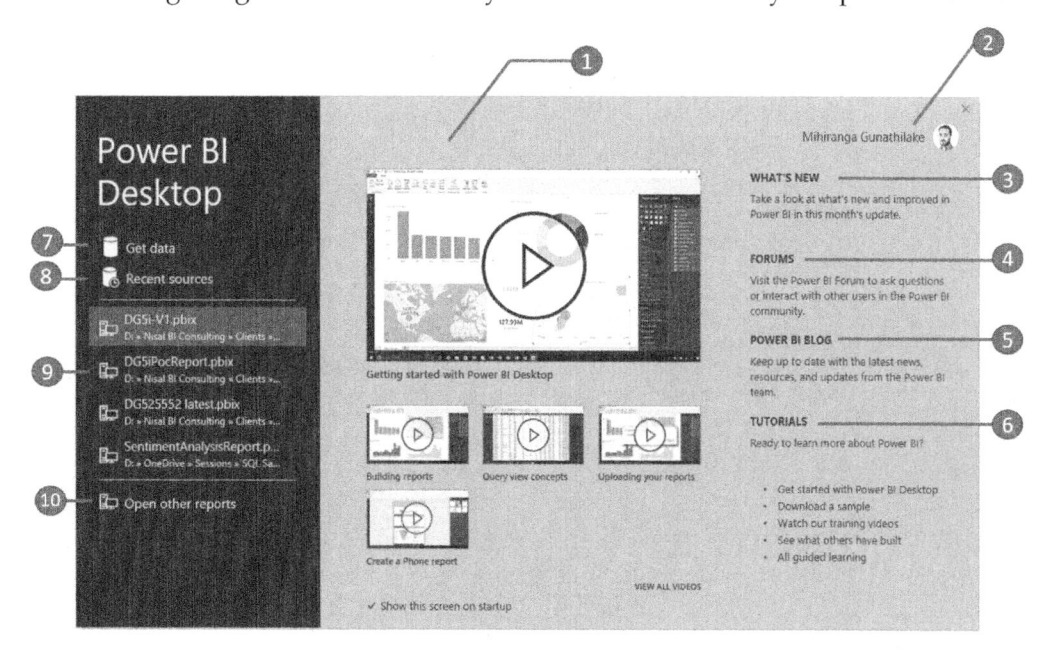

Figure 2.2: Power BI desktop startup screen

If you are a newbie to the Power BI, this start-up screen itself provides guidance to get started with:

1. You can get started with video tutorials.

2. This shows the person who logged in with Power BI. This is crucial, especially when communicating Power BI desktop with other services like Power BI service.

3. **What's New** link will bring the announcements page in the Power BI, which helps you to get up-to-date with the latest features, and so on.

4. A forum is a place where you can share your ideas, raise concerns, give feedback, and engage with various activities.

5. **Power BI blog** is also a repository with all the resources such as release notes, road maps, and announcements.

6. You will get access to guided learning tutorials in the Power BI.

7. **Get Data** will open the *75+ data source connectors* provided by Power BI. These connectors vary from simple text or CSV files to Big Data storage such as Apache Spark or Azure Data Lake.

8. This link will open the most recent data sources you have been working on in this machine.

9. These list items are the recent **Power BI work files (pbix)**.

You can start with the **Get Data** option or just close the screen, then it will appear in the Power BI desktop window, as in *figure 2.3*.

Let us have a walk-through on the Power BI desktop. Then you will get an understanding of its features and will help to remember those:

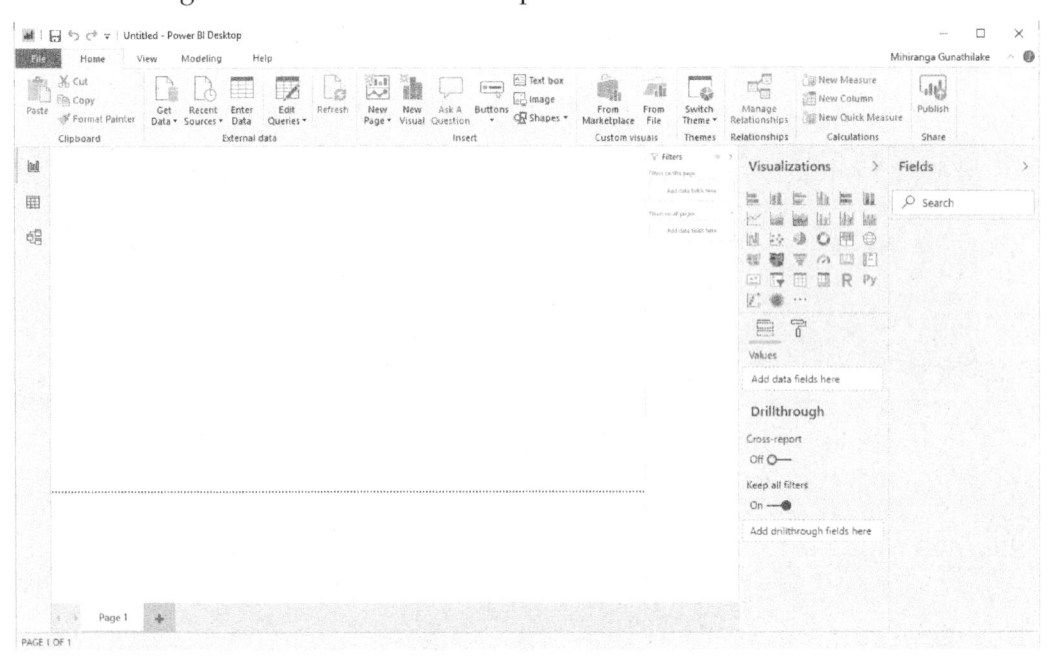

Figure 2.3: Power BI desktop

In the top *menu* ribbon, you can see there are four tabs: **Home**, **View**, **Modeling**, and **Help**. This menu bar contains all the actions you could perform essentially and will go into detail later in this chapter.

The **Visualizations** section contains *32 built-in visuals* at the moment writing this book. Perhaps you will get more visuals added in the future. However, these built-in visuals get a lot of flexibility and allow you to perform advanced configurations. You will learn how to use some of these visuals in *Chapter 4, My First Power BI Dashboard*.

Fields area that shows you the tables, fields, hierarchies, and measures in your data set. As a report developer, you have to deal with this area for easy drags and drops through your work. You may find out it is more comfortable and interesting when you start using it.

> Hierarchies enable self-service BI users to navigate and analyze data easily. As a Power BI user, you can create your own hierarchy using the data set. Once you create a hierarchy, it will appear a symbol like ⧈ front of the hierarchy, which also allows any other BI user in your team to find it quickly. You will learn how to create hierarchy in Chapter 4, My First Power BI Dashboard.

- **Home tab**: Consist with most frequently accessed menu items:

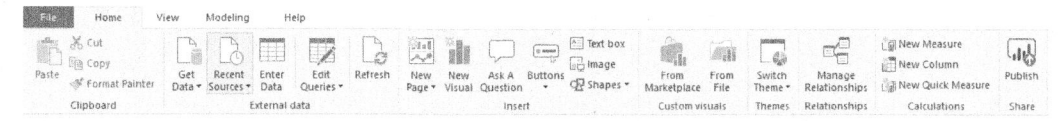

Figure 2.4: Power BI desktop home tab

  o **Clipboard**: In this option, you can find similar other Microsoft office products.

  o **Get Data**: Where you can ingest data into a Power BI file by connecting different sources.

  o **Recent Sources**: Link to open the most recent data sources you have been working on.

  o **Enter Data**: This will open a new window to enter data manually and create a table.

  o **Edit Queries**: This will open the Power Query window. Most cleansing and transformations are done using this window (will talk about these menu items in detail in *Chapter 4, My First Power BI Dashboard*).

  o **Refresh**: You can refresh all the tables in the model with the latest data from the source. This feature gives real validity when you import the data into the model, where the Power BI model and the source have two different versions.

  o **New Page**: From this button, you can add a new report page to your Power BI workspace.

  o **New Visual**: By clicking, you can add a new visual to the **Report** page.

> You also can straightaway add a new visual by dragging and dropping a visual item from the visualizations list. In this way, you are one step ahead. Because otherwise, you have to click the New Visual button in the menu bar, then select the visual type from the visualizations.

- o **Ask A Question**: Using this feature, you can ask questions against the data in the model in natural language. Answers will be generated in a visual manner.

- o **Buttons**: This is where you can add buttons to your report. Once you add buttons, you can configure different actions for them as desired.

- o **Insert Text box**, **Image**, and **Shapes**: You also can add text elements, images, and different shapes in order to generate visually rich reports.

- o **Custom visuals**: Other than the *32+ build-in visuals* provided, the Power BI ecosystem allows third-party developers to build custom visuals. Those built custom visuals you can download and add to your Power BI report.

- o **Switch Theme**: By changing the theme, you can add variety to your Power BI reports. There are pre-built themes you can quickly change.

- o **Manage Relationships**: This opens a window to create and manage relationships built between tables. You can define the cardinality and the cross-filter direction type in the relationships you build.

- o **New Measure**: Using DAX queries, you can create new (pre-calculated) measures in your model. This type of calculation is useful when you need to create aggregations that do not require to evaluate row-by-row. Calculated measures are evaluated during the query execution. DAX stands for **Data Analysis Expression**, the language for querying and build calculations in Power BI.

- o **New Column**: Again, you will be using DAX expressions to create calculated columns. These calculated columns are a little different from to calculated columns you create in SQL. Those T-SQL calculated columns are defined and evaluated during query execution, whereas calculated columns you create in Power BI evaluate during the model processing time and save the values in the model. Those are evaluated row by row.

- o **New Quick Measure**: Allows quickly creating a measure based on the measures and numerical columns in the table.

- **View tab**: Consists with a set of items along with check-boxes. You can enable those whenever you need to work with them:

Figure 2.5: Power BI desktop view tab

o **Phone Layout**: It will enable mobile view, then you can arrange visual elements the way you want to see in a mobile device.

o **Page View**: This page view helps you to change into different reporting layouts.

o **Show Gridlines**: This is a very helpful tool to show a grid in the report layer. After you create the visuals, this will help you to do the final touch by align the visuals perfectly.

o **Snap Objects to Grid**: This option always moves with the preceding **Show Gridlines** feature. You may have encountered this feature in other office products too. Once this is enabled, when you move, the visual objects are always aligned with one of the grid points.

o **Lock Objects**: Even if you perfectly align your visuals after everything is finished, there is a chance that these objects can move here and there by touching. So, by this option, you can ensure nothing is moved.

o **Bookmarks Pane**: This bookmarking feature was introduced in the *Power BI desktop 2017 October* release. This works like a snapshot; you can bookmark (save) your report objects with different filters and interactions.

o **Selection Pane**: Selection pane feature is also mostly used with bookmarking feature. You will be able to configure the visibility of objects for different bookmarks.

o **Sync slicers**: This is a very important feature. This allows you to select one of many slicers in your report page and start to work those slices across multiple pages.

o **Performance Analyzer**: This is a new feature added to the *Microsoft Power BI with May 2019 Update*. This enables you to trace time information for DAX queries and visual loading. Further, this allows you to identify the DAX query behind each visual, which you can use for further performance tuning.

Did you know that Power BI has great community support and a wider range of experts all over the world who can help you when you find it difficult in your work? **Power BI community forum is the place you can raise any questions related to your work and get answers.**

- **Modeling tab**: Consisting with features that allow you to do a lot of data shaping and build models in your Power BI workbook:

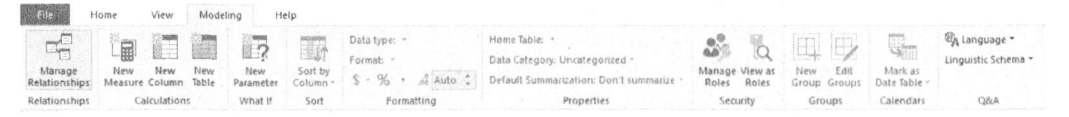

Figure 2.6: Power BI desktop modeling tab

  o **Manage Relationships**, **New Measure**, and **New Column**: These features are the same as mentioned previously in this chapter, as in the **Home** tab.

  o **New Table**: You can create your own table using DAX, which cannot produce from the source. The date table is a very good example of the calculated table you can define using various DAX formulas.

  o **New Parameter**: You can perform a *what-if analysis* and create a parameter from here. Values for the parameter can be set using a slicer.

  o **Sort by Column**: You can sort a data set by a column in your model.

  o **Formatting**: You require to select the data types and formats precisely in order to perform the model and visualizations work well. Further, you can set precisions and add symbols into the fields.

  o **Properties**: This section allows us to configure field properties. Especially when you work with special data like spatial data or Web URLs, you can define whether the field is an address, city, country, Web URL, and so on.

  o **Manage Roles**: You can create roles and define the row-level security in your Power BI model.

  o **View as Roles**: Once you properly configure the roles, you can check those and view them for validating the logic using this option.

  o **Grouping**: You can create custom groups by combining multiple values.

  o **Mark as a Date Table**: We rarely find a data set without a **date** table. You can mark your calendar or date table, which allows to enable time intelligence functions, and so on.

o **Q&A**: Question and answer is an *AI feature* you will find in Power BI to convert your data model and allow BI users to through questions in natural language and generate answers. You can configure the language support for Q&A.

- **Help tab**: Containing various options to help you through work in the Power BI ecosystem:

Figure 2.7: Power BI desktop help tab

o **Guided Learning**: Once again, you will redirect to the guided learning video tutorials section in Power BI. Visit the following link:

https://docs.microsoft.com/en-us/power-bi/guided-learning/

o **Documentation**: This link redirects to the `Getting started` article series. If you are good at learning, this is for you. Visit the following link:

https://docs.microsoft.com/en-us/power-bi/desktop-getting-started

o **Training Videos**: You will redirect to the Power BI YouTube channel from this link.

o **Support**: This link will bring you to the Power BI support page. This is the place you can ask for support.

o **About**: This will open small windows containing the version, user ID, session ID, and so on:

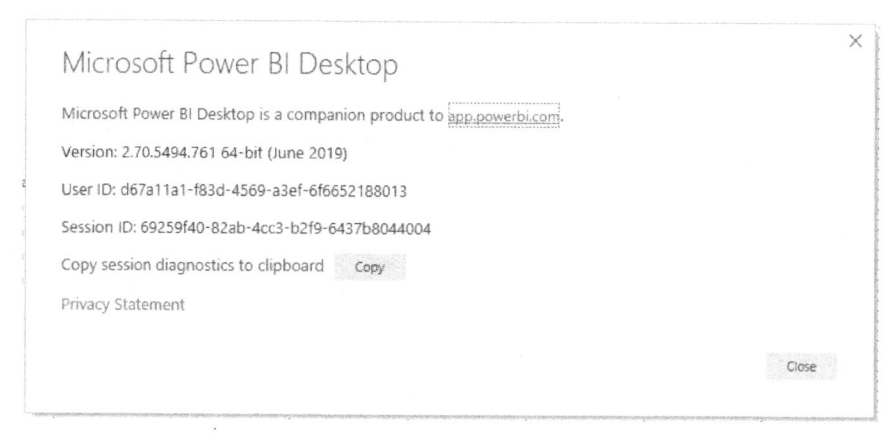

Figure 2.8: About Window

- **Power BI Blog**: Like in the start-up screen, you can access the Power BI blog for the latest products and feature updates. Visit the following link:

  https://powerbi.microsoft.com/en-us/blog/

- **Community**: You can connect with a very large community base where all the peers and experts are live in. That is the place you can raise your concerns and ask questions. Visit the following link:

  https://community.powerbi.com/

- **Power BI for developers**: This link brings you to the **Power BI developer** page, where you can start to build custom visuals, embedding, and automate tasks like duplicate Power BI workspace automatically. Visit the following link:

  https://powerbi.microsoft.com/en-us/developers/

- **Samples**: Another good way to start to learn is by looking at existing work done by others. You can find download Power BI sample work files. Visit the following link:

  https://powerbi.microsoft.com/en-us/developers/

- **Community Galleries**: You can view the Power BI reports gallery done by experts.

- **Submit an Idea**: It does not matter you are an expert or a newbie. There is always a place where you can submit your own idea, which is possible to become a reality.

- **Partner Showcase**: This link redirects to the **Partners** page, where you can view existing partners for implementing your BI solution, or you can become.

- **Consulting Services**: You will redirect to paid and free consulting/workshops for Power BI:

Power BI Ecosystem ■ 23

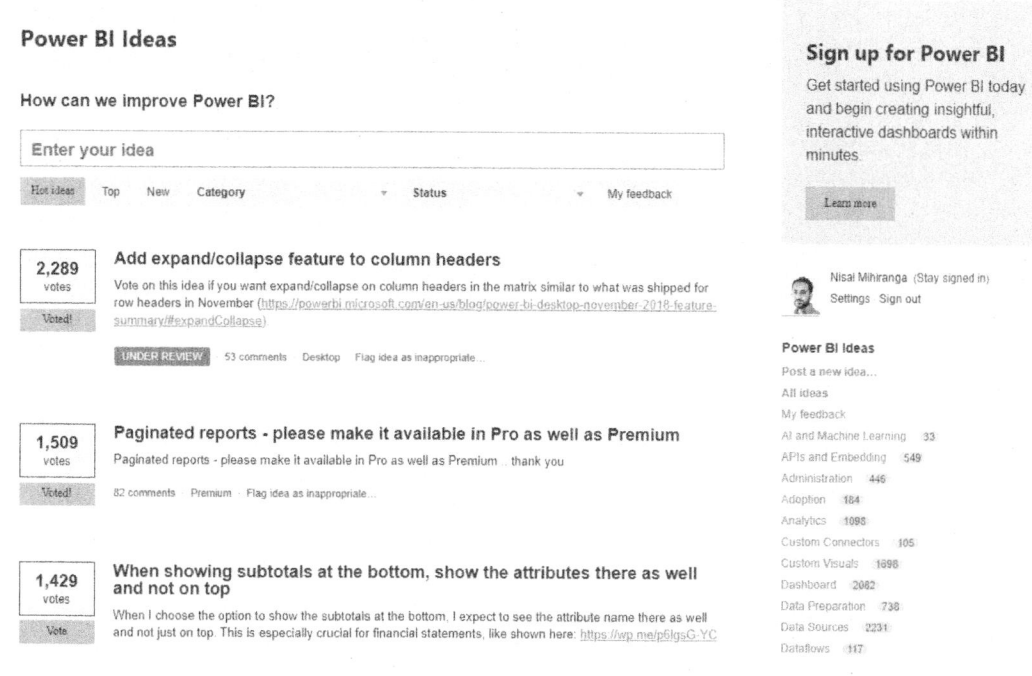

Figure 2.9: Submit an idea portal

Data tab

So far, you have been in the *Report* tab. You can move to the *Data* tab by clicking the *table* icon in the left vertical menu bar:

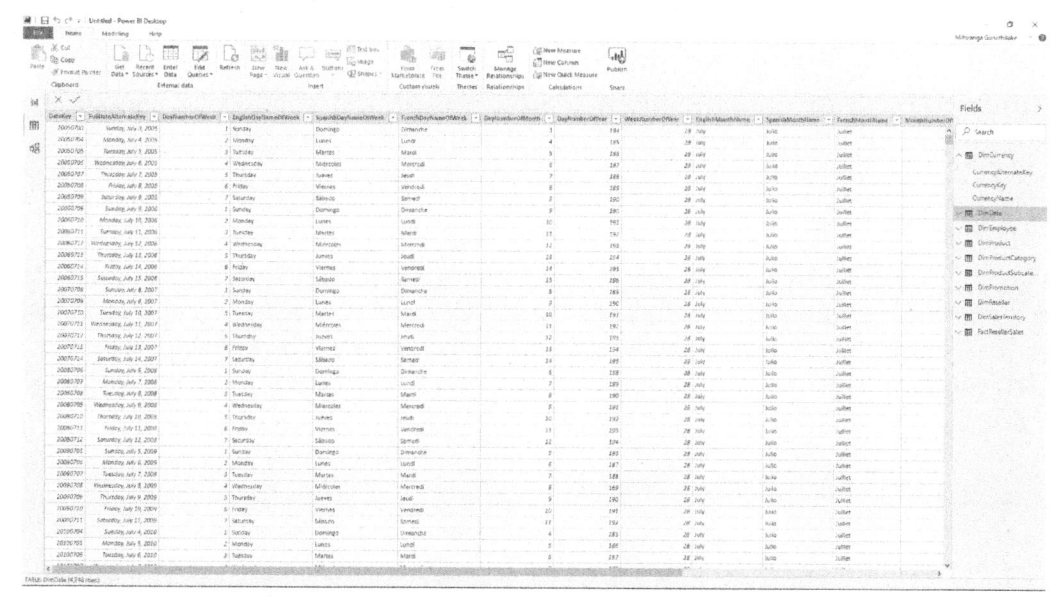

Figure 2.10: Data tab

This view is similar to the view we can see in Microsoft Excel. You can click the dropdown button in each field in order to do changes to the data set, such as sorting, filtering, and so on:

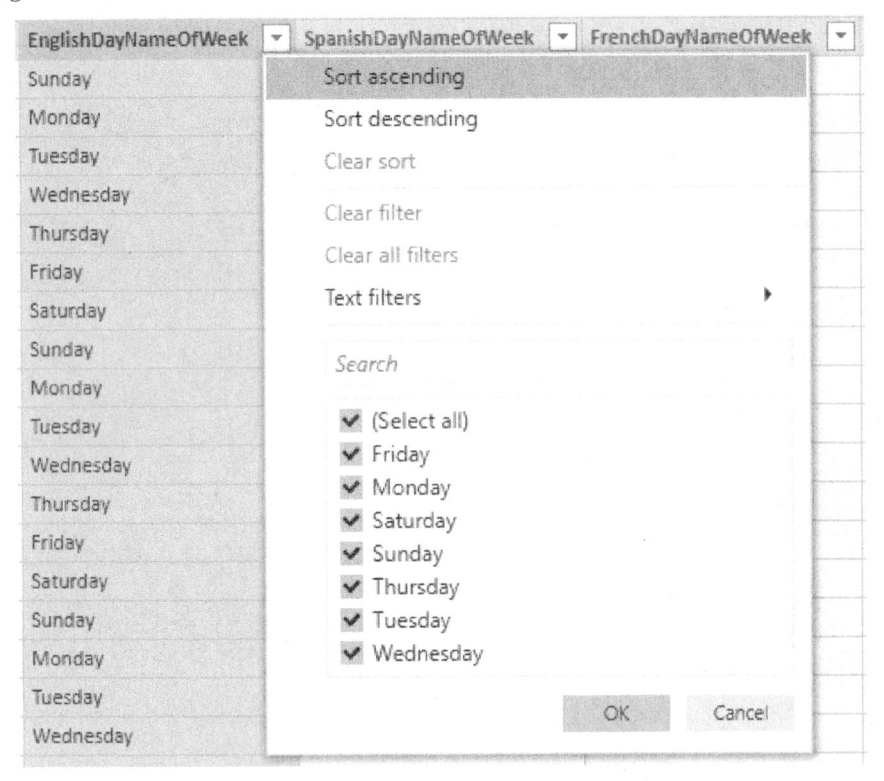

Figure 2.11: Dropdown for sorting and filtering

Model tab

The model tab is where you can view your **star schema** or **snowflake** structure of the model. Further, this view helps you to build relationships, especially when you have many tables.

This is also the ideal place to do advanced configurations like aggregations. You will learn more details of how to configure relationships and how to design aggregations in later chapters. The star schema and snowflake are the two most popular data modelling techniques you can find. You will learn about it in detail in *Chapter 5, Introducing BI Building Blocks: Dimensional Modeling Concepts*.

> Aggregations help you to improve the performance over Big Data. Pre-aggregated data can be configured and reduce the cache size and engine to choose the execution path based on the required data set by the query. You will learn how to implement aggregations in *Chapter 14, Incremental Refresh for Data Models*.

The *model view* tab exhibits all the tables and the relationships. You can see the model tab in the following *figure 2.12*:

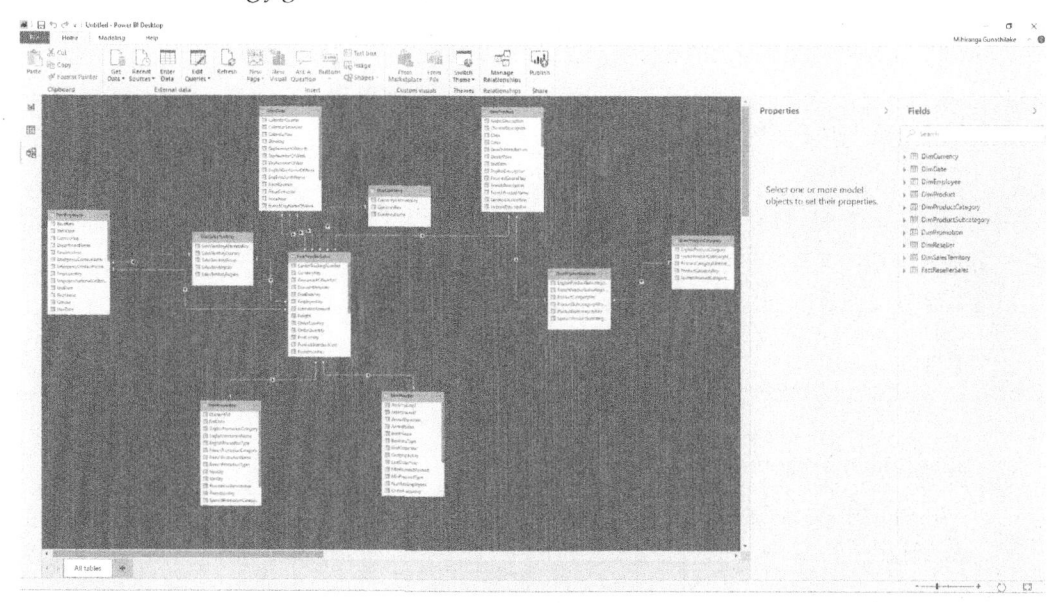

Figure 2.12: Model tab

Power BI service

Power BI service has been implemented on top of Microsoft Azure services. Once you have successfully modeled and created the reports, you have to publish your report into the Power BI service in order to do advanced collaborations and create dashboards; you can sign in to the Power BI service using the following link:

https://powerbi.microsoft.com/en-us/

The Power BI service is a Web-based cloud application you can access through your favorite browser. The preview of the Power BI service you can see in *figure 2.13*:

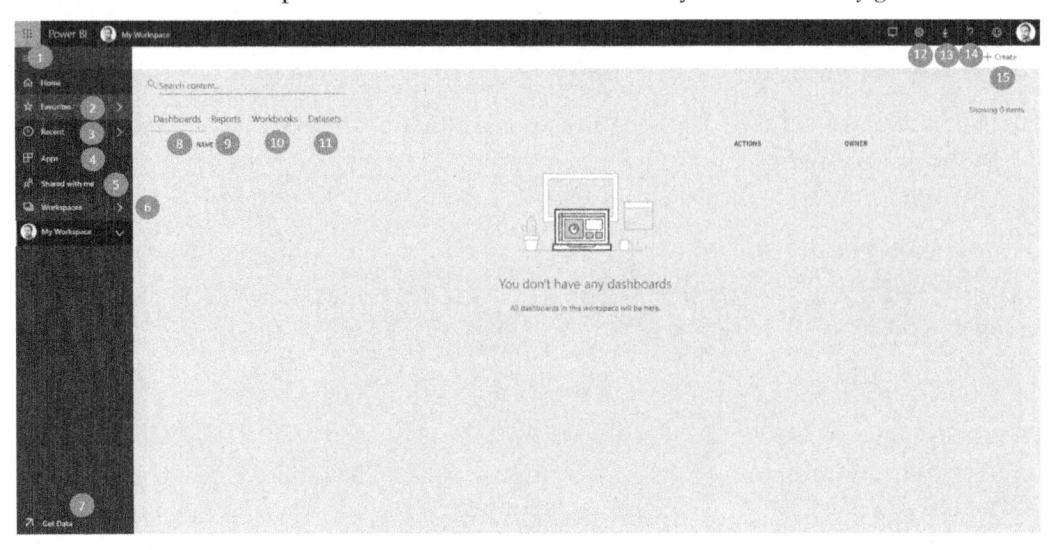

Figure 2.13: Power BI service

The tasks of each option are listed as follows:

1. This will open other Microsoft apps which connect with your Power BI account.
2. You can mark your favorite work, reports/dashboards, and so on.
3. Your recent work can be accessed from here.
4. Once you publish your work in service, you can combine related reports and dashboards and create an app, for example, **finance**. In this manner, you can easily control access to a group of content rather than individuals.
5. Content shared with you can see from this link.
6. In the Power BI service, all the content you publish will be hosted in a workspace. The default workspace is **My Workspace**. But you can always create a custom workspace and control access for them.
7. You can get data and start to create reports/dashboards from this link.
8. You can create dashboards using **Reports** by pin the most important visuals such as cards and KPIs. Those dashboards will be list in here.
9. After you have published your report, you can list it under **Reports**.
10. Excel workbooks you published will be list in here.

11. Every report creates on top of the data set. Those data sets will be listed in this section.

12. You can navigate to the admin portal, settings, manage gateways from this *gear* icon. You will get a better understanding of each in later chapters in this book.

13. In the **Download** section, you can download the data gateway setup, Power BI mobile, and so on.

14. **Help and support** link works in a similar way as in Power BI desktop help works. You can connect with the community, get tutorials, and so on.

15. **+ Create** button allows you to create a new report, dashboard, data set, or streaming data set.

There are many advanced configurations in the data set settings. You can configure the data gateway that connects the Power BI report with the data source, schedule the data refresh, and so on. You will get an in-depth understanding of how these features work in the later chapters of this book.

Power BI mobile

Power BI mobile app allows users to get insights into their fingers tip. It supports all the following mobile platforms:

- iPhones
- iPads
- Android phones
- Android tabs
- Windows mobile devices

In Power BI mobile, you can only view and interact with reports. In other terms, cannot develop reports. That makes sense because it would be hard to do any sort of development via a small device like a mobile. The mobile version is always a better way of getting insights into the business to the fingertip. For example, a company

28 ■ *Power BI Data Modeling*

CEO may check the status of the company profit margins via his mobile phone while traveling to the office:

Figure 2.14: Mobile dashboard sample

The menu of the Power BI mobile reporting is as follows as in *figure 2.16*:

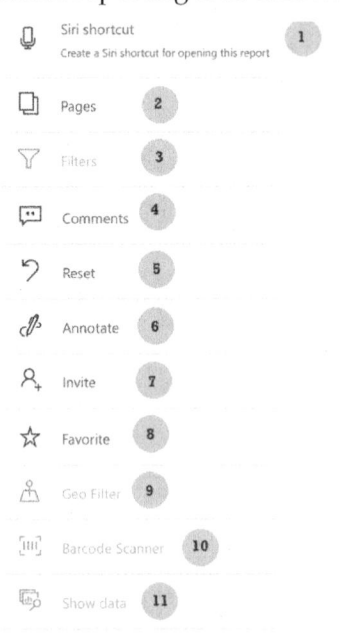

Figure 2.15: Mobile reporting menu

Each menu item serves a specific task for the mobile user as listed here:

1. This is an OS-specific feature where you can create shortcuts for opening the report.
2. You can navigate to different pages.
3. To add filters to the report.
4. You can add comments to the report.
5. Reset the filters and selections to the default state.
6. You can take a screen capture, annotate, and directly share from your mobile.
7. Invite and share with other users.
8. Mark as favorite and unselect.
9. Filter the report based on the geo-location you are in.
10. Scan the barcode to filter the data in the report.
11. Display the data in the report.

Conclusion

In this chapter, first, we discussed the Power BI ecosystem and its components. Then run through the features of Power BI desktop, service, and mobile. Furthermore, we discussed about advanced analytics features like built-in machine learning capabilities. This helps the audience to understand the big picture of it before moving to advanced topics.

Questions

1. **What is the name of the AI feature offered in Power BI that you can communicate with the data set in natural language?**

    A. Quick Insight

    B. Key Influencer

    C. Ask a Question (Q&A)

2. **How to maintain the connectivity among two tables in the data model?**

    A. Hierarchies

    B. Edit interactions

    C. New table

    D. Edit relationships

3. Assume that after you work for a certain period of time, you got a new idea that can be super, and you think if that can be real, the Power BI would be even better. What do you do about it?

Answers

1. C
2. D
3. Click **Help and Submit an Idea** button, go to the Power BI community portal, and validate the idea (whether the idea is an original one or an existing one). If that exists, vote for the idea. If that is the unique original one, submit it as a new idea.

CHAPTER 3
Getting Started with Power BI and Connect with Data

When it comes to self-service BI, connecting to data, modeling, and visualization are the three key pillars you can find. In this chapter, we are going to start with how to connect with data using Power BI. There are various methods to do that, and it is the right time to have a good understanding of how to connect with data using connectors in Power BI. In this chapter, you will learn about the data source connectors and connection types with advanced configurations.

Structure

The following topics will be covered during this chapter:

- Power BI connectors
- Connection types

Objective

The objective of this chapter is to get a high-level understanding of Power BI connectors offered and connection types. It is important to have a clear picture of the connection types. Because then you can choose wisely the appropriate connection type for your scenario.

Get data

In order to connect with any data source, first, you need to click the **Get Data** button in the **Home** tab in the *top menu bar* in the Power BI desktop:

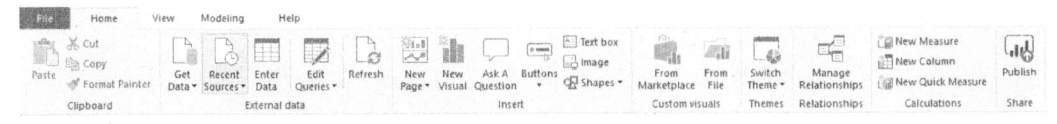

Figure 3.1: Top menu bar

Once you click the **Get Data** button, it will open the **Get Data** window, which gives a huge list of sources:

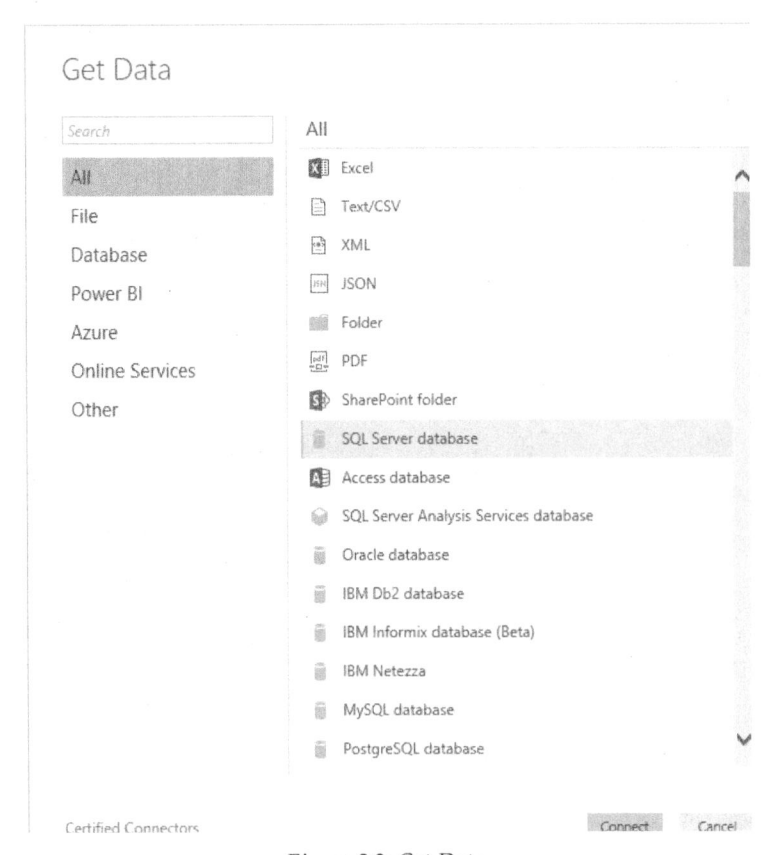

Figure 3.2: Get Data

Power BI connectors

Microsoft Power BI offers a range of connectors, starting from text documents/CSV files to Big Data sources like **Hadoop File Systems** (**HDFS**). The Power BI team

Getting Started with Power BI and Connect with Data ■ 33

keeps adding new data connectors to the Power BI. You can develop your own connector, which does not exist currently. Power BI provided the Power Query SDK to develop it. You can read more in the following link on how to develop your own custom data connector:

https://github.com/Microsoft/DataConnectors

The following diagram demonstrates the list of connectors available in the Power BI. However, this is not the completed list. It is mainly classified for types such as `File`, `Database`, `Power BI`, `Azure`, and `Online Services`:

Power BI Supporting Data Sources

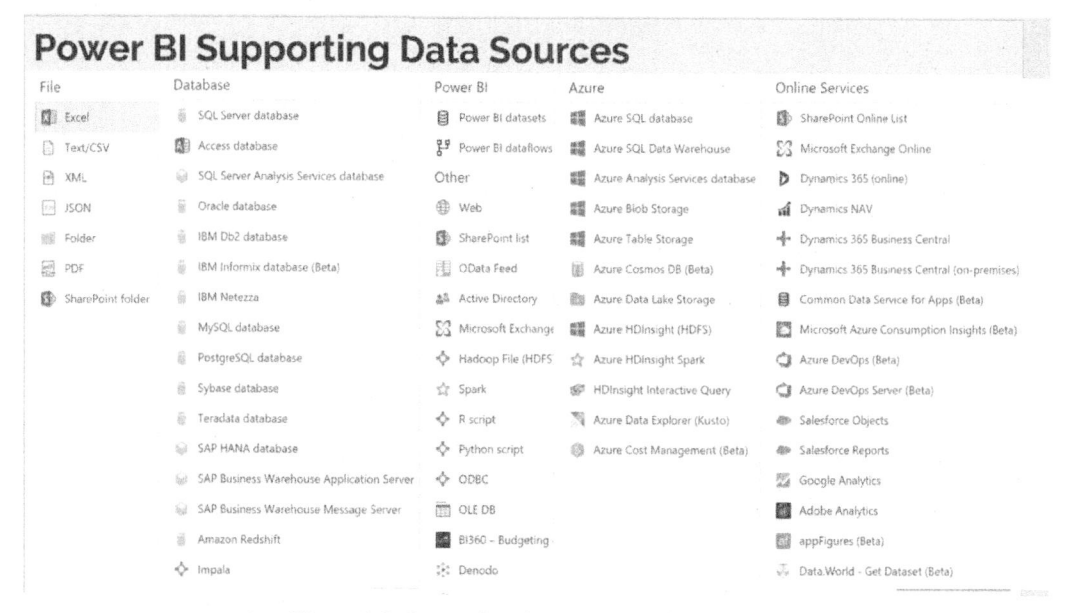

File	Database	Power BI	Azure	Online Services
Excel	SQL Server database	Power BI datasets	Azure SQL database	SharePoint Online List
Text/CSV	Access database	Power BI dataflows	Azure SQL Data Warehouse	Microsoft Exchange Online
XML	SQL Server Analysis Services database	Other	Azure Analysis Services database	Dynamics 365 (online)
JSON	Oracle database	Web	Azure Blob Storage	Dynamics NAV
Folder	IBM Db2 database	SharePoint list	Azure Table Storage	Dynamics 365 Business Central
PDF	IBM Informix database (Beta)	OData Feed	Azure Cosmos DB (Beta)	Dynamics 365 Business Central (on-premises)
SharePoint folder	IBM Netezza	Active Directory	Azure Data Lake Storage	Common Data Service for Apps (Beta)
	MySQL database	Microsoft Exchange	Azure HDInsight (HDFS)	Microsoft Azure Consumption Insights (Beta)
	PostgreSQL database	Hadoop File (HDFS)	Azure HDInsight Spark	Azure DevOps (Beta)
	Sybase database	Spark	HDInsight Interactive Query	Azure DevOps Server (Beta)
	Teradata database	R script	Azure Data Explorer (Kusto)	Salesforce Objects
	SAP HANA database	Python script	Azure Cost Management (Beta)	Salesforce Reports
	SAP Business Warehouse Application Server	ODBC		Google Analytics
	SAP Business Warehouse Message Server	OLE DB		Adobe Analytics
	Amazon Redshift	BI360 - Budgeting		appFigures (Beta)
	Impala	Denodo		Data.World - Get Dataset (Beta)

Figure 3.3: Supporting data connectors by Power BI

However, the way of connecting data is different from connector to connector. Predominantly, we can group them into three connection types.

Connection types

Connection types are the methods of connecting to data sources. There are two main types of connections you can see in Power BI:

- **Import**: In the `Import` connection type, when you connect any data source, the data will be imported into the Power BI. You can experience this when you try to connect to text/CSV or Excel data sources or even in Microsoft SQL Server connector. While you are importing data into the Power BI, it will show up a window with the load status along with the list of data sets.

You can see a sample of loading data for a few tables with the status in the following *figure 3.4*:

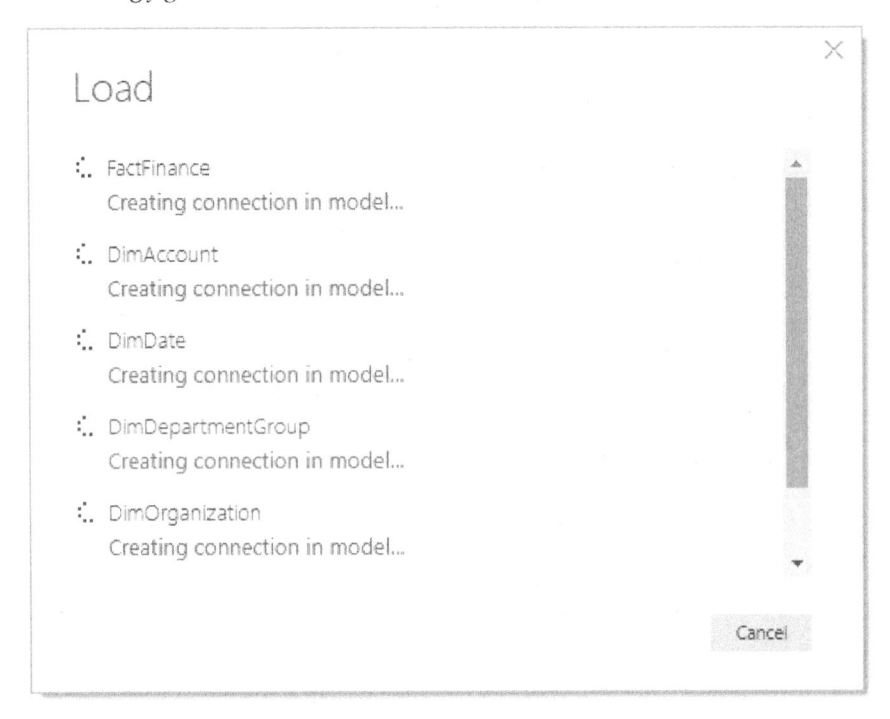

Figure 3.4: Load data in import mode

For this illustration, I used the **AdventureWorks** sample demo database as a source to connect.

When you import data from the Power BI storage engine, **Vertipaq** compresses and stores your data in-memory. That memory is the machine you are holding the Power BI file. Once you publish the report into the Power BI service, it consumes the memory of the server, the Power BI service host. There is an upper limit of the import data in Power BI. Especially, when you publish the report into the Power BI service, it has a 1 GB data limit per data set.

You can find the **Microsoft SQL Analysis Services** instance under the Power BI Desktop task in `Task Manager,` where your imported data holds in-memory. In other words, Power BI uses SSAS tabular **Vertipaq** in-memory storage engine behind the scene to store data in the `Import` connection mode:

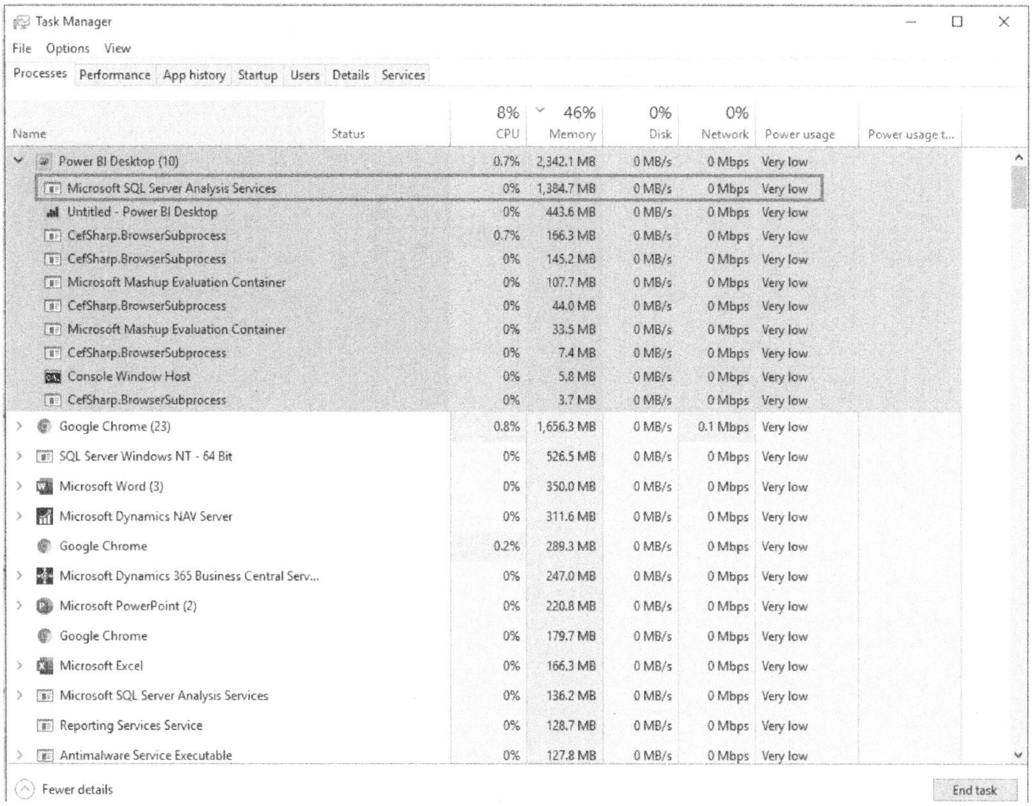

Figure 3.5: SSAS instance uses for store import data in-memory

In general, the data is always updated from time to time. Once you import the data, it is obvious the version of the source data, and your power BI may be different. There is an option offered in Power BI called **schedule-refresh**. By using schedule-refresh, you can bring your data to live; in other words, keep up-to-date with your data.

- **DirectQuery**: `DirectQuery` is another option available to connect with data. The main difference with the direct query is that it only makes the connection between Power BI and your source. The data does not import to the Power BI. When you visualize the data using this connection type, it does live query the back-end source and fetch the live data. So, you are always seeing the latest data as one of the benefits of the `DirectQuery` connection type. But from the performance point of view, `DirectQuery` mode is a little slower than the `Import` (in-memory Vertipaq). Because in `DirectQuery`, it does query in real-time on the source system. So, many factors will decide the performance of your visualization, such as data source performance, network latency, and so on. That is not the case with **Import** mode, where all data is compressed and stored in-memory. So, it gives more performance than a source where data is stored in files.

When you try to connect with the **SQL Server** database, the connector offers both **Import** and **DirectQuery** options. Because you may require to choose the option based on your scenario.

For example, *figure 3.6* shows connecting to SQL Server database in the **Import** mode. Here, the **NISAL-WS\MSSQL17** is the SQL Server instance name. In this case, the version is **2017**. However, Power BI supports all the SQL Server versions without fail:

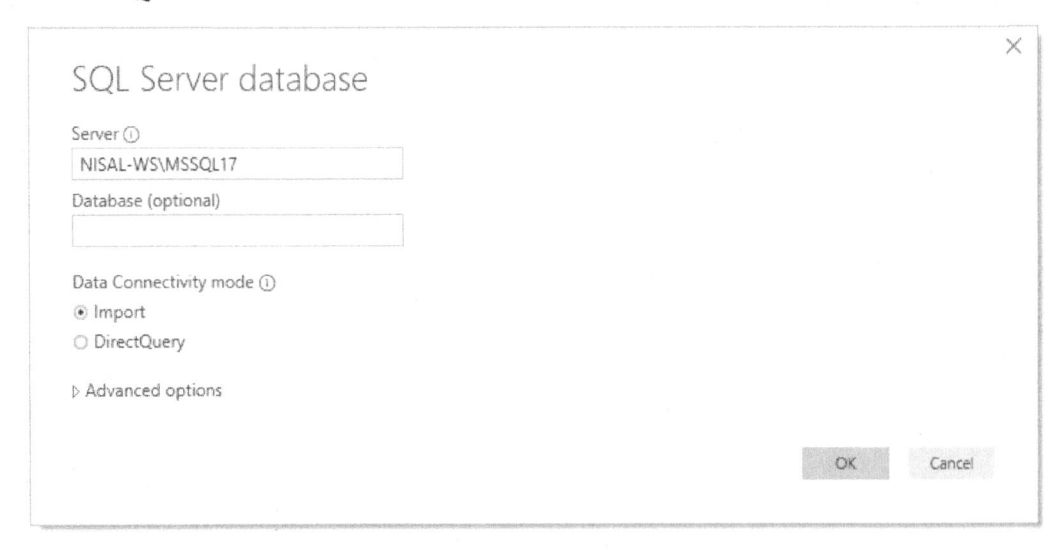

Figure 3.6: SQL server database data connectivity modes

As an example, just assume that you are doing a **Proof of Concept** (**PoC**), and you connected to the strange database in your client environment; you do not know the quality of the data, how many numbers tables are in the database, how accurate the data. In that case, you may require to do some data transformation and convert it in a way that the data is cleaner and make it simple by creating a data model to analyze the data. So, in this case, the **Import** mode is a good option. But if you try to connect with a source like a data warehouse before it made all the different kinds of data transformation cleansing has made. And also, it would not be possible to import an entire data warehouse database. So, in this second case, **DirectQuery** is the way to move.

Another noticeable thing in `DirectQuery` is once you selected the data source, instead of loading data, it appears to `Create connections` in the window shown as follows:

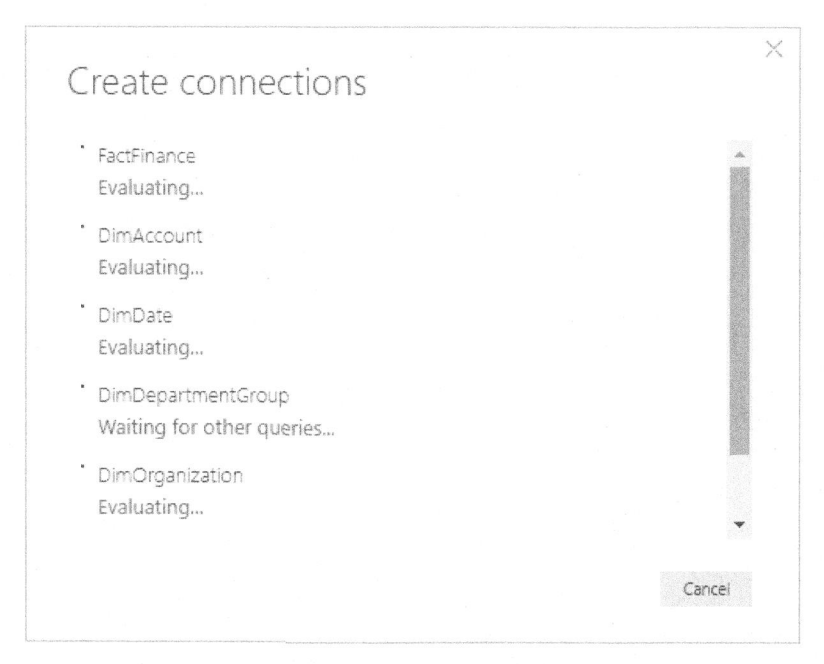

Figure 3.7: Create connections status in DirectQuery mode

As in the DirectQuery mode, only the connection is made, and no data will be loaded to the Power BI; once you save, your `pbix` file size is relatively low. One advantage of the DirectQuery mode is you do not need to schedule the refresh. Because, anyway, it fetches the real-time data by querying the underneath source database.

In *figure 3.7*, you can see two Power BI files along with the respective file size where the crated same set of tables. Once file used Import and another used DirectQuery connection type. You can see the **Import** mode takes more volume, **776 KB,** whereas the report file made with **DirectQuery** connection is just **35 KB**:

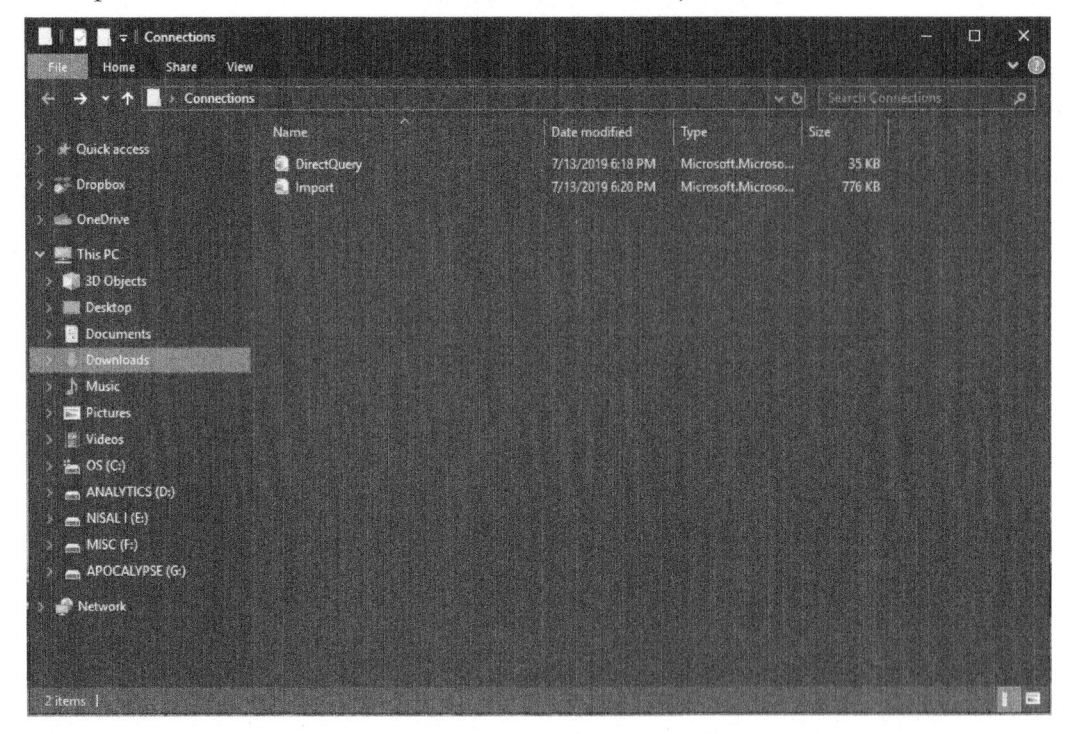

Figure 3.8: DirectQuery versus import Power BI file storage size

> **You can also see the storage mode (connection type) you have used in the bottom right corner in the report tab. You can change the mode from DirectQuery to Import if you want by double-clicking the status area. But not vice versa. You will learn more about storage modes during** *Chapter 14, Composite Models and Implement Aggregations* **to improve query performance in this book.**

Whenever you try to change the storage mode from **DirectQuery** to **Import**, you will see this message box as follows. You can click the **Switch all tables to Import** button and turn all the queries to the **Import** mode. But, as mentioned in the diagram, once you turn to `Import` mode, you cannot reverse it to the `DirectQuery` mode. So, just be make sure before you do:

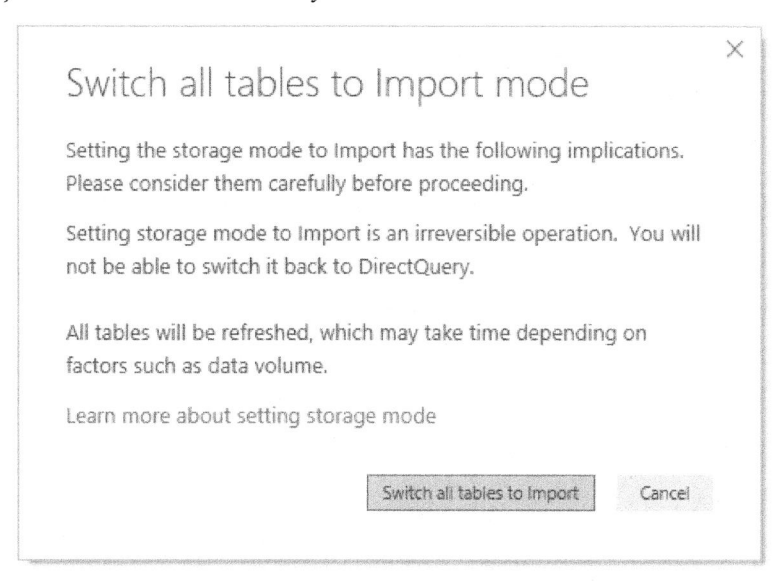

Figure 3.9: Change the storage mode from DirectQuery to import

Live connection

In the `Import` mode, you may notice that there is a limitation of you can import data, especially when you publish a report into the Power BI service where the data volume exceeds the *1 GB* limit. *What about the large volume of data?* Power BI never puts limits to analyze data. That is where the **SQL Server Analysis Services Tabular** database comes into the picture. As I mentioned earlier, in this book, Microsoft Power BI and SQL Server Analysis Services Tabular use the same storage engine technology called **Vertipaq**.

In a corporate BI projects, if you are a BI Engineer, you may require to implement data warehouses for clients. After you load the data into a relational data warehouse, either you can connect Power BI directly and analyze or create a semantic data model. That is what we call the **SSAS database** (tabular database). One of the main reasons out of many to implement this database is to improve the user experience of the Business Intelligence user. There are many similarities of the things you can do in the Power BI and SSAS tabular. In this book, we are not going to cover about SSAS tabular. However, for you to get a high-level understanding of a data warehouse environment, please refer to the following diagram:

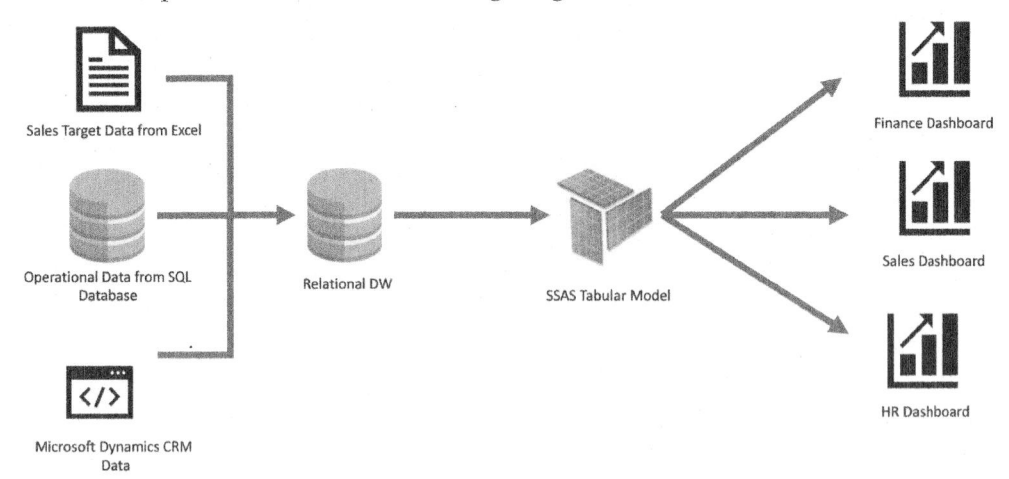

Figure 3.10: Classic DW architecture demonstrating the involvement of SSAS tabular database

In this reference diagram, it pulls the operational data from the SQL server database, whereas retrieving master data from dynamics CRM and sales target data from Excel files. Once implement the data warehouse using SQL Server, we implement the **SSAS Tabular** data model. The tabular database is an **in-memory database** that consumes the deployed server memory. It does not have any upper limit of memory expansion. So, this pushes the limits of having a *1 GB* data limit in the `Import` mode. In this solution, the Power BI works as a reporting tool. Not a data transformation/modeling tool. If you pay attention closely, you will realize that those steps are already taken in the relational data warehouse and the SSAS Tabular model.

When you try to connect to the **SQL Server Analysis Services Tabular** database, in the connector provides both `Import` and `Connect live` connection. But, in reality, it is not recommended to import the data from the tabular model. Because then, you are importing data from again an in-memory database:

Figure 3.11: SQL server analysis services tabular database connector connectivity modes

In the **DirectQuery** mode, you cannot see the *Data* tab or view data, just like in the **Import** mode. You only see the *Report* tab and the *Model* tab. In the **Connect live** mode, only have the *Report* tab. Because, as I said in the **Connect live** mode, Power BI is merely used for reporting:

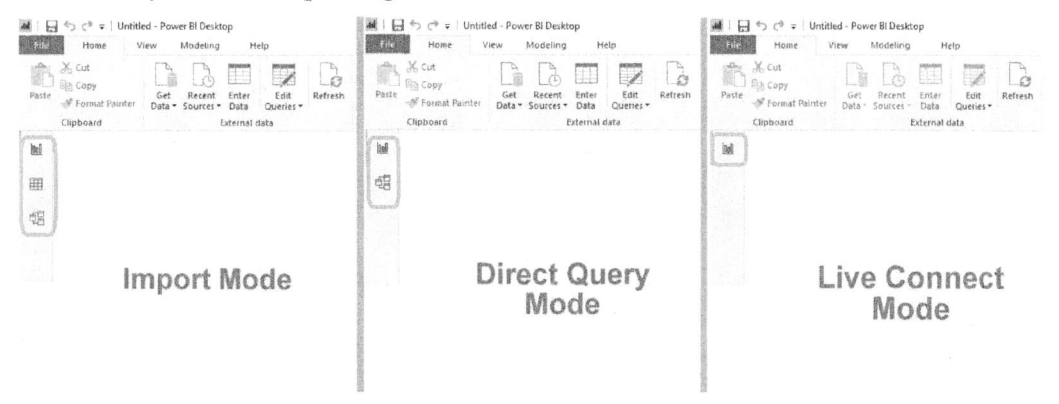

Figure 3.12: Import versus DirectQuery versus connect live comparison

You can have the summary of features and capabilities of all three connections as in the following table:

Import	DirectQuery	Live
Limited to 1 GB	Query live data	Query live data
Data resides in-memory	Less flexibility	Less flexibility
Query last refreshed data	Slower than Import and Live	Faster than DirectQuery
Faster than DirectQuery	Data resides in source DB	Data reside in-memory
Can transform and model data as desire Schedule-refresh required	Schedule-refresh not required	Schedule refresh not required

Conclusion

In this chapter, you learned about Power BI connectors and connection types. Now, you have a better understanding of each connector and when you have to use each of them. In the upcoming chapter, we are going to connect with data and create our first Power BI report.

Questions

1. You have a set of Excel files to process and analyze. What is the connection type used in Power BI to connect with Excel?

    A. Connect Live

    B. Import

    C. DirectQuery

    D. Cache

2. You have a SQL Server database that stores the operational data with *200 MB*. You know it will grow over time, but you require to do a Proof of concept analysis using Power BI. You realized a lot of transformation needs to be done as the data is not of good quality, and the table structure is also not user friendly. What is the suitable connection type you are going to use?

    A. Connect Live

    B. Cache

    C. Import

    D. DirectQuery

Answers

1. C
2. C

CHAPTER 4
My First Power BI Report

You have been learning about the Business Intelligence, Power BI ecosystem, and how to ingest the data into Power BI. Now it is time to get your hands dirty. In this chapter, we are going to discuss about data transformations with practical steps. It is really important to learn how to perform data transformations. This chapter is dedicated to explore various data cleansing and transformations which you can easily perform using Power Query.

Structure

This chapter will cover the following topics:

- Connect with Excel data
- Clean and transform data
- Visualize data in Power BI

Objective

The objective of this chapter is to teach you how to get data, shape, and visualize despite the background you are from. So, you do not need to wait until the end of the book to learn how to create reports in Microsoft Power BI.

Download the demo materials

In this chapter, we are going to read data from Excel files and create the first report. So, you have to first locate the demo folder from this path and download the demo files:

https://drive.google.com/drive/folders/1AHMRVGw1JSJcbLpeXS1Sp8DCSIbEIIDi?usp=sharing

You will find three CSV files in the demo folder. The **DimProduct.csv** that contains the product information, **DimSalesTerritory.csv** is a master data file for geographical data and **FactInternetSales.csv** file. When we prepared for this, I extracted these data files from **AdventureWorksDW** popular demo data warehouse database. At the moment, we would suggest you to do not much worry about the file names and prefixes. Those **Dim** and **Fact** are the naming conventions in data warehousing. However, you will get more understanding about those names in *Chapter 5, Introduction to BI Building Blocks and Dimensional Mod Concepts*.

Try to open the CSV files by double-clicking. Hope you have Microsoft Excel been installed on your computer.

Load data into Power BI

Let us get started to load excel data into the Power BI desktop. There are a few steps to follow in order to load the data in the demo file successfully. First, open the Power BI desktop and let us load the data files into Power BI. Click the **Get Data** option in the top menu bar as shown in the following screenshot:

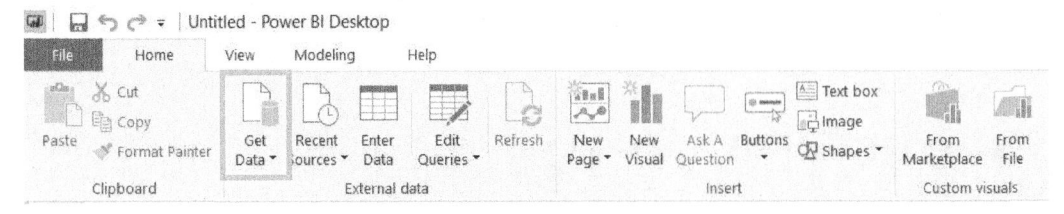

Figure 4.1: Get data from CSV

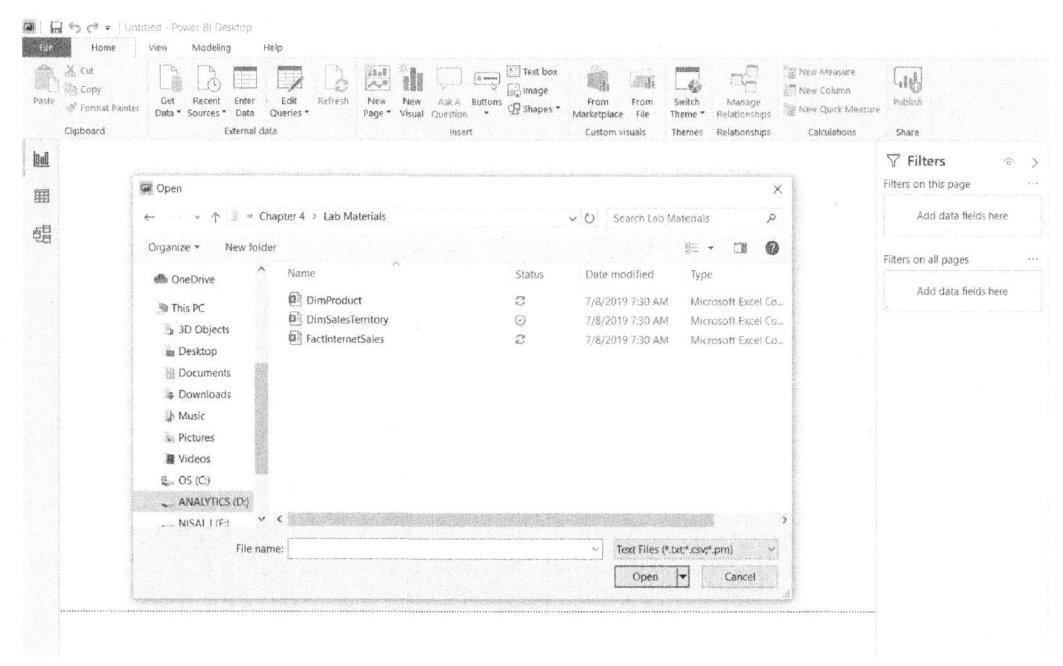

Then select the connection as text/CSV and locate the downloaded lab materials:

Figure 4.2: Select the CSV demo files you downloaded

Hence, these files are CSV files; you have to open them one by one.

- Once you open one file, you will bring it to the file preview, where you can do configurations like change the **file origin** format (this setting is related to internationalization; basically, Power BI gets your Windows operating system settings. But if you are from a different region/culture the open is always available to change).

- The next configuration is you can choose the **delimiter**. Power BI automatically selected the comma as delimiter of this file based on the metadata (you can check that by trying to open one of the data files from Notepad. You will see in the data columns are comma separated).

- The third configuration is **data type detection**. This is where you can give how many rows to analyze and detect the data types of each column in your data set. The default configuration is *200 rows*.

You can either click the **Load** button in order to load the data into Power BI or select **Edit** to open the Power Query window. This is the place you can do transformations into your data. (You can remove unwanted fields by selecting the column you want to remove and click the **Remove column** button, or you can do it later together after by loading other files:

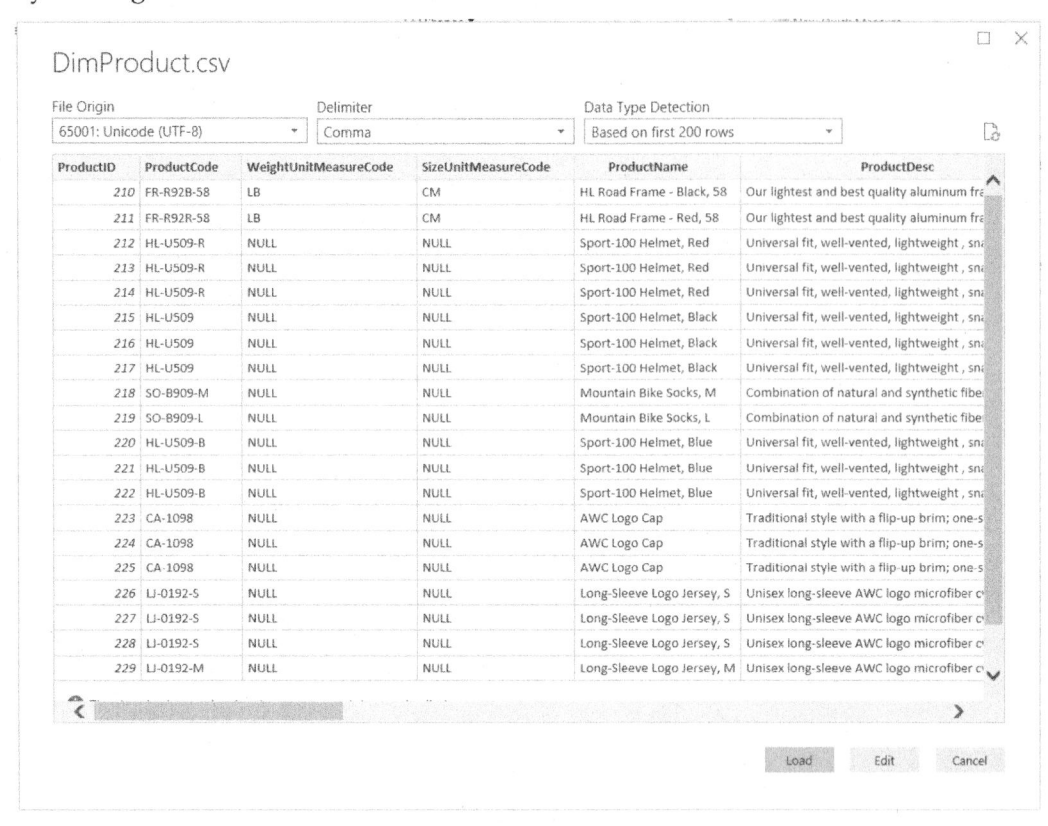

Figure 4.3: Power query preview

Follow the same way and load the other two files to the Power BI. Once you load the data successfully, you can see the tables in the **Fields** area:

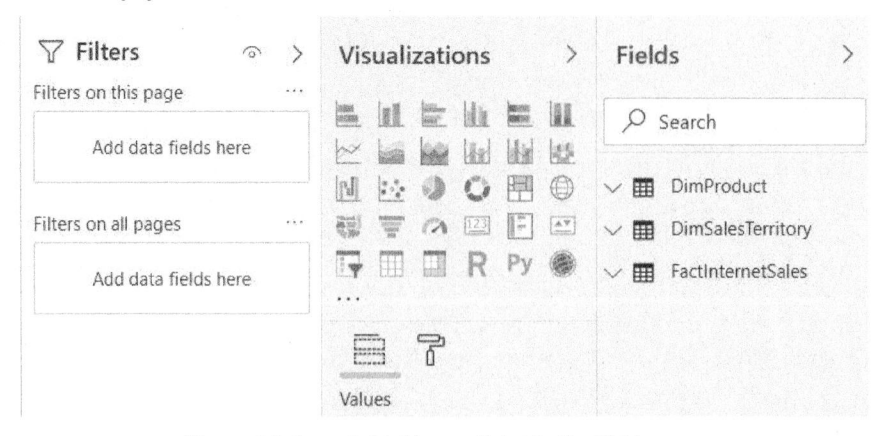

Figure 4.4: Imported tables are listed in the Fields pane

If you go to the *model* tab, you can see the three data sets are already connected. You may wonder how it happened. Actually, Power BI does automatically detect the relationships based on the column names, data types, and the data:

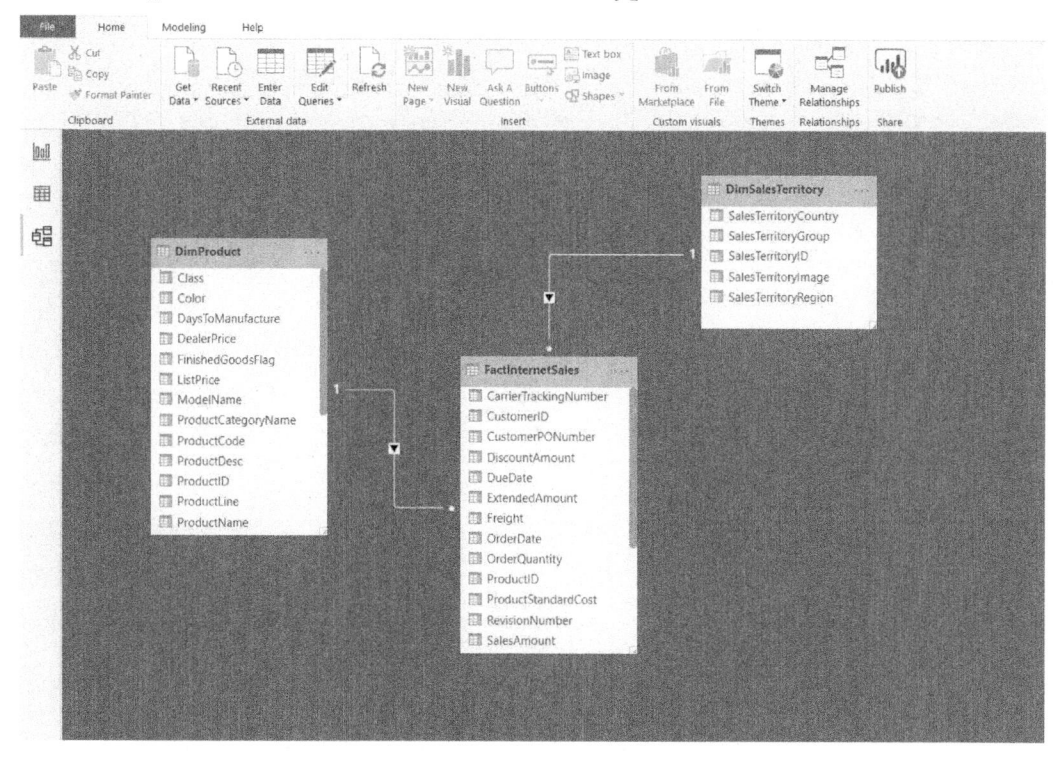

Figure 4.5: Model tab with imported tables

48 ■ Power BI Data Modeling

Even before performing cleanses data, the very first thing you need to do after the import is to observe your data set. You can switch to the *Data* tab to do that:

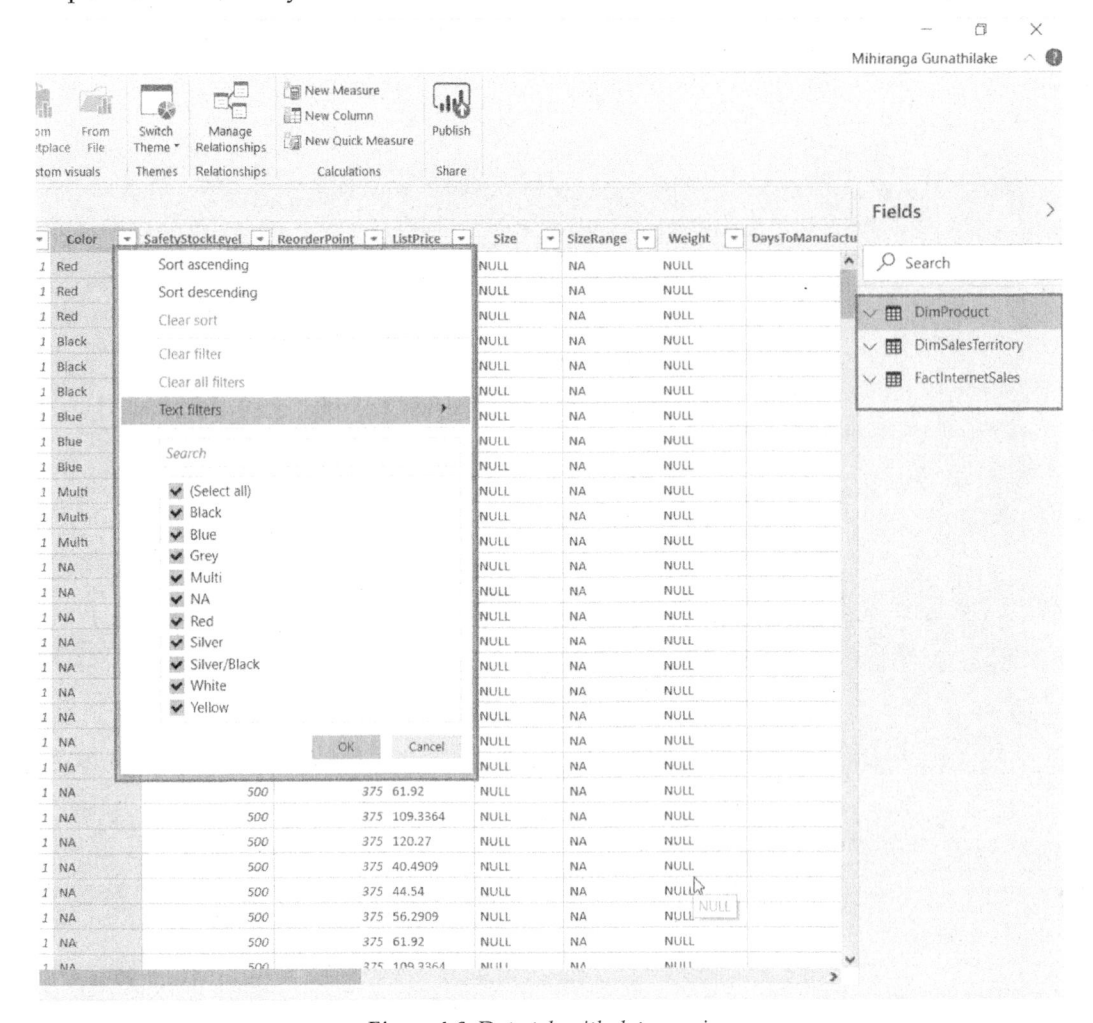

Figure 4.6: Data tab with data preview

In the *Data* tab, you can switch between data sets and view the data. Here, the experience you get the pretty much similar to Microsoft Excel. You can click the down arrow for each column and perform various tasks such as filter, sort, and search. Even you can delete a column by right-clicking from the *mouse* pointer to a particular column and then clicking the **Delete column** option. The column will get removed from the table.

At this point, we are not going to perform any task here, but we are going to do a lot more in the Power Query editor.

Data cleansing and blending

Data transformation is the process of converting data into a required structure by performing cleansing activities and applying business logic to it. Here we are going to discuss how we can perform data transformations using Power Query—the **ETL technology** inside Power BI. In order to get started with transformation activities, click the **Edit Queries** button in the top menu bar, then it will open the **Power Query Editor** window, which is another window you can do various transformations for your data.

> **Power Query is the Microsoft data connectivity, and data preparation technology that allows business users to seamlessly engage with data ingest and preparation tasks. Usually, 80% of the time is taken to connect and prepare data. Because code-free graphical user experience in Power Query allows to fast track the data preparation process. You can see the Power Query in many Microsoft products such as Power BI, Excel, Azure Data Factory, and so on.**

- **Rename the queries**: The prefix **Dim** and **Fact** are more useful in data warehouse terminology. But you can always use a simple naming convention for the end-user. So, first thing, I am going to rename the queries. To do that, right-click one of the tables in the left pane and select **Rename**. Rename the **DimProduct** as **Product**, **DimSalesTerritory** as **SalesTerritory**, and **FactInternetSales** as just **InternetSales**:

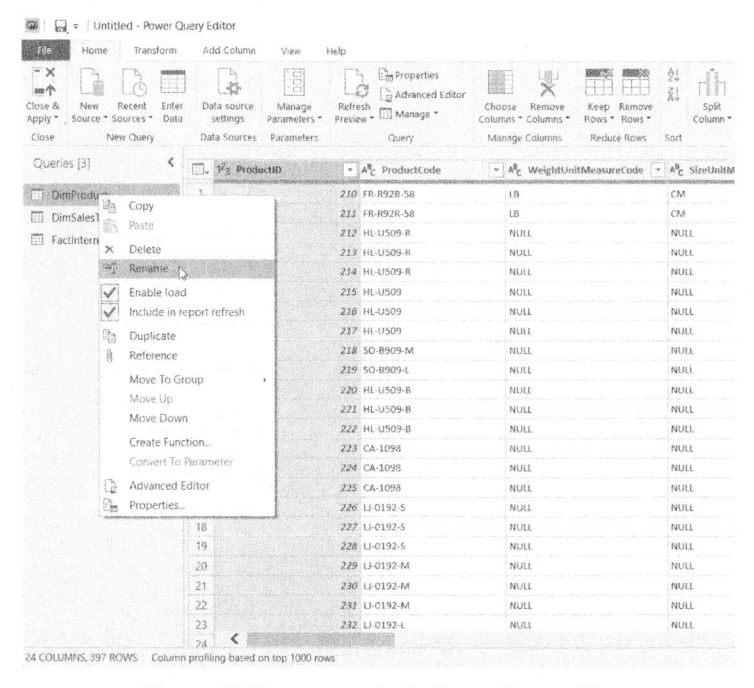

Figure 4.7: Rename queries in Power Query editor

- **Assign appropriate data types**: It is really important to assign appropriate data types for each column. You can select the column you want to change the data type and select the data type in the top menu bar, or else you can right-click and change the data types:

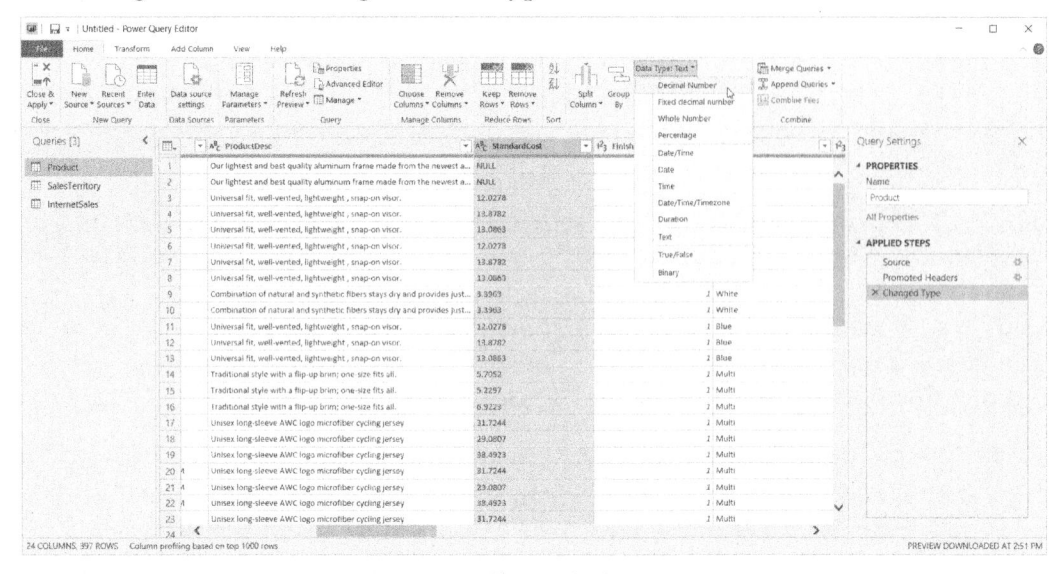

Figure 4.8: Change the data types

Here, I am going to change the data type of the **StandardCost** column into **Decimal**. By default, it was in **Text**:

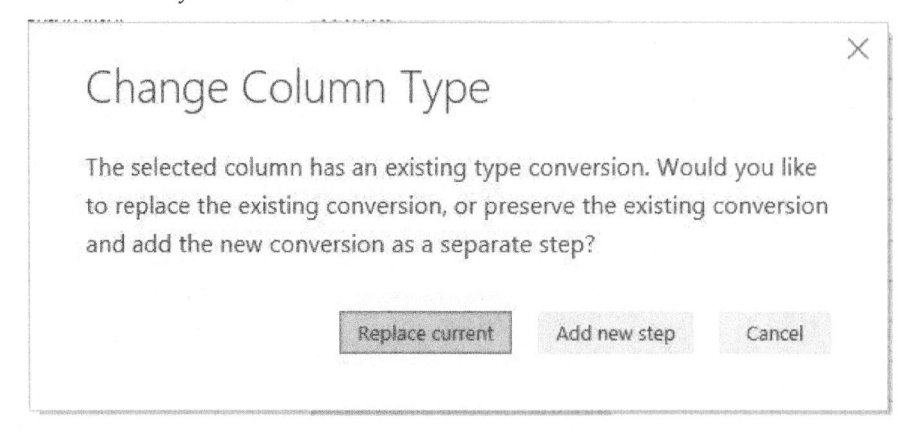

Figure 4.9: Add a new step in Power Query

It will pop up a message box and ask *whether you want to replace the existing one or convert it into a new data type as a new step. What is this?* This means Power Query has a feature to track your changes. Whatever the changes you made, it will show at the right-hand pane—**APPLIED STEPS**. The advantage of having this feature is you can **UNDO** by going back to the previous step at any time, especially when you do errors mistakenly:

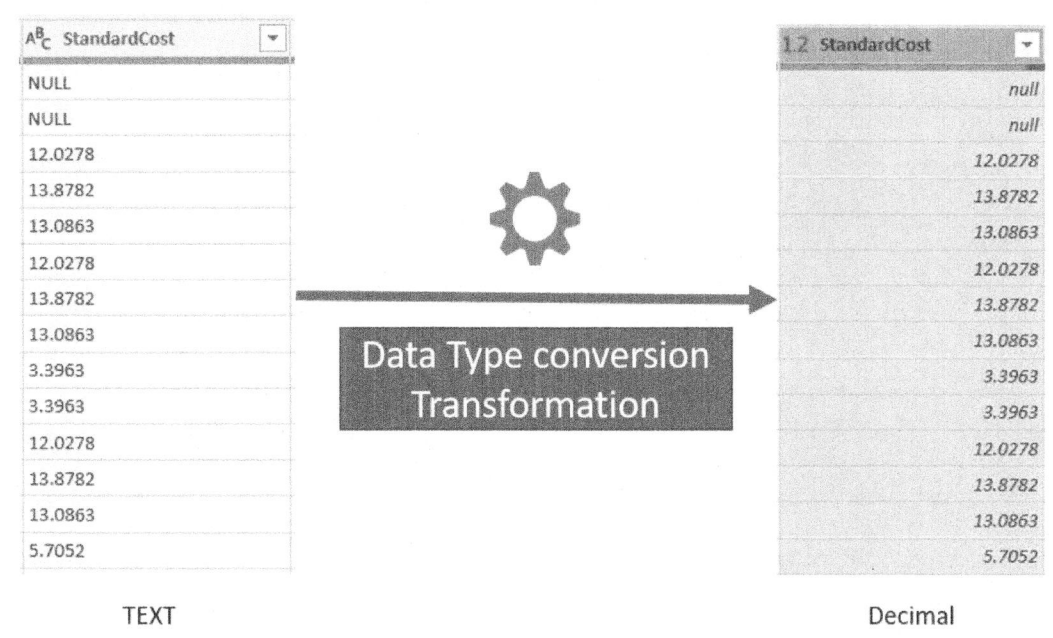

Figure 4.10: Data type conversion transformation

Similarly, change the appropriate data types for other columns in the **Product** table. Change the `ListPrice`, `Weight` data type into decimal.

Add a new column

In this step, we are going to add a new column into the **Product** table using existing columns. I am going to add a new column, `FullProductName,` by concatenating **ProductCode** and **ProductName**. To add a new column, go to the **Add Column** tab in the top menu and select **Add a Custom Column**.

You can select columns by clicking the `Available columns` box or drag and drop to formulate the expression:

ProductFullName = [ProductCode] &" "&[ProductName]

52 ■ Power BI Data Modeling

These expressions can be written in *M* formulas; *M* is the language behind Power Query:

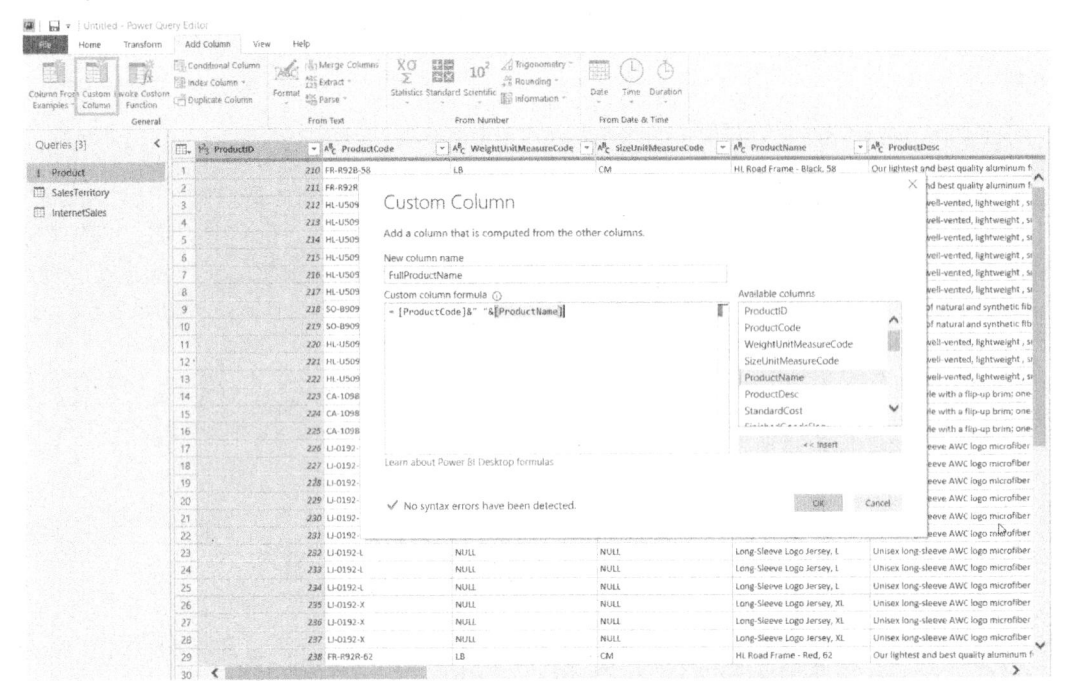

Figure 4.11: Concatenate columns using Power Query formula

Replace values

Replace the value **NULL** with **NA** in the product **Size** column. In order to do that, right-click on the column and select the **Replace Values** option:

Figure 4.12: Replace values

Remove columns

`LargePhoto` column in the **Product** table I am not going to use in this report. So, remove it from the data set. To remove the `LargePhoto` column, select the column and click the **Remove Columns** button at the top of the menu bar.

> In Power BI, it is important to remove unwanted columns from the data set. Hence, Power BI store your data in-memory; to keep unwanted data might hinder the performance in the reports. So, it is always better to report the fields that are not going to use in your report.

Let us move to the `SalesTerritory` data set (you can click the `SalesTerritory` from your left menu to switch to the data set):

- In the `SalesTerritory` table, just remove the column, `SalesTerritoryImage`.
- Switch to the `InternetSales` table remove `careertracker` and `customerphonenumber` columns. Because those columns contain just **NULL** values.
- You would notice, `OrderDate`, `DueDate`, `ShipDate` have the `DateTime` data type, but in the data time information is not there. So we can convert the `DateTime` into date format:

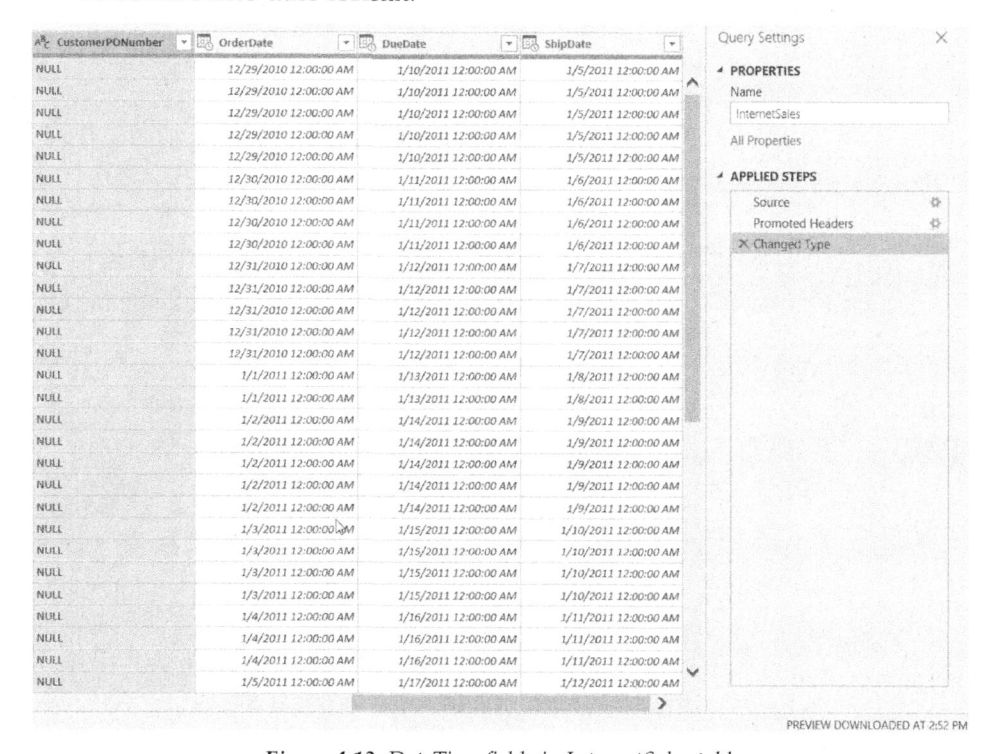

Figure 4.13: *DateTime fields in InternetSales table*

After you have completed the transformation steps, click the `Close and Apply` button in the **Home** tab to save the steps into your Power BI file.

> During the data transformation in the Power Query Editor, all the steps you performed did not persist until you selected Apply. Once you apply only, it will be saved to the Power BI file, which actually affects the data set, and it will be there even you open it next time.

Create product hierarchy

Hierarchy is a logical structure you can create on the data that enable the user to navigate through data easily. Most of the Business Intelligence tools support hierarchies.

Think about a scenario like in your organization. There will be a CEO at the top level. Then there may be different departments such as **Production, Sales, Marketing,** and **Finance**. There will be managers who manage and are accountable for each department. Also, the employees who work under those managers. We can name this as organization hierarchy, which demonstrates the organizational structure that is easy to understand; for example, if anyone wants to know about an employee who belongs to which department and how is his manager. It is quite easy to find an answer. This is illustrated in the following diagram:

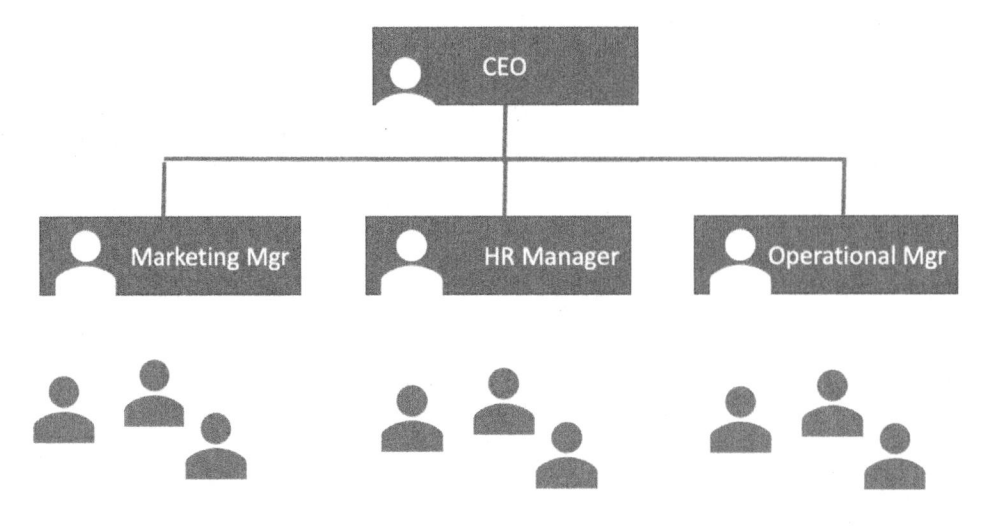

Figure 4.14: DateTime fields in InternetSales table

So, in our data set, we have the `Product` table, which contains three columns, we can build a hierarchy. In order to do so, go to the *Report* tab in the Power BI. Expand the

`Product` table in the `Fields` pane. Find the `ProductName` and select, then drag and drop on top of `ProductSubCategoryName`:

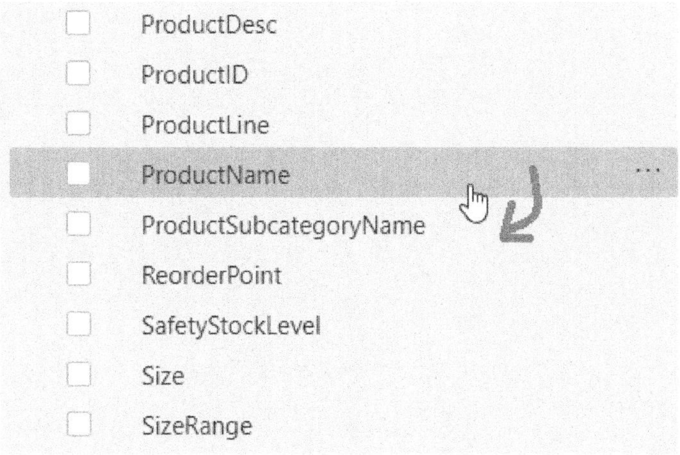

Figure 4.15: Create a hierarchy

As soon as you drop the field, automatically, it will create another row with a hierarchy called `ProductSubcategoryName Hierarchy`. You can see with little indentation `ProductSubCategoryName` and `ProductName` fields are listed under that. The last field is `ProductCategory`. Find the `ProductCategory` column and drag and drop on top of the hierarchy. Do not worry if the fields are not in proper order. You can always rearrange it at any time. You can just drag and move up and down:

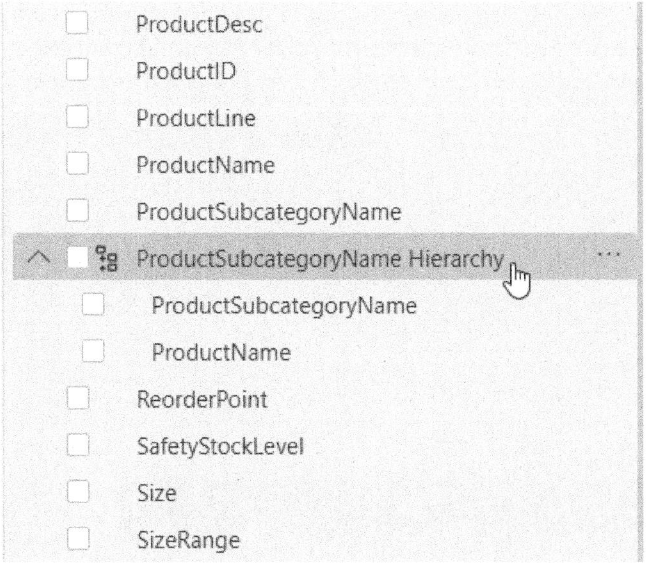

Figure 4.16: Hierarchy created with indication

56 ■ Power BI Data Modeling

After that, I renamed my hierarchy as **Product Hierarchy**, which is convenient:

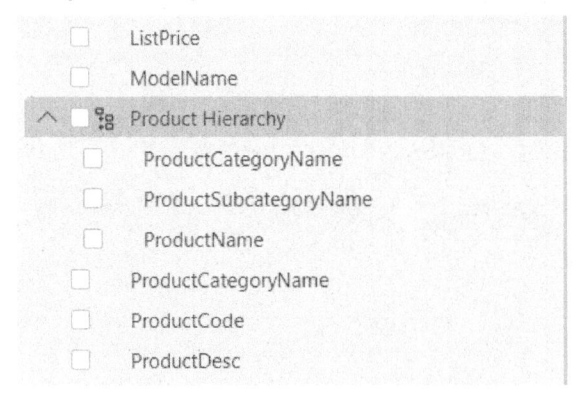

Figure 4.17: Completed product hierarchy

Create calculations

> You also can directly add a new visual by dragging and dropping a visual item from the visualizations list. In this way, you are one step ahead. Because otherwise, you have to click the New Visual button in the menu bar, then select the visual type from the visualizations.

Data visualizing

In this section, I will guide you on how to add visualizations quickly to create an insightful report. We can start with the basics. Every report needs a heading that explains what the report visuals say about. Here, we are going to create a sales report. So, you can add a text from the top menu and name it **Sales Analysis**:

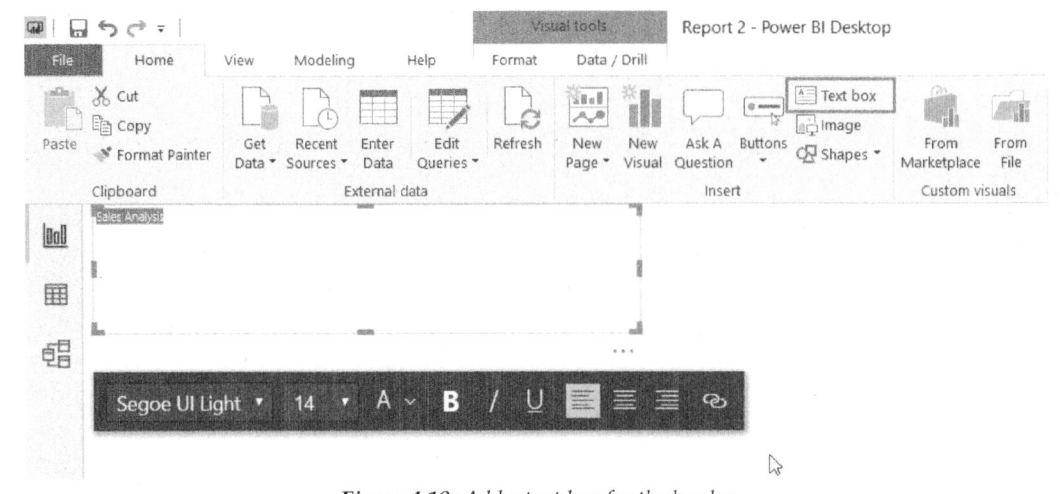

Figure 4.18: Add a text box for the header

My First Power BI Report ■ 57

You can increase the font size and change the font and color. The default font size is **14**, which is very small. Make it like **44,** at least. Next to the text box visual at the top menu, as in *figure 4.18*, you can click the *Image* icon to add an image into your report canvas. If you are thinking of doing branding for your reports, you can add the company brand logo:

Figure 4.19: Add an image for branding

Add card visuals

Card visual always shows a numerical value. You can add filters to the card visual. I am going to add a card and show the sales amount. Click *Card visual* from the **Visualizations** menu:

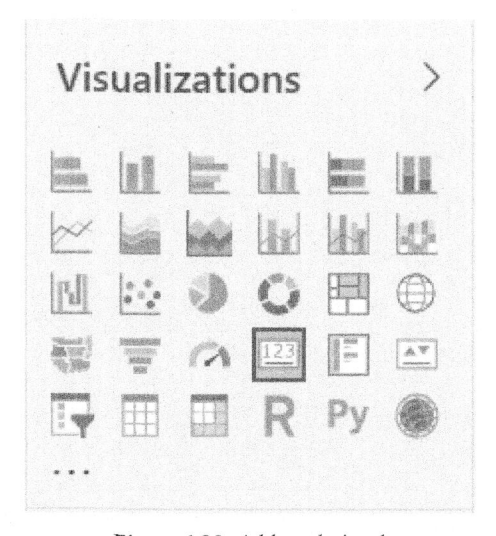

Figure 4.20: Add card visual

58 ■ *Power BI Data Modeling*

Then go to the **InternetSales** data set and click **SalesAmount**. You can see there is a sigma sign in front of the **SalesAmount** field, which indicates it is a numerical measure. Also, *yellow color right sign* in the **InternetSales** and **SalesAmount**. This indicates selected visual has been created using the *yellow right* indicated data set and field:

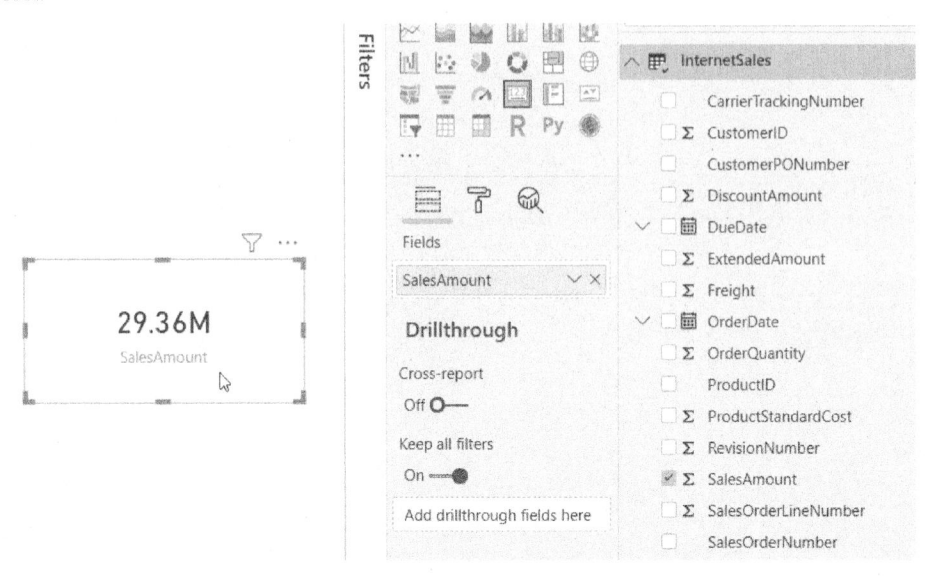

Figure 4.21: Represent the sales amount in card visual

Now, we are going to add a filter to this card. Go to **SalesTerritory** and drag and drop **SalesTerritoryCountry** filed into the filters pane:

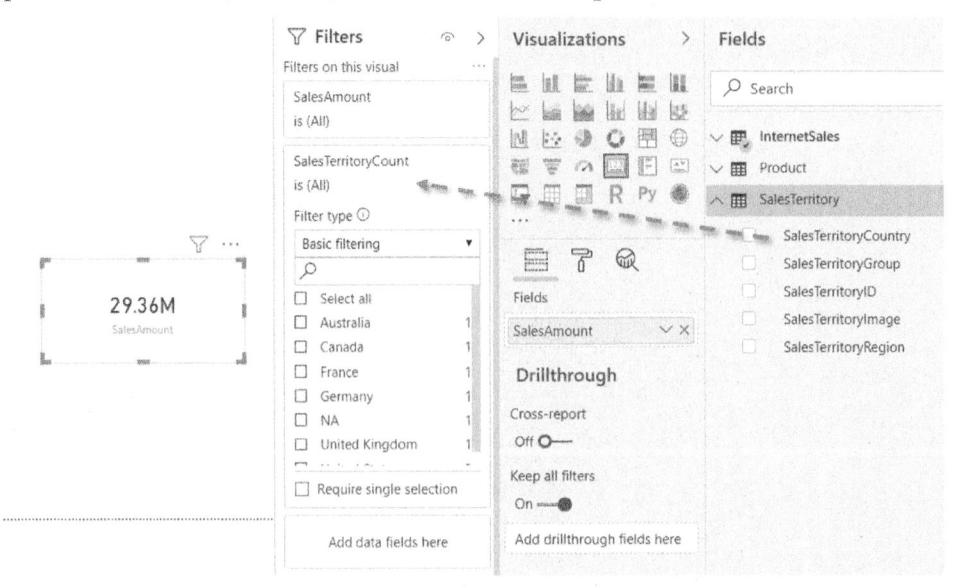

Figure 4.22: Add a visual level filter into the card

Then in the **Filters** list, select the **United Kingdom** checkbox. Then you can see the **29.3 M** initial figure changed to **3.39 M** after applying the filter:

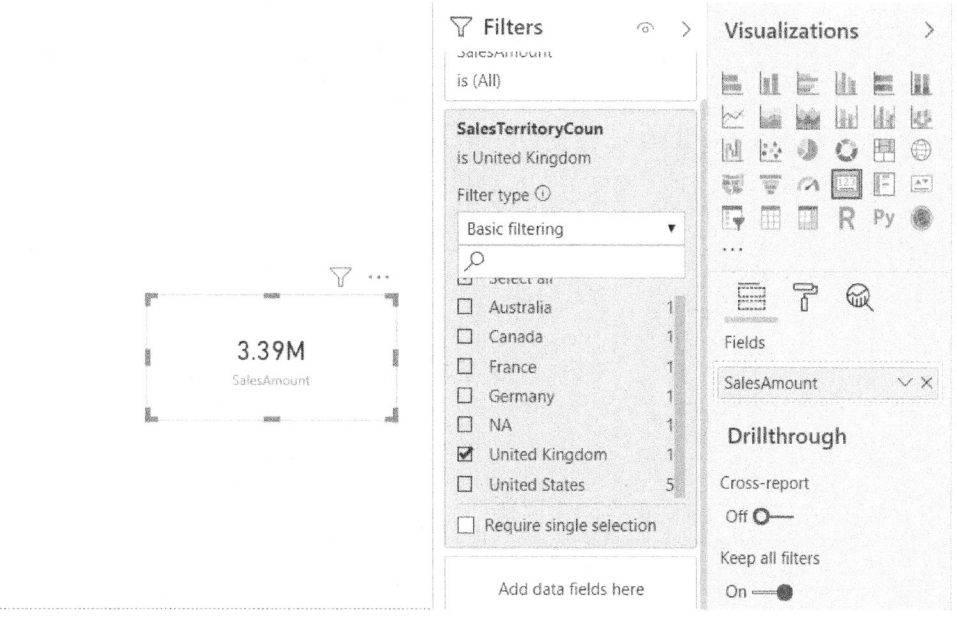

Figure 4.23: Sales amount filtered by the United Kingdom

It is a bit misleading to leave the card for United Kingdom sales with the name **SalesAmount**. So, let us rename it as **UK Sales**. Double click the fields **SalesAmount** placeholder and rename it as **UK Sales**:

Figure 4.24: Rename the fields

Another alternative is enabling the **Title** property and giving a name. You can find the **Title** property in the **Format** tab.

> When we talk about filters predominantly, there are three types of filters. Those are visual level filters, page-level filters, and report level filters. The visual level filter is the one you applied to the card previously. The page-level filter is only applicable for a particular page when applied. The report level filter is applied for every page in the report, which is also considered as a data set filter.

Figure 4.25: Add a title

You can make copies of visuals rather than create one by one. By selecting *Ctrl + C*, copy the particular visual, and paste by *Ctrl + V*. In this manner, we have reduced my effort making sales cards for each country. We changed the filter and field name for each country:

ADVENTURE WORKS Sales Analysis

3.39M	9.39M	9.06M	2.64M	1.98M	2.89M
UK Sales	US Sales	Australia Sales	France Sales	Canada Sales	Germany Sales

Figure 4.26: Copy and paste visuals to duplicate

Enabling gridlines by clicking the check box in the **View** tab helps you to align the visuals nicely.

Add a map visual

Add a **map** in **Visualizations** and configure the fields like this. For **Location**, drag and drop the **SalesTerritoryCountry**, **SalesAmount** in the **Size** place holder and **ProductCategory** in **Legend**:

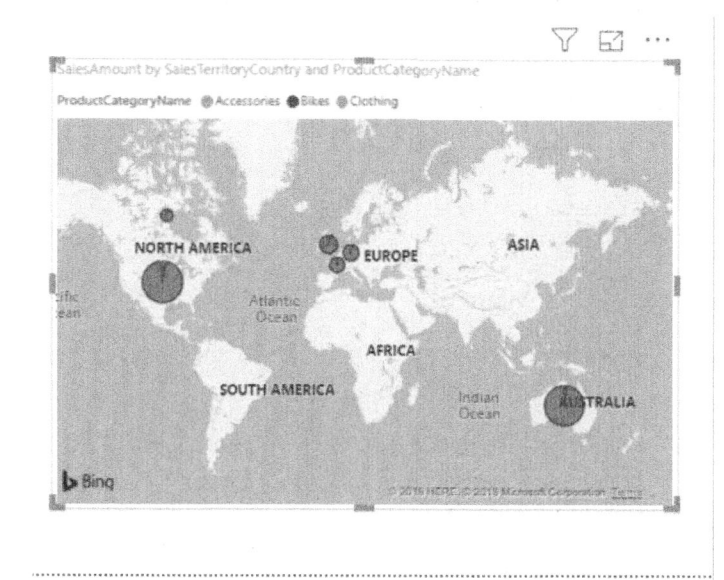

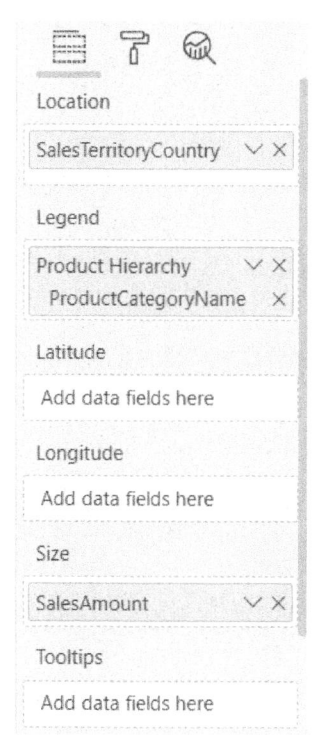

Figure 4.27: Add map visual

You may wonder about the **Latitude** and **Longitude** placeholders. Actually, if you have that information, also you can configure and draw the map more precisely.

Add a clustered column chart

Add a clustered column chart into the canvas. The purpose is to show a high-level understanding of how the sales have varied across countries. Even though we added sales cards, when it shows visually, the end-users can compare and have an understanding easily. That is why visual representation is more important than tabular representation (flat reports).

If you want you can give different colors for each country. For that, switch to the *Format* tab and expand the data colors. Then you can change the colors as desired:

Figure 4.28: Add a clustered column chart

Add a matrix visual

Among built-in Power BI visuals, there are two ways you can represent the data in tabular. By using a **Table** or a **Matrix**. I am going to add a matrix visual into the canvas and display product standard cost, quantity, discount, and sales amount along with the product hierarchy. You need to add product hierarchy to the **Rows** place holder and measures into the **Values** place holder. You can change the grid style as preferred. I have used the default style in the diagram:

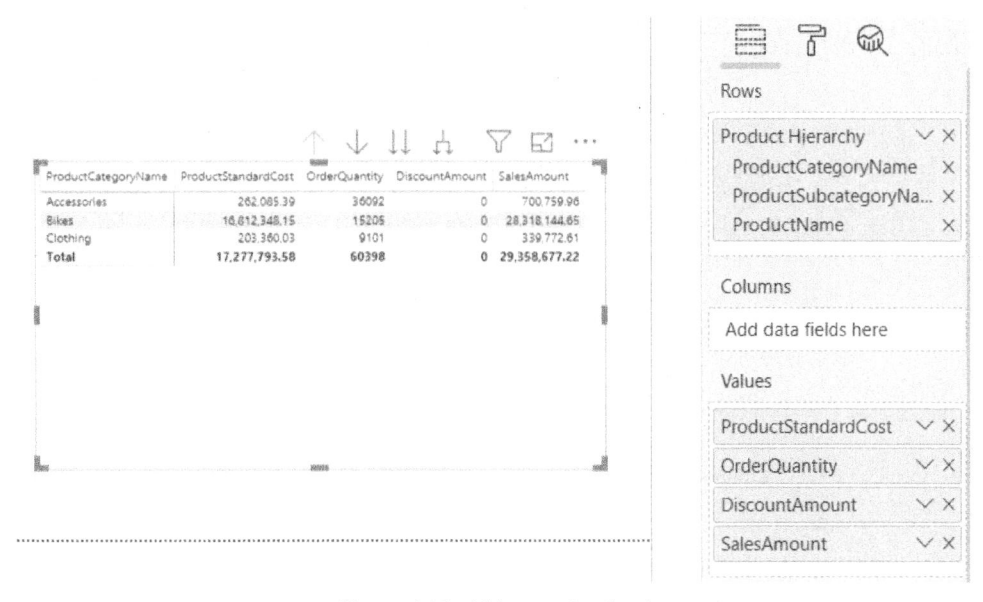

Figure 4.29: Add a matrix visual

You can enable conditional formatting to color the cell or font color based on the figure in each cell. In order to enable conditional formatting, go to *Format* tab, `Conditional formatting`, and then select the column you want to enable it:

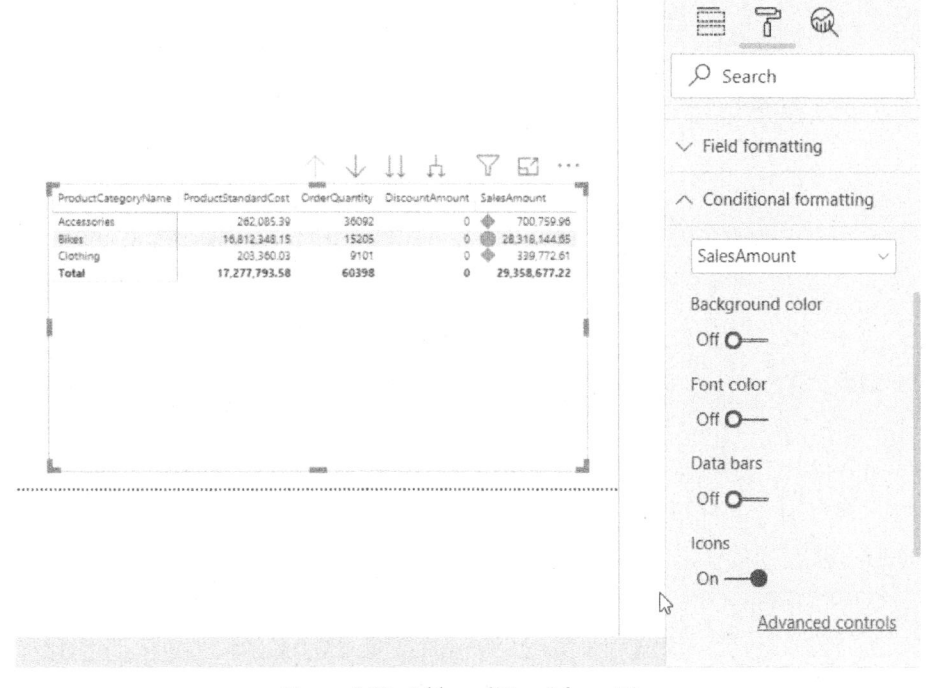

Figure 4.30: Add conditional formatting

64 ■ *Power BI Data Modeling*

Cross filtering

Cross filtering is the default behavior in Power BI. It means when you select a whole or part of any visual in the canvas, all other visuals in the report page will be filtered based on the filter criteria.

For example, I selected the `United States` column in the column chart. So, all other visuals in the report were filtered by the United States. When you need to go back to the earlier state, select any other area in the chart. It will remove the cross-filter you made:

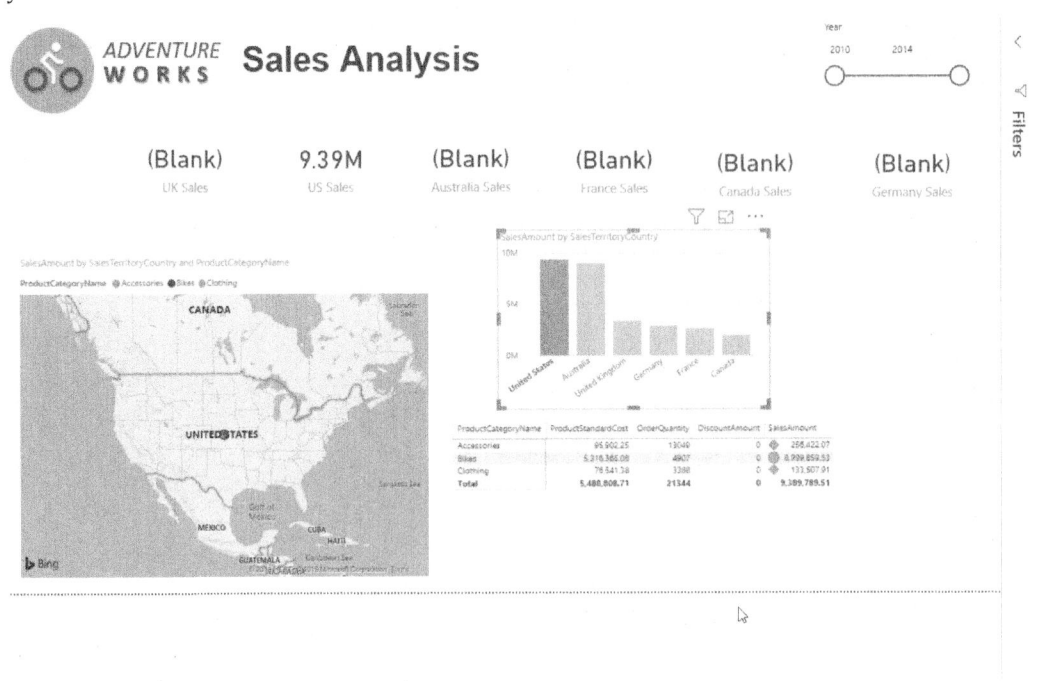

Figure 4.31: Cross filtered by US sales

Drill-down

Drill down feature will enable whenever you use a hierarchy in your visual. Not all visuals enable drill down at the beginning until you add hierarchy fields such as `Date Hierarchy`, `Product Hierarchy`, and so on.

In our matrix visual, we have used `Product Hierarchy`. So, you would notice there are additional three-down arrow icons at the top right corner in the matrix visual. This means you can drill down the data into a granular level through product hierarchy. You can enable drill down by clicking the down arrow once (you can disable the *drill down* if you click again):

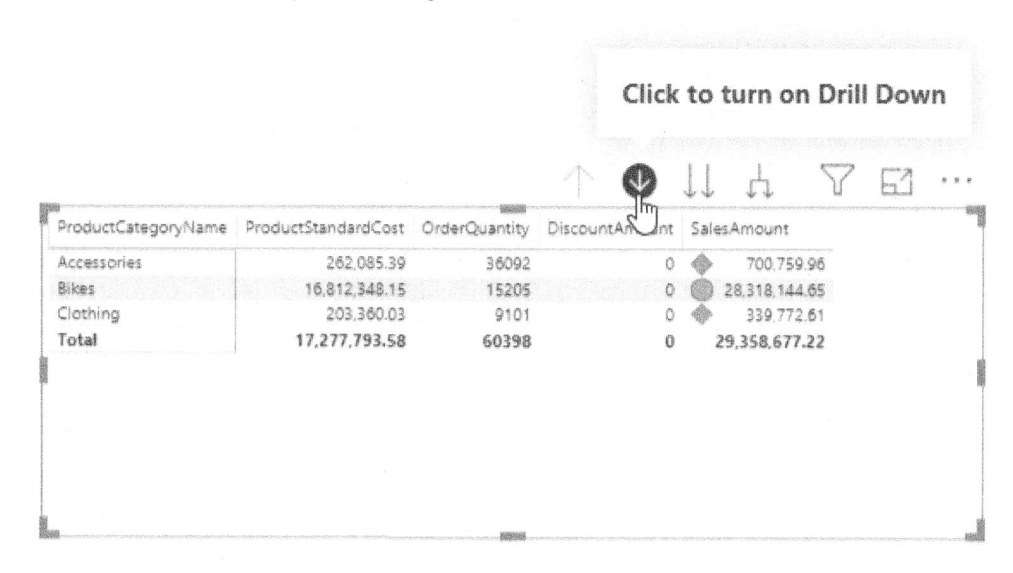

Figure 4.32: Enabled drill down

Click one of the cells in the `ProductCategoryName` column. We selected the `Accessories` cell; then it expands to all accessories:

Figure 4.33: Click to expand to the next level

Add a slicer

You can filter all the visuals or specific visuals on the report page using a slicer. In order to add a slicer, drag and drop the slicer visual from the **Visualization** pane.

Select the order date; then, the slicer automatically changes to a date range. In the **Fields** pane, **OrderDate**, click the down arrow and change to a date hierarchy. Then the slicer will turn into a **Year** range:

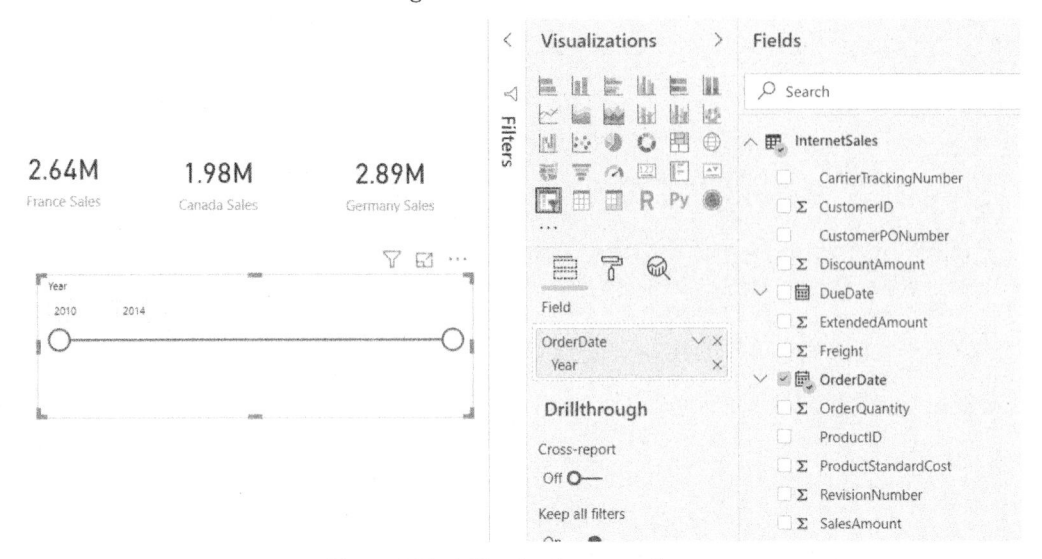

Figure 4.34: Add order date year slicer

Apart from that, you can perform various other formattings into your report such as add shapes and add background colors:

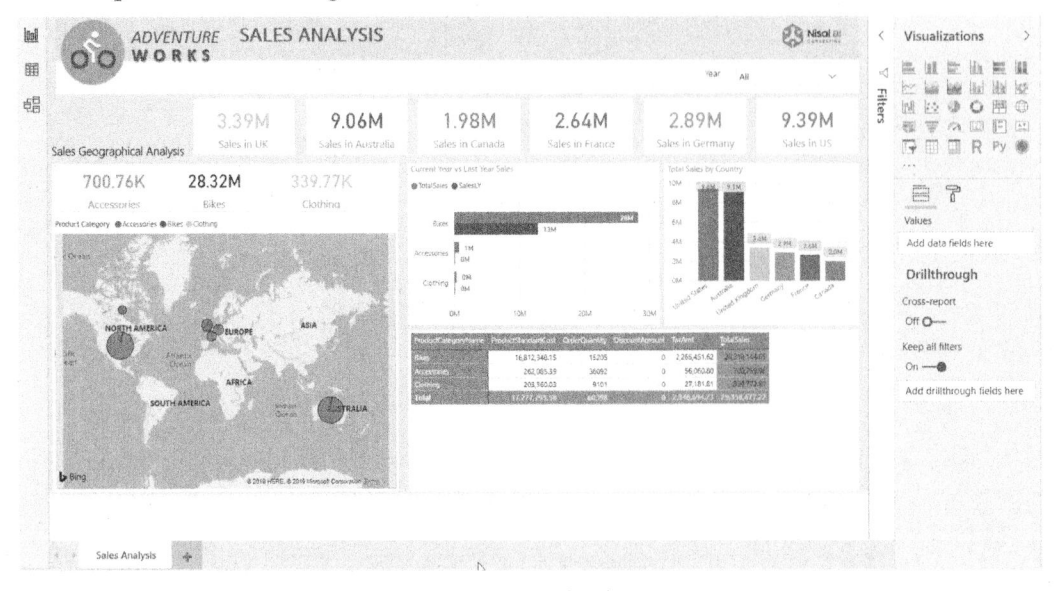

Figure 4.35: Completed report

Let us publish the report into the Power BI service.

My First Power BI Report ■ 67

In order to publish the report, you need to sign in with your Power BI account. This account makes the connection between your Power BI desktop report and the service when you publish the report:

Figure 4.36: Publish report

When you publish, it will ask about the destination of the workspace you need to publish the report. By default, it has selected **My workspace,** which is the default workspace.

You have to log in to http://powerbi.microsoft.com site using your Power BI account. Then you can see the published report:

Figure 4.37: Published report in Power BI service

Conclusion

In this chapter, you learned how to connect with CSV data, transform data, and build the first report in this book. There are a set of transformation steps discussed during the chapter, such as remove unwanted columns and replace values. Then we discussed user-defined hierarchies and created calculations. Finally, you learned how to publish the report you created into the Power BI service. In the upcoming chapter, we are going to discuss an important aspect of BI, data modeling. You will get more understanding about those names during the upcoming chapter.

Questions

1. Which language Power BI does not support for the data transformation?
   A. Python
   B. M
   C. R
   D. Q

2. Which feature allows you to select any visual area and filter all other visuals on the page based on the filter criteria?
   A. Cross-filter
   B. Slicer
   C. Drill-down filter
   D. Drill-through filter

Answers

1. D
2. A

CHAPTER 5
Introducing BI Building Blocks: Dimensional Modeling Concepts

So far, throughout this book, you have learned how to connect to the data source, the link between tables, create visuals, and publish the report into the Power BI service. In this chapter, we are going to discuss an important aspect of the BI, data modeling concepts. Data modeling is a key concept of data warehousing and Business Intelligence projects. Once you learn about this, it will help you to build a more robust Power BI implementation for the longer run. This also helps for better optimizations of the data structure.

Structure

The following topics will be covered during this chapter:

- *What is data modelling, and why?*
- Classic self-service BI approach versus data modeling
- Facts and dimensions
- Star schema and snowflake schema

Objective

The objective of this chapter is to provide high-level knowledge about the data modeling concepts and explain how it is different from the classic report development approach. Further, where you can apply data modeling techniques, data model design, facts, and dimensions. Knowing these concepts and practices will be beneficial when you develop Power BI reports in the real world. We always need to take the best approach when implementing Power BI reports in order to make it and explain to you about many advantages of following the modern BI approach.

What is data modeling, and why?

Data modeling is the process of designing a logical structure to store data in the form of a database. In this process, you may consider various aspects such as accessibility, optimization, and so on. Dimensional modeling is a subset of data modelling specifically designing for report databases or rather data warehouses. In the next few sections of this chapter, we will discuss what is meant by the classical approach and data modeling approach and what are the benefits in a detailed manner.

Classic BI approach

We assume that you may deal with many data source systems by now. Those could be in different domains such as sales, marketing, finance, HR, health care, logistics, and so on. The systems which record those data we call them as **Online Transactional Processing (OLTP)** systems. Those systems or databases are highly normalized and optimized for transaction recording. If you already have connected to one of those and try to draw visuals, which means knowing or without knowing, you could have followed the classic BI approach. The classic BI approach, it only contains three steps. You just connect to the data source, define metrics, and create interactive visuals:

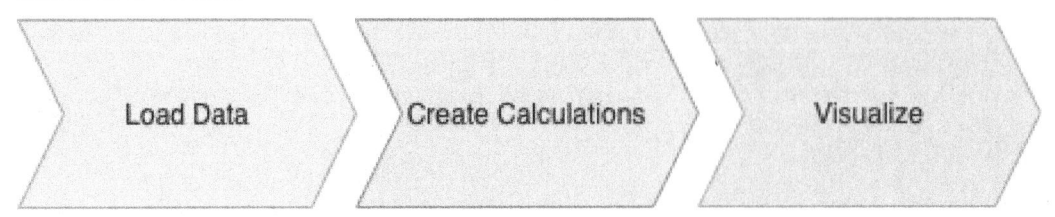

Figure 5.1: Classic BI approach

This is the traditional report development approach. Each of these steps is explained as follows:

- **Loading data**: Connect to the data source and load data into your Power BI file. There could be a single table or multiple tables. If you have to load multiple tables into the Power BI, you may think to connect those tables by building relationships in order to make filters work properly.

- **Create calculations**: Typically, after loading data, usually you define calculations or matrices which can be used during visualizations.

- **Create visuals**: This is nothing but creates interactive visuals using available data.

However, this approach is working fine with certain scenarios. For instance, if you have a simple data set with few tables and the data volume is also considerably low, then this approach would be fine. But, how about if you connect to a data source that contains *50+ tables*. Some operational databases may contain a couple of hundreds of tables. Sooner, you will find yourself it is hard to analyze when there are many tables in your Power BI file. Not only that but also a scenario where the data is volume is relatively large. If you tried out with large data sets like *approximately 1 GB* data volume, you might need to follow optimization in order to deliver a more robust BI solution to the end-user.

It is always required to follow the best storage and memory optimization practices during the model design. Then when the data grows over the period, your data model will perform well as earlier. It will be discussed about storage optimizations and memory optimization techniques during *Chapter 11, Row-Level Security in Power BI* and *Chapter 12, Calculation Groups in Power BI*.

Those systems have been optimized for transaction processing. You will find many much smaller tables with few records. But, when you perform reporting, you need to create relationships for each table. Not only that, you need to drag and drop the fields from all those tables. You would find it as a tedious task very soon.

Think about a scenario you connect with an OLTP system that contains more than fifty to hundreds of odd tables. After you connect to the source, you may find it yourself hard to go through and analyze data because of the table has already been overloaded. On the other hand, in a self-service BI system, analyzing and visualizing is not a one-time task.

This is the list of scenarios where the classic approach is not going to work:

- Connect with a source where having complex relational mapping.

- OLTP systems are not optimized for self-service reporting.

- Legacy source systems which are also normalized contains *100+ tables*. For example, ERP systems and legacy database systems.

- Though the structure is straightforward with the minimum number of tables, still you may require transforming it to a different format in order to serve self-service business intelligence users.

Modern self-service BI approach

In order to overcome the preceding limitations, we can create another layer in between imported data and the defined metrics phases, which is called as create a **data model** or **dimension model**.

Data modeling or dimension modeling is a design practice that enables the end-user to have a simplified data structure, which optimized for analytics. This methodology not only makes your data model simpler but also lead to perform well for large data volumes:

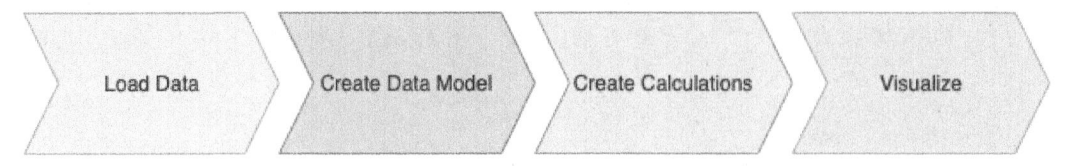

Figure 5.2: Modern self-service BI approach

This intermediate data model works as a data warehouse for the self-service Power BI reporting. It also transforms your source tables into facts and dimension tables, which is optimized for reporting.

End-to-end BI with Microsoft Power BI

If you are in the Business Intelligence arena and have worked for a couple of years, you might know in and out of BI stack by now. In the corporate BI, using Microsoft BI provides end-to-end BI for even large data volumes seamlessly and provides various analytics on top of that. With the arrival of Power BI now, not only data warehousing and BI experts but also people who are from other fields can easily do self-service BI through Power BI. The following table is shown how traditional corporate BI phases replaced with Power BI:

Phase	Corporate BI with SQL Server	Power BI
Data extract/load	SSIS	Power BI Power Query
Data Modeling	SSAS tabular/multidimensional	Power BI
Metrics	SSAS (DAX/MDX)	Power BI DAX
Reporting	Power BI	Power BI
Collaborating	Power BI service/embedding	Power BI service/embedding

Table 5.1: Traditional corporate BI phases replaced with Power BI

In the corporate BI with SQL Server, the data expectation, transform, and load or rather ETL is done by **SQL Server Integration** services. In Power BI, this can be done using **Powerful Power Query** language. Implementing a data warehouse with facts and dimensions will be done in SQL Server Analysis services using either **Tabular** or **Multidimensional** database engines in the traditional method. As I mentioned earlier, this can be served in Power BI. The only difference will be the way you form your tables. Defining metrics is a task of semantic modelling. This is what you are doing in DAX or MDX query language. In Power BI, you can use DAX for it. By now, reporting will be the same for traditional corporate BI and self-service BI. Power BI is used by both. Sharing reports is also the same.

Both multidimensional cubes and SSAS tabular are analysis databases. Both have similarities like can be implemented advanced calculations, KPIs, and hierarchies. Tabular is the latest in-memory database technology preceding by multidimensional. Both have unique programming languages for defining calculations by expressions and querying data. For multidimensional cubes, it is MDX, whereas when it comes to tabular, the language is called DAX. As mentioned before, Power BI is influenced by tabular database technology. So, you will learn on DAX in order to work with Power BI.

You cannot replace corporate BI using Power BI. But for some scenarios, Power BI works well. If you are developing a proof of concept for a data warehouse within a short time period, the go-to option is Power BI. Also, without doing further configuring, if you want to deliver a specific solution for a subset of users, this works perfectly. Always Power BI is a good test lab for connecting to new data sources and doing modeling. Power BI is also a candidate for delivering targeted solutions to the target audience as a cost-effective method where corporate BI is expensive.

However, Power BI is not limiting for your data volumes. You can go for Power BI Premium, which has dedicated storage of 1 TB and do Big Data processing. You can use Power BI dataflow, which is a good candidate for self-service ETLing. We are going to discuss about data flows in *Chapter 15, Composite Models and Perform Aggregations to Improve Query Performance*.

I am going to explain to you some key elements of data warehousing which are important to understand the concepts of BI.

Data warehouse

Typical OLTP database systems are highly normalized and optimized for transaction recording. So, when we try to use OLTP databases for reporting, we face many challenges like the slowness of query execution, lack of consistency, and so on. So, in order to overcome these problems, we create a separate database that is dedicated to reporting and analytics. You will find two types of tables in a data warehouse. Those are **fact tables** and **dimension tables**.

Dimensional model also identified as **data warehouse structure**. In other words, we are creating a data warehouse inside Power BI. Typically, during a data warehouse implementation, during the design phase, we create a **bus matrix** or **enterprise bus architecture**, which is a design artifact for the data warehouse. Bus matrix is a table matrix with a mapping between business processes in an organization against the dimensions.

Bus matrix architecture

The bus matrix architecture is a blueprint for enterprise-level dimensional modeling. It is a matrix consisting of all the dimensions and business processes that maintain the linkage between them. This makes it easy to understand how each business process interacts with dimensions. You can see a sample bus matrix as follows in *figure 5.3*:

BUSINESS PROCESSES	Date	Product	Customer	Sales Person	Location	Vendor
Sales Order	X	X	X	X		
Product Inventory	X	X			X	
Purchase Order	X	X				X

Figure 5.3: Bus matrix architecture

During the **source data analysis**, all the business processes or events are listed down on the left-hand side, and common dimensions are on the right-hand side. Against each business process, linked dimensions are checked in order to indicate a number of dimensions and granularity for each process.

For instance, the sales order process recorded the date-time information, product, customer, and salesperson. Even though other dimensions like location and vendor are defined in the system, those are not relevant to the sales order business process.

Similarly, product inventory is linked with a date-time dimension, a product of course, and location dimension.

Fact tables

Fact tables are a type of tables in a data warehouse that store all the business processes, events, or transactions. For example, let us assume we are going to capture employee attendance events. So, we can record all the attendance information in the **Attendance** fact table. Similarly, order transactions we could capture in the **Order** fact table. Usually, in a fact table, there are two column types:

- **Surrogate keys**: Keys that reference linked dimensions. Example: **Employee attendance** fact table there can be linked dimensions like employee, date, time, department, reporting manager, and so on. So, this enables the analysis of attendance information using all these dimensions.

- **Measures**: Numerical values or facts generated during the event. Scenarios like sales in a supermarket, those measures will be unit price, order quantity, and sales amount:

OnlineSalesKey	DateKey	StoreKey	ProductKey	CustomerKey	SalesQuantity	SalesAmount	DiscountQuantity	DiscountAmount	TotalCost	UnitCost	UnitPrice
19560484	2007-01-01 00:00:00.000	306	782	333	1	10.36	1	2.59	6.60	6.60	12.95
19560485	2007-01-01 00:00:00.000	306	782	334	1	10.36	1	2.59	6.60	6.60	12.95
19560486	2007-01-01 00:00:00.000	306	782	335	1	10.36	1	2.59	6.60	6.60	12.95
19560487	2007-01-01 00:00:00.000	306	782	336	1	10.36	1	2.59	6.60	6.60	12.95
19560488	2007-01-01 00:00:00.000	306	782	337	1	10.36	1	2.59	6.60	6.60	12.95
19560489	2007-01-01 00:00:00.000	306	1701	333	1	3.984	1	0.996	2.54	2.54	4.98
19560490	2007-01-01 00:00:00.000	306	1701	334	1	3.984	1	0.996	2.54	2.54	4.98
19560491	2007-01-01 00:00:00.000	306	1701	335	1	3.984	1	0.996	2.54	2.54	4.98
19560492	2007-01-01 00:00:00.000	306	1701	336	1	3.984	1	0.996	2.54	2.54	4.98
19560493	2007-01-01 00:00:00.000	306	1701	337	1	3.984	1	0.996	2.54	2.54	4.98
19560494	2007-01-01 00:00:00.000	306	1701	338	1	3.984	1	0.996	2.54	2.54	4.98
19560495	2007-01-01 00:00:00.000	306	1701	339	1	3.984	1	0.996	2.54	2.54	4.98
19560496	2007-01-01 00:00:00.000	306	1701	340	1	3.984	1	0.996	2.54	2.54	4.98
19560497	2007-01-01 00:00:00.000	306	1701	341	1	3.984	1	0.996	2.54	2.54	4.98
19560498	2007-01-01 00:00:00.000	306	1701	342	1	3.984	1	0.996	2.54	2.54	4.98
19560499	2007-01-01 00:00:00.000	306	1701	343	1	3.984	1	0.996	2.54	2.54	4.98
19560500	2007-01-01 00:00:00.000	306	1701	344	1	3.984	1	0.996	2.54	2.54	4.98
19560501	2007-01-01 00:00:00.000	306	1701	345	1	3.984	1	0.996	2.54	2.54	4.98
19560502	2007-01-01 00:00:00.000	306	1701	346	1	3.984	1	0.996	2.54	2.54	4.98

Figure 5.4: Sample fact table which holds sales data

Usually, fact tables are relatively larger than dimension tables. So that is why only store numerical values in the fact table, which consume lesser storage space. So, when you design fact tables using Power BI, make sure you can assign relevant data types.

Dimension tables

All the textual data and the entities map are dimensions. In a supermarket scenario, product, product category, salesmen, customer, and most importantly, date and time are the dimensions. You will find three main components in a dimension table:

- **Surrogate key**: This is an auto-increment numeric field that is created to maintain the uniqueness of records. This field works as the primary key for the dimension.

- **Business key**: This is the unique key when the data is in the source. This can be duplicated, especially if you maintain history records in your dimension table.
- **Dimension attributes**: Textual fields as dimension attributes.

The idea is the business user will be able to analyze order information using different dimensions. You can analyze daily sales by joining date dimension and sales order fact table and aggregate sales amount and apply a filter in date dimension, date attribute which equal to any particular date if you want or else you can have daily sales:

ProductKey	ProductLabel	ProductName	ProductDescription	Manufacturer	BrandName	ClassName	StyleName	ColorName
1	0101001	Contoso 512MB MP3 Player E51 Silver	512MB USB driver plays MP3 and WMA	Contoso, Ltd	Contoso	Economy	Product0101001	Silver
2	0101002	Contoso 512MB MP3 Player E51 Blue	512MB USB driver plays MP3 and WMA	Contoso, Ltd	Contoso	Economy	Product0101002	Blue
3	0101003	Contoso 1G MP3 Player E100 White	1GB flash memory and USB driver plays MP3 and WMA	Contoso, Ltd	Contoso	Economy	Product0101003	White
4	0101004	Contoso 2G MP3 Player E200 Silver	2GB flash memory, LCD display, plays MP3 and WMA	Contoso, Ltd	Contoso	Economy	Product0101004	Silver
5	0101005	Contoso 2G MP3 Player E200 Red	2GB flash memory, LCD display, plays MP3 and WMA	Contoso, Ltd	Contoso	Economy	Product0101005	Red
6	0101006	Contoso 2G MP3 Player E200 Black	2GB flash memory, LCD display, plays MP3 and WMA	Contoso, Ltd	Contoso	Economy	Product0101006	Black
7	0101007	Contoso 2G MP3 Player E200 Blue	2GB flash memory, LCD display, plays MP3 and WMA	Contoso, Ltd	Contoso	Economy	Product0101007	Blue
8	0101008	Contoso 4G MP3 Player E400 Silver	4GB flash memory and FM Radio, LCD Display with 7-...	Contoso, Ltd	Contoso	Economy	Product0101008	Silver
9	0101009	Contoso 4G MP3 Player E400 Black	4GB flash memory and FM Radio, LCD Display with 7-...	Contoso, Ltd	Contoso	Economy	Product0101009	Black
10	0101010	Contoso 4G MP3 Player E400 Green	4GB flash memory and FM Radio, LCD Display with 7-...	Contoso, Ltd	Contoso	Economy	Product0101010	Green
11	0101011	Contoso 4G MP3 Player E400 Orange	4GB flash memory and FM Radio, LCD Display with 7-...	Contoso, Ltd	Contoso	Economy	Product0101011	Orange
12	0101012	Contoso 4GB Flash MP3 Player E401 Blue	1.8" color LCD, play MP3, WMA and Video MTV, and...	Contoso, Ltd	Contoso	Economy	Product0101012	Blue
13	0101013	Contoso 4GB Flash MP3 Player E401 Black	1.8" color LCD, play MP3, WMA and Video MTV, and...	Contoso, Ltd	Contoso	Economy	Product0101013	Black
14	0101014	Contoso 4GB Flash MP3 Player E401 Silver	1.8" color LCD, play MP3, WMA and Video MTV, and...	Contoso, Ltd	Contoso	Economy	Product0101014	Silver
15	0101015	Contoso 4GB Flash MP3 Player E401 White	1.8" color LCD, play MP3, WMA and Video MTV, and...	Contoso, Ltd	Contoso	Economy	Product0101015	White
16	0101016	Contoso 8GB Super-Slim MP3/Video Player M800 White	2" color LCD, Touchpad, Plays music, video, photos ...	Contoso, Ltd	Contoso	Regular	Product0101016	White
17	0101017	Contoso 8GB Super-Slim MP3/Video Player M800 Red	2" color LCD, Touchpad, Plays music, video, photos ...	Contoso, Ltd	Contoso	Regular	Product0101017	Red

Figure 5.5: Sample product dimension table

Granularities

Granularity is the number of dimensions linked to a fact. As mentioned before, if we have recorded customer, product, location, date, a salesperson with sales amount, then the granularity is **five**.

Star schema

If you are designing a data warehouse or dimension model in Power BI, it should be either **star-schema** or **snowflake schema**. Star schema is a structure in data warehousing where the fact table is in the middle and surrounded by all dimensions:

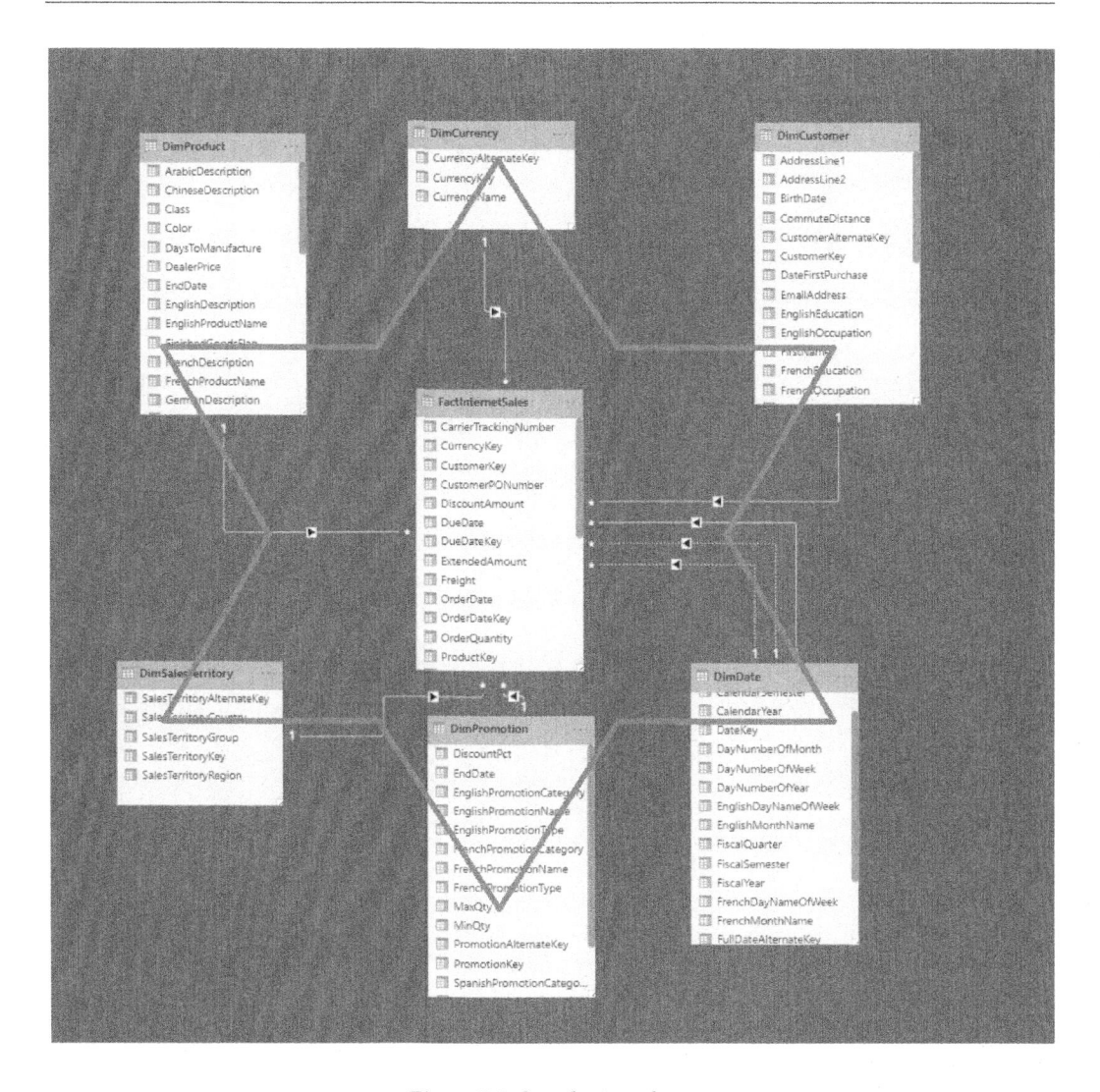

Figure 5.6: Sample star schema

Snowflake schema

In the **snowflake schema**, the fact will be surrounded by dimensions, and there will be other dimensions that connect with dimensions; for example, **Sales** fact can be linked to the **Product** dimension. **Product** dimension linked to **Product Subcategory** dimension. Product Subcategory linked again with **Product category** dimension:

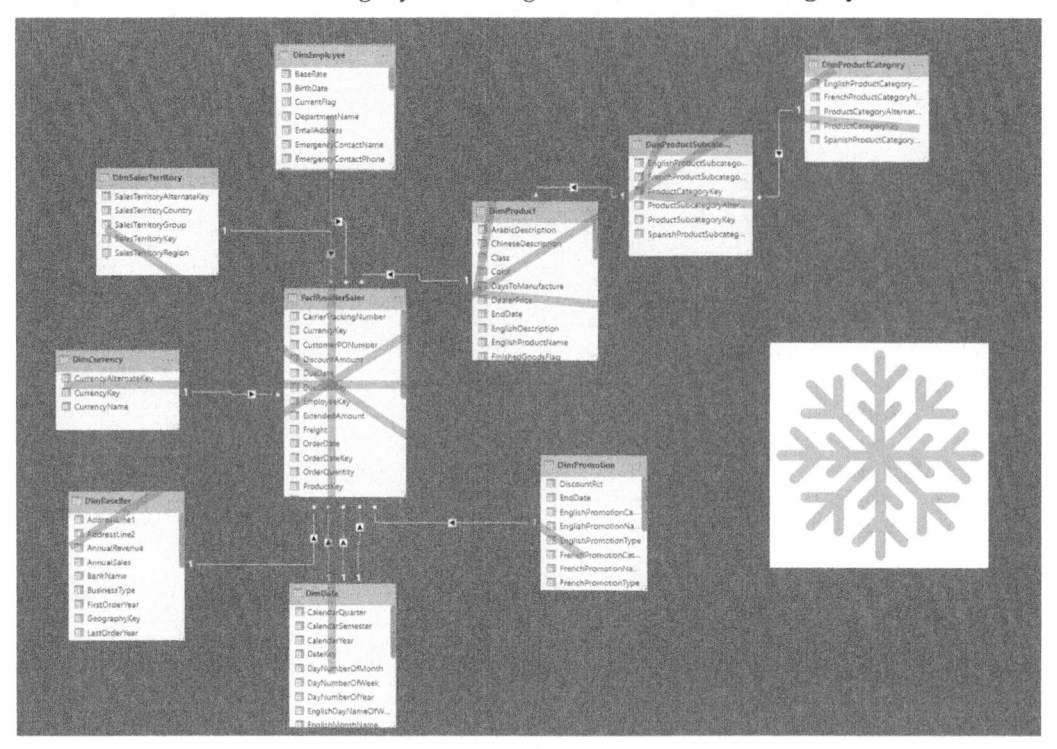

Figure 5.7: Snowflake schema

You would notice that the main difference in **star schema** versus **snowflake** is in snowflake hierarchies divided into separate tables, whereas star schema does not. Star schema is always a simple design structure compared with the snowflake. Suppose that the product hierarchy without splitting to individual tables, having in same **Product** table in star schema leads to high data redundancy. However, due to **Vertipaq** engine behavior, which would not be an issue. Star schema gives a much clearer picture of your data model because of less number of tables. We will talk more about storage optimization in *Chapter 11, Row-Level Security in Power BI*.

The objective of this chapter is not to teach you all the data warehousing and dimensional modeling concepts because it is a broad topic, and there are several books on it.

Conclusion

In this chapter, we discussed what data modeling is and why it is important as a Power BI report developer.

Here, you learned about the difference between the traditional report development approach and the modern approach with data modelling. Further, facts and dimensions; tables and schemas.

In the next chapter, you will learn how to work with relational database data sources like SQL Server.

Questions

1. **What is the name of the key, which maintains the uniqueness of records in a dimension?**

   A. Surrogate key

   B. Business key

   C. Primary key

   D. Candidate key

2. **Bus matrix is the main design artifact of a data warehouse solution. What are the main components in a bus matrix design?**

   A. Dimensions and facts

   B. Dimensions and business processes

   C. Dimensions and measures

   D. Dimensions and metrics

3. Research on creating a comprehensive data model and state here the benefits of creating rather than following a traditional approach.

4. In this chapter, we mostly talked about designing the data model. Discuss on how to implement a data model with available features in Power BI.

5. Discuss about star schema and snowflake schema and when to use each of them.

Answers

1. A
2. B

CHAPTER 6
Get Data from Relational Databases

In the previous chapters, you learned about how to connect with data and data modeling concepts, which is key to the self-service BI. Though the basic concept is covered in dimension modeling, you will require to learn more on that area to master it. However, this is not the main objective of this book; we cover as much as possible, which helps you to get in started with data modeling.

Structure

The following topics will be covered during this chapter:

- Relational database connectors
- Ingesting data from SQL databases
- DirectQuery and Import connectivity
- Best practices

Objective

The objective of this chapter is to teach you how to connect to database sources using provided connectors and some best practices you can follow when data loading from relational databases.

In the previous chapter, you learned the difference between the classic self-service BI approach and the modern self-service BI approach with data modeling concepts. In this chapter, we will be more focused on getting data from relational databases. This is one of the most common use cases, even when you are using Power BI in the cloud. However, Power BI is not limited to relational database sources.

In this chapter, for the demo purpose, I have used `AdventureWorksLT` sample relational database. You can download it from the Web:

https://github.com/Microsoft/sql-server-samples/releases/tag/adventureworks

Relational database connectors

Power BI supports a range of relational database connectors. You can see the list of connectors under the **Database** tab. Not all the connectors are in the relational database category. For example, **SQL Server Analysis Services** and **SAP Hana** are types of databases, which are fully or partially in-memory. In order to get the window, select the `Get Data` option and then select the **Database** tab as in *figure 6.1*:

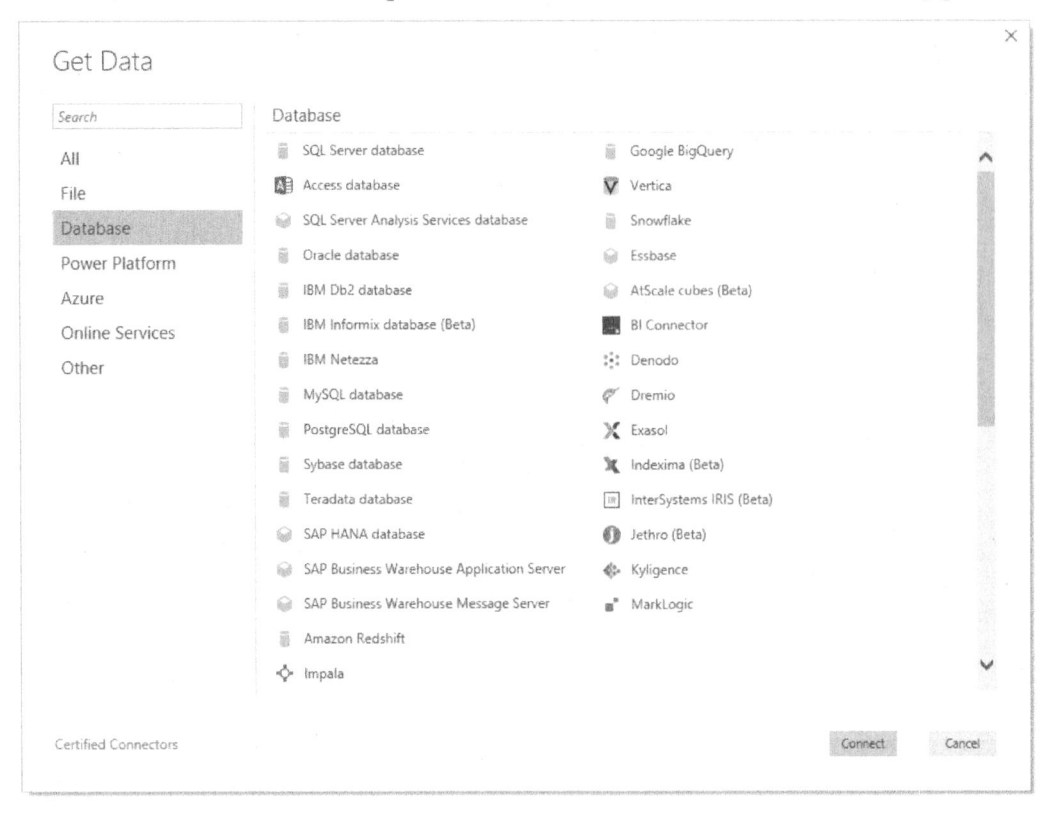

Figure 6.1: Database connectors in Power BI

Maybe you are connecting to an ERP system with many tables; sometimes, you may connect to a CRM database or any other operational database using Power BI. All these systems use relational databases to store data. Further, after going through certain processes to implement a relational data warehouse, we will be using the same source. Whatever the relational source mentioned, Power BI serves the self-service and semantic model requirement.

Getting data with SQL Server database

In order to connect to SQL Server data source, select the get data from the **Home** tab, then select the **Database** tab. Then select `SQL Server Database`. You can see a window where you can configure the database settings as shown in *figure 6.2*:

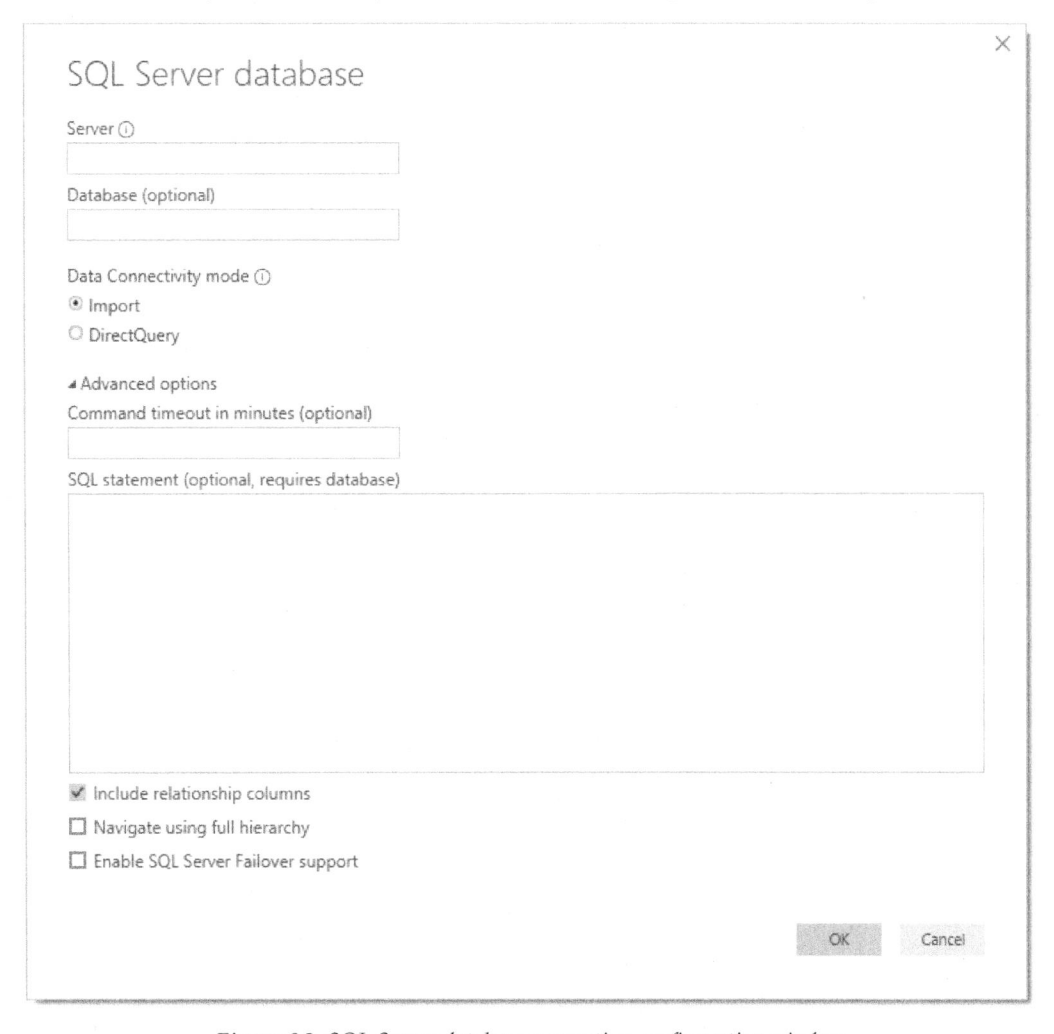

Figure 6.2: SQL Server database connection configuration window

Each configuration setting option is explained as follows:

- **Server**: This is the SQL server instance name that you are going to connect.
- **Database**: Database name you are planning to connect. As mentioned, this is optional. If you did not provide the database name, then it will show the list of databases in the server to choose from in the wizard.
- **Data Connectivity mode**: This is the most crucial configuration in this window. Why? Because this decides whether you are using **DirectQuery** connection or **Import**. Both are widely used in different scenarios.

For example, you can use the **Import** mode option to connect if you see there are many more transformations that need to be done in order to model and visualize data. If you can remember, in the previous chapter, one of the data modeling requirements is when you have a source like an ERP system with many more tables, but still, you do not want to expose them as is to the analytical user. Because it is time-consuming to analyze data as is. So, you may need to consolidate and aggregate to a certain degree in order to serve it to the end-users.

DirectQuery mode will be useful when your source is a reporting database or a relational data warehouse, where you expect all the consolidation cleansing work already done when loading from the original source to the warehouse. As shown in *figure 6.3*, the data warehouse consists of already pre-processed data to consume. So, Power BI will use the **DirectQuery** option just to read and visualize the data. In this method, data importing and storing do not happen:

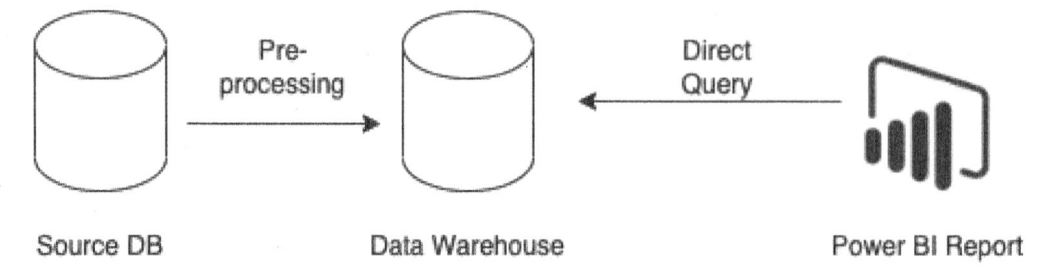

Figure 6.3: DirectQuery from the data warehouse

Advanced options

The following are the set of options/configurations that has been provided apart from the basic configurations:

- **Command timeout in minutes(optional)**: This option will be useful, especially when your queries take more time to refresh. In that case, you can set the time out in minutes.

- **SQL statement (optional, requires database)**: In this option, you can write a T-SQL statement that references a table, set of tables by **JOIN** condition, a view, or procedure, and so on:

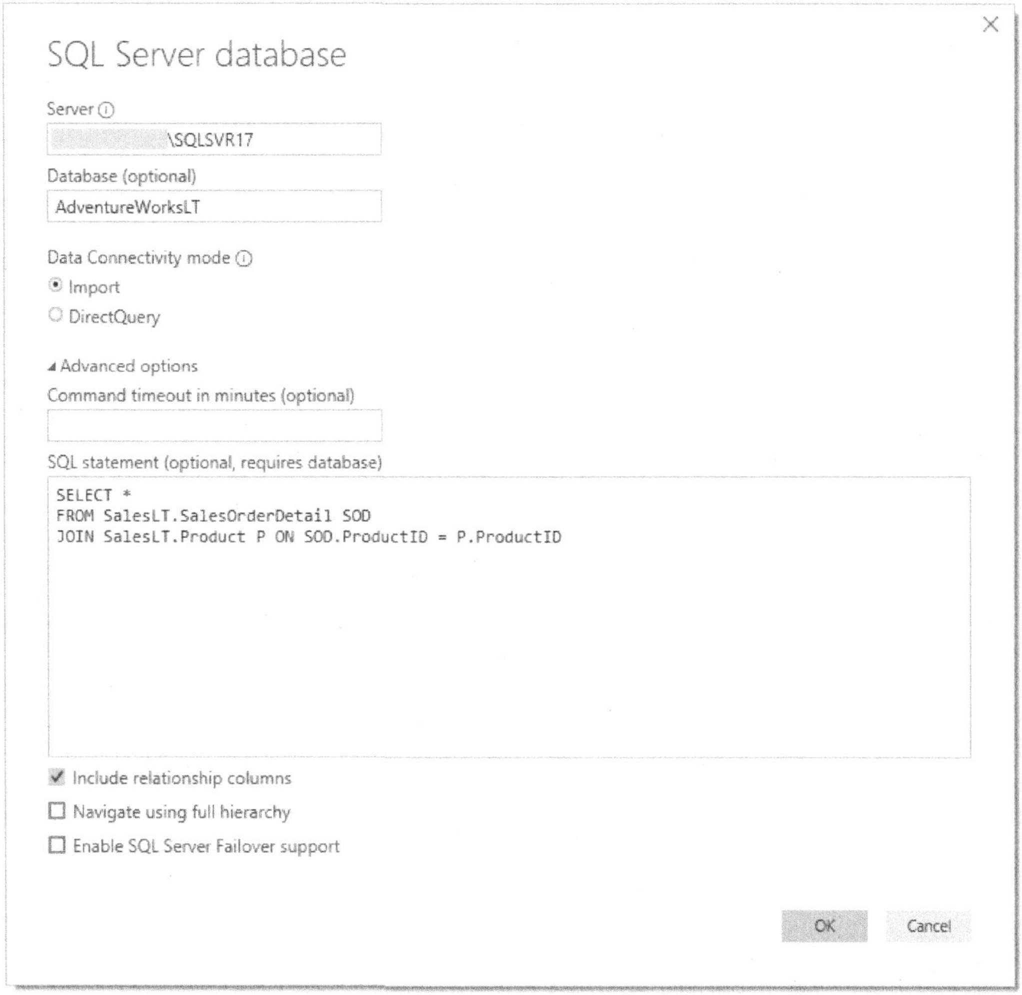

Figure 6.4: SQL statement provided to get data from two tables

T-SQL or Transact SQL is an extension to the Structured Query Language (SQL), the language we use to engage with relational databases like SQL Server. Apart from the standard SQL, T-SQL includes procedural programming build-in functions for the date, string, and mathematical processing. There are many more enhancements you can find in T-SQL as opposed to SQL.

Include relationship columns

By default, this option has been checked. Here, it reads the relationship metadata, including the primary key and foreign key of your selected tables. One advantage is you can apply the related tables option, which selects the relation tables to your selected table.

Here, first, select **SalesLT.SalesOrderDetail** table and then select the **Select Related Tables** option. Then it will automatically select the related two tables: **SalesOrderHeader** and **Product** table:

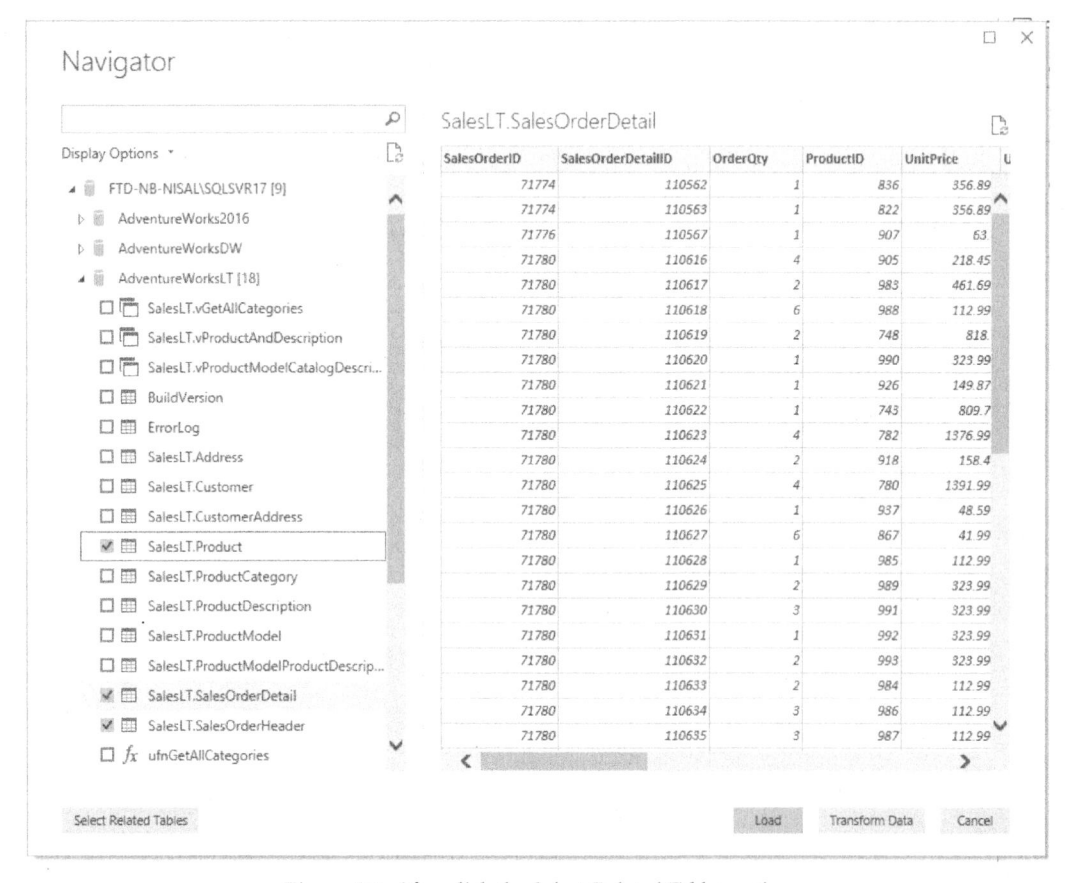

Figure 6.5: After click the Select Related Tables option

If you deselect **Include relationship columns**, the Power BI tool is unable to find related tables. So, in such case, you will get a message like: **We didn't find any more related tables** as shown in the following screenshot:

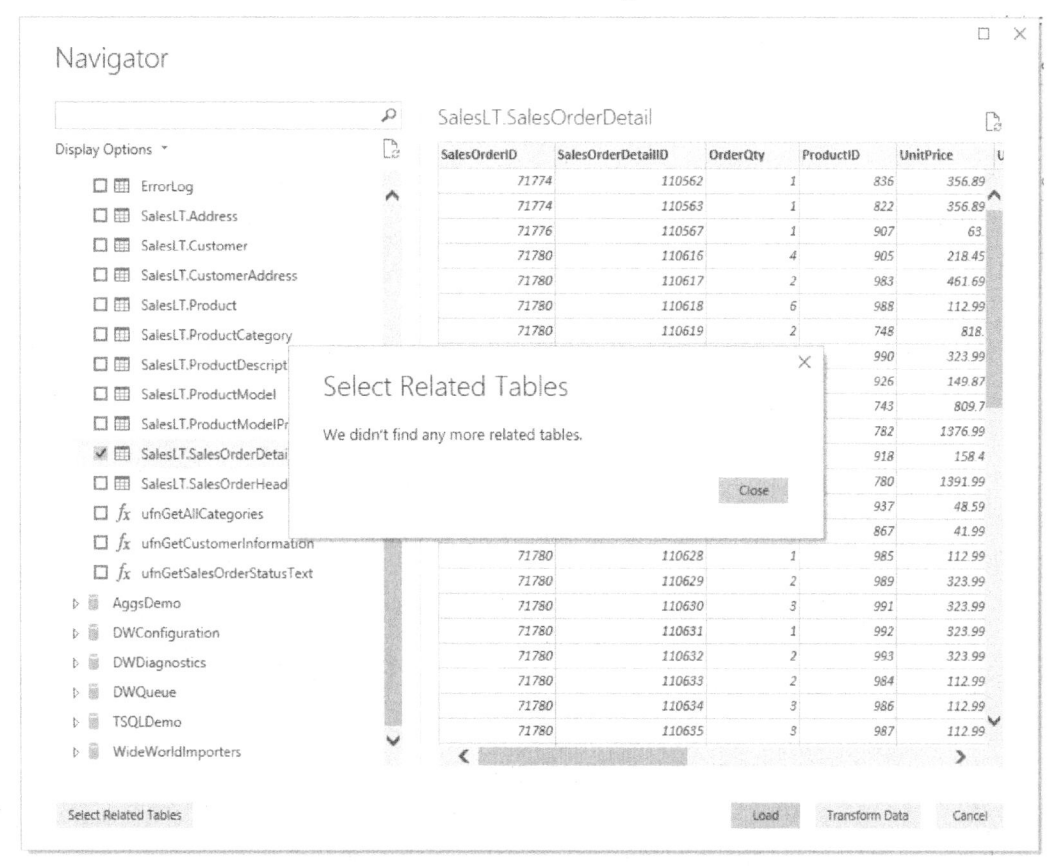

Figure 6.6: Select related tables option is not working

If you have checked, the same option will be helpful to automatically detect the filter relationships in your *Model* tab immediately after you imported your data into Power BI:

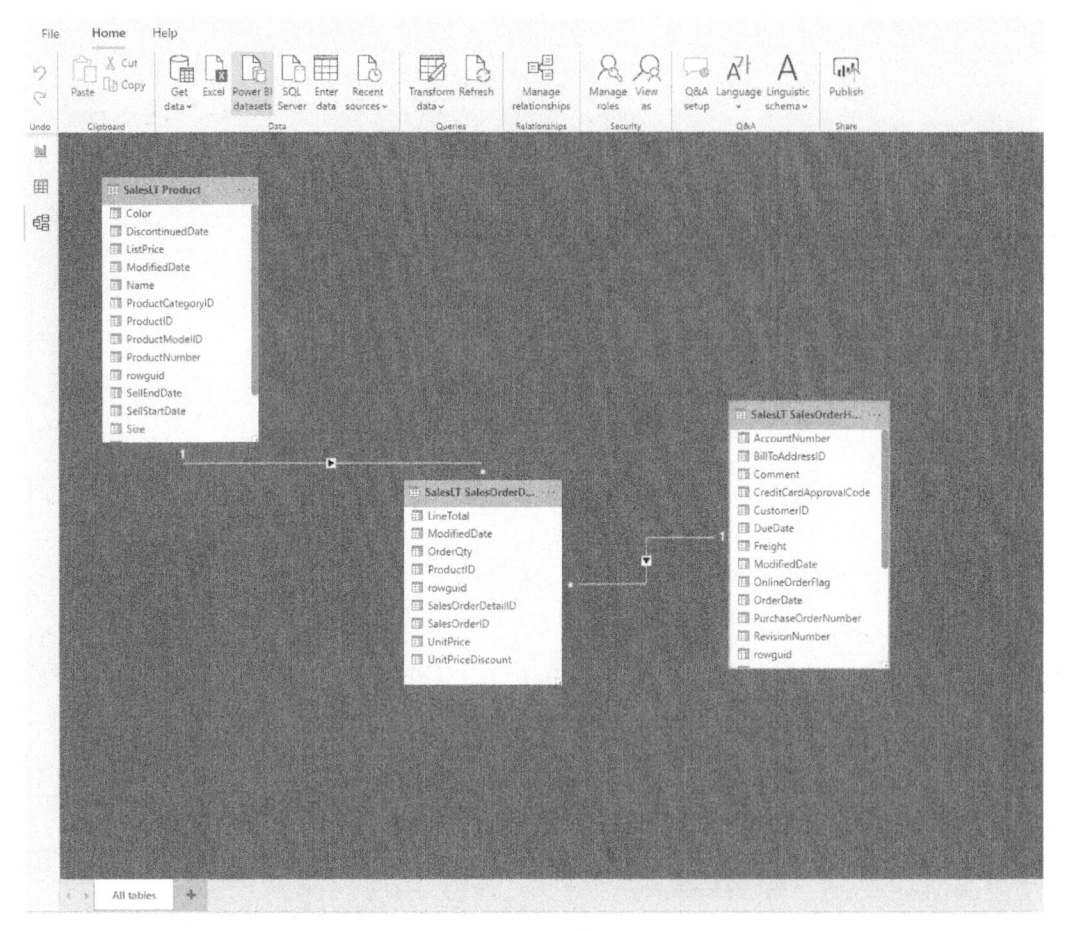

Figure 6.7: Detect relationships automatically

Assume that you have just selected one table from your relational database, that is, the `SalesOrderDetails` table. The other noticeable feature is when you go to the `Transform Data` option (edit queries), you can see special kinds of columns that are not supposed to be in your table. Basically, if you cross-check with the source SQL table, you cannot find such columns.

These are the linked columns based on the relationship you have in your selected table, **SalesLT.SalesOrderDetail** with other tables:

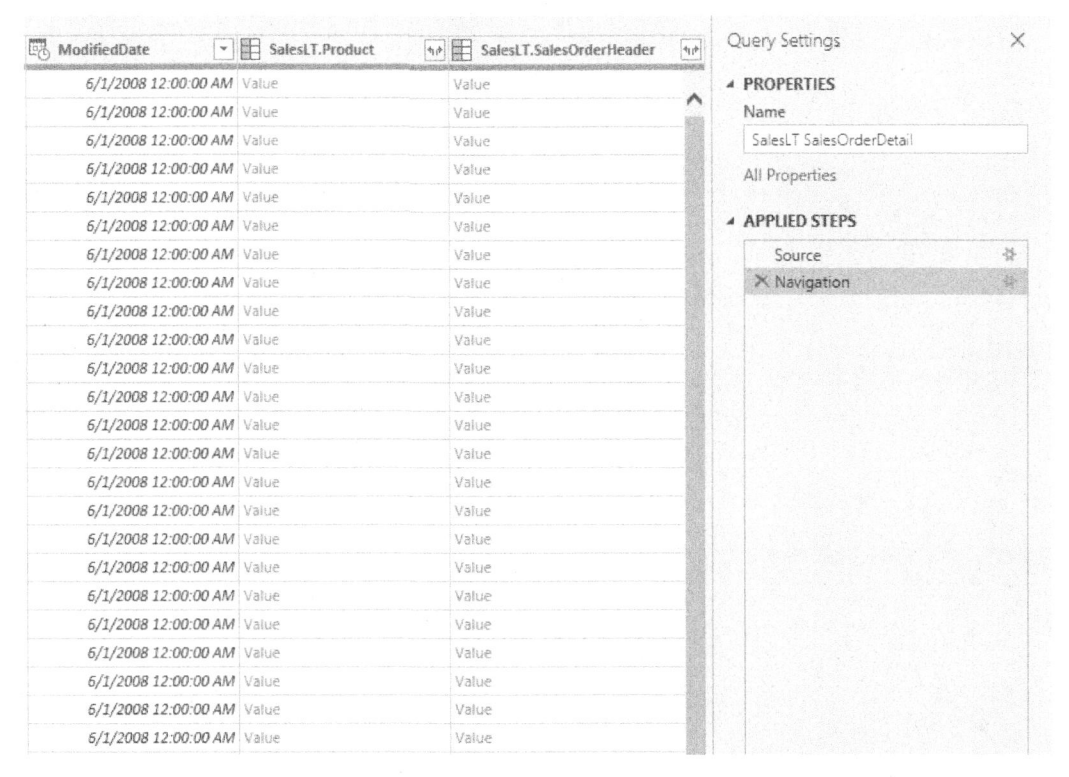

Figure 6.8: Show related table links in transform data

If you click the *double arrow* button at the corner in the column header, you can expand and see the columns in the related table. If you want, you can add those columns too into the existing query even though you have not added that table when you are loading data:

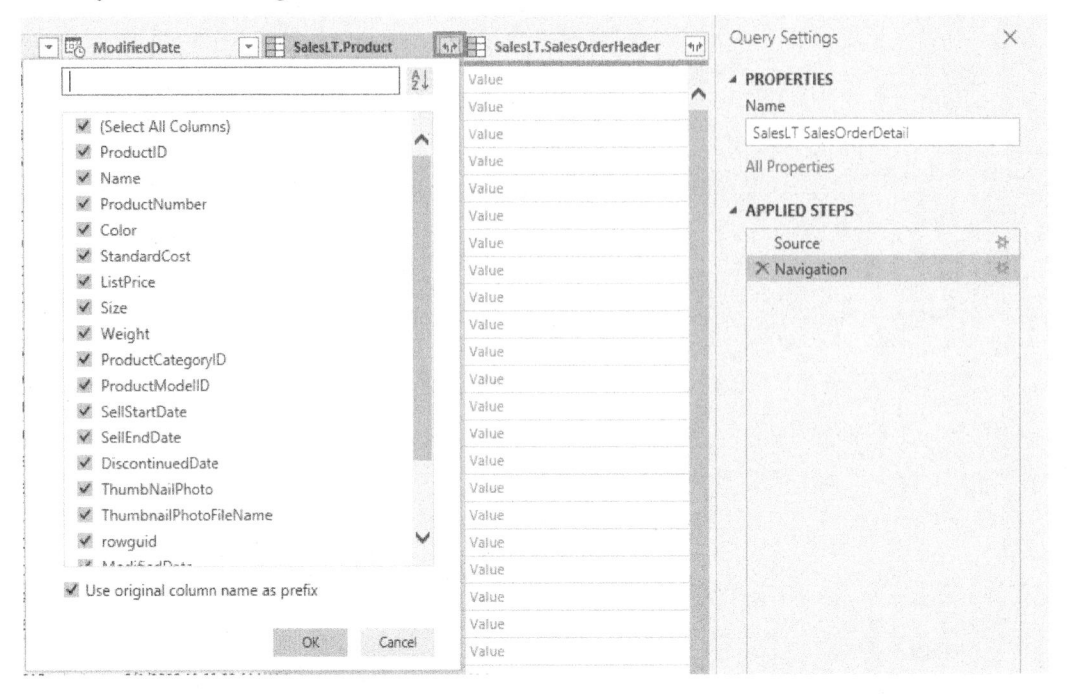

Figure 6.9: Expand and view the columns in related tables

Navigate using the full hierarchy

When you select this option, you can navigate through the database object hierarchy. Please refer to the following screenshot for comparison:

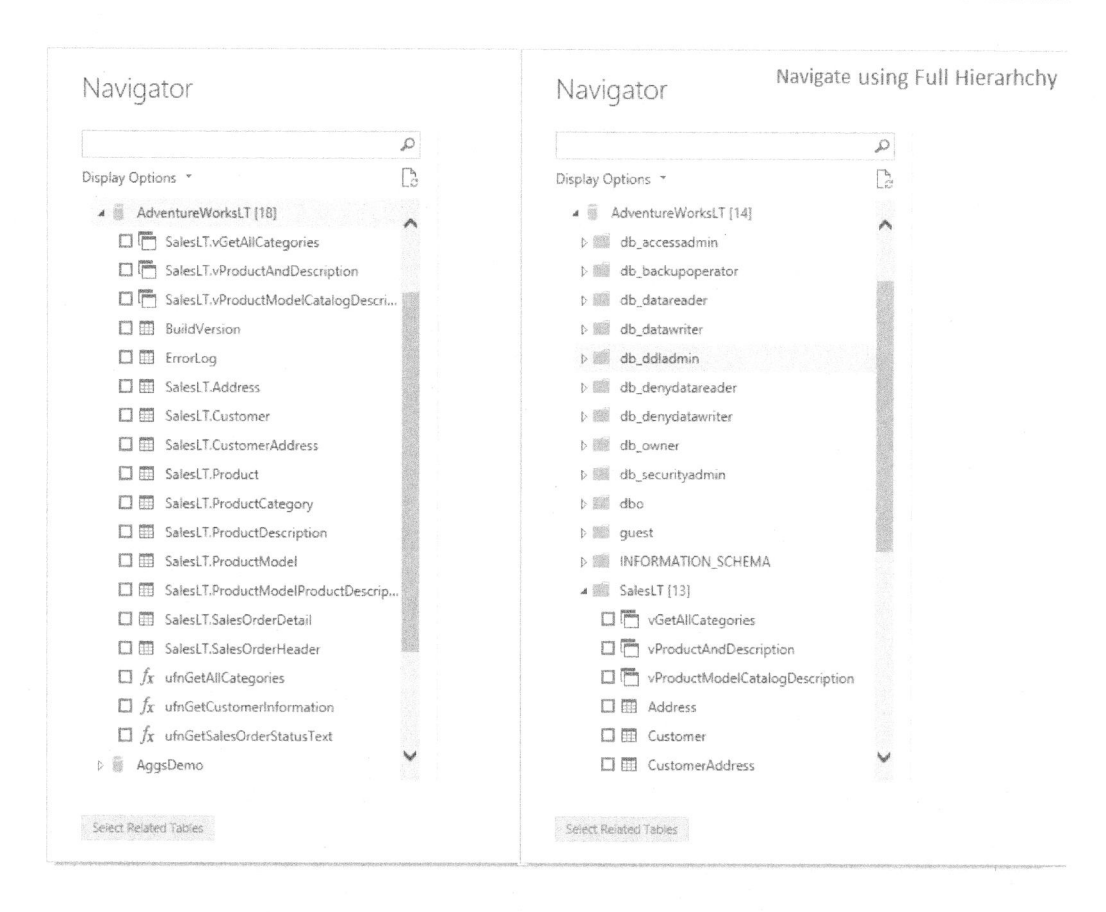

Figure 6.10: Compare normal behavior and when you select Navigate using the full hierarchy option

Enable SQL Server failover support

Once this option is checked, it will add **MultiSubnetFailoverSupport= True** and **ApplicationIntent = Read-only**. It means this option supports faster failover for all availability groups.

Disaster recovery and failover is a separate branch of SQL Server database administration, which is not planned to go into detail in this book.

92 ■ *Power BI Data Modeling*

Once you configure the initial window, you can click the **OK** button in order to move to the next window. Over there, you can select tables to load into the Power BI:

Figure 6.11: Click the Transform Data option in the wizard

You can directly click the **Load** button to load selected queries (tables) into the Power BI, or else you can select the `Transform Data` to open the `Transform` window to perform the necessary transformation before loading data into the Power BI file:

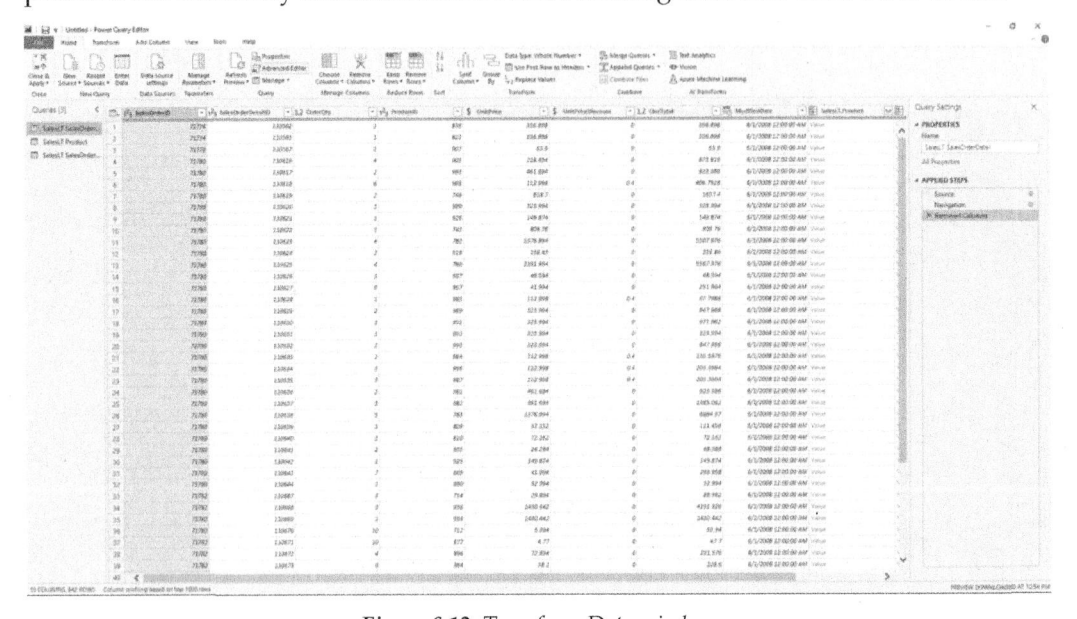

Figure 6.12: Transform Data window

There will not be much difference even when you do the transformation after the loading.

The database used for the Power BI is Vertipaq which is an in-memory database. It is important to choose the right data when you are loading to the Power BI. Sometimes you can skip unnecessary columns for the analytics to reduce the size of the memory usage for storing data. Try to make the model much simple as possible.

Conclusion

Apart from the flat file data, relational data sources are one of the most common data sources we have to deal with day in and day out. Therefore, we focused on how to set configurations to connect with relational sources, especially SQL Server data sources, and load them into the Power BI. Having this knowledge helps us to configure other relational data sources such as MySQL, Oracle, and so on. In the upcoming chapter, we will discuss about how to perform data transformation using Power Query.

Questions

1. Explain the importance of the Command Timeout option. What are the different use cases using that configuration?
2. Try out and find different options you can use the SQL statement option.

CHAPTER 7
Cleansing, Blending, and Transforming Data Using Power Query

In the previous chapter, you learned how to ingest data from the relational data source into the Power BI. In this chapter, you will learn more about how to perform various transformations to cleanse the data. Then eventually, how to convert it into a data model. First, we will go through how to work with the Power Query editor and see how we can interact with the UI to do various transformations. Then about data types and combine tables with Joins provided. This will be a starting point to explore the available data transformation options in Power BI.

Structure

The following topics will be covered in this chapter:

- Introduction to Power Query
- Cleansing data
- Blending data
- Select appropriate data types
- Merge queries using joins
- Add new columns, pivot, and unpivot

Objective

In *Chapter 6, Get Data from Relational Databases*, you learned how to ingest data from relational data sources. That is the extract step of **Extract-Transform-Load** (**ETL**). Once you decide right data to pull in, you can follow the data ingestion steps and extract the relevant data into your Power BI model. The next most important phase is to cleanse and transform your data into a structure that gives more performance and usability for analysis. Power Query is the technique in Power BI that offers for the self-service BI users to do the data extract, cleansing, and transformations. **M** language or **Mashup** language is the programming language behind the Power Query, which means for every task you perform in the Power Query interface, there is a programming code snippet executing behind. At the end of this chapter, you will learn various data transformation methods.

Introducing Power Query

Power Query is the technology behind the data connectivity and transformation for Microsoft Power BI, analysis services, and Excel. Now Power Query has become more versatile, and you will meet Power Query in **Power BI dataflows** and dataflows in **Azure Data Factory**, the Microsoft Azure cloud service for data integration.

Using Power Query, you can filter, combine, and transform your data as per the business requirement. Power Query is a **Graphical User Interface** (**GUI**) based platform so a variety of users can easily interact and fulfill their business needs. M formula language or Mashup language is the programming language behind the tasks you perform using Power Query.

> Power BI dataflows are features inside Power BI that enable self-service data warehousing capabilities in Power BI at a scale. You will learn about Power BI dataflows in *Chapter 13, Self Service AI Capabilities in Power BI*.

Business scenario

The case study we are referring to in this chapter is a data set that is derived from the popular **AdventureWorks** sample database. You can download the demo database from this link.

This demo database **PBIDataModels** contains six tables with sales data as in the following diagram:

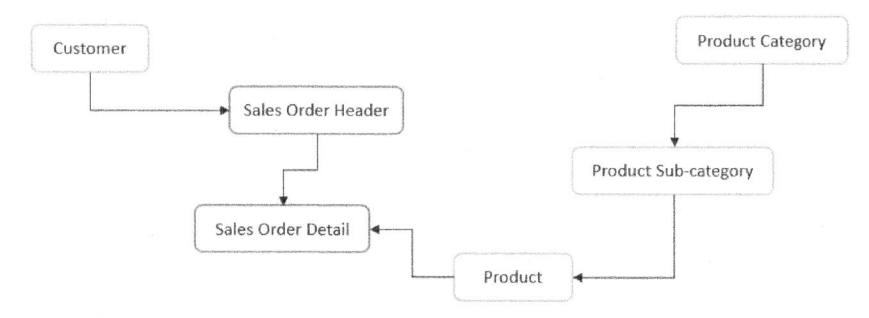

Figure 7.1: Tables mapping for sales order data

Connect to the database and extract tables

Download the demo database backup from the following link:

https://drive.google.com/drive/folders/1RezMTS0sEXcT1PoxZwC1UWbflV_1sioo?usp=sharing

In the previous chapter, you learned how to connect to a relational source using Power BI and ingest data into a model. You can follow the lessons learned to load the preceding tables into the Power BI model.

Data cleansing

Let us perform data profiling for each query (table) and cleanse the data. **The customer** table contains the basic customer information, first name, last name, company name, and so on:

Figure 7.2: Customer data in the Data tab

Power BI Data Modeling

You can click the **Transform Data** button, earlier known as **Edit Queries**, to enable profiling to your customer query:

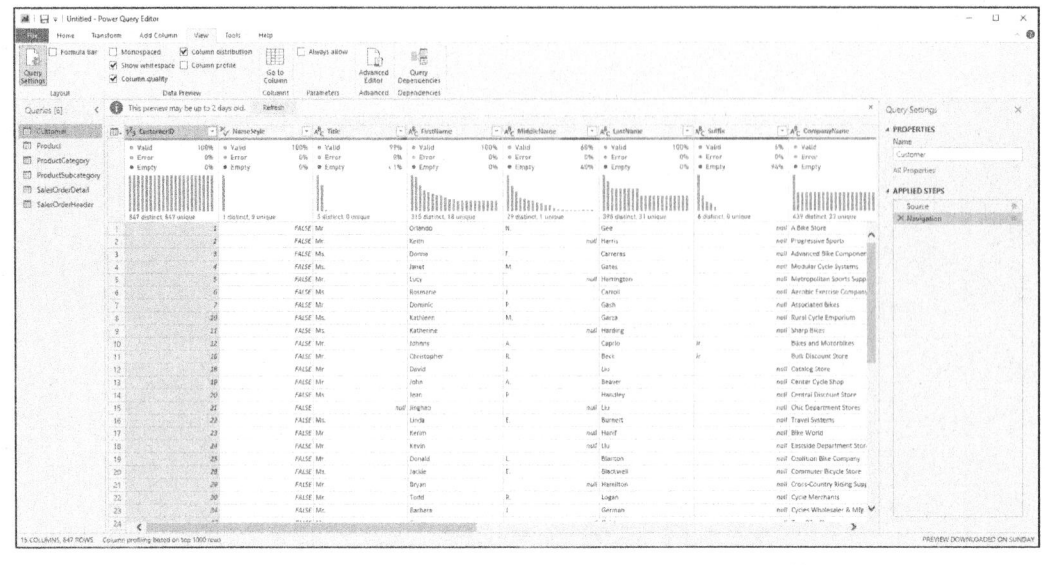

Figure 7.3: Transform data using Power Query and data profiling

Just like in Excel, the *bottom status* bar shows the number of rows and columns in this customer query. You can enable the dataset profiling by the switch to the **View** tab and tick the column distribution, column quality, and column profile:

- There are *847 rows* in the customer query, *847 distinct records*, and also *847 unique* in the **Customer ID** column. Distinct means the total number of distinct values can be found in the column. The total number of unique values represent by the **Unique** count. According to the stats, there is nothing wrong with the **Customer ID** column. You can proceed with looking at other fields.

- Next column is **NameStyle**. In theory, you cannot find any value other than false in this column. Which means you cannot generate any insight from it. You can probably remove that column from the query.

- In the **Title** column, there are *seven* null value rows. In order to make easy future transformations like concatenating, you can replace the **NULL** with an empty string.

- If you look at the statistics of the **MiddleName** column, *40%* of the records the column is *null*. But this column is useful when we form the **FullName** column. So, in order to get used to it, you can replace the **NULL** values with blank. Then, when we concatenate the columns in order to make a new column, the expression will be simple.

- You can apply the same transformation for the **Suffix** column.

- **PasswordHash** and **PasswordSalt** columns can be removed as they are not necessary for the analysis. Usually, these kinds of fields you can expect from the operational source system. Those are stored only for operational purposes:

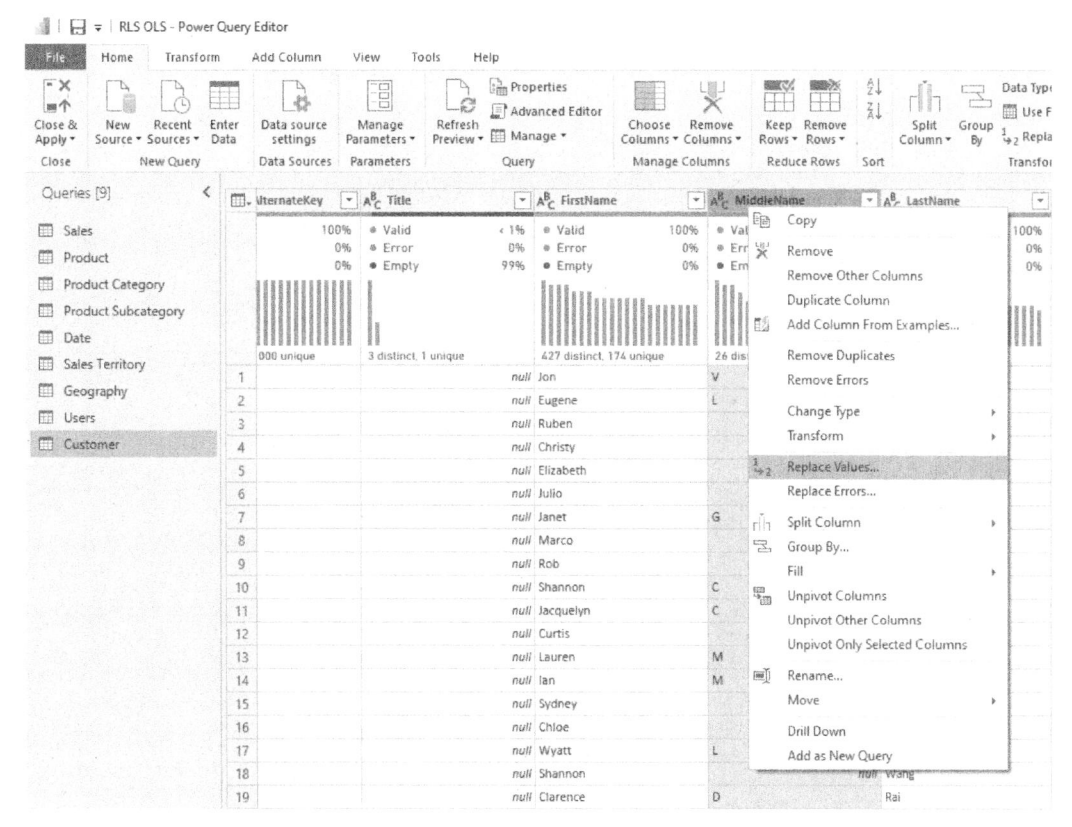

Figure 7.4: Replace values

Once you click the **Replace Values** option, you will see a window where you can configure the value you want to replace and which value you want to replace with, as shown in *figure 7.5*:

Figure 7.5: Replace values window

Then remove the **rowguid** field, which is also not required. **ModifiedDate** column is the **DateTime** data type even though it only contains date information. So, you can change the data type.

At the right-hand corner, you can see the applied steps you performed through Power Query. You can revert the changes at any time if you want:

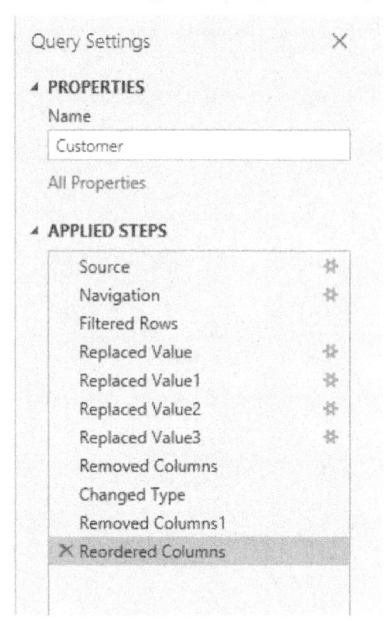

Figure 7.6: Applied steps

As mentioned previously, Power Query is a GUI-based technology built in order to ensure that this feature will reach a wider audience. However, there may be advanced users who are coming from a computer programming background. For them, M language, which is behind the Power Query, gives more control over the data transformations space.

You can open the M language query edition by clicking the **Advanced Editor** icon at the top menu bar:

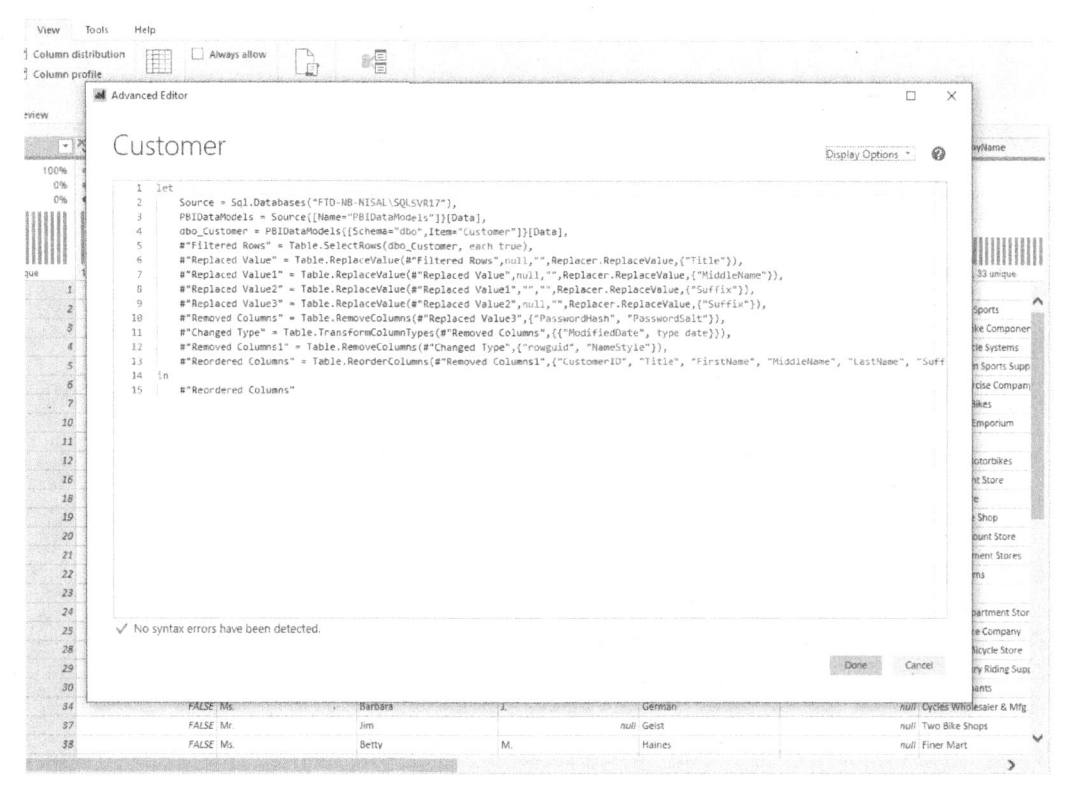

Cleansing, Blending, and Transforming Data Using Power Query   101

Figure 7.7: Advanced editor

Previously, we replaced the **NULL** values in the **Title** column with blank. You can see it in line *Number 6*.

> You can also enable the formula bar, which displays the M code for each step you select, which is a handy way of accessing the M expressions without opening Advanced Editor.

Once you have completed, click the **Close and Apply** button in order to apply those transformations. You should get a cleansed customer table at the end like this:

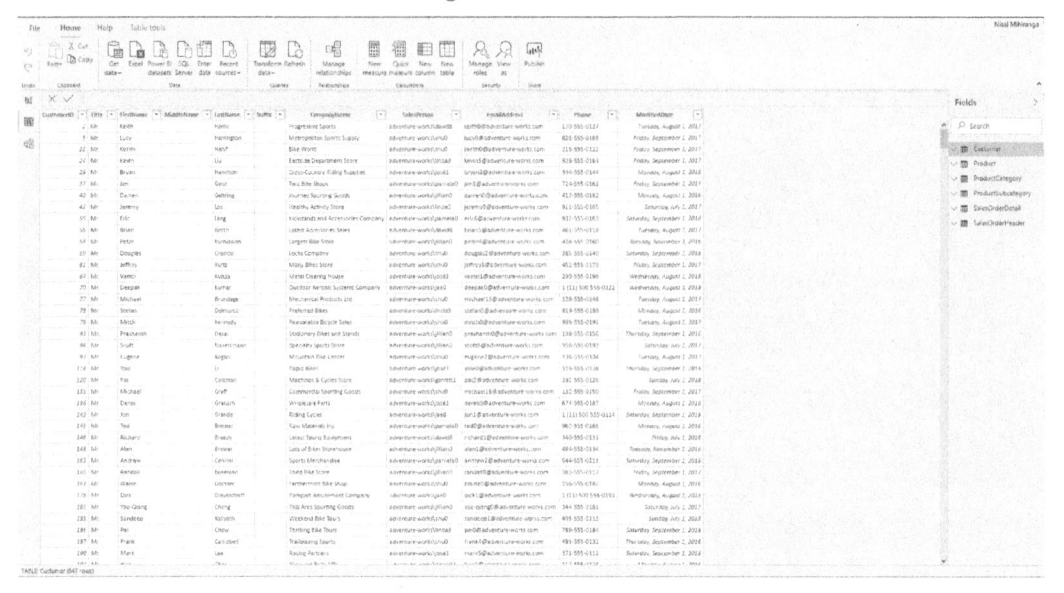

Figure 7.8: Completed customer table

Next, move to the product query, which contains more attributes than the customer:

- A total of 49% of the records are empty in the **Color** column. We will replace the **NULL** values as **N/A** in here. Then when we do visualize data, all the **NULL** values will be represented as **N/A**, which is logically true as representation.

- **Size**, **SizeUnitMeasureCode**, and **WeightUnitMeasureCode** fields also we can replace the **NULL** values with **N/A**.

- Handling **NULL** values in the **Weight** column will be a bit tricky. Common practices are dropping the records where **NULL** values or replacing them with mean, median, or mode would be an option. However, in this particular scenario, we are not supposed to aggregate this **Weight** column in our analysis, and replacing it by mean or median will be misrepresenting the facts. So, either you can leave it or replace it with **0**.

- **ProductLine**, **Class**, and **Style** columns can be replaced with **N/A**. Here, **ProductSubcategoryID** is the foreign key for the **ProductSubcategory** table. So, I will leave it as it is. There are many **NULL** values in **SellEndDate** and **DiscoutinuedDate**.

- Let us remove the **rowguid** column and change the data type of **ModifiedDate** as **Date**.

- In the **ProductCategory** query also, remove the **rowguid** column, and change the data type of **ModifiedDate**:

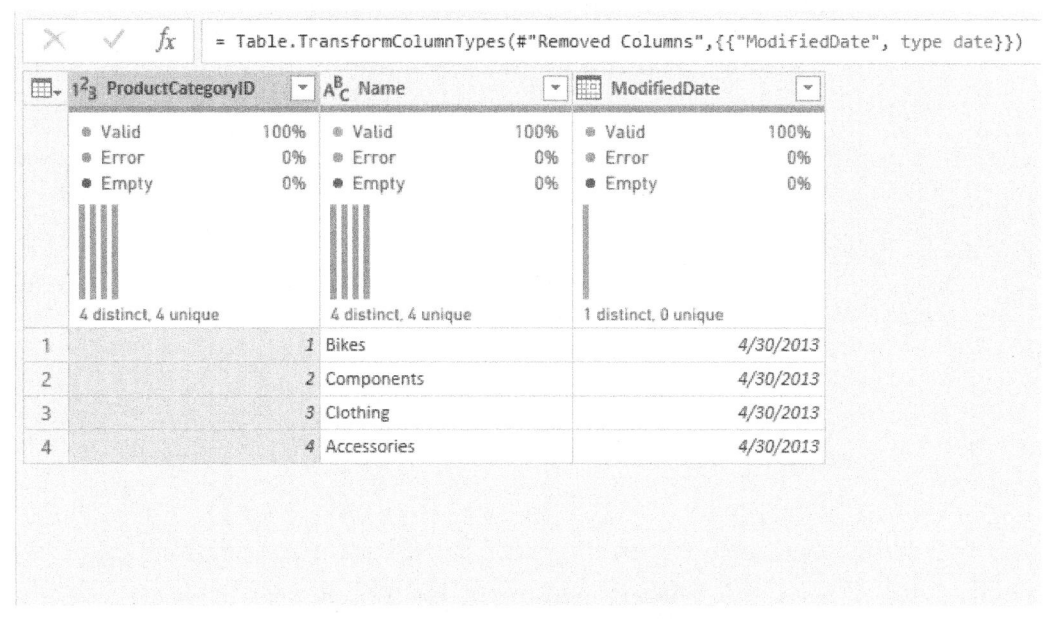

Figure 7.9: ProductCategory table

- The query of the **ProductSubCategory** table is also similar to the previous one. You can follow the same steps to get rid of **rowguid** column and change the data type of the **ModifiedDate** column.

Similar steps you can apply for other tables also, including **SalesOrderHeader** and **SalesOrderDetails**.

- In the **SalesOrderHeader** table, **OrderDate**, **DueDate**, and **ShipDate** columns are in the **DateTime** data type. Change them to just **Date**. There are *70% of the records* that are **NULL** for the **PurchaseOrderNumber** field. You can replace them with **N/A**. A similar transformation you can apply for the **SalesPersonID** column. Usually, in data warehousing, maintaining a specific value to represent the **NULL**. So, you can maintain the value and description in the reference dimension table. However, in our demo database, the **SalesPerson** dimension table is not included. So, you can ignore that step. You can get rid of the **Comment** column as it is all **NULL**.

- If you can recall your memory on *Chapter 4, Dimensional Modeling Practices,* when we define facts based on the business process. According to the demo dataset, a sales order is the business process. So, the sales order business process is represented by both **SalesOrderHeader** and **SalesOrderDetails** tables. Actually, our source is a relational database. So, the tables are highly normalized. However, when we transform it into a data model for reporting, it will become denormalized. Therefore, we shall combine **SalesOrderHeader** and **SalesOrderDetails** tables into one fact as **Sales**.

- Select the **SalesOrderHeader** table in the Power Query editor and select **Merge Queries** in the top menu to combine it with **SalesOrderDetails**.

- When merging tables, select the **SalesOrderID** from the **SalesOrderHeader** table and select **SalesOrderID** from the **SalesOrderDetails** table. Then click **OK**.

- We are going to bring all the columns in the **SalesOrderDetails** table into **SalesOrderHeader**:

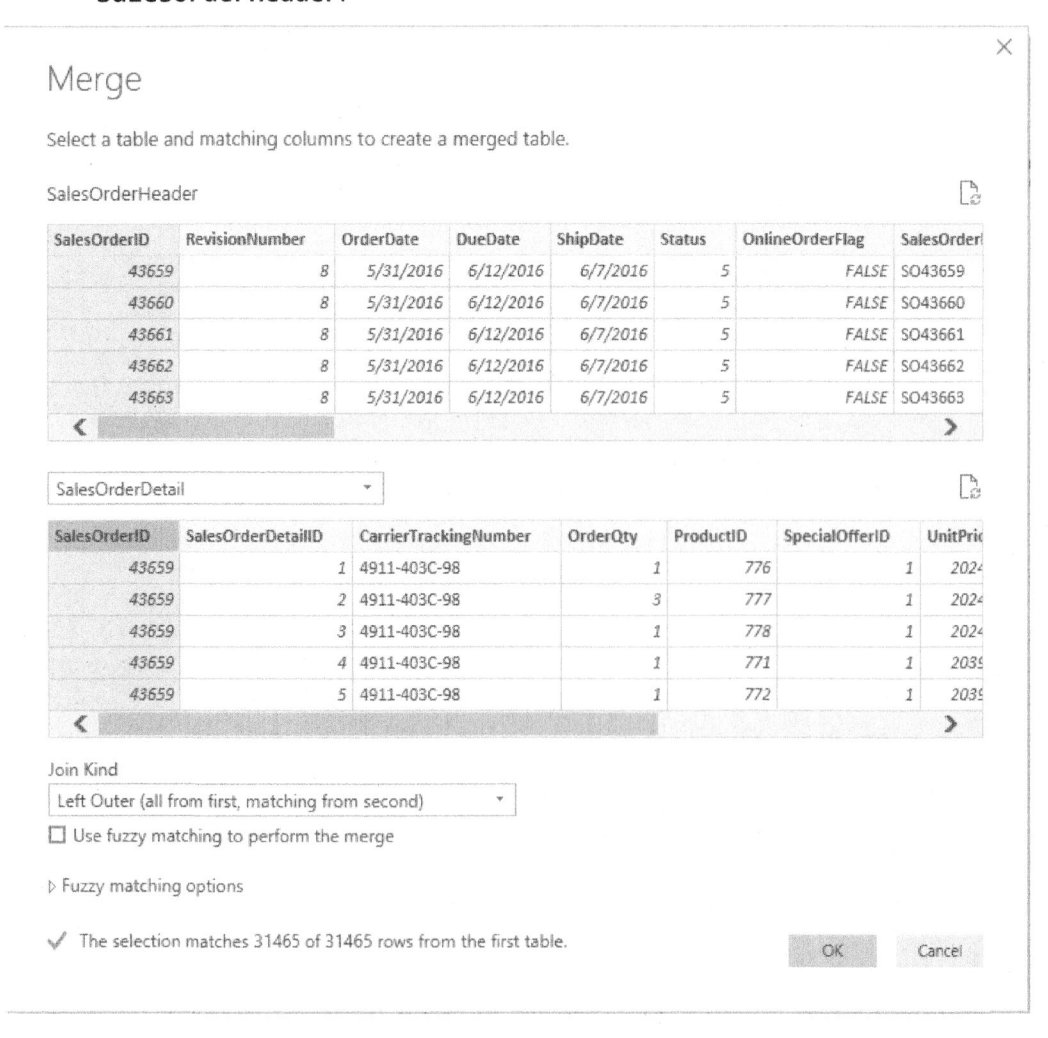

Figure 7.10: Merge queries – SalesOrderHeader and SalesOrderDetails

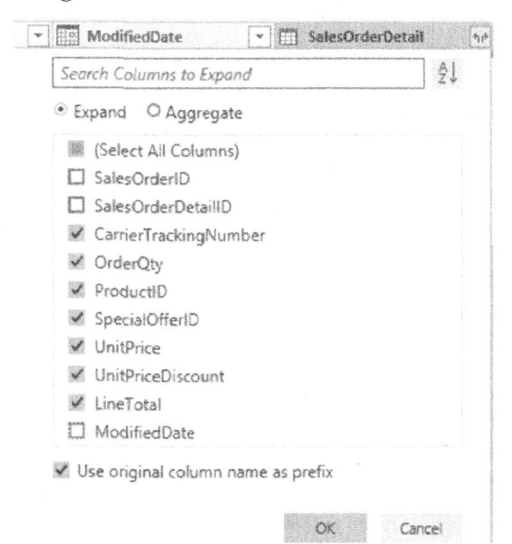

Select the following list of columns and click **OK**:

Figure 7.11: Select required columns

- Rename your **SalesOrderHeader** table as just **Sales**. We must cleanse a lot in the newly formed **Sales** table.

- Right-click the **SalesOrderDetails** query and uncheck the **Enable load** option. We have just disabled the loading of **SalesOrderDetails** into the report. It is just remaining behind and support to perform the merge and to populate the sales:

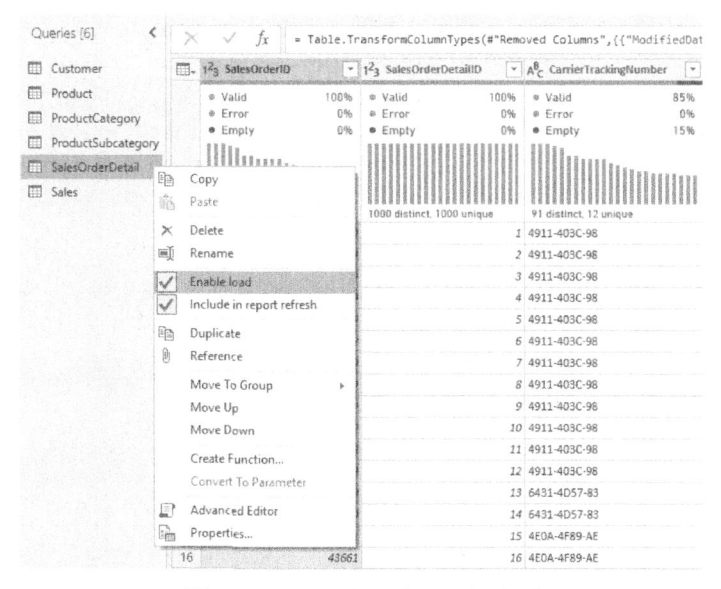

Figure 7.12: Uncheck the Enable load

- Once you uncheck the **Enable load** option, the file name will turn to *italic*.
- If you added prefix from the **SalesOrderDetail** table, then rename those columns, and make them proper names. Now the least granularity of the **Sales** table is product level.
- **CurrencyRateID** column contains **NULL** values of more than *61%*; also, the related master table is not there in the database. We can remove that column if we are not wished to use it for the analysis.
- **SalesOrderNumber**, **PurchaseOrderNumber**, and **CarrierTrackingNumber** fields act as degenerated dimensions. So, we can leave them for analysis purposes.

> Degenerated dimensions are a type of dimension where only a single attribute, for example, has SalesOrderNumber. If, we consider SalesOrderNumber, which we can use for the analysis or filtrations. But then again, we cannot find any other attribute in that dimension. So, this kind of special dimension is named as degenerated dimensions.

- Removed the **RevisionNumber**, **Status**, and **SpecialOfferID** columns, which do not show a valid point to maintain for analysis.
- You can get rid of the **SubTotal** column which came from **SalesOrderHeader**, anyway, is the sum of **LineTotal**.

We have cleansed the **Sales** related data by now.

Work with budget data

You may find an Excel file in the link named as **Budget**. Download the **Budget** Excel file, which is related to the budget information. Once you imported the sales information from the **PBIDataModel** database, import the budget information from Excel:

BudgetMonth	Clothing	Accessories	Components	Bikes
2016-05	1253049.248	861939.9944	1804164.242	4580565.233
2016-06	NULL	NULL	NULL	532451.2925
2016-07	4610550.65	2566164.573	6006120.967	14202655.88
2016-08	6003432.209	3907508.974	9154402.182	20845114.22
2016-09	NULL	NULL	NULL	582531.1886
2016-10	13040524.46	7889447.817	20349255.11	48747641.17
2016-11	NULL	NULL	NULL	856078.666
2016-12	1410600.5	352874.7362	1061381.837	8704466.556
2017-01	8004787.706	3699379.042	7880704.213	40725370.21
2017-02	2784580.768	1381514.868	3632889.407	11022803.55
2017-03	7659641.011	4412624.982	11023265.4	28641702.86
2017-04	3473375.668	2223935.707	6199512.104	15467270.24
2017-05	26961029.51	8668396.94	46539049.06	43025447.84
2017-06	37200658.99	12870114.7	64769622.56	62342851.37
2017-07	32319174.93	9990322.007	58151825.53	48033611.26
2017-08	17179026.53	5975603.57	24923646.18	31287455.21
2017-09	26749265.89	9863038.662	39305329.76	52503179.04
2017-10	21334551.94	7122913.226	30021803.46	34991592.18
2017-11	9023030.984	2858836.184	7936914.859	21946244.96
2017-12	12984748.36	3575808.648	11519846.84	41207909.4
2018-01	10433838.36	3158992.825	10242725.21	24164101.38
2018-02	19469792.17	7055397.362	26920624.38	32007189.7
2018-03	27213719.88	9815351.793	36402231.28	50774438.71
2018-04	20684170.71	6739247.401	26637605	31918304.63
2018-05	23185991.25	12435616.08	55173031.92	43893871.59
2018-06	35117859.63	19170993.21	82880212.88	68898787.26
2018-07	31805255.75	17834268.99	85664444.03	66908428.94
2018-08	19225154.22	11287712.34	31312375.16	36474682.54

Figure 7.13: Budget Excel file

Let us move the budget data which we extracted from Excel and do some necessary cleansing. You would notice there are **NULL** values for budgets under the **Clothing**, **Accessories**, **Components**, and **Bikes** columns. Let us replace them with **0**.

Then, we need the budget table in a format similar to the sales actuals, which we can link the data with dimensions:

ProductCategoty	BudgetMonth	Amount
Clothing	2018-11	10827107.09
Accessories	2018-05	12435616.08
Accessories	2017-10	7122913.226
Accessories	2017-12	3575808.648
Bikes	2017-11	21946244.96
Clothing	2018-07	31805255.75
Accessories	2016-05	861939.9944
Accessories	2017-03	4412624.982
Components	2017-07	58151825.53
Accessories	2017-05	8668396.94
Accessories	2017-02	1381514.868
Components	2017-04	6199512.104
Components	2018-09	48062791.33
Clothing	2019-02	560726.0485

Figure 7.14: Required format

108 ■ Power BI Data Modeling

We are expecting the table to look like the preceding figure. In order to do that, select all four columns, **Clothing**, **Accessories**, **Components**, and **Bikes** columns, and select the `Unpivot Only Selected Columns` option:

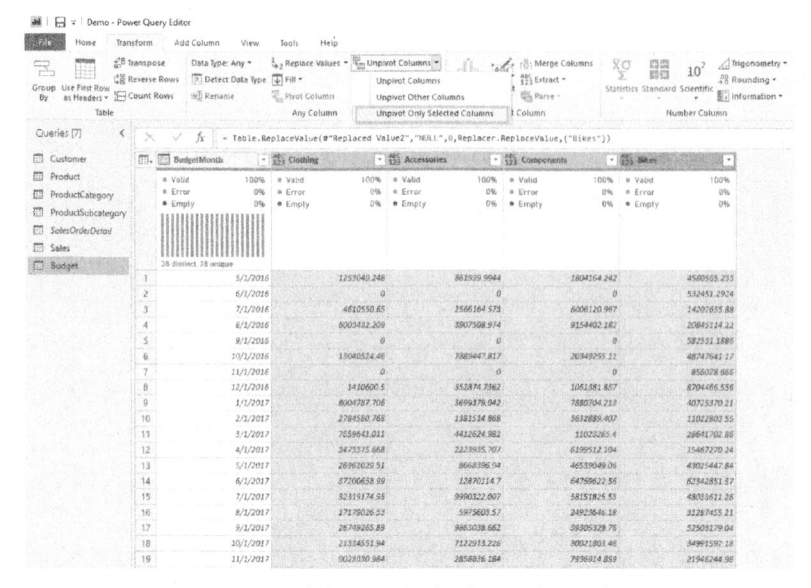

Figure 7.15: Select required columns for unpivot

Then unpivot the table successfully. You can rename the newly created column as **Category**:

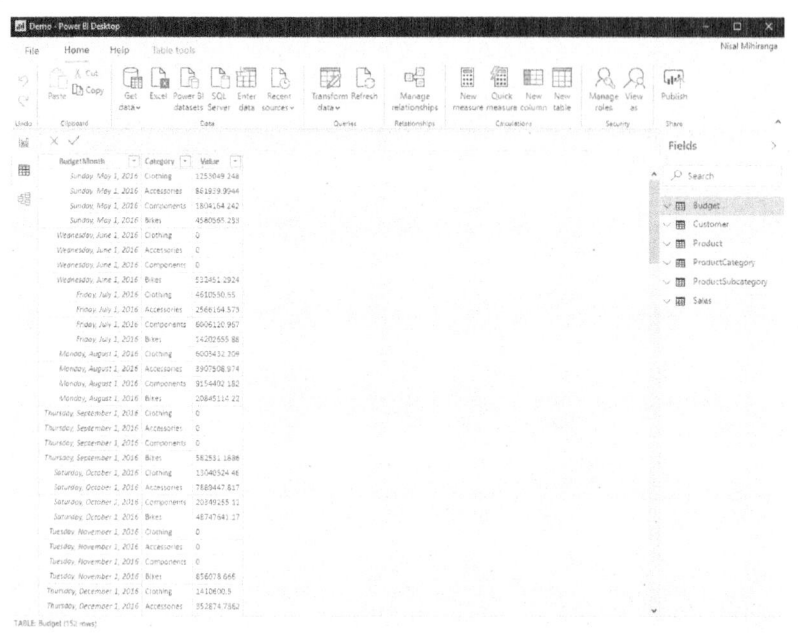

Figure 7.16: Formatted budget query

We have successfully transformed our data set in a way we can build a data model for analysis.

Conclusion

In this chapter, we learned how to extract source data and cleanse it from using various data cleansing and transformation techniques offered in Power Query. We also learned how to unpivot transformation, merge two queries, and so on. However, there are a lot more available to do transformations. We may use them in the future for a different purpose. In the upcoming chapter, we will discuss about how to connect these queries by making relationships among them.

Questions

1. Which one of Microsoft products do not use Power Query technology?

    A. Power BI

    B. Excel

    C. Azure Databricks

    D. Power BI dataflows

    E. Data factory dataflows

2. In this chapter, we replace the budget values where **NULL** with **0**s. If we require you to replace them with average budget value for each category, explain how you are going to achieve it.

Answer

1. C

CHAPTER 8
Build Relationships

In the previous chapter, you learned how to cleanse and transform the data in Power BI. I believe that you have followed the steps to create the data structure manner in order to complete the data model. However, sometimes we may work with a single query/table. Sometimes we create a data model with multiple tables. When our data model comprises with multiple tables, it is vital to make them connect to each other in order to filter and analyze data across the model. As a result, this chapter will be focused on how to build different types of relationships in the Power BI.

Structure

The following topics will be covered in this chapter:

- Relationships in Power BI
- Methods of building relationships
- Select cardinality
- Select cross filter direction

Objective

The objective of this chapter is to teach you how to build relationships in order to create a data model in Power BI. In Power BI jargon, it does not matter you are working with a single table or multiple tables; we call them as a data model. But there is a definite advantage of having multiple tables connected with rather having one big table. We believe we already talked about it in previous chapters. In this chapter, we will discuss further different methods of defining relationships and how they basically affect them for the filtering data. Filter directions and cardinality. Finally, we will talk about active/in-active relationships.

Relationships in Power BI

First, we will discuss *why we need to have relationships in Power BI*. If you are maintaining one large table or your few tables are not related to each other, which means you are not planning to draw visuals combining them because those are not related, then you may not have to create relationships. But, in most of the time, you are working with relational data. Every table you are bringing into your model has some kind of relationship with others. Then, definitely you need to tell the engine that has related each other in order to make filters work properly in the report view. This is the idea of relationships. There are a few advantages as well having smaller tables than maintaining one giant table:

- End-users will have a better understanding of categorical data for filter purposes.
- The design itself can help to reduce the cost of space and memory.

You may have learned about the term **Entity Relational** modeling if you are coming from a database development background. In relational database development, you can create relationships among tables using *foreign key* constraints. The same concept will apply here with Power BI when it comes to relationships. Instead of creating foreign key constraints, you may create relationships with Power BI. In order to manage relationships, you have to switch to the *Model* tab.

We assume that you have completed the previous lab, *Chapter 7, Cleansing, Blending, and Transforming Data using Power Query*. You may open the file using Power BI. Readers who have not completed the previous chapter; you can download the Power BI file from this link:

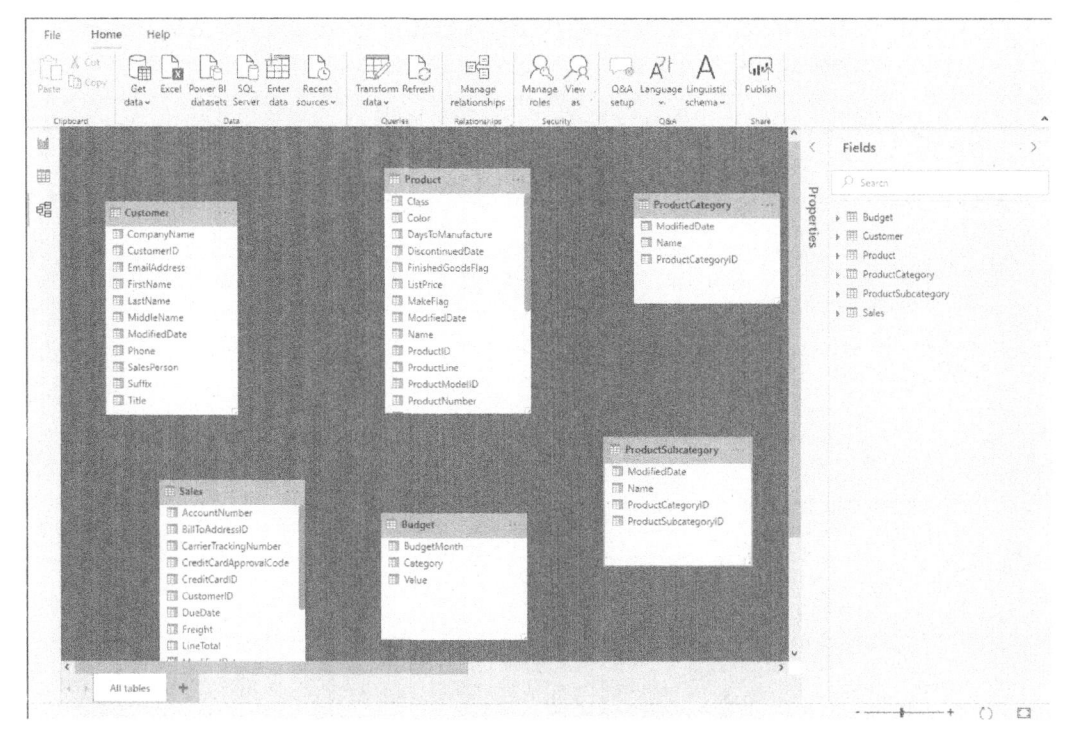

Figure 8.1: Model tab

Methods of creating relationships

There are mainly two ways of creating relationships in Power BI. Even before you create the relationship, you need to understand how these relationships work. You may have both distinct values in columns in the two tables you are going to create the relationship, or only one side has the distinct values, and the other side has many values then you should select the many sides table column first:

1. **Drag and drop from UI**: Select column from the side and drag into over the second table column and drop. It will automatically draw a line between two tables. This is the easiest way of creating relationships. Let us take **ProductCategory** and **ProductSubCategory** tables. Both have **ProductCategoryID** in common. Actually, in simple terms, **ProductCategoryID** in the **ProductCategory** table is the unique key column.

On the other hand, **ProductCategoryID** in the **ProductSubCategory** table is a reference key column that you can use to build the relationship:

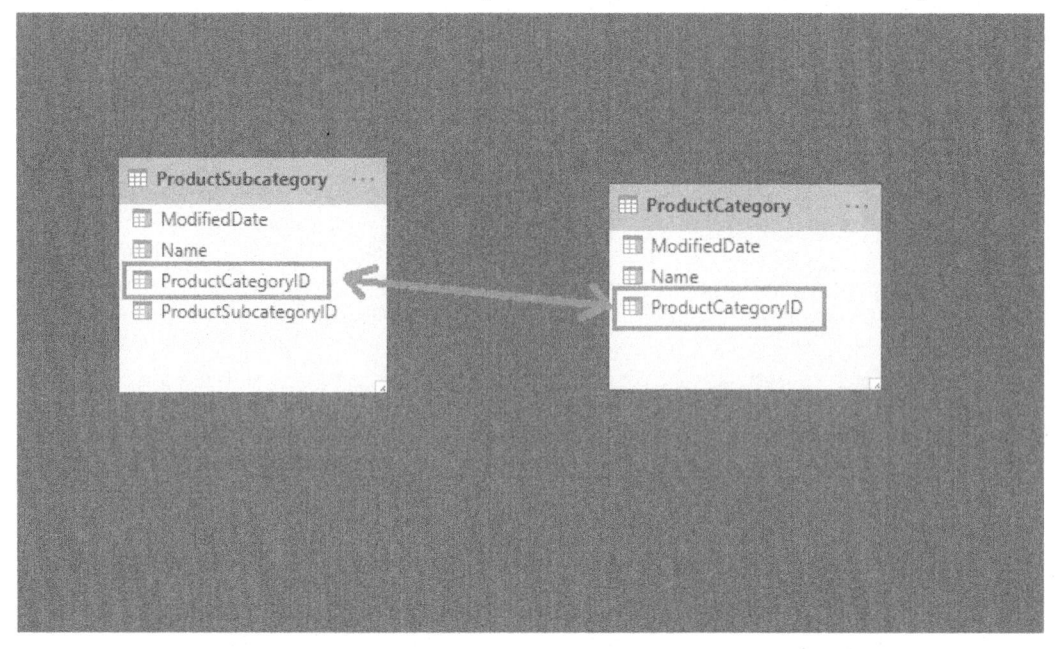

Figure 8.2: Relationship fields product category and subcategory

You can simply drag and drop to create the relationship between these two tables. Always start with a small table when drawing the relationship. In this case, I have to choose the **ProductCategory** table:

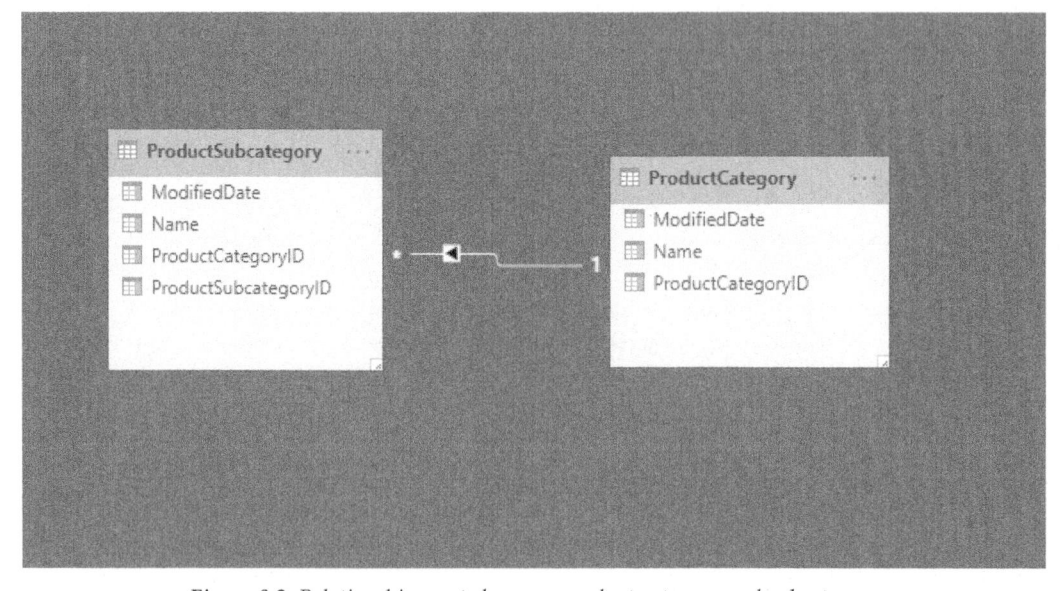

Figure 8.3: Relationship created among product category and subcategory

1. **Using manage relationships**: You can go to the **Menu** tab and click the **Manage relationships** button in order to create a relationship:

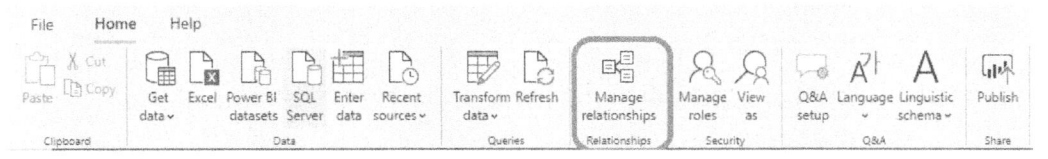

Figure 8.4: Manage relationship button at the main menu

Then you will see a window where you can manage relationships. If you have already created any relationship, then you will be able to see those in the list. But if no relationships exist and you are going to create it for the first time, then you will see an empty list:

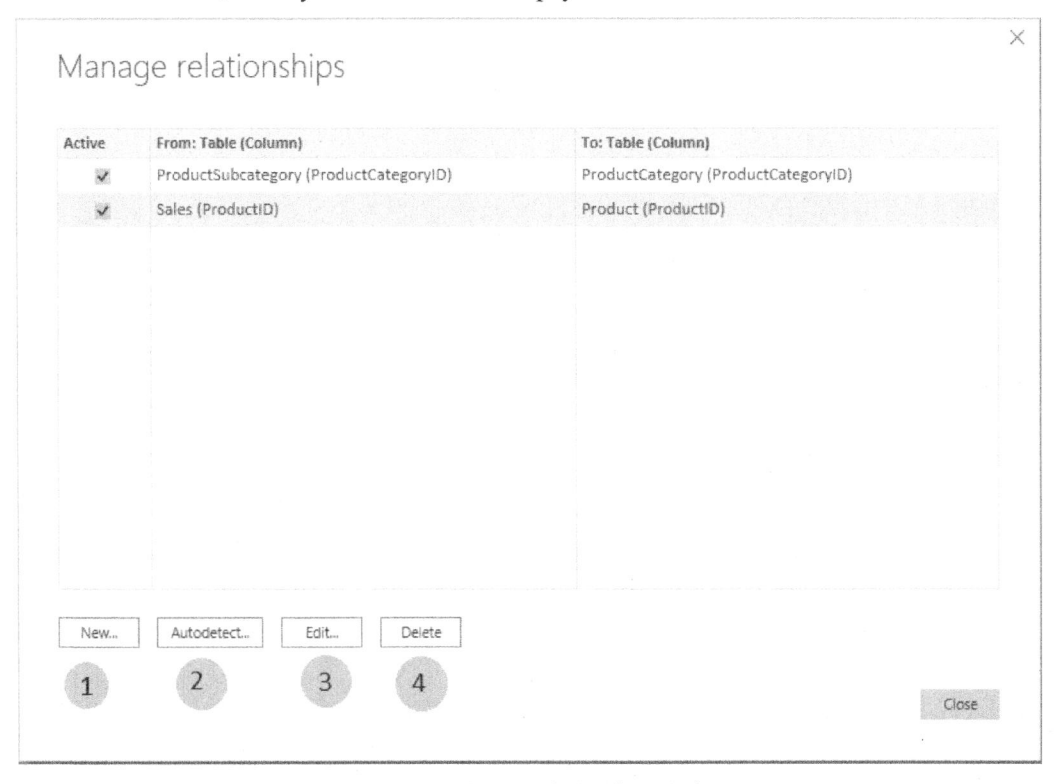

Figure 8.5: Manage relationship window

You can create and modify relationships by clicking the buttons in the window shown in *figure 8.5*. Actions you can perform by clicking each button are explained as follows:

- **New...:** For creating a new relationship in the model.

- **Autodetect…**: This will automatically detect the relationships based on the metadata, such as column names, data types, and data, of course.
- **Edit…**: This allows you to edit existing relationships. For that, you need to select the particular relationship if it is listed many.
- **Delete…**: If you want to delete the relationships, you can select this option to delete.

Demystify relationships in Power BI

Many people get confused with relationships with join datasets. Actually, there is a valid reason for that. If you can remember, in the previous chapter, UI is pretty much the same in the `Edit relationship` and `Merge queries`.

You can see the `Edit relationship` view for the tables **ProductSubCategory** and **ProductCategory**. Using this window, you can select any two tables to build your relationship:

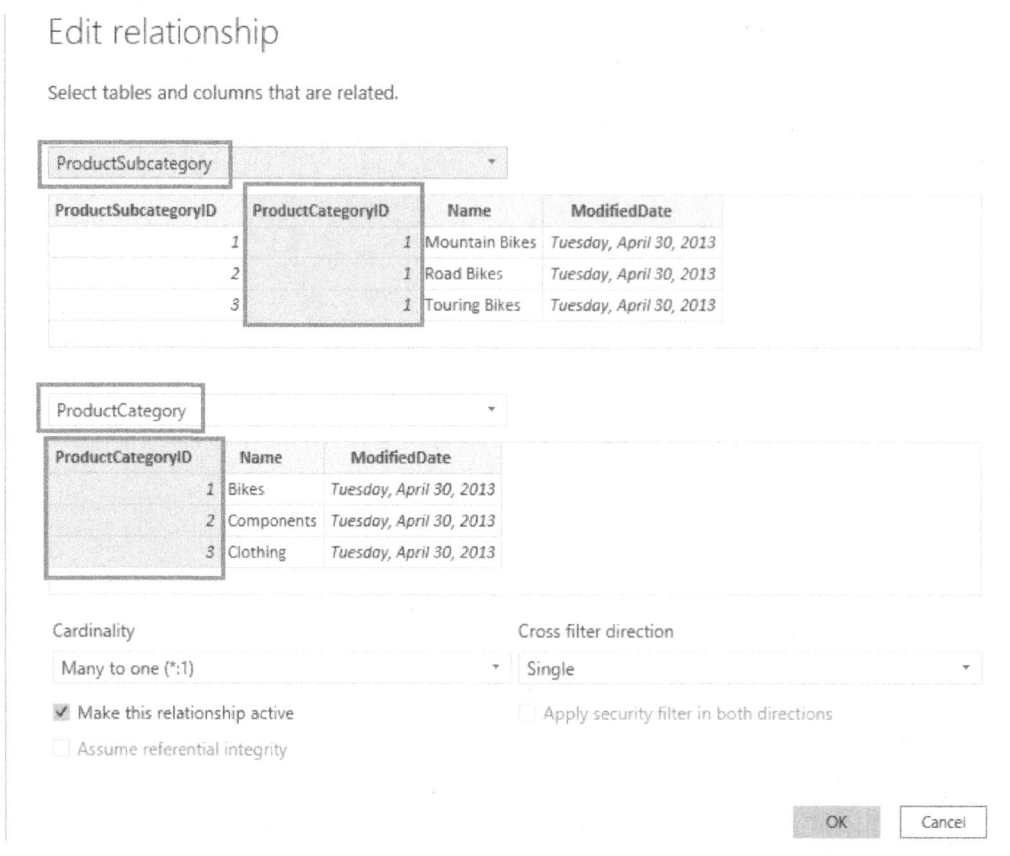

Figure 8.6: Edit relationship window

Select cardinality of a relationship

In the previous section, you learned how to create a relationship. Before we continue with the lab session, it will be beneficial to learn about another concept—**cardinality**. We actually did quick touch on this. But here, we will learn in detail about *what cardinality of relationship is* and how to select the cardinality properly. Because without selecting the right cardinality, it will lead to unexpected issues in your visuals.

- **Many to One (*:1)**: This means your left side column has many values, and the right side has unique values. So, this will work as a typical many to one relationship:

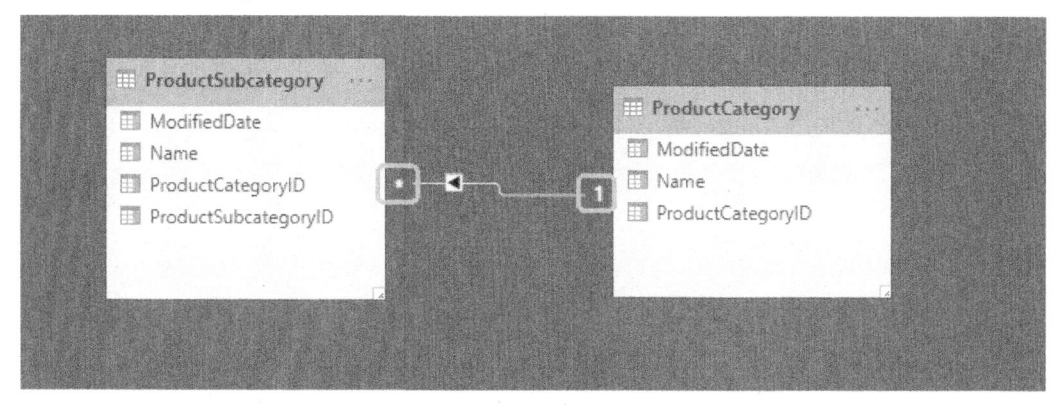

Figure 8.7: Many to one relationship

For example, two tables have parent-child attributes such as `ProductCategory` and `ProductSubcategory`.

- **One to Many (1:*)**: This cardinality represents the left side has unique values, whereas the right side has many values.

These are the two types of cardinality we experience the most in common.

- **One to One (1:1)**: This means both sides of tables have unique fields. See the following image for the one-to-one relationship:

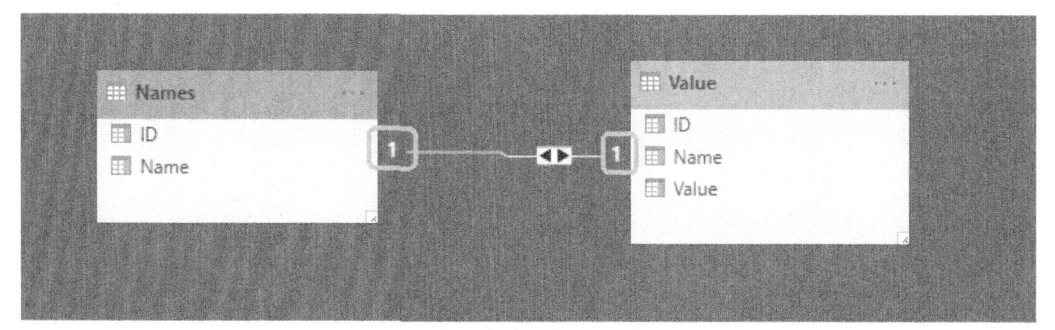

Figure 8.8: One to one relationship

For example, this is less often used. Imagine you have two tables that contain an equal number of rows, the same data with an ID column and having different attributes. In such a case, you need to extend one table with the second table attribute.

- **Many to Many (*:*)**: This kind of relationship has both sides with more than one unique value. See the following image for many-to-many relationship:

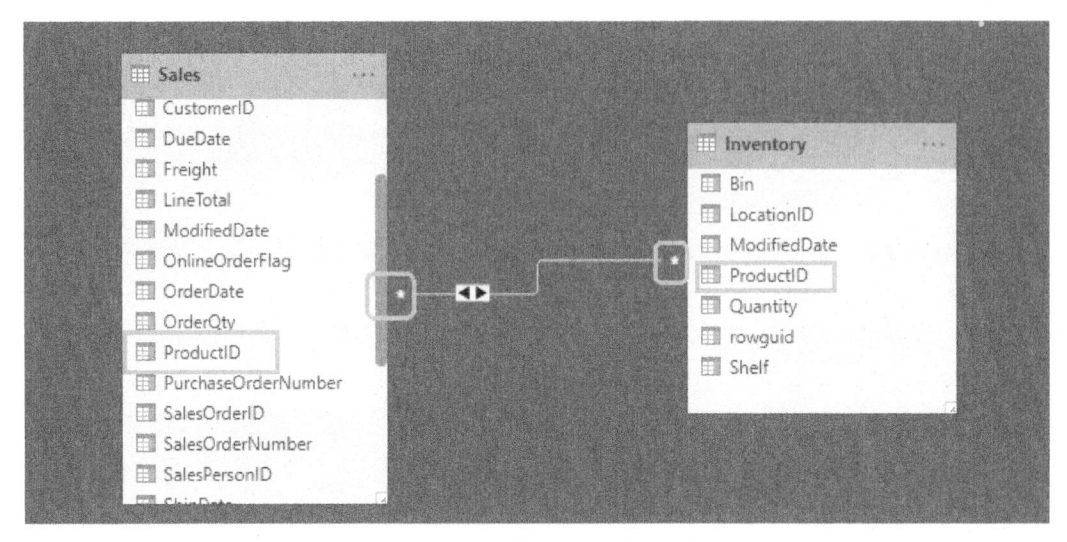

Figure 8.9: Many to many relationships

For example, think about a scenario you have two different transaction tables. These two tables have common attributes like the **product**. Let us say, you need to visualize these numerical data in the same chart with the product. In such a case, you must combine them like the preceding *figure 8.9*.

Some scenario such as **Sales** and **Inventory,** where both tables have duplicate product IDs, gives an example for the many to many relationships:

Build Relationships ■ 119

Create relationship

Select tables and columns that are related.

Sales							
TaxAmt	Freight	TotalDue	ModifiedDate	CarrierTrackingNumber	OrderQty	ProductID	Un
11,751.9938	$3,672.4981	$135,606.6769	Tuesday, June 6, 2017	C1B5-40D6-8D	14	801	
11,751.9938	$3,672.4981	$135,606.6769	Tuesday, June 6, 2017	C1B5-40D6-8D	14	760	
11,751.9938	$3,672.4981	$135,606.6769	Tuesday, June 6, 2017	C1B5-40D6-8D	11	765	

Inventory						
ProductID	LocationID	Shelf	Bin	Quantity	rowguid	ModifiedDate
864	7	N/A	0	180	93EBCE66-E74B-4134-BCA6-33B4B1EAEAC8	4/30/2013 12:00:00
865	7	N/A	0	216	8FF570BB-B9EE-4FE8-9ECE-20D33EE99F43	4/30/2013 12:00:00
866	7	N/A	0	252	838E81A3-3B2A-4CCA-9FCB-5F0EC5186957	4/30/2013 12:00:00

Cardinality | Cross filter direction
Many to Many (*:*) | Both

☑ Make this relationship active ☐ Apply security filter in both directions
☐ Assume referential integrity

⚠ This relationship has cardinality Many-Many. This should only be used if it is expected that neither column (ProductID and ProductID) contains unique values, and that the significantly different behavior of Many-many relationships is understood. Learn more

OK   Cancel

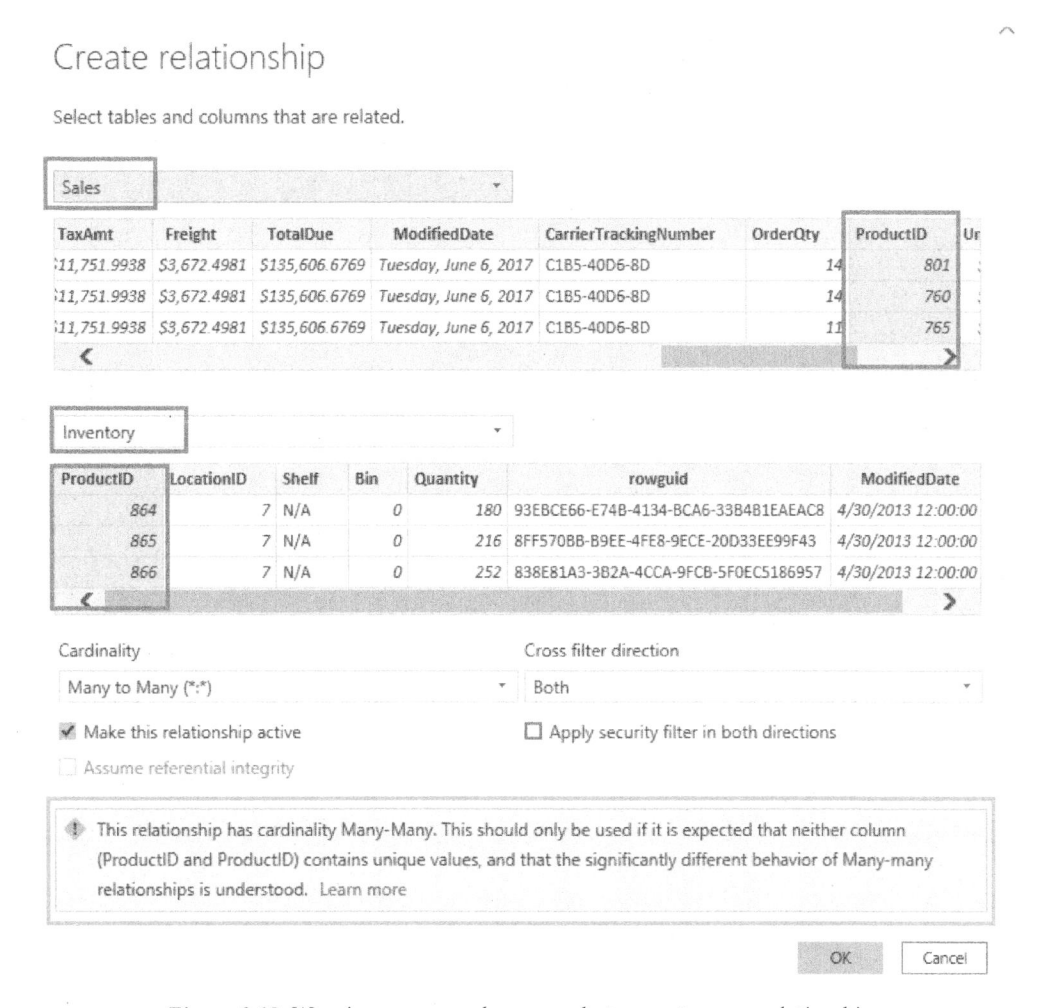

Figure 8.10: Warning message when you select many to many relationships

You need to be careful, especially when you are working with many-to-many relationships in your model. It is always additional testing required. As a practice, try to use one or too many relationships as much as possible.

Select cross filter direction

In theory, when you create relationships in your data model, it allows you to make cross filtering in the nice visuals you are creating. So, in this section, we will talk about what is cross filter direction and why we need to be alert on this.

When you create a relationship apart from the cardinality, it shows the cross-filter direction as well. In the *arrowhead of the relationship line*, indicate which direction the filtration is happening. You can see in the following image it is flowing through from

ProductCategory to **ProductSubcategory**, which means **ProductCategory** filter the **ProductSubcategory** table values:

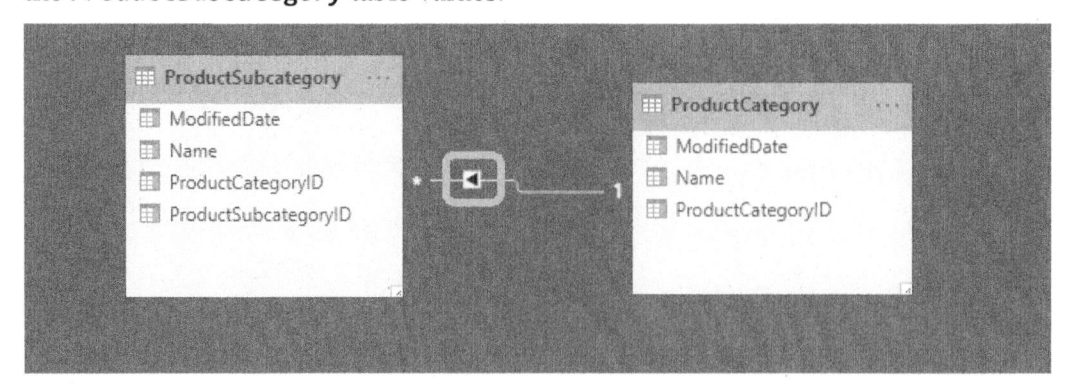

Figure 8.11: Single direction

The same information is given when you open the double click arrow and open the **Edit relationship** window:

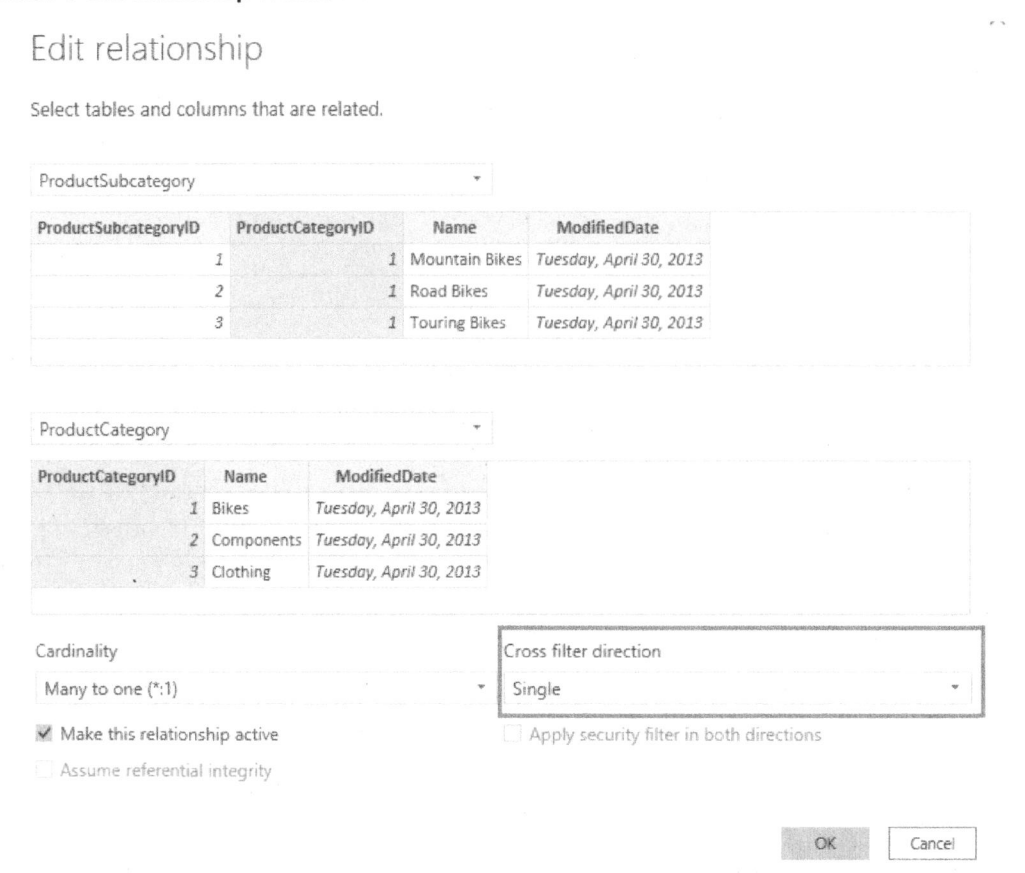

Figure 8.12: Cross filter direction option

Build Relationships 121

If you select a many-to-many or one-to-one relationship by default, it is *bi-directional*. You can see in the following diagram arrowhead goes to both sides, which represent the *bi-directional*:

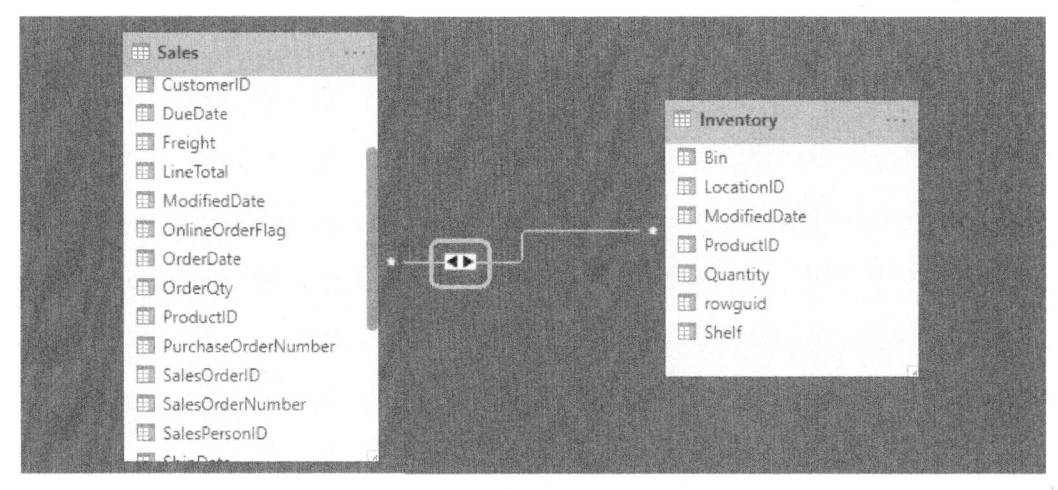

Figure 8.13: Bi-directional arrowhead

In the **Edit relationship** window, it is displayed as *bi-directional*. So, this is the place where you can configure the cross-filter direction:

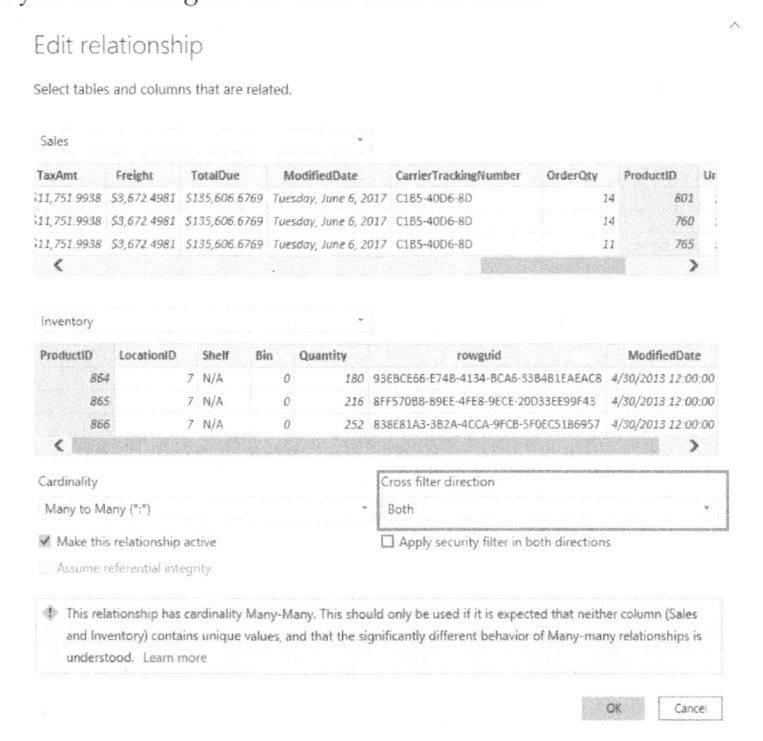

Figure 8.14: Cross filter direction option selected as both

Active and inactive relationships

When you create relationships by default, it is active. Straight-line indication it is as an active relationship. However, when there are situations, you come across with role-playing dimension scenarios. This means if you take two tables, there are multiple columns; you can also connect to those that are useful at different times. The classic example would be the **Sales** table and **Date** table. You have **OrderDate** and **ShipDate** in the **Sales** table; both columns can connect with the **Date** table **DateKey**:

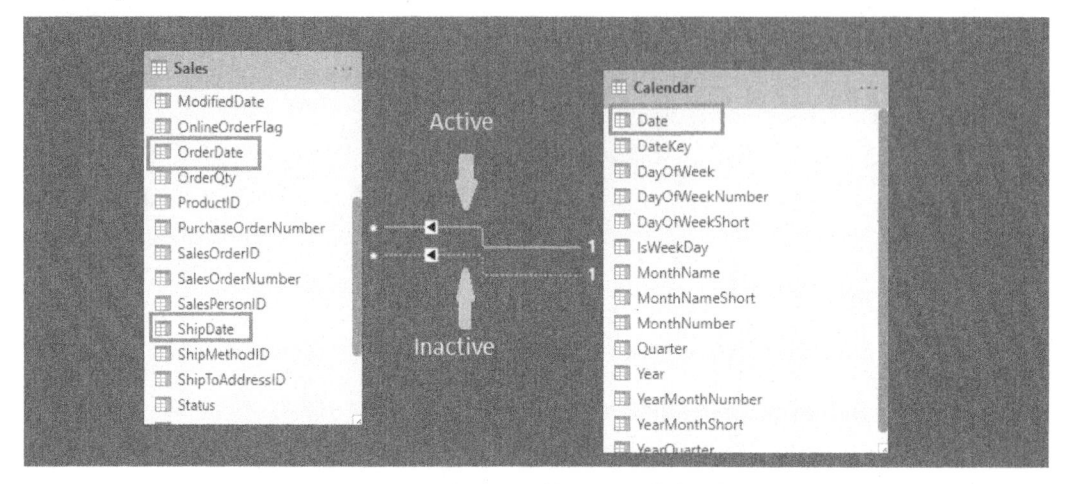

Figure 8.15: Active and inactive relationship

In this scenario, **OrderDate** is my main date key because we are analyzing the sales information here. So, it makes active, whereas the relationship with **ShipDate** is inactive. If you try to make that relationship also active, it will not allow doing in Power BI.

This inactive relationship means if you try to draw a visual with the **Sales** and **Calendar** table to analyze by ship date wise, *it will not filter because it is inactive*. Then, what is the purpose of having inactive relationships. You can make them active dynamically using DAX. We will talk about that in the upcoming chapters:

Figure 8.16: Inactive relationships when you make active, you will get the message like this

Conclusion

We started off by talking about relationships in Power BI, *why we need to create them*, and so on. Then we discussed different methods of creating relationships. Also, more importantly, we discussed different cardinality types. Later on in this chapter, we discussed filter direction and active/inactive relationships. Hope, this will educate you to build relationships among tables in your data model. In the upcoming chapter, we will focus on how to implement calculations in your data models using DAX.

Questions

1. **Open your Power BI file you completed in the previous chapter and start to create relationships among tables (still, you will not be able to create any relationships for dates as we did not create it yet):**

   A. ProductCategory table and ProductSubcategory table

   B. Product Subcategory table and Product table

   C. Product table and Sales table

   D. Customer table and Sales table

2. What is an active relationship in Power BI, and explain why you cannot create two active relationships between two tables?

CHAPTER 9
Introducing DAX, Calculated Columns, Calculated Measures, and Hierarchies

If you are reading this book without skipping any chapter, you will understand that we have started with the introduction to Power BI and gradually moved to learn how to connect with data, then learned data transformation, and so on.

Now, it is time to dig into calculations in Power BI. We start off with the importance of implementing calculations in the Power BI model then talk about different methods we can use to implement them. Later in this chapter, also we talk about the main differences between them and when to use each of them.

Structure

The following topics will be covered during this chapter:

- Calculated measures
- Calculated columns
- Calculated tables
- Hierarchies

Objective

It is vital to have knowledge of DAX programming and the related concepts when working with Power BI data models. This chapter is dedicated for you to acquire the ground for calculations using DAX.

Calculations in Power BI

If you have a closer look at the data model you built so far, you can see that you have connected multiple tables using relationships, the knowledge you grasped in the previous chapter. Each table may contain different columns with different data types. Fields may be text fields, geoinformation fields, date fields mainly you can use to analyze numerical data. But if you look at the **Sales** table, for instance, which contains a lot of numerical fields, with a *Sigma* sign in front of which indicates metric values.

You can see such numerical base measures in *figure 9.1*:

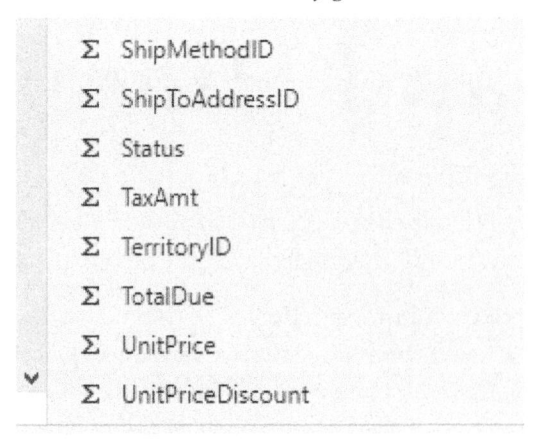

Figure 9.1: Base measures

These numeric values we can use to visualize data by drag and drop into the value area of the visual. Sometimes, you may require implementing complex calculations using existing data. So calculated objects allow further extending the capability of implementing business logic in power.

The **Data Analysis Expressions (DAX)** is the programming language to build calculations in Power BI data models and similar products such as Excel, SSAS Tabular, and Azure Analysis Services. These products share the same internal engine called **tabular**. Therefore, knowing DAX is versatile. You can learn about the official reference guide via the following link:

https://docs.microsoft.com/en-us/dax/

Calculated columns

Calculated columns are logical objects you can define inside a table in your Power BI model in order to extend the tables further. You can create a calculated column using the DAX language expression.

These calculated columns you create are evaluated by row by row. This means each row calculate individually.

Imagine you have an **Employee** table in your model. Your **Employee** table has the joining date of each employee. Let us say you need to have information about their **service period**. Basically, you can derive the service period by calculating the difference between the join date and today's date. Again, you cannot store this information or read from the source as it keeps changing as the days are spent off. The best way to handle this is to create a calculated column.

Service Period = Today() – Employee[Join Date]

There are multiple ways you can follow in order to create a calculated column in the model.

If you are in the *Report* tab, then you can create a calculated column by switching to the **Modeling** tab and selecting the **New column**. You can see the option to create a new column in the following *figure 9.2*:

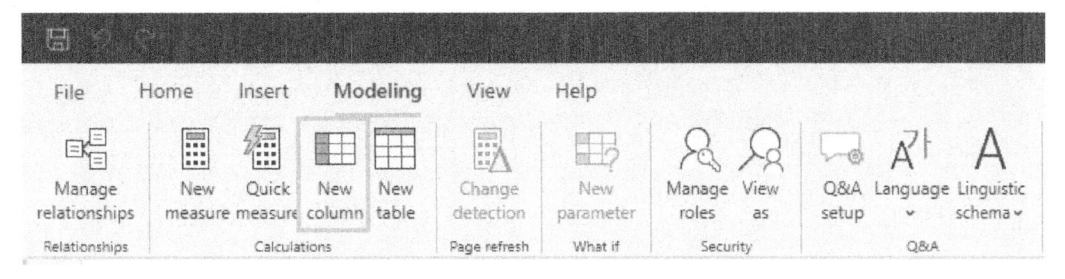

Figure 9.2: Create a new calculated column

You also can add a new calculated column by clicking the ellipse button (...) you want to add the column, then select the **New column** option as shown in *figure 9.3*:

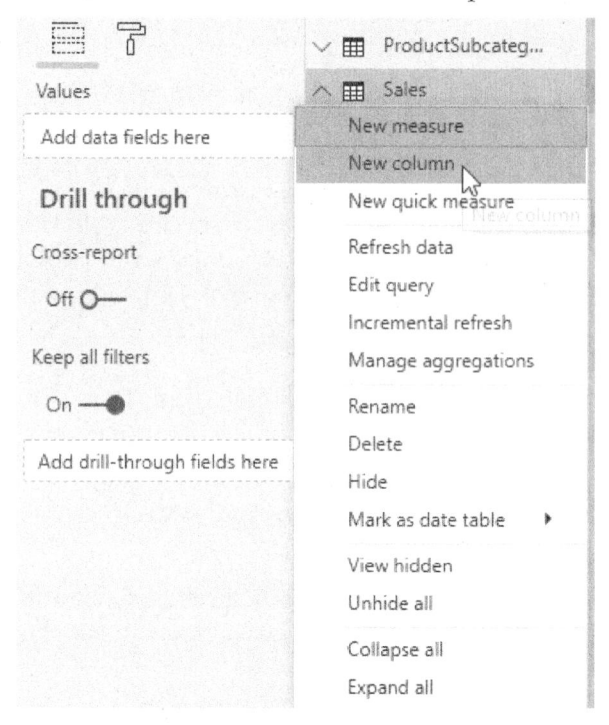

Figure 9.3: Another way of creating a calculated column

As soon as you click, you will see the formula bar to enter the DAX expression. For the learning purpose, let us say we want to calculate the sales line amount. The formula for this calculation is *Unit Price x Quantity*. So, we can create a calculated column like this. The name of the column is also specified in the formula. You can see the sample line amount calculated column DAX expression put in the formula bar as shown in *figure 9.4*:

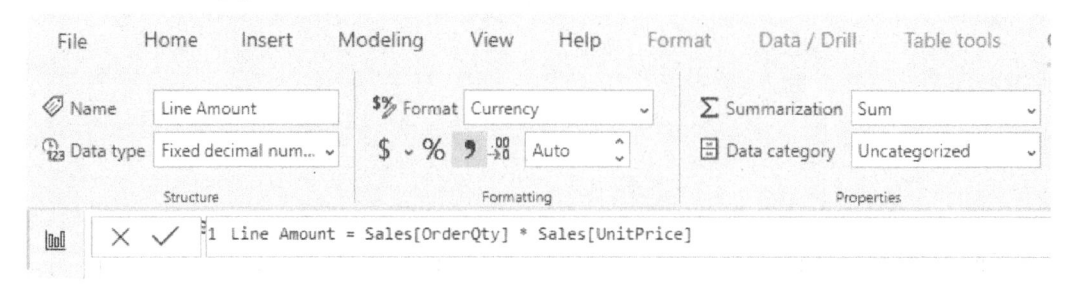

Figure 9.4: DAX expression for calculating line total

If you go to the **Data** tab, you can see the newly created column data in the tabular view:

Introducing DAX, Calculated Columns, Calculated Measures, and Hierarchies ■ 129

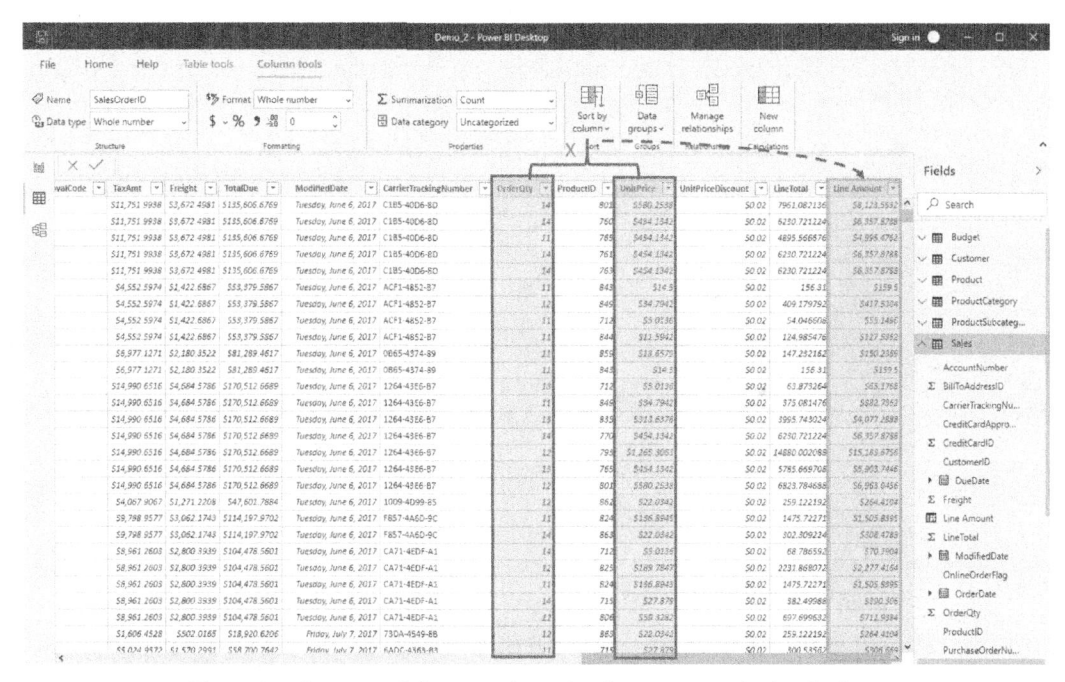

Figure 9.5: Conceptual diagram of creating line amount calculated column

Calculated measures

Calculated measures are another way of creating calculations in Power BI. You can define calculations using DAX. There are slight changes in defining calculated measures than calculated columns. Every time you create a calculated measure; you aggregate the values in a column and do. However, the way of behaving during the visualization is pretty much similar.

You can create a new measure by clicking the **New measure** icon in the top tab:

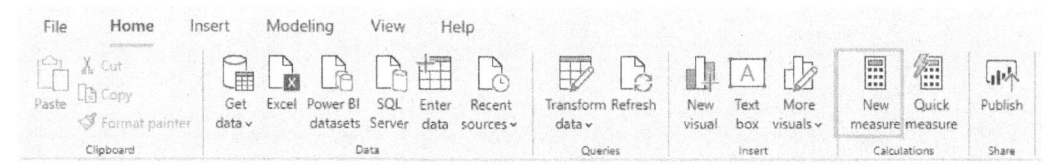

Figure 9.6: Create a calculated measure

The concept of calculated columns, calculated measures, and calculated tables are the same across different platforms such as Microsoft Power BI, Microsoft Excel Power Pivot, and SSAS Tabular. So, once you are comfortable with these concepts, including DAX, you can perform tasks hand-in-hand with them.

You can define a calculation for total sales by aggregating the `Line Amount` column created before. Similar to the calculated column, you need to select the table you want to hold the calculated measure:

Total Sales = SUM(Sales[Line Amount])

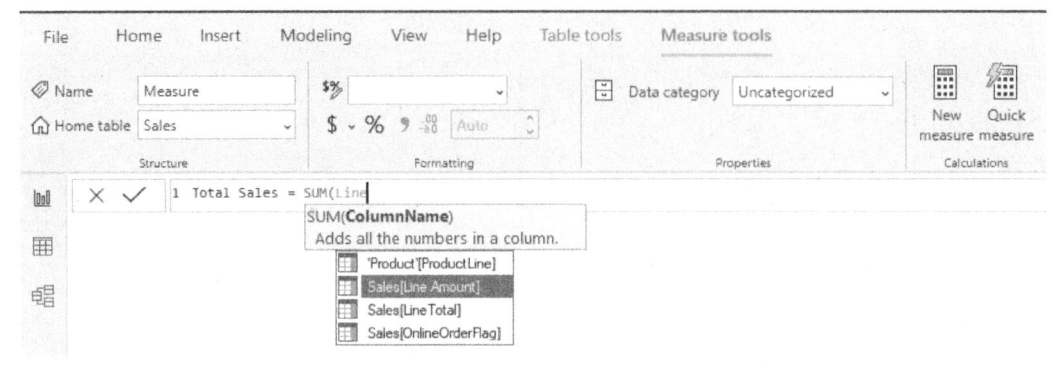

Figure 9.7: IntelliSense support

You can see when you type function names in the formula bar; Power BI suggests *IntelliSense* for you. This is very helpful to learn the DAX formula quickly.

Now, we have been created a calculated column and calculated measure. Let us do some analysis of *what the differences between them are?*

If you look at the diagram, you can see in the visualized matrix the result of the calculated column, `Line Amount,` and the measure `Total Sales` is the same. As mentioned before, numerical fields, which are denoted by *Sigma*, by default aggregate during the visualization. Oppose to the definition of a calculated column, in the measure; we have summarized the values by using an aggregation function – `Sum( )`. Therefore, in terms of visualizing data, you see the same results. But the way it works internally and storing data is completely different:

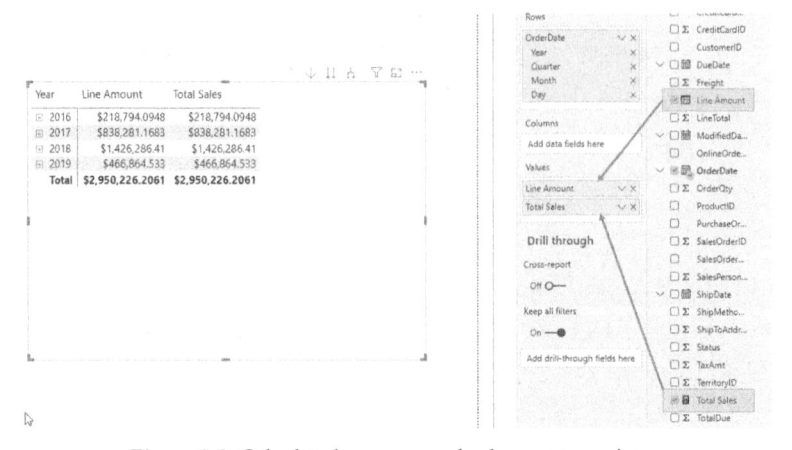

Figure 9.8: Calculated measure and column comparison

Calculated columns are evaluated row-wise and consume space for storing the cell values in the memory. While calculated measures just store the formula only. Whenever a request comes, it evaluates using a *calculated engine* inside the Power BI database, and picks the right cell information from *storage engine* data, and returns it to the client.

So, it is always important to be conscious about the decisions to make these objects in the model. Because, in the end, the performance of the model is totally depending on the way you create these objects. However, we will talk about details of internal architecture in later chapters in this book.

You can perform a lot more than just basic calculations. Assume that you need to filter certain information in your model. We know that we have a **base measure** in our model called `OrderQty`, which holds the sales ordered quantity of products in each transaction. If you want to analyze *how many bikes have been sold?* To answer such a question, there are multiple ways it can handle. One simple way is to drag and drop the `OrderQty` field into the model and apply a filter using a category the `Filter` pane. But you would notice that process is a bit cumbersome when it comes to the practical world. If you see the most frequent type of questions throwing by analytics users, rather let them follow this:

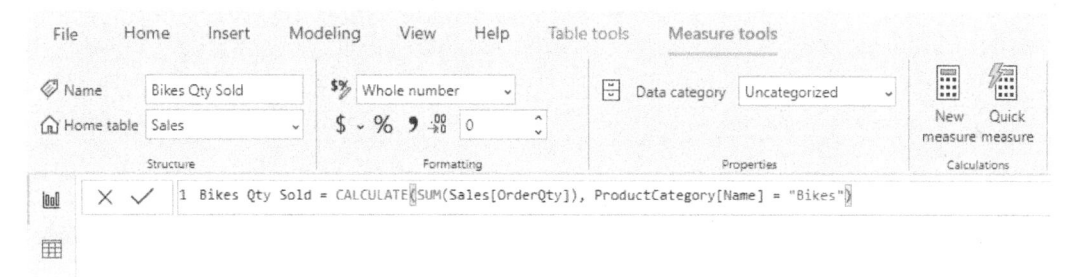

Figure 9.9: Filtered calculated measure

Calculated tables

When you import data or use DirectQuery, individual tables from the source saving as tables (queries) in the Power BI model. However, Power BI allows us to create extended tables using DAX, which means with existing values or without, we can define new tables in the model using DAX expressions. Every time the DAX expression returns a dataset. The classic example is the **Date** table.

When we analyze data most of the time, we perform analysis against a particular date or time. Every transaction we can consider as an event occurs in the real world. If you purchase some goods at glossary, even once you do a bank transaction, you do it at a particular date and time. Those dates and times will be recorded in your bank transaction history or in the bill issued by the glossary. The same information will be useful to perform analysis by bank, How many transactions, per day, in the morning and how much. How many sales are done per day, and so on.

So, by looking at these real-world scenarios, you can realize date and time play a vital role in data analytics. This is the same reason why in data warehousing, creating a separate dimension table for the calendar. Then the user can easily perform time-intelligence analysis.

You can create a calculated table by going to the **Modeling** tab clicking the **New table** option shown as follows. You can write a DAX query to generate a new **Calendar** table:

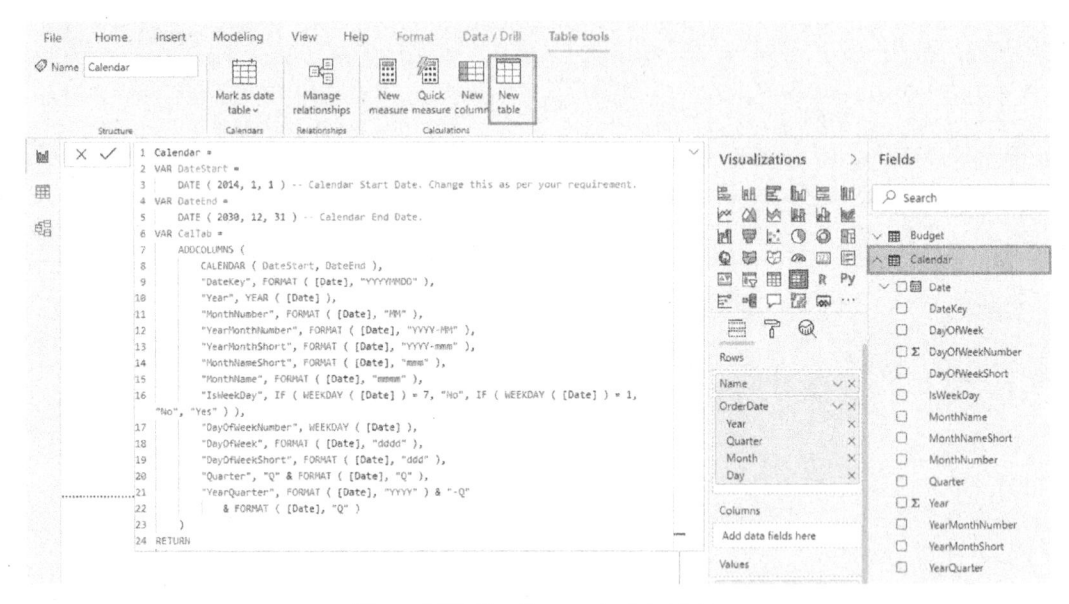

Figure 9.10: Creating a calculated table

You can write a DAX query as follows in your formula bar in order to create a new table for holding calendar information. As soon as you create, you will notice there is a new table created and listed in the **Fields** area. Here in the query, date start and date end are two variables you can define the range you want to generate dates. In our data model, it contains data with order dates from **2016** to **2019**. So, we generate it between **2014** and **2030** by meaning in future dates also captured in this **Calendar** table:

Introducing DAX, Calculated Columns, Calculated Measures, and Hierarchies ■ 133

Figure 9.11: Calendar table

The DAX query for populating the **Calendar** table is as follows. You can refer to the code then modify it in order to create your own **Calendar** table using DAX:

```
Calendar =

VAR DateStart =
    DATE ( 2014, 1, 1 ) -- Calen-
dar Start Date. Change this as per your requirement.
VAR DateEnd =
    DATE ( 2030, 12, 31 ) -- Calendar End Date.
VAR CalTab =
    ADDCOLUMNS (
        CALENDAR ( DateStart, DateEnd ),
        "DateKey", FORMAT ( [Date], "YYYYMMDD" ),
        "Year", YEAR ( [Date] ),
        "MonthNumber", FORMAT ( [Date], "MM" ),
        "YearMonthNumber", FORMAT ( [Date], "YYYY-MM" ),
        "YearMonthShort", FORMAT ( [Date], "YYYY-mmm" ),
        "MonthNameShort", FORMAT ( [Date], "mmm" ),
        "MonthName", FORMAT ( [Date], "mmmm" ),
        "IsWeekDay", IF ( WEEKDAY ( [Date] ) = 7, "No", IF ( WEEK-
DAY ( [Date] ) = 1, "No", "Yes" ) ),
        "DayOfWeekNumber", WEEKDAY ( [Date] ),
        "DayOfWeek", FORMAT ( [Date], "dddd" ),
        "DayOfWeekShort", FORMAT ( [Date], "ddd" ),
        "Quarter", "Q" & FORMAT ( [Date], "Q" ),
        "YearQuarter", FORMAT ( [Date], "YYYY" ) & "-Q"
            & FORMAT ( [Date], "Q" )
    )
RETURN
    CalTab
```

Because you have created a **Calendar** table, utilizing the knowledge of creating relationships you learned from the previous chapter, you can create a relationship between **Calendar** tables date and **Sales** order date field:

```
1 Sales by Shipped Date = CALCULATE([Total Sales], USERELATIONSHIP(Sales[ShipDate], 'Calendar'[Date]))
```

Figure 9.13: Build relationships for Sales and Calendar tables

You can see in this data model we have a **Sales** transaction table and **Date** dimension table. If you look closely, the **Sales** table contains three **Date** columns, **OrderDate**, **DueDate**, and **ShippedDate**. But, in theory, we cannot have all of them as active relationships. This means only one relationship filter can apply in your report. In this case, you can only visualize the **Sales** data using the **OrderDate**. Because it is the active relationship in this model. Even the relationship exists for the **DueDate** and **ShippedDate** because it is *inactive*; we cannot use them for visualization. This means the filtration does not work.

So, in this model, the **Date** table works as a role-playing dimension. At a time, it plays the **OrderDate** role and, at another time, the role of the **DueDate** and **ShippedDate**. However, once you establish a relationship, you can make them active programmatically using DAX. For that, you have to use the **USERELATIONSHIP** DAX function:

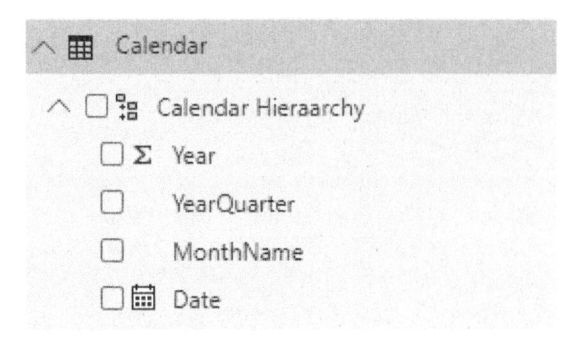

Figure 9.14: DAX expression for creating sales by Shipped Date measure

Hierarchies

In Power BI, you can create hierarchies in your model. The main objective is to give users more accessibility to their analysis. Once you have hierarchies, more functionalities will enable, like the drill-down option in visual charts. *What are the hierarchies you can find in general?* In many scenarios, we can see organizational hierarchies, product hierarchies, and so on.

Hierarchies enable self-service BI users to navigate and analyze data easily. As a Power BI user, you can create your own hierarchy using the dataset. Once you create a hierarchy, it will appear a symbol like front of the hierarchy, which also allows any other BI user in your team to find it quickly. You will learn how to create a hierarchy in *Chapter 4, My First Power BI Report*.

If you closely look at our `Calendar` table we created in the previous step; we can see a hierarchy:

Year >> Quarter >> Month >> Date

Let us create a hierarchy for the `Calendar` table.

In the field list, click **Quarter** and drag and drop atop of **Year**. As soon as you do it, it will automatically create a hierarchy. And the symbol also changed to a *hierarchy* symbol:

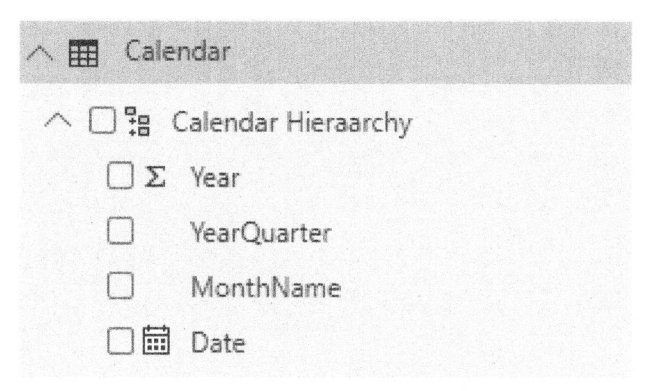

Figure 9.15: Calendar hierarchy

Following the same pattern, you can add a month and date and create the hierarchy. In the end, you can rename it also as you prefer.

Once we create a hierarchy, it will give more analytics power to the business user. So as a best proactive, you can hide existing fields in the table and make only hierarchy visible. Otherwise, it also creates some confusion for the user.

Conclusion

In this chapter, we went a little deep into the theoretical aspect and learned about the basics of DAX language, calculated columns, measures, and tables. Later in the chapter, we also learned about hierarchies and created a hierarchy through a calendar table.

Questions

1. Discuss about the differences between calculated columns and calculated measures and use cases of them.

2. In the chapter, we discussed about one scenario for the calculated table and calendar table. Discuss about another usage of creating calculate tables.

CHAPTER 10
Creating Insightful Reports Using Visualization Techniques

By reading this book chronologically, you already know that Power BI is not just visualizing tool. You can also perform various tasks like data cleansing, shaping, and profiling. However, once the data is ready to consume, the next important task would be how we can serve the insights precisely to the end-user. Hence, Power BI is a self-service BI tool; this is not a difficult task anyway. Anyone with little prior knowledge to work with data can easily download Power BI desktop and play around with data by creating visuals as desired. The main objective of this chapter is to create reports by using the right visuals, which is a skill you need to develop. In this chapter, you will learn the data visualization best practices, how to select visual type for each KPI, and the visual features offer in Power BI.

Structure

The following topics will be covered in this chapter:

- Data visualization best practices
- Designing the report
- Filtrations
- Drill-down visuals
- Drill-through visuals and reports

- Mobile layout and theming

Objective

The objective of this chapter is to teach how to visualize and generate insights effectively. First, you will understand the business requirement, what sort of questions to pick in order to answer through visuals, then how to transform the data model into insightful visuals using data visualization techniques, and then you can deliver the right information in the right manner.

Data visualization practices

We can always follow the best practices when doing the visualization. It is important to go through the data model one last time and identify the business problems before starting to do any visualization. It is a good practice to jot down the number of questions you are going to answer via BI reporting. So, it is a process of identifying the business queries, sketching the report design, and visualizing. You can see the process workflow in *figure 10.1*:

Figure 10.1: Visualization process

Once you have the list of questions, then it is time to sketch how you are going to represent it. To sketch the reports, you can use various tools out there. My preferred tool is **drow.io**. But you can do it even with PowerPoint. The main idea here is to reserve spaces for visuals. If you are developing reports for client requirements, you can send them for feedback before implementing them.

The final step is to visualize using various built-in and third-party visuals. We can make a template to sketch the canvas as follows in order to design the visuals in a convenient manner. It's always your choice to decide the structure of the report:

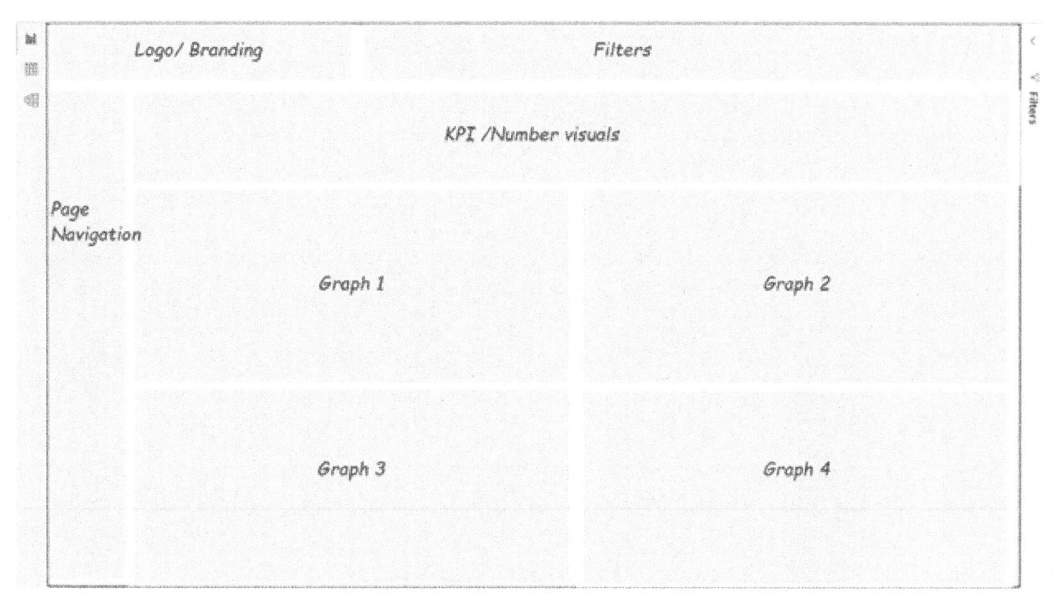

Figure 10.2: Report structure layout

Of course, we must give a name, add a logo, and apply brandings for the report. The first-place holder is all about that. In the top right corner, we can consume mandatory filters for the report. This is the most common position for placing the filters. You can use the left narrow area also the area we used for page navigations. These two areas have been interchangeably used for the filters for a long time. One main reason I can highlight is this is the way our brains used to read and left to right and top to bottom. So, it is a common practice to place filters that are frequently used visual throughout the report here.

Page navigation: As you know, we can have multiple pages in the Power BI report file. You can add buttons and make your report more sophisticated when the user wants to navigate to different pages. This gives the user clearer visibility of what includes in the report from the very beginning.

> **By default, Power BI provides the ability to navigate across pages. But you can make use of buttons and allow users to navigate through them, which enhances the user experience. We will learn how to use buttons to navigate pages later in this chapter.**

Designing the report

Let us get started with designing the report. When we design the visuals on the canvas, we have to know certain elements and features in order to finalize the design as per the requirement.

Filtrations

When it comes to filtration, there are multiple ways you can apply filters in the report. You can see the filter pane as shown in *figure 10.3*:

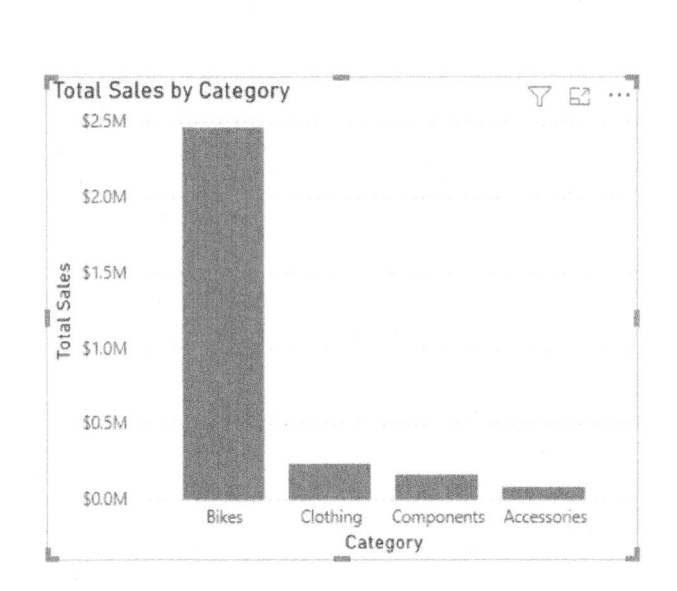

Figure 10.3: Report filters

Filter pane filter types will be explained as follows:

- **Visual level filter**: This is the type of filter we can use to filter the visual selected. We can add one or more visuals to it.

- **Page level filter**: When you drag and drop a field into the page level filter, it is only get filtered all the visuals on the current page.

- **Filters on all pages**: Most of the time, you may need to add multiple pages to your report. In that situation, if you want to add a filter into the global scope, it means applying that filter across all the pages that you can.

There are mainly three types of filters in common: **basic filtering**, **advanced filtering**, and **Top N**. You can see the filter types in *figure 10.4*:

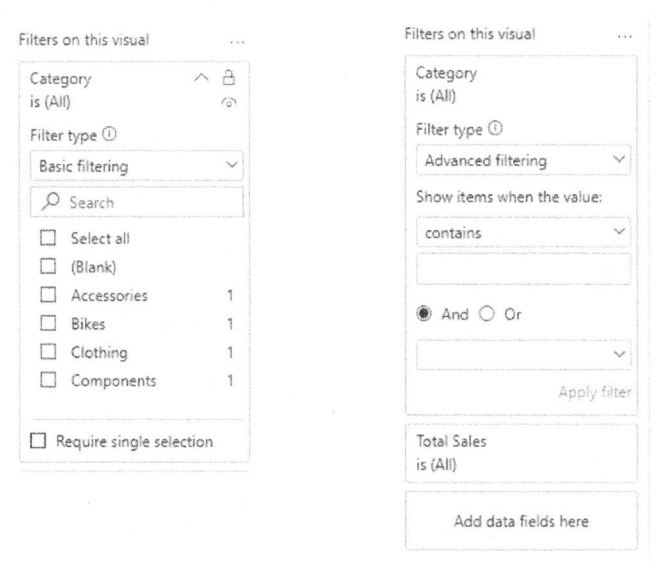

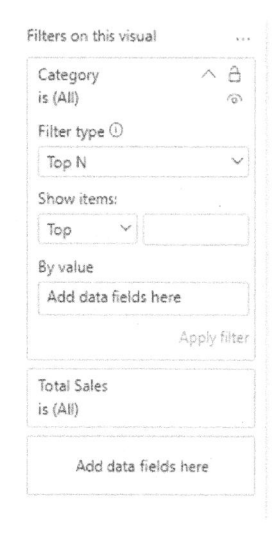

Figure 10.4: Filter types

Use slicers in the report

Another way to filter visuals is using a slicer. **Slicer** is a special kind of visual in the gallery that acts as a filter. Depending on the data type, you can choose the type for the filter; for example, **Date** data type, you can use all kinds of filters, including range. Range slider with the date you can see in the following screenshot:

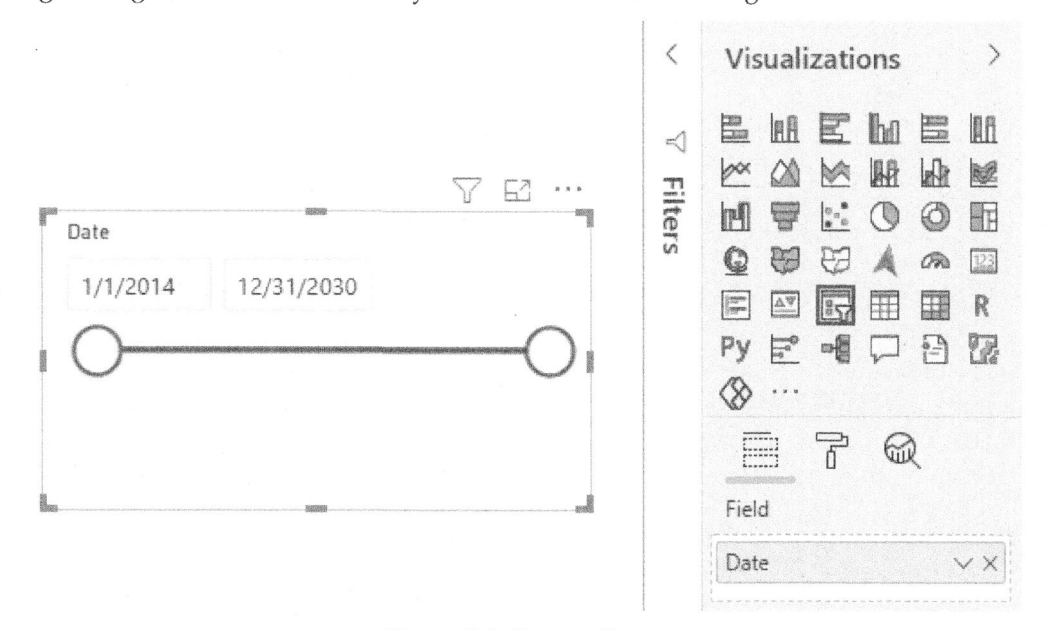

Figure 10.5: Using a slicer

Cross-filtering

Cross-filtering is the default behavior of filter automatically all other visuals when you select some area of one visual. Basically, it will get filtered and leave the portion which contributes to the selected criteria and grey out the rest. For example, assume that we have sales by **category** column chart and sales by **region**, donut chart as follows:

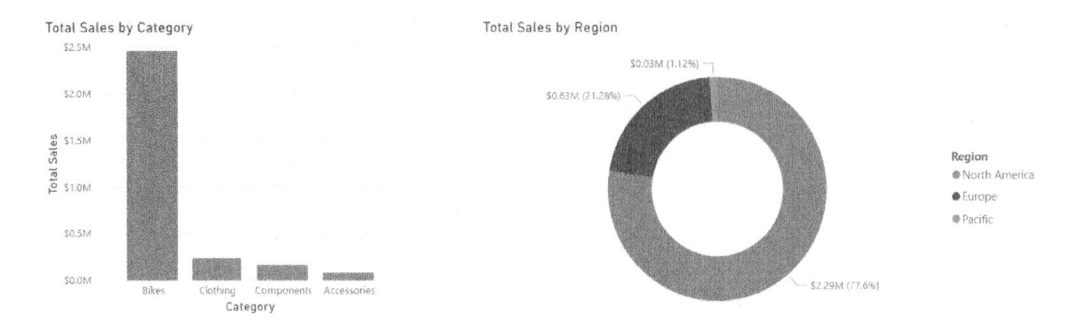

Figure 10.6: Column chart and donut chart as default

Then, if you click one of the areas of the donut chart, you will see it will affect not only the donut chart but also the column chart on the left-hand side:

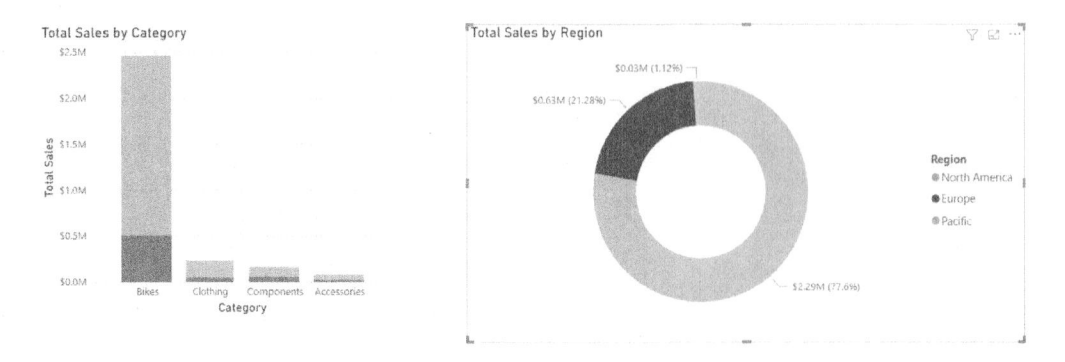

Figure 10.7: Column chart and donut chart as default with cross filter

This will be the same for all the charts you created in the report canvas. However, the option is provided to stop this behavior. You can go to the **Format** menu and click the `Edit interactions` option to change this behavior:

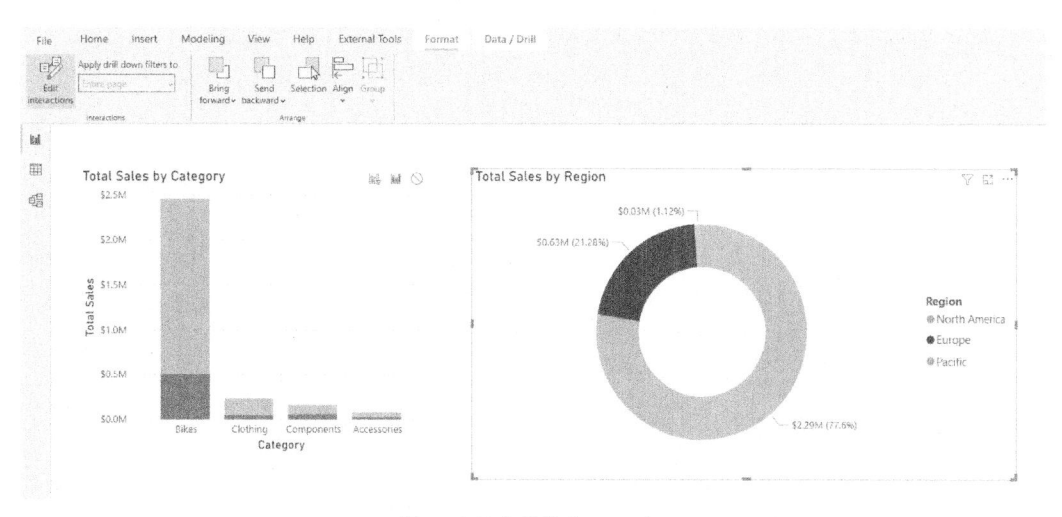

Figure 10.8: Edit interaction

Drill-down visuals

As you know, you can create hierarchies in your model, which we have already discussed in the previous chapter. Either you use a logical hierarchy, or you have fields that behave like a hierarchy; you can add those fields into an axis in the visual. A very good example would be, let us a closer look into the column chart:

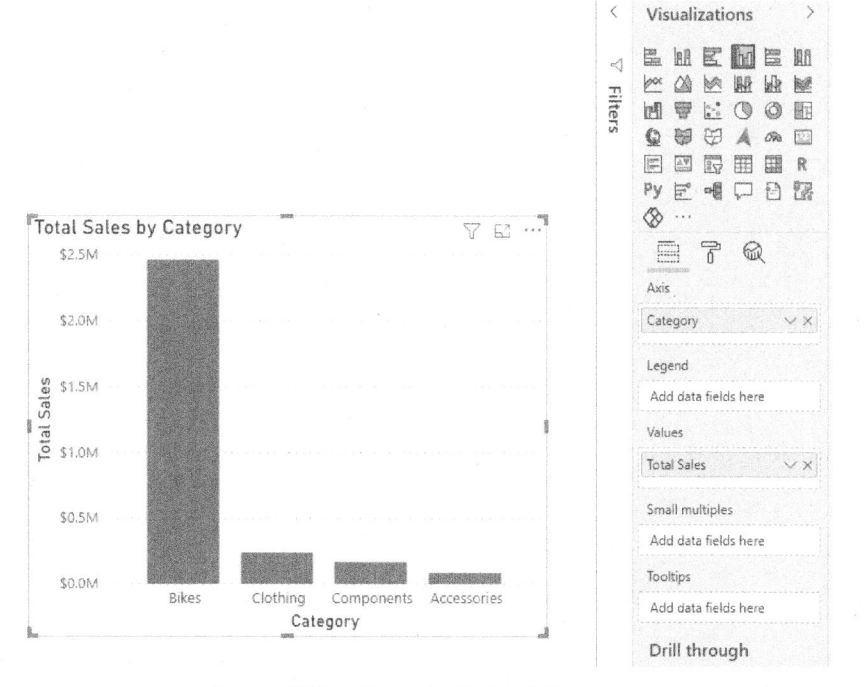

Figure 10.9: Column chart with fields menu

Basically, this chart has been drawn using total sales and product category. In the data model we build, there are many hierarchies we can see. One of the most common hierarchies is the **Product Hierarchy**. Let us add the next level of the product category: the product sub-category field, into the axis. As soon as we add, we can see there are new icons start to appear in the top left corner of the chart:

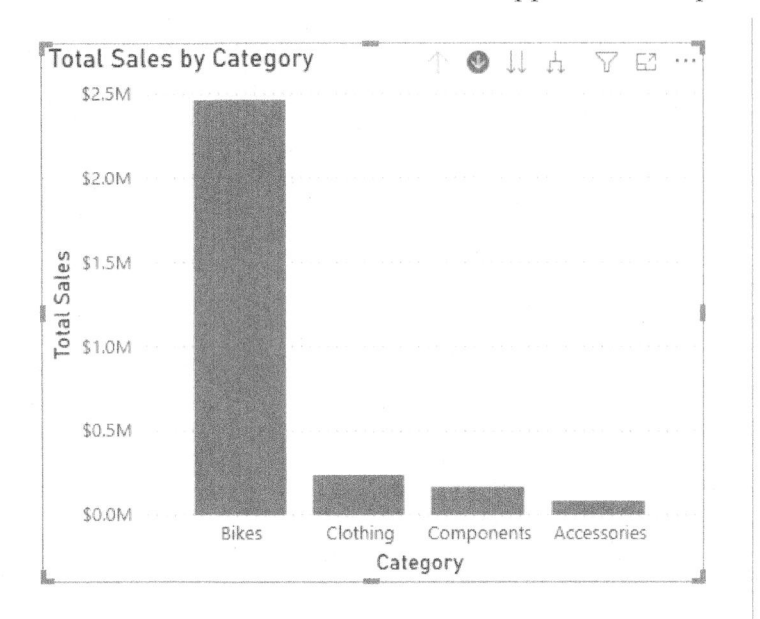

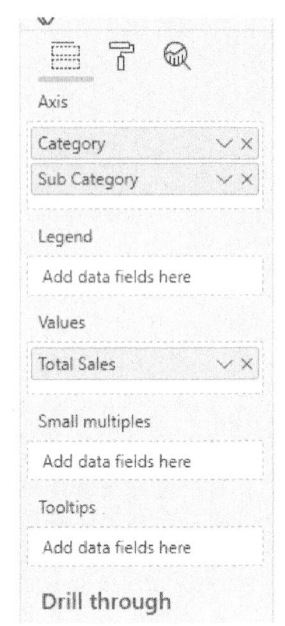

Figure 10.10: Column chart with drill-down filter

We can click the single down arrow and click one of the columns. Then, it will drill down into the product sub-category level:

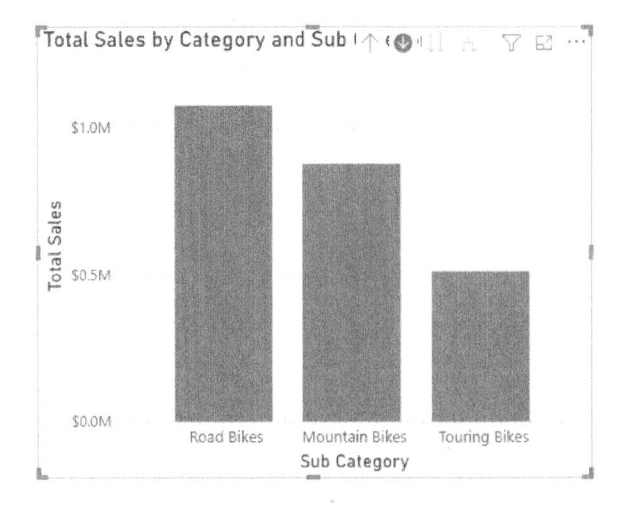

Figure 10.11: Drill down into sub-category

Hierarchies enable self-service BI users to navigate and analyze data easily. As a Power BI user, you can create your own hierarchy using the data set. Once you create a hierarchy, it will appear a symbol like ⁞⁞ front of the hierarchy.

Drill-through visuals

Drill-through report filters are another way of enhancing the user analytics experience in Power BI. Here, we add a filter in the drill-through fields places holder in the `Fields` tab. This is what we do for the destination report page. Assume you do have a summary report page and detail report page in your Power BI file:

- **Summary page**: Contain visuals data at a higher level, mostly cards, and few visuals.
- **Detail page**: Contain the detailed analysis information that are derived from a summary.

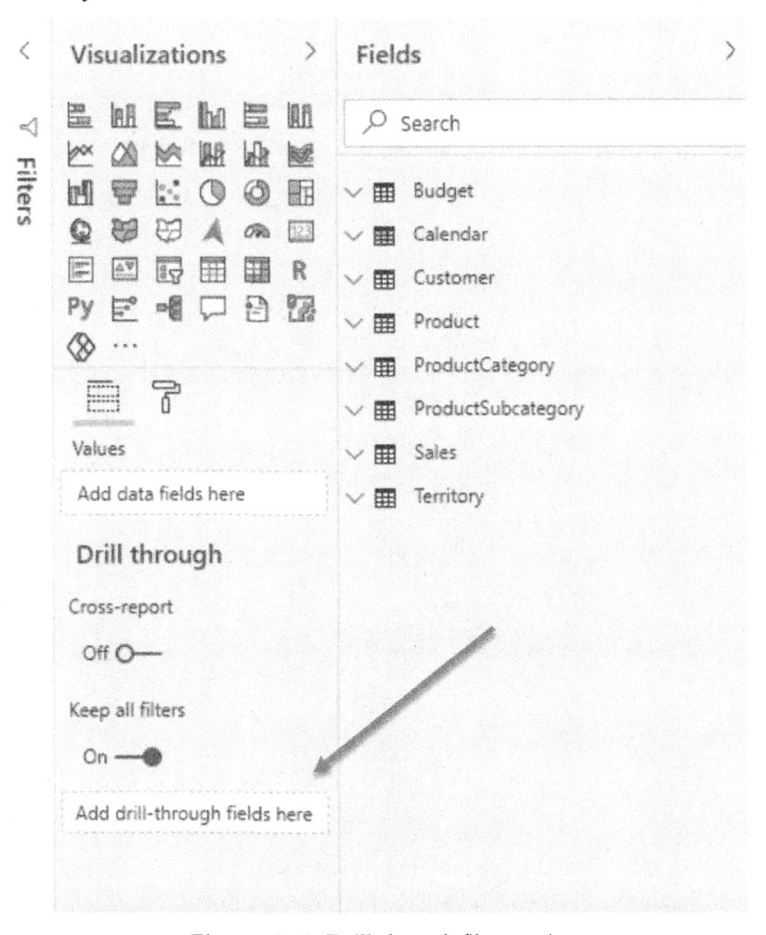

Figure 10.12: Drill-through filter section

146 ■ *Power BI Data Modeling*

Now drag and drop a field; in this case, we will add a **Region** field into the drill-through filter placeholder. As soon as you add the drill through the filter, in the canvas, a new button with a *left arrow* will appear in the top left corner for the return page:

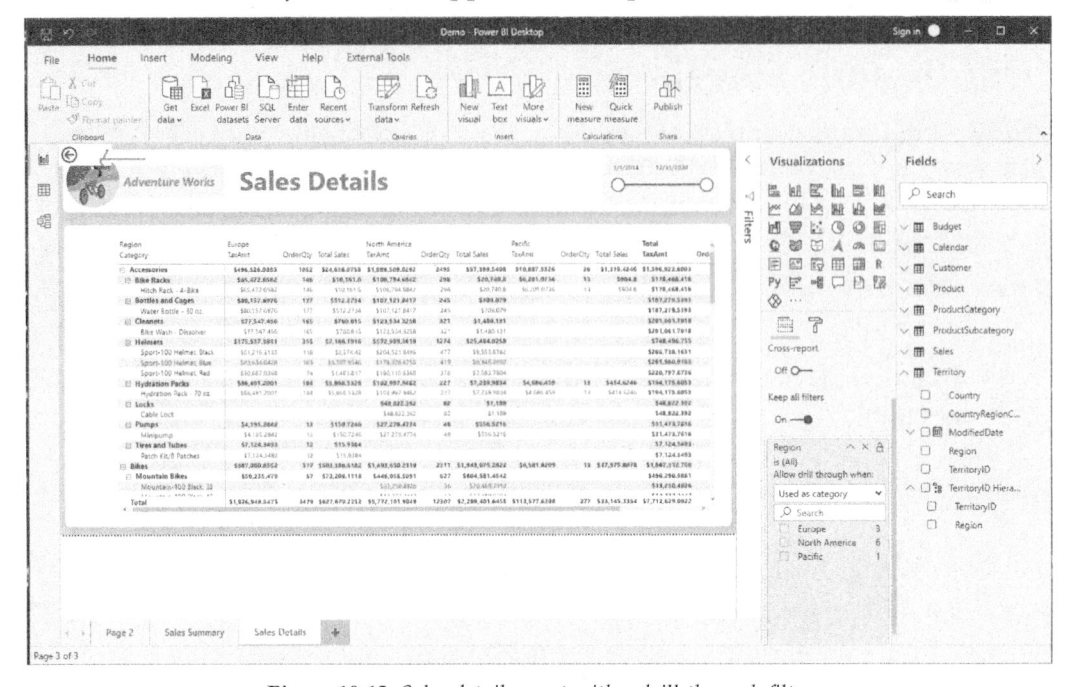

Figure 10.13: *Sales detail report with a drill-through filter*

The idea here is whenever you use the *region* in other report pages, which enables you to drill through to this detail report page; for example, I will move to the summary page and I have a donut chart of sales by region. I can right-click by selecting one of the regions and click the **Drill-through** option to navigate to the detail page:

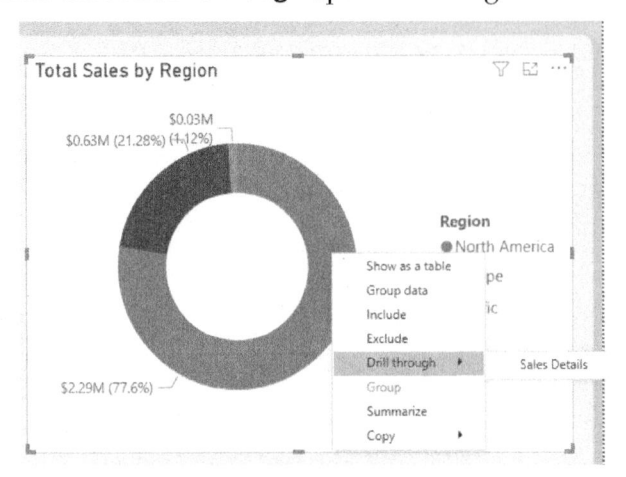

Figure 10.14: *Apply the drill-through filter*

Creating Insightful Reports Using Visualization Techniques ■ 147

Once you select **Sales Details** (the drill-through report page name), this report will re-direct to the **Sales Details** page and filter all the visuals on that page from **North America,** which I selected from the donut chart:

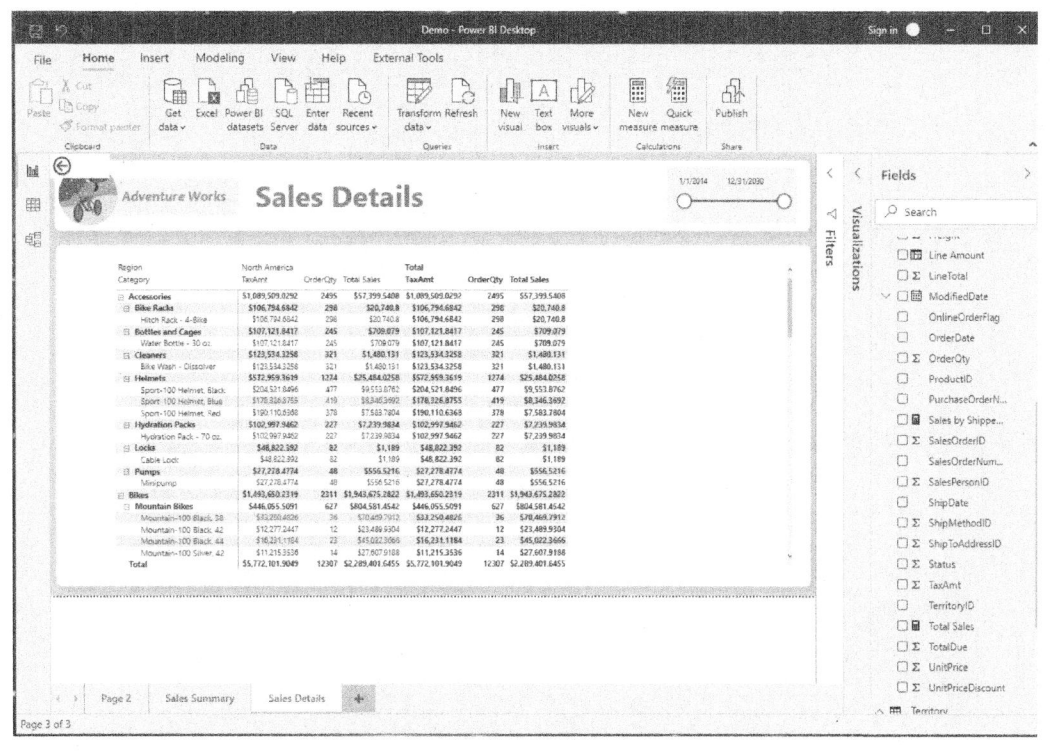

Figure 10.15: *After applying the drill-through filter*

Theming

You can choose different themes and configure custom themes if you want. This flexibility has been given by Power BI as default. You can change the themes by going to the **View** tab and selecting the theme you want:

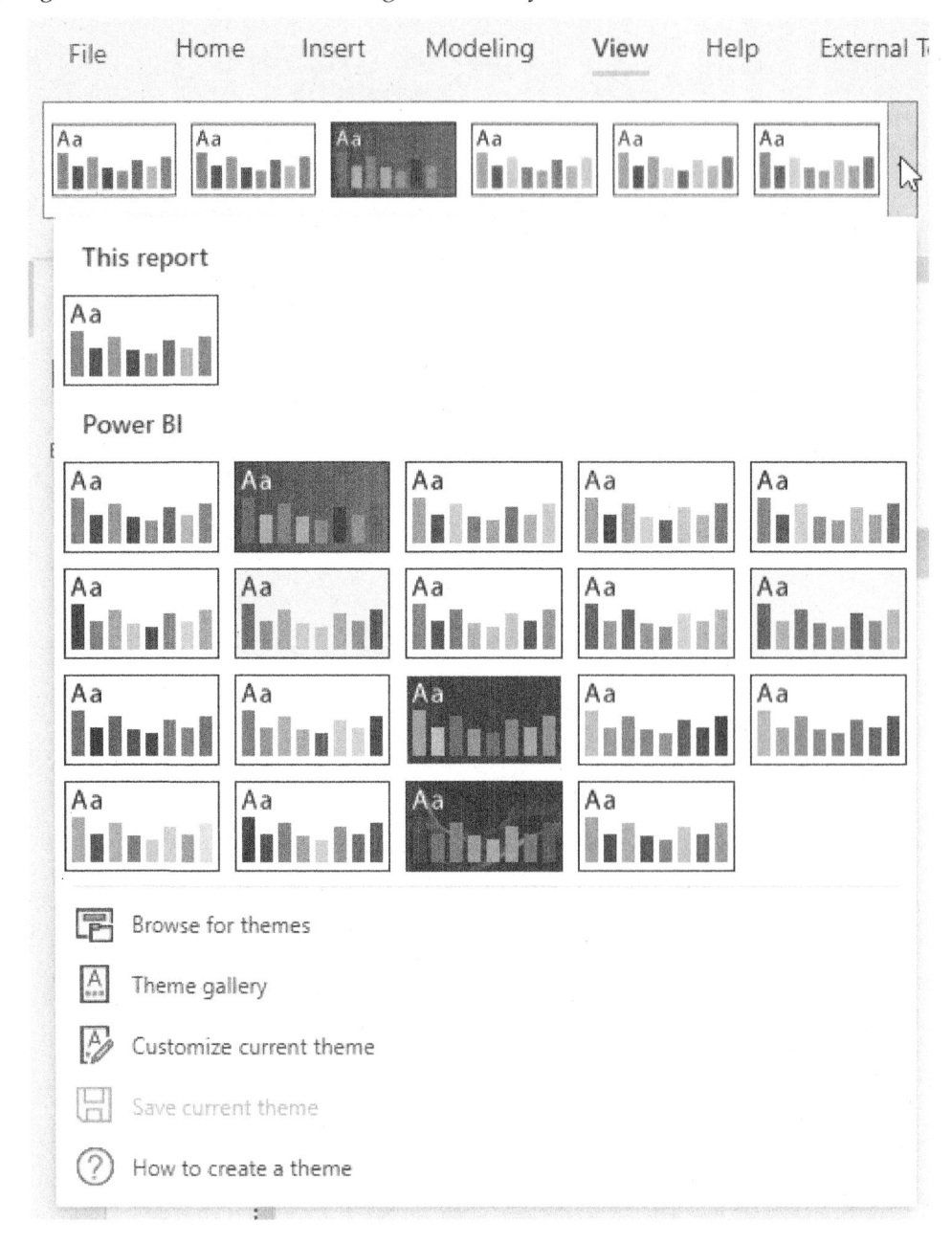

Figure 10.16: Theming

Gridlines and lock object options are also helpful to make the visuals perfect. You can perfectly align all the visuals in the report with the help of gridlines:

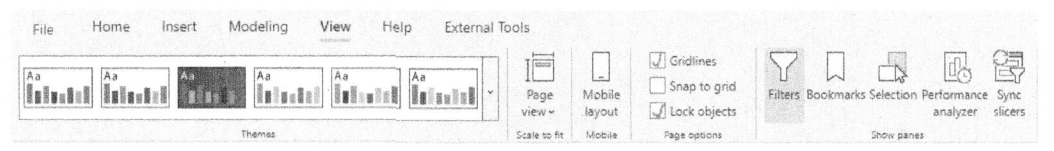

Figure 10.17: View tab with gridlines and lock objects

Our objective in this chapter is not to discuss all the possibilities we can go with when we do the visualizations but to discuss the most important features that are available with Power BI today. Again, these features are changing time-to-time; they add more and more new features every time to give the best self-service analytics experience to the Power BI users.

Mobile layout

This is another cool feature in Power BI that allows you to rearrange the way you want visuals how it should appear when looking at from mobile devices:

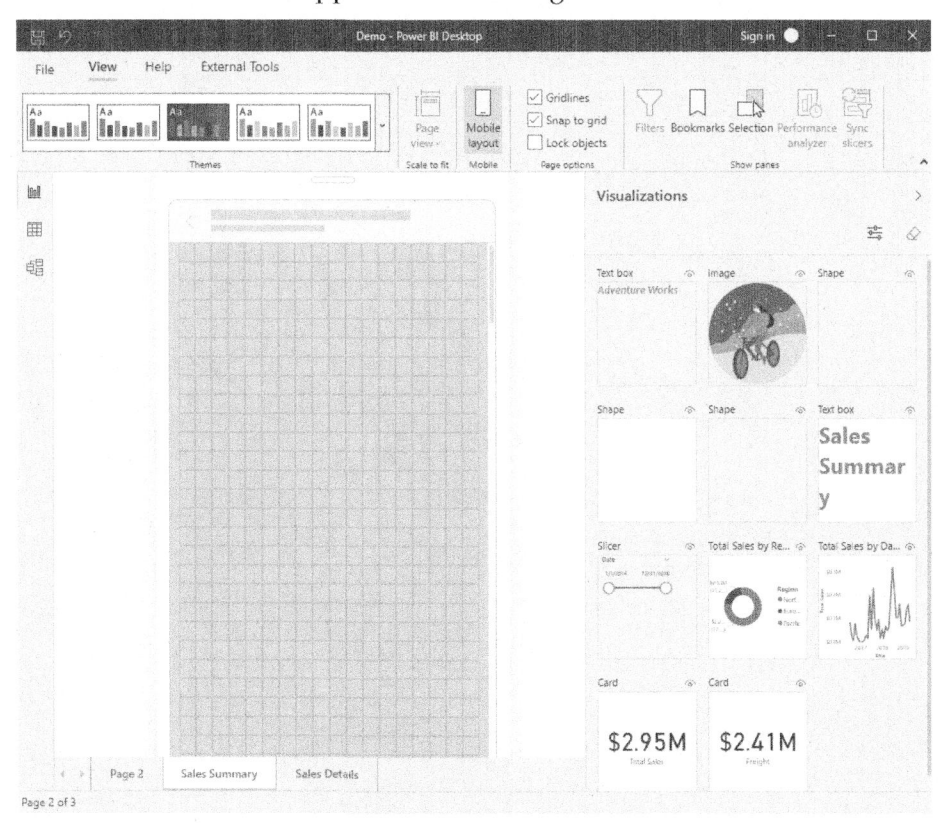

Figure 10.18: Mobile layout

Conclusion

In this chapter, we focused on the visualization aspect of the Power BI development. However, we understood it is vital to have the knowledge of features available in Power BI. We discussed about how to apply visual filters, drill-down filters, and drill-through filters. Also, some features which can enrich your reports, such as the mobile layout and grid layout. Because we have discussed the model and report development, the upcoming chapter will focus on how to implement security in the Power BI model.

Questions

1. Explain three ways of applying filters to a report page in Power BI.
2. Theming is important, especially when you consider brandings. Discuss how to configure custom theming in your report.

CHAPTER 11
Row-Level Security in Power BI

You have learned to build beautiful data models and reports with the experience you gained by reading the past chapters. Now is the right time to focus on more advanced concepts in Power BI. In the modern-day, data is a more valuable asset than anything out there. Furthermore, collecting data and storing it in a secure manner is more important in any organization. Power BI itself came up with features to handle the complex security requirements in the organizations. In this chapter, you are going to learn how to implement security in your data model.

Structure

The following topics will be covered in this chapter:

- Security overview
- Role-based security
- Implement row-level security
- *How to test row-level security?*

Objective

The objective of this chapter is to give you thorough knowledge on how to implement row-level security in your Power BI models.

Security overview

When we talk about security, many things may come to your mind. Power BI manages security through Azure Services and **Active Directory** (**AD**). Azure AD is used to store and manage users in your organization uniquely. About how it manages and detail technicality, you can learn more in this white paper:

https://docs.microsoft.com/en-us/power-bi/guidance/whitepaper-powerbi-security

This explains how Power BI as a SaaS product secures your data from external threats.

However, as report developers or BI engineers, our responsibility is to implement the business logic for data access. This is where row-level security comes into the picture. In this section, we will be going to discuss about two aspects of it: **static RLS—role-based** and **dynamic RLS**.

> **In this chapter, we only cover the row-level security we can implement in Power BI. But that does not mean the capabilities are limiting to it. Similar approach can be taken in SQL Server Analysis Services Tabular databases to implement row-level security using DAX.**

Static row-level security—role-based

We will require adding another file to our data model. Because we feel we can demonstrate the real use of row-level security in a more sensible manner.

As the first step, download the `Territory.csv` file from this demo files link and download it into your PC (refer to *figure 11.1*). Then open the demo Power BI file and import it into your data model:

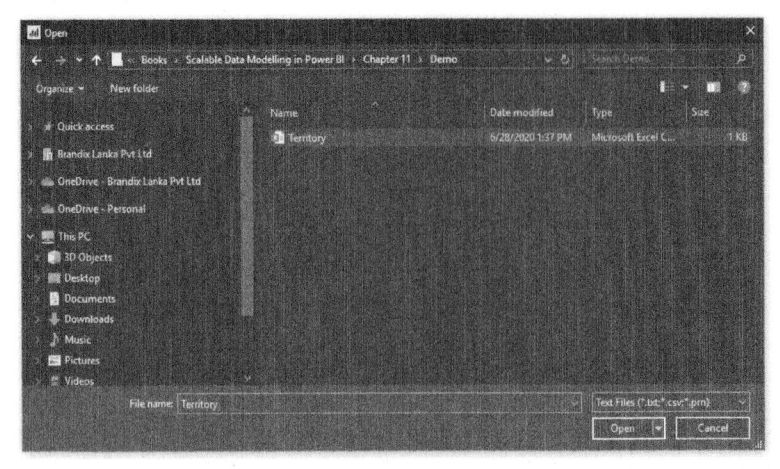

Figure 11.1: Import sales Territory CSV file

The same way you imported previous data, use the **Get Data** option to load this file into the model:

Figure 11.2: Transform the query using Power Query

Click **Transform data** straight away to go to the Power Query editor to make changes to this query. We do not need **rowguid** so, remove that column. Once completed, click **Close & Apply** to apply the changes to the model:

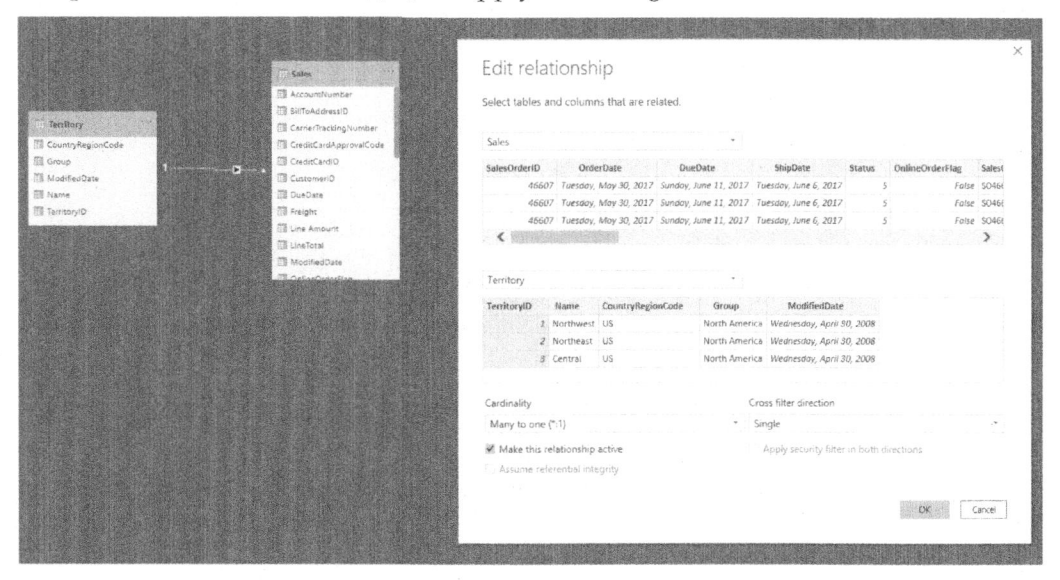

Figure 11.3: Build a relationship with territory query with sales

154 ■ *Power BI Data Modeling*

Territory table will connect with the existing **Sales** table. Now, we have done the data modeling part required to implement static row-level security.

We have created a simple report with a few visuals to elaborate on the row-level security and how it looks once it is applied. You can do the same with the previous chapter, visualizing the experience you had. We are not going to repeat those steps as you are already familiar with it:

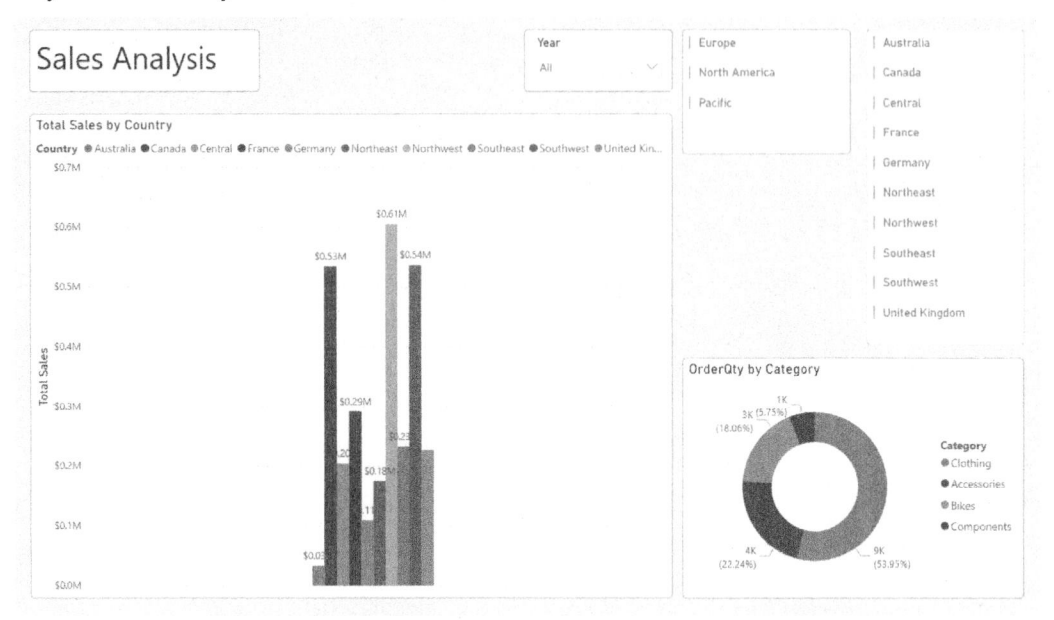

Figure 11.4: Sample report created to demonstrate row-level security

This report shows a column chart with sales for each country. Also, a donut chart has been created to visualize sold quantity based on the product category.

Creating roles

Now, it is time to create roles in the data model. We are going to create different roles for each territory group. You can see there are three main territory groups in the model. **Europe**, **North America**, and **Pacific**. So, we are going to create roles for each.

In order to create roles, go to the *top menu bar* tab in the Power BI desktop, and switch to the **Modeling** tab:

Row-Level Security in Power BI ■ 155

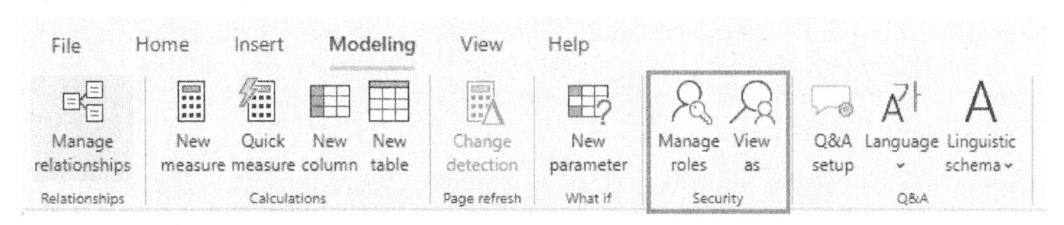

Figure 11.5: Menu bar options to implement and test RLS

Click the **Manage roles** button in the menu. You will see a window as shown here:

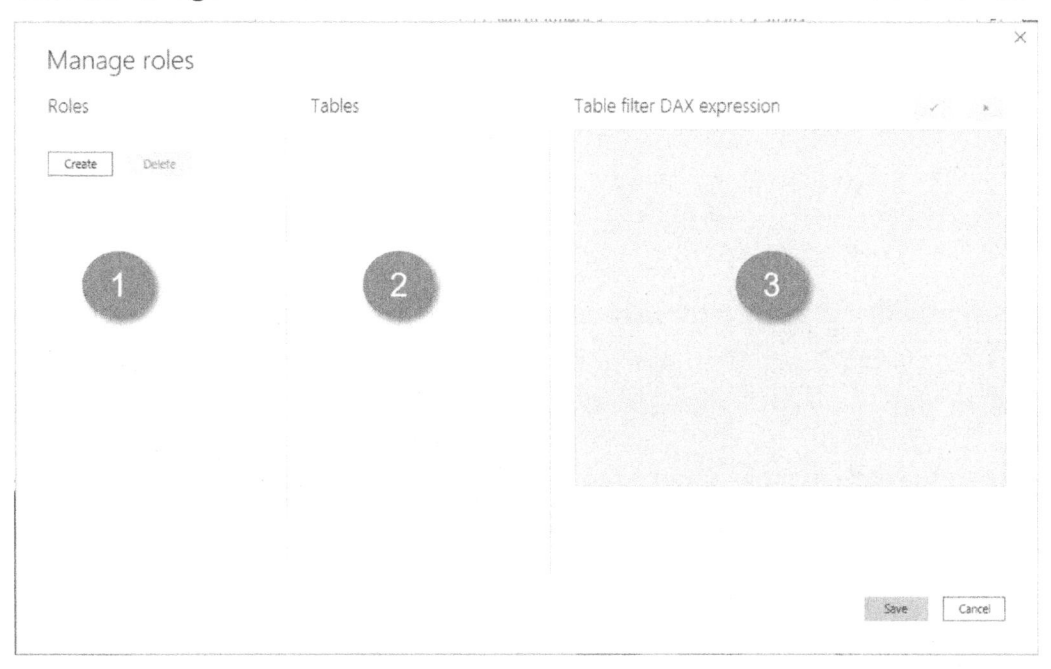

Figure 11.6: Manage roles window

- In the **Manage roles** window, you can create roles as required to apply the security for certain data in your data model. Delete button you can use to delete the roles.

- Once you create a role, you will see that all tables are listed in the **Tables** area. You can select the table you need to filter data that match the role; for example, you can create a role, for **Bikes Department Manager** and filter only the data where product category is **Bikes** for that role. This way, the report user in that role only can see the relevant data for bikes.

- Table filter DAX expression is the area where you define the filter using DAX.

Assume that you need to create a role as **US Sales Manager,** which only can see US sales data:

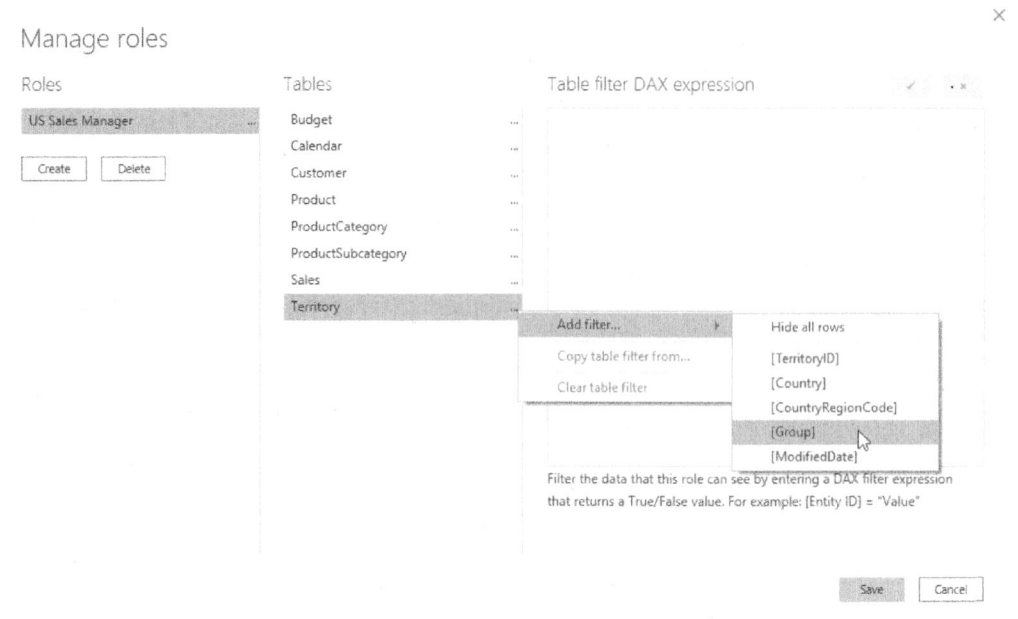

Figure 11.7: *Add filters based on the logic*

In order to create the role, we need to add **Territory [CountryRegionCode]** as a field to apply the filter:

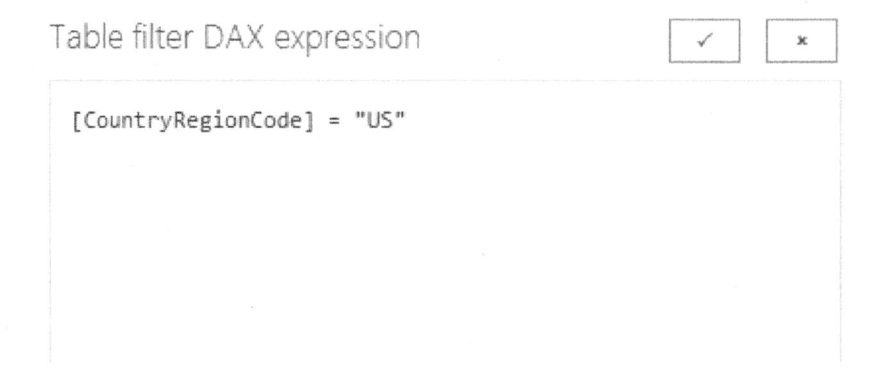

Figure 11.8: *DAX expression for filter US data for the role*

How to test raw-level security?

In the menu bar, select the **View as roles** button to tick this **US Sales Manager** role. Then the report will filter from US data:

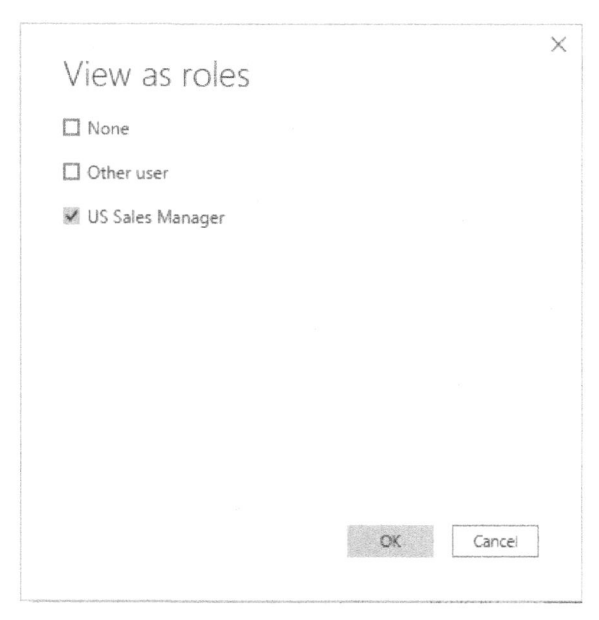

Figure 11.9: Test the RLS using View as roles option

You can then view the report only filtered by US data. Because the role you are viewing is the **US Sales Manager**. Similarly, you can add more and more roles based on different logics:

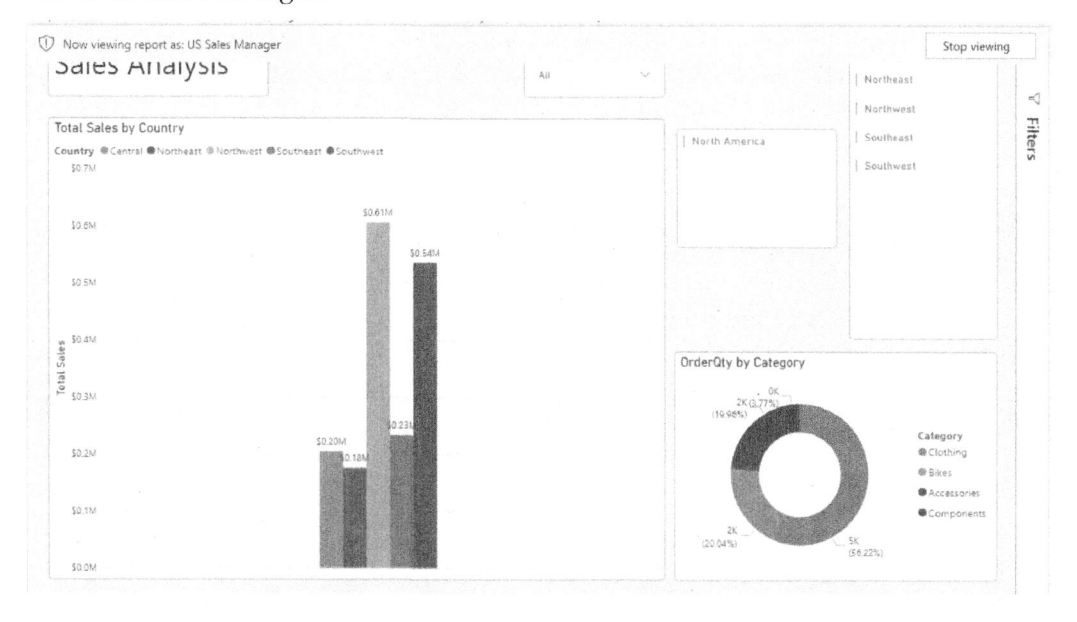

Figure 11.10: Viewed as US Sales Manager role

158 ■ *Power BI Data Modeling*

You can go back to the previous mode by clicking the `Stop viewing` button. This is the predominant way of implementing row-level security. You must add users to the roles once you have published this into the service.

Let us publish the report into the Power BI service. Once you have published the report, you must go to your data set, click the *ellipse* button, and go to **Security,** as shown in the following diagram:

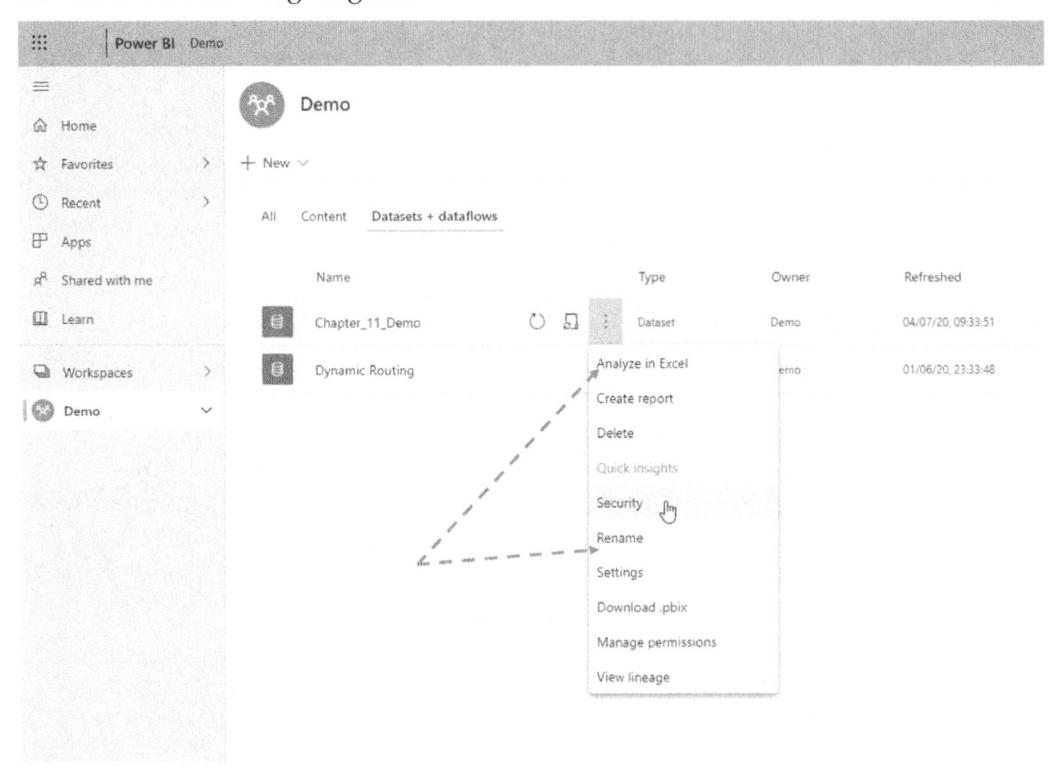

Figure 11.11: Configure security in service

Then it will redirect to the `Row-Level Security` tab. This is where you can add report users or groups into this role where the row-level security role applies.

You can also test the role by clicking the *ellipse* button in front of the role you created:

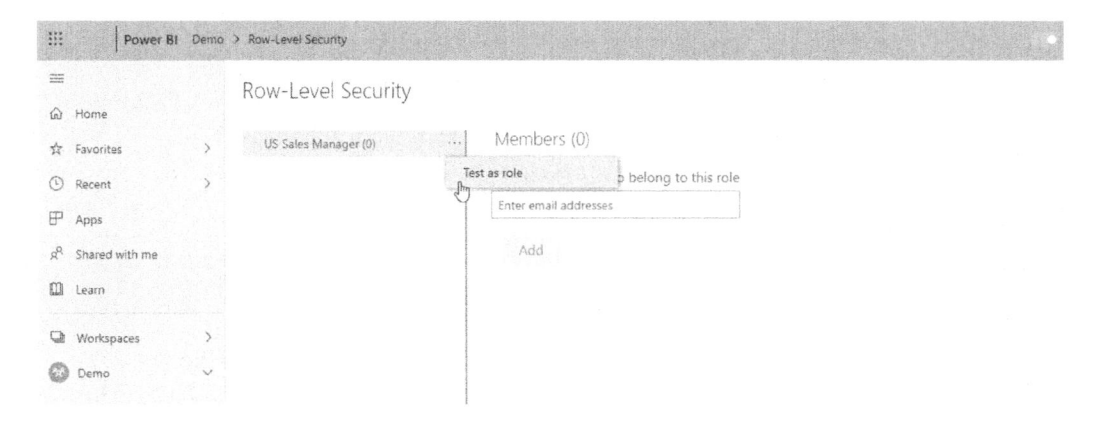

Figure 11.12: Test the role in PBI service

Then, you can view the report as per the role in the Power BI service. By testing this, you can ensure that whoever falls to this role will get filtered by US region data:

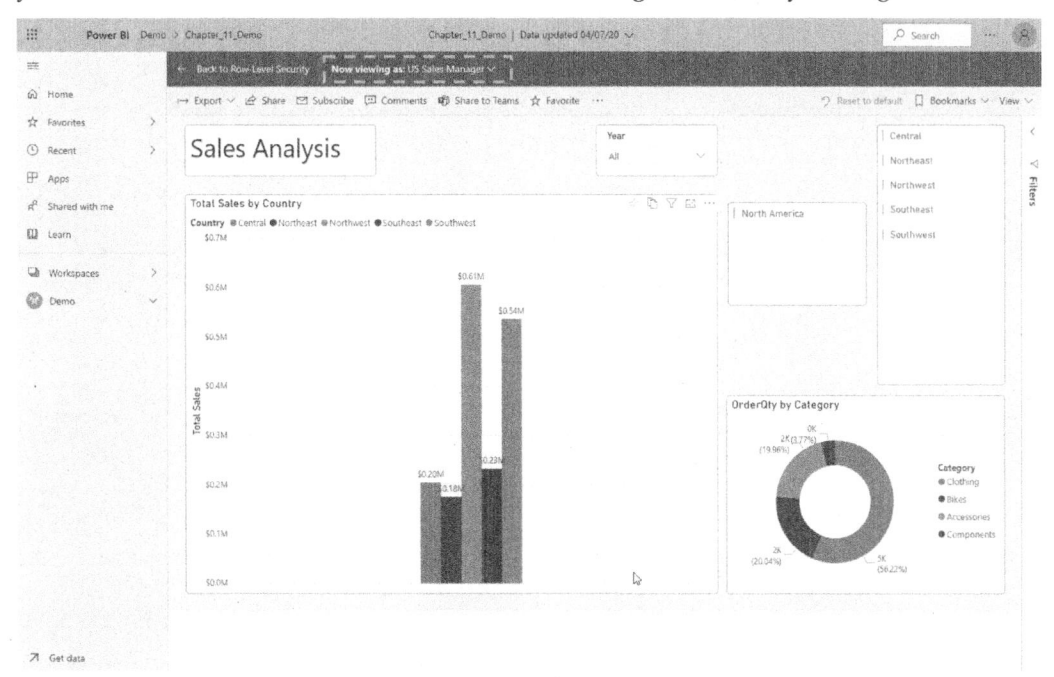

Figure 11.13: Viewed result in Power BI service

In this case, you can create different groups for different regions according to this scenario or, for example, create finance users' role, operational users' role, marketing users' role likewise, and add all relevant AD accounts to it. Then those groups will persist, and you do not need to create when authoring each report.

Dynamic row-level security

So far in this chapter, the way we set up the security is not dynamic. This means for the report user, based on his or her user information, if the user is assigned to a specific country, region, or department, based on that only he can see the relevant data. For your information, Power BI authentication and authorization are based on Azure AD. So, we can integrate the user accounts into the model in order to implement the dynamic row-level security:

Figure 11.14: Create user table

For the demo purpose, I created a table and added user accounts. But in the real case, you can extract this information from master data in the organization. Here, we are not holding any sensitive data like passwords. Active Directory and Power BI service will take care of it.

Let us try to implement the dynamic row-level security for the same scenario. In this case, you may need to have a bridge table where each user mapped to a specific country region code:

Create Table

	UserId	TerritoryID
1	1	1
2	1	2
3	1	3
4	1	4
5	1	5
6	2	6
7	2	7
8	2	8
9	2	9
10	2	10

Name: UserTerritoryMap

Figure 11.15: Create user and territory mapping bridge table

Then, you have to connect these user tables and mapping tables into the model:

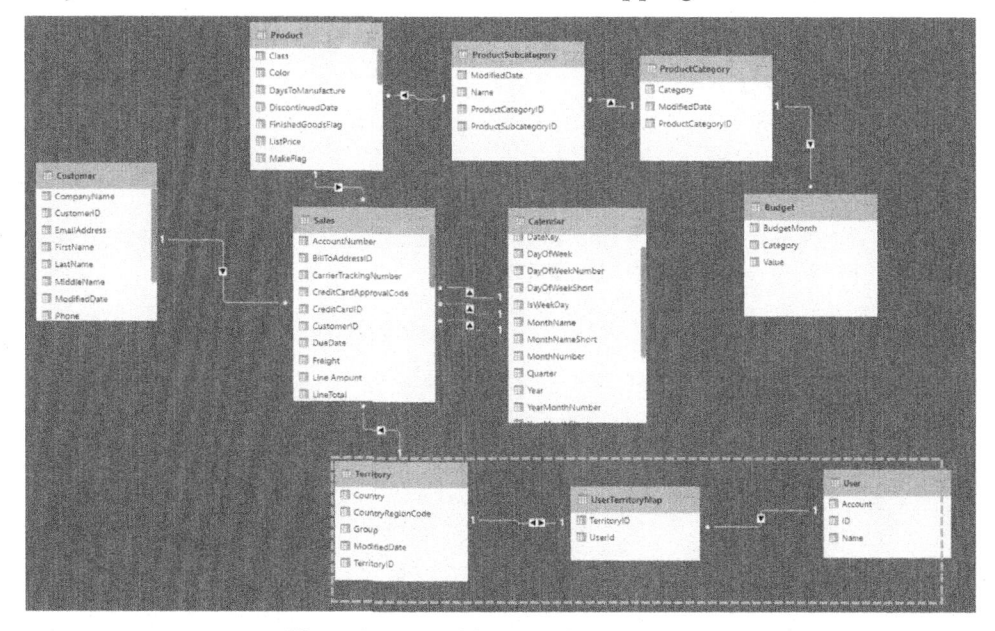

Figure 11.16: Model view with security tables

Here, you need to keep in mind in order to work with the security properly; you must make the checkbox **Apply security filter in both directions** in the relationship between `Territory` and `UserTerritoryMap` tables:

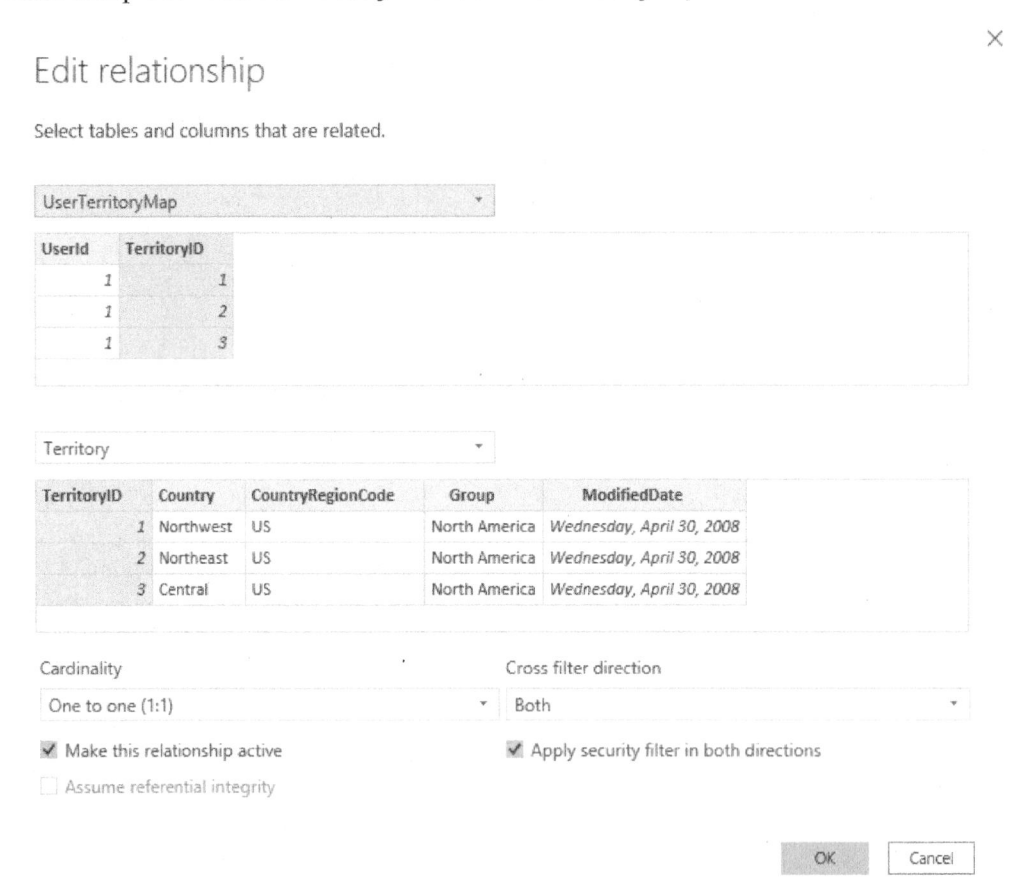

Figure 11.17: Apply security option in the relationship

Then, you can implement the dynamic row-level security role using DAX functions such as `USERNAME()` and `USERPRINCIPALNAME()`:

Figure 11.18: Dynamic RLS expression

Now, you have successfully implemented the dynamic row-level security. Similarly, you deployed and configured the user buckets you can put into this role. But the difference here is that the data is filtering according to the logic or the mapping in the `UserTerritoryMap` table.

Conclusion

In this chapter, we discussed about the ways to implement row-level security. Then using the existing model, we implemented static and dynamic row-level security. Also, in this chapter, we deployed the model into the Power BI service and learned how to configure the security at the service level. We will discuss about more internals of Power BI in the upcoming chapter.

Questions

1. Explain the different ways of implementing the security in Power BI?
2. Describe the advantages of dynamic row-level security and usage by taking real-world scenarios.

CHAPTER 12
Calculation Groups in Power BI

In this chapter, we are going to discuss a more advanced feature in Power BI. When the growth of the complexity of the data models and the calculations, maintainability is something we need to worry about. In this chapter, we are going to focus on a feature called **calculation groups**, which helps you to reduce redundant measures. Eventually, it also helps to make a simplified model and consider this feature as a time saver.

Structure

The following topics will be covered in this chapter:
- Calculation groups requirement
- Calculation groups and how it works?
- Create calculation groups in Power BI
- Sort the calculation items
- Limitations in calculation groups

Objective

Calculation groups are some advanced topics yet essential for Power BI development. The objective of this chapter is to explain it in a simpler manner in order to use it in your development more frequently.

Calculation groups requirement

In order to cater to self-service BI requirements, we develop semantic models using Power BI. If the requirement is more complex, then we might need to go for a corporate BI solution. We can achieve that requirement with technology such as **SQL Server Analysis Services** or **Azure Analysis Services**. Both Power BI data models and Analysis Services data models face a common specific type of problem. When the growth of the number of calculations increases, the complexity of the model also increases. Complexity is not just in terms of usability but also in terms of development and maintainability effort.

Imagine you have a data model with a few simple calculated measures:

1. Sales Amount := SUMX(Sales, Sales[OrderQty] * Sales[UnitPrice])
2. Total Cost:= SUMX (Sales), Sales[OrderQty] * Sales[UnitCost])
3. Sales GP:= [Sales Amount] – [Total Cost]
4. Sales Quantity := SUM(Sales[OrderQty])

Figure 12.1: Basic measures

How it will be if you require to apply time-intelligence functionality for the preceding measures? You must apply time intelligence and create separate measures individually:

- PY, YTD, QTD, MTD, YOY, YOY %
- [Sales Amount] Measure :
  - [Sales Amount PY], [Sales Amount YTD], [Sales Amount QTD], [Sales Amount MTD], [Sales Amount YOY], [Sales Amount YOY %]
- [Order Qty] Measure :
  - [Order Qty PY], [Order Qty YTD], [Order Qty QTD], [Order Qty MTD], [Order Qty YOY], [Order Qty YOY %]

Figure 12.2: Apply time-intelligence

Just imagine you have *10* measures in the model. You require to apply five-time intelligence functions to the model. After you apply, you need to maintain *60 odd measures*, which is a cumbersome task. In reality, for four base measures, you require to create and maintain such a list of measures in the following figure:

- Sales
  - Sales Amount
  - Sales Cost
  - Sales GP
  - Sales Qty
  - Time Intelligence
    - Sales Amount MTD
    - Sales Amount PY
    - Sales Amount QTD
    - Sales Amount YTD
    - Sales Cost MTD
    - Sales Cost PY
    - Sales Cost QTD
    - Sales Cost YTD
    - Sales GP MTD
    - Sales GP PY
    - Sales GP QTD
    - Sales GP YTD
    - Sales Qty MTD
    - Sales Qty PY
    - Sales Qty QTD
    - Sales Qty YTD
- Budget
- Calendar
- Customer
- Product

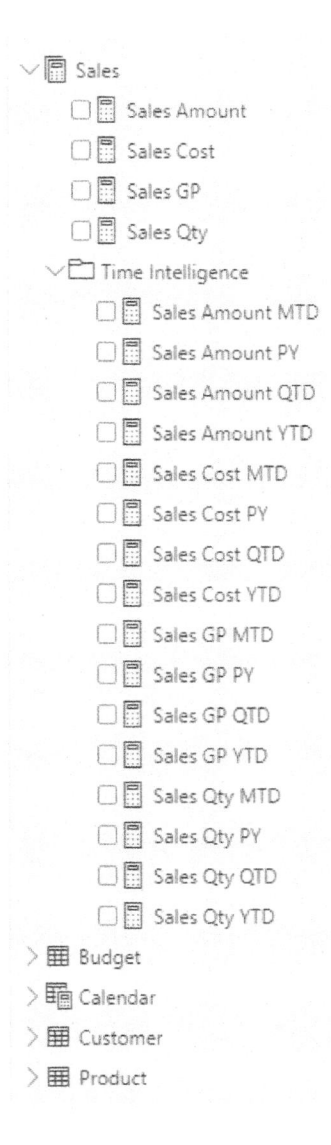

Figure 12.3: *Time intelligence measures*

This is where the calculation groups feature really helps to get rid of the pain.

Calculation groups and how it works?

Calculations groups are not a brand-new concept for semantic data modeling. Similar functionality was there in the multi-dimensional cubes with the name of calculation members. **Calculation groups** are a technique to reduce the number of redundant measures significantly. Calculation groups are supported in tabular models at *1500* or higher compatibility levels. There are four main DAX functions introduced:

- **SELECTEDMEASURE**: Return the measure in the current context.
- **SELECTEDMEASURENAME**: Return the measure name in the current context.
- **ISSELECTEDMEASURE**: Return **TRUE** if one of the listed measures is evaluated in the current context.
- **SELECTEDMEASUREFORMATSTRING**: Return the measure format string that is evaluated in the current context.

Let us see how we can use the above functions to get rid of measures redundancy. Imagine you would apply the time intelligence function **YTD** to the previous four measures:

1. YTD Sales Amount := CALCULATE (Sales Amount], DATESYTD ('Date'[Date])
2. YTD Total Cost:= CALCULATE ([Total Cost], DATESYTD ('Date'[Date])
3. YTD Sales GP:= CALCULATE ([Sales GP], DATESYTD ('Date'[Date])
4. YTD Sales Quantity := CALCULATE ([Sales Quantity], DATESYTD ('Date'[Date])

Figure 12.4: Time intelligence measures with YTD

We just applied **YTD** into base measures. Similarly, we can apply **MTD** time intelligence using the **DATESMYD( )** function:

1. MTD Sales Amount := CALCULATE (Sales Amount], DATESMTD ('Date'[Date])
2. MTD Total Cost:= CALCULATE ([Total Cost], DATESMTD ('Date'[Date])
3. MTD Sales GP:= CALCULATE ([Sales GP], DATESMTD ('Date'[Date])
4. MTD Sales Quantity := CALCULATE ([Sales Quantity], DATESMTD ('Date'[Date])

Figure 12.5: Time intelligence measures with MTD

You may notice there is a common pattern we can identify in this set of calculations. For a specific set of measures, time intelligence function is common:

```
YTD <Measure> :=
CALCULATE (
    <Measure>,
    DATESYTD ( 'Date'[Date] )
)
```

Figure 12.6: Calculation pattern

So, if we can identify the calculated measure, then it will be evaluated in the next section.

Creating calculation groups in Power BI

There are mainly two ways we can find to create calculation groups. If you are creating calculation groups in the analysis service model, you can try both **Visual Studio** and **Tabular Editor**. For the Power BI models, you can only use the Tabular Editor. **Tabular Editor** is a free and open-source tool you can download and use:

Figure 12.7: Tabular Editor and Visual Studio as tools

Because this book is more focused on Power BI data models development, we are going to explain to you how to create calculation groups using Tabular Editor, which is the tool you can use for Power BI.

> **Tabular Editor is a free and open-source tool that you can download and perform various tasks over analysis services and Power BI data models. It is a great tool in which you can easily build and maintain tabular models. It is a simple yet robust tool with a bunch of features to help you to boost productivity. You can download it from the website: https://tabulareditor.com/.**

If you have already downloaded and installed the Tabular Editor, you will see a tab called `External Tools` in the Power BI tabs:

Figure 12.8: Tabular Editor as External Tools tab

170 ■ *Power BI Data Modeling*

You are just required to click the **Tabular Editor** Icon in order to open it in a separate window connected to your Power BI model:

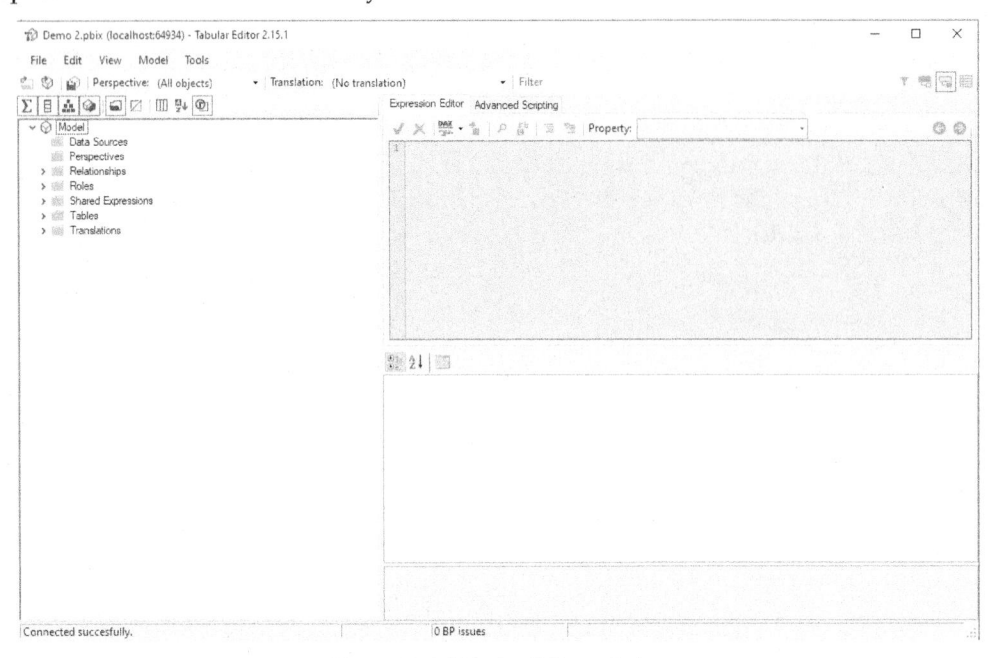

Figure 12.9: *Tabular Editor window*

You can see the Tabular Editor in the preceding screen. You have an object browser along with other folders. You have **Expression Editor** on the right-hand side and a **Property** window in the next line.

The process of creating calculation groups is a pretty straightforward task. You have to right-click the **Tables** folder and click on **Calculation Groups**. Then, it will create a one. You can name it as you want. Here, I named the calculation group I created as **Time Intelligence**. This will be the name of the table at the end:

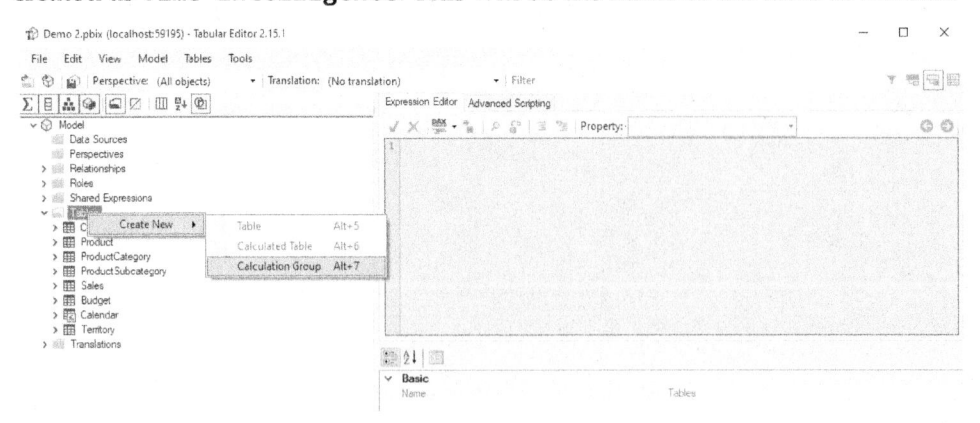

Figure 12.10: *Creating calculation groups*

Calculation Groups in Power BI ▪ 171

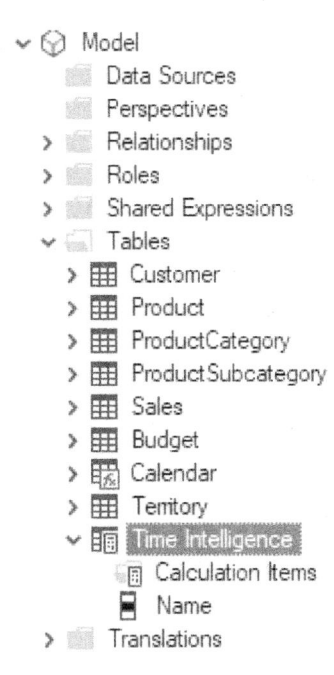

```
∨ ◯ Model
      Data Sources
      Perspectives
   >  Relationships
   >  Roles
   >  Shared Expressions
   ∨  Tables
      >  Customer
      >  Product
      >  ProductCategory
      >  ProductSubcategory
      >  Sales
      >  Budget
      >  Calendar
      >  Territory
      ∨  Time Intelligence
            Calculation Items
            Name
   >  Translations
```

Figure 12.11: Calculation groups structure in the Tabular Editor

Once you have created the calculation group, you can see there are two items under that:

- **Calculation Items**: These are the individual measures you are going to create. For example, **YTD**, **MTD**, **QTD**, and so on.
- **Name**: This will be the group of fields those calculation items reside.

You can right-click the **Calculation Items** folder and create items individually. You can name it the way you want. So, each item has a specific **Expression Editor** window. You have to select the calculation item individually and write the code.

Figure 12.12 demonstrates how it looks when you write the expression. It shows how to write the **YTD** time intelligence function:

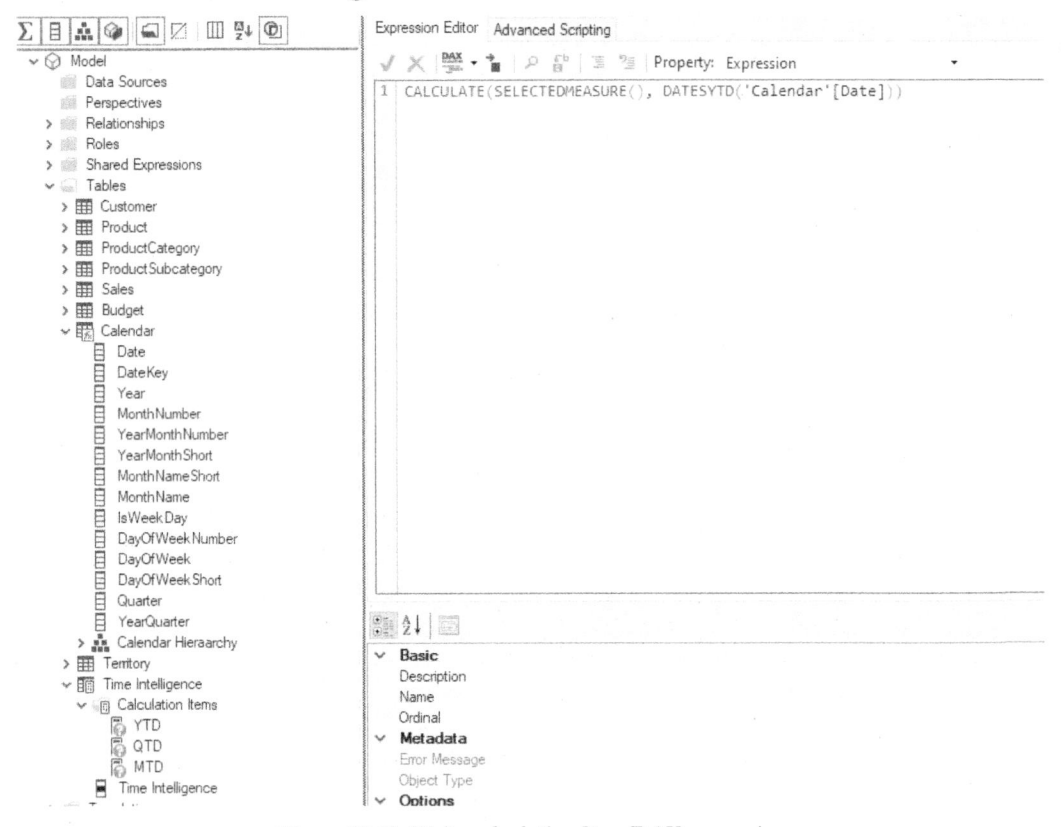

Figure 12.12: Write calculation Item DAX expression

Once you have created the calculation group, you need to save it in order to reflect them into your model:

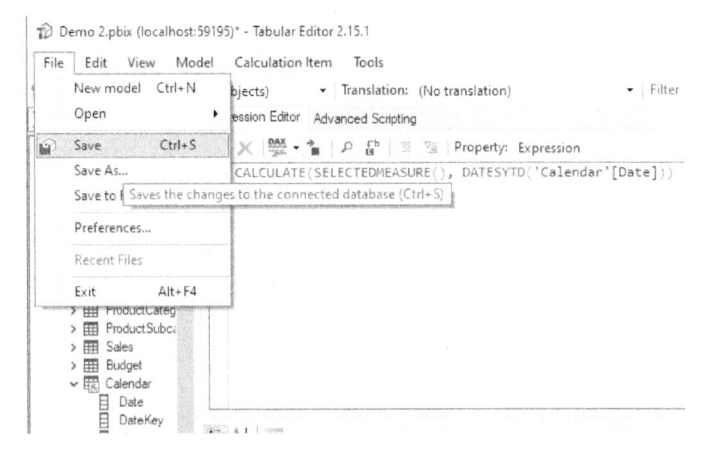

Figure 12.13: Save changes into the original model

Calculation Groups in Power BI   173

Just go to the **File** menu, click the **Save** button, or press *Ctrl + S* in order to save the model changes into your actual Power BI model.

Then you can go back to your Power BI desktop window and start to use the calculation groups you just created. In the Power BI window, you can see a *yellow color message bar* with a **Refresh now** button. You need to click this button in order to reflect your changes to the model and select **Time Intelligence** table. See *figure 12.14*:

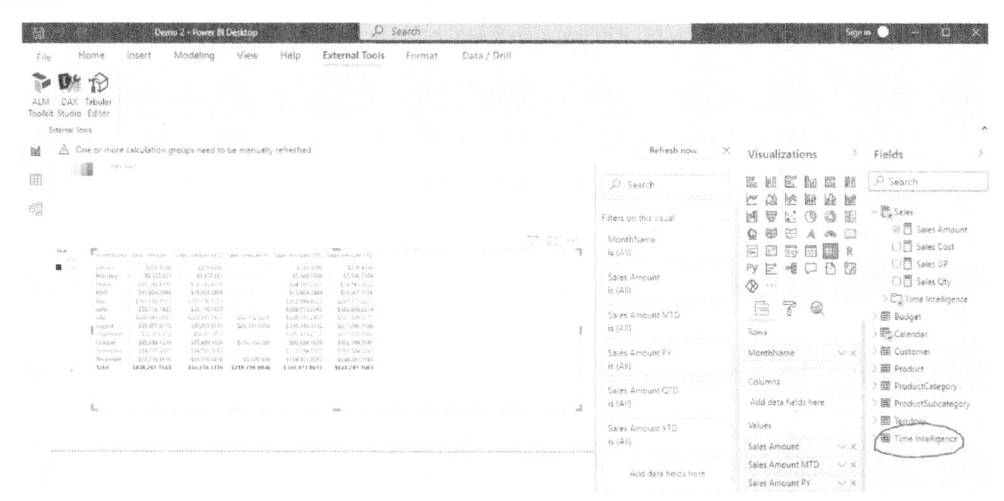

Figure 12.14: Click "Refresh now" in yellow bar and select the Time Intelligence table

You can drag and drop the column and visualize it as shown in *figure 12.15*:

Figure 12.15: Visualize calculated groups

Sorting the calculated items

As this is works as a table, you may wonder how to change the order of the columns. That is also possible to do in both tools. You can select an individual calculation item in the Tabular Editor and change the **Ordinal** attribute. It is an integer property with a default value of **-1** for all items. But you can set the order by ascending:

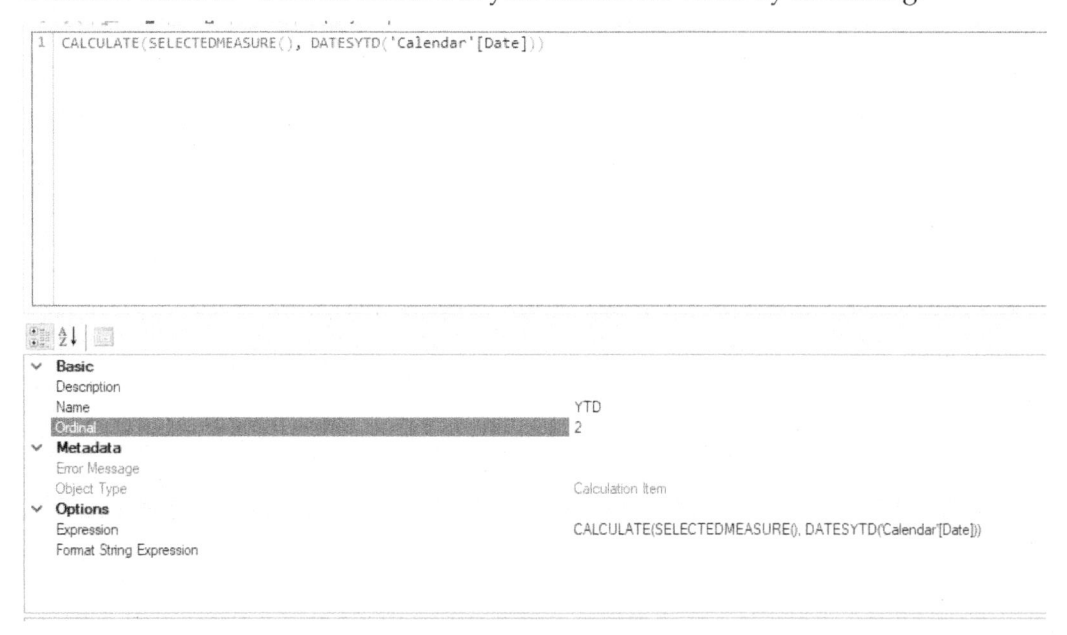

Figure 12.16: Configure the ordinal property

Limitations in calculation groups

This is a sort of new feature, and there are some limitations better go know them when you are using it:

- **Object level Security (OLS)** does not work: If you are using calculation groups and use object-level security for tables or columns that do not work.

- **Row-level Security (RLS)** does not support: The same thing for row-level security also, which does not work with the calculation groups.

- **Detail rows expressions are not supported**: Detail rows expressions are also not supported with calculation groups.

- **Smart narrative visuals** in Power BI have not been supported: Smart narrative is an AI feature that produces a summary of the visual or page you create. If you are using calculation group items that down not compatible with it.

Conclusion

In this chapter, we learned why we require to use calculation groups and the available options we can use to create calculation groups. Also, we discussed how to use Tabular Editor, which is a free tool to make our development work easier. At the end of the chapter, we talked about some advanced topics like ordering calculation items and the limitations. In the upcoming chapter, we will talk about AI features in Power BI.

Questions

1. Discuss about other possible use cases for calculation groups other than time intelligence.

2. How can we use the **SELECTEDMEASUREFORMATSTRING** DAX function?

Chapter 13
Self-service AI Capabilities in Power BI

Artificial Intelligence (AI) and **Machine Learning (ML)** are the most popular buzzwords in the decade of the Data Science world. Accessing the AI tools and getting the benefit from them is limited due to the complexity. Only a limited audience, such as AI and ML engineers, used to do magical things in it. However, the Power BI team has been working tirelessly to bring AI capabilities for business users through Power BI. There could be more features introduced in future. In this chapter, we will explore the AI features they have already introduced into the Power BI desktop and service.

Structure

The following topics will be covered during this chapter:

- Intro to AI capabilities in Power BI
- Quick insights
- Q&A visual in Power BI
- Decomposition tree visual
- Key influencer visual
- Smart narrative visual

- Perform text analytics and integrate with cognitive services
- R and Python integration

Objectives

The objective of this chapter is to get a high-level understanding of AI-related feature offerings in Power BI.

Introducing AI capabilities in Power BI

The world is moving to new innovations along with big data processing, artificial intelligence, and machine learning capabilities invented in the recent past. It is rare to find any data product without AI or ML capabilities. In terms of Microsoft Power BI, as a self-service BI tool, it offers a rich experience to use AI-related features; more of them are free to use. We are going to discuss what these offerings are and how we can use them in our analysis.

Quick insights

The **Quick Insights** is a visual one of the AI features introduced in the Power BI. This visual is the best fit for when you have a completely new dataset. Then you can run the Quick Insights to see what possible outcomes can be generated through the help of AI behind the Power BI.

Once you implement the data model (it could be a single table or star schema model), you must publish it to the Power BI service. The message you get after the successful publish is as follows:

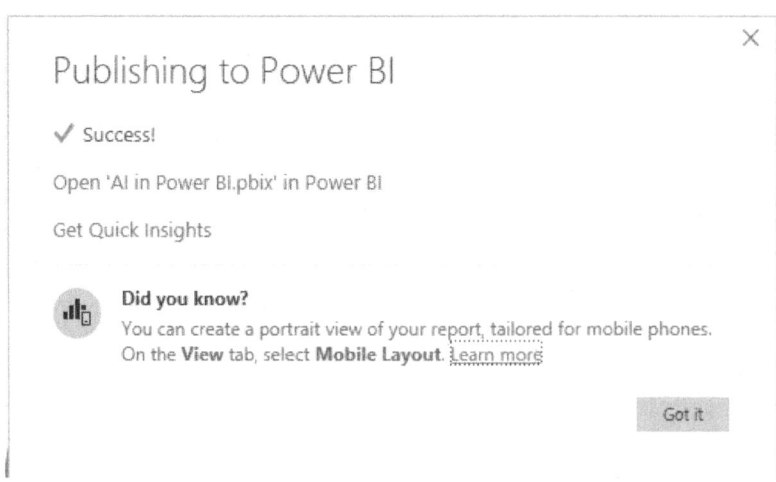

Figure 13.1: Publish data model

There are two options given. You can open the report you published by clicking the first link. The second link is for **Get Quick Insights**.

After you click, it will bring you to the web browser where the insights generation process happens:

Searching for insights...

This could take a little while. We will notify you when your insights are ready.

Figure 13.2: Searching for insights

It takes a while to generate insights autonomously using the Power BI AI algorithms:

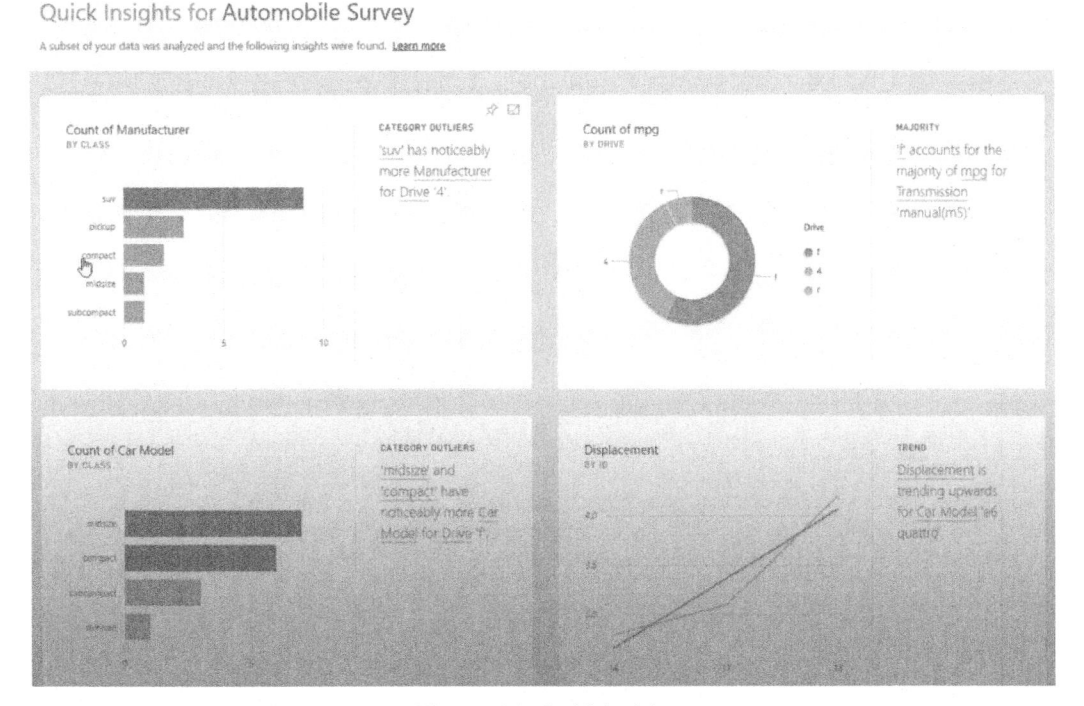

Figure 13.3: Quick insights

Remember, these are generated autonomously through the program. So, all the visuals it generates may not be useful. But it helps to uncover hidden insights indeed. You can pin those visuals into a dashboard if you want.

However, there are a few guidelines you must follow in order to get the maximum out of this feature:

- Use meaningful table names and column names
- Use relevant data types
- Handling NULL values

Q&A visual in Power BI

This is another AI featured visual type introduced very early days. However, it has gotten better over the period of time. You will find the **Q&A** bar when you create a dashboard. Also, you can add **Q&A** visuals to your report. Though the way it works is similar in terms of functionality-wise, they are two different. Especially, Q&A visual has more capabilities, and you have more control to customize it. The idea is you can ask questions using natural conversation and get relevant answers in a visual manner.

You can see the Q&A in the dashboard where you can type questions to get answers:

Figure 13.4: Q&A in dashboard

When you type, it will pop up to a new window, as shown in *figure 13.5*; you can see the suggestions based on the existing data. You can click those or type your own question:

Self-service AI Capabilities in Power BI ■ 181

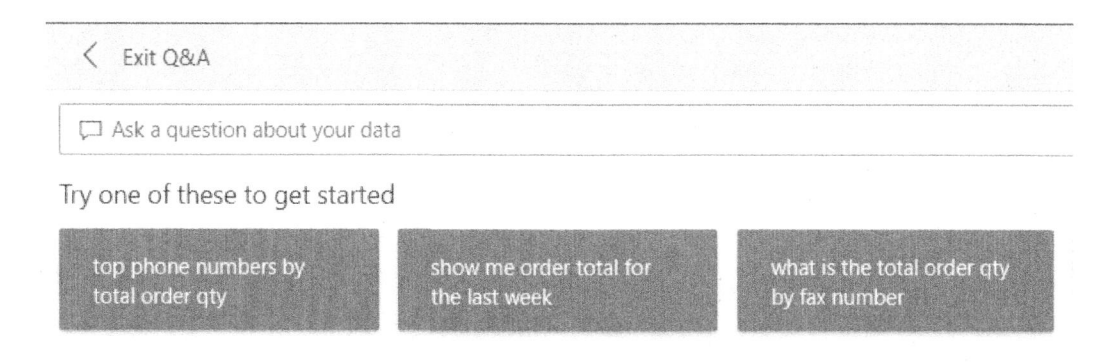

Figure 13.5: Overview of Q&A in dashboard

Q&A visual in the Power BI desktop

Q&A in the Power BI desktop works as a visual similar to other visuals in the gallery. You can add Q&A from the **Insert** tab and select and drag and drop **Q&A** to the canvas that is under the **AI visuals** category. Nevertheless, if you want to add the **Q&A** visual into the canvas, you can find it at the AI visuals area in the **Insert** tab, as shown in *figure 13.6*:

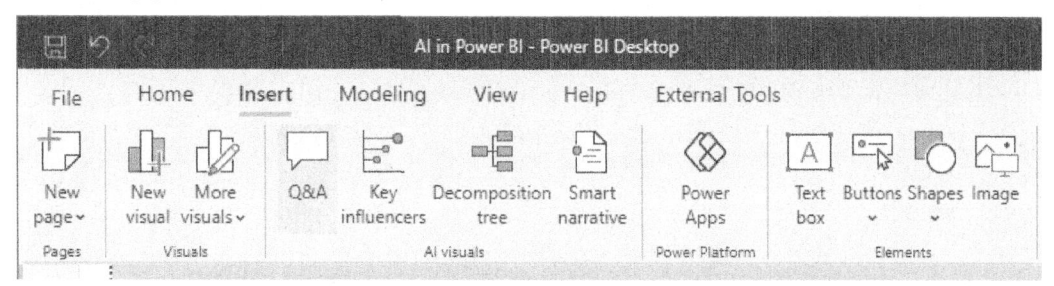

Figure 13.6: Insert tab with AI visuals

By default, the look and feel are pretty much similar to the Q&A in the dashboard. You will see the text box where you can type questions and a *little gear icon* where you can explore the advanced settings. At the bottom, you can see the suggestions in blue color text boxes. You can change the color of this if required.

182 ■ Power BI Data Modeling

You can see the text box for search keywords along with a list of keyword phrases listed. Those keyword phrases are generated automatically based on the learning by the AI from your data set. You can see the outlook of it in *figure 13.7*:

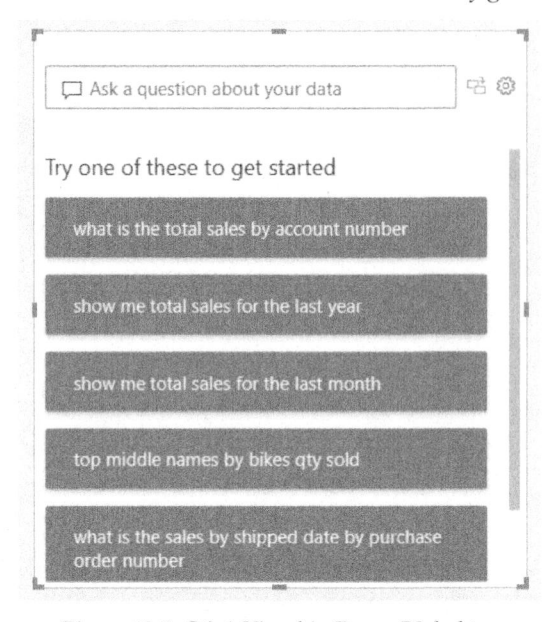

Figure 13.7: Q&A Visual in Power BI desktop

You can type a question like *show me total sales for the country*. It will understand the intent of the question and return a bar chart of sales by country as follows:

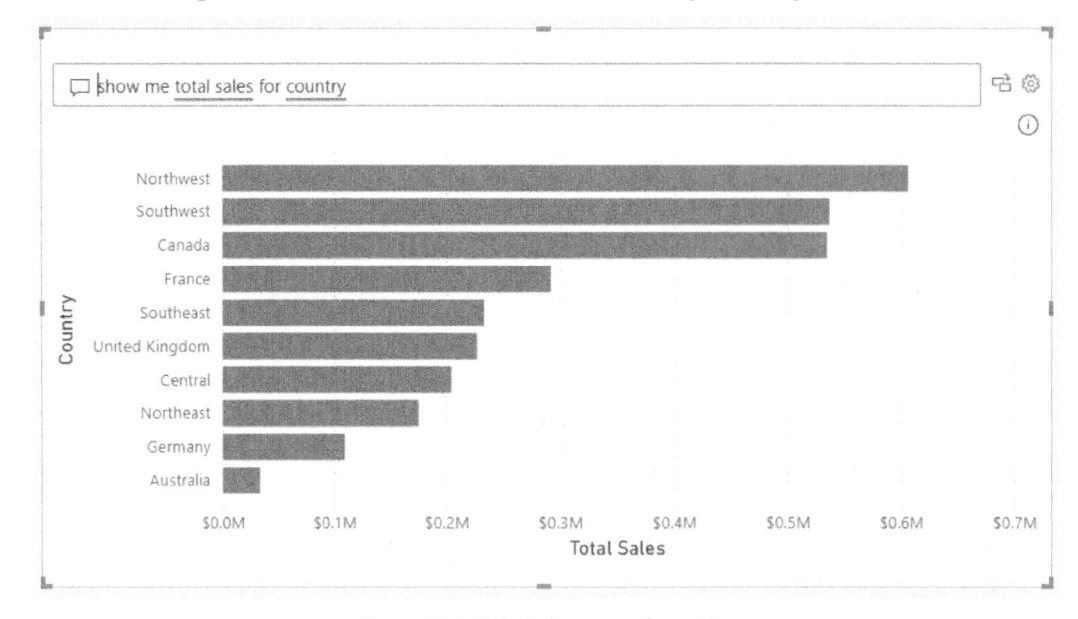

Figure 13.8: Selected suggested question

Further to explore this visual, you can click the *gear icon* to go to advanced settings. It will open another window with multiple tabs:

- The first tab, of course, will be for learning how to utilize this Q&A visual.

- In the second tab, you can configure **Field synonyms** (refer to *figure 13.9*). It will show you the list of tables in the data model. You can expand each of these and show the fields where you can introduce synonyms. This impact to ask questions by referring to similar field name keywords.

For example, the **customer** term in the **Customer** table shows suggested terms such as consumer, user, client, buyer, and so on:

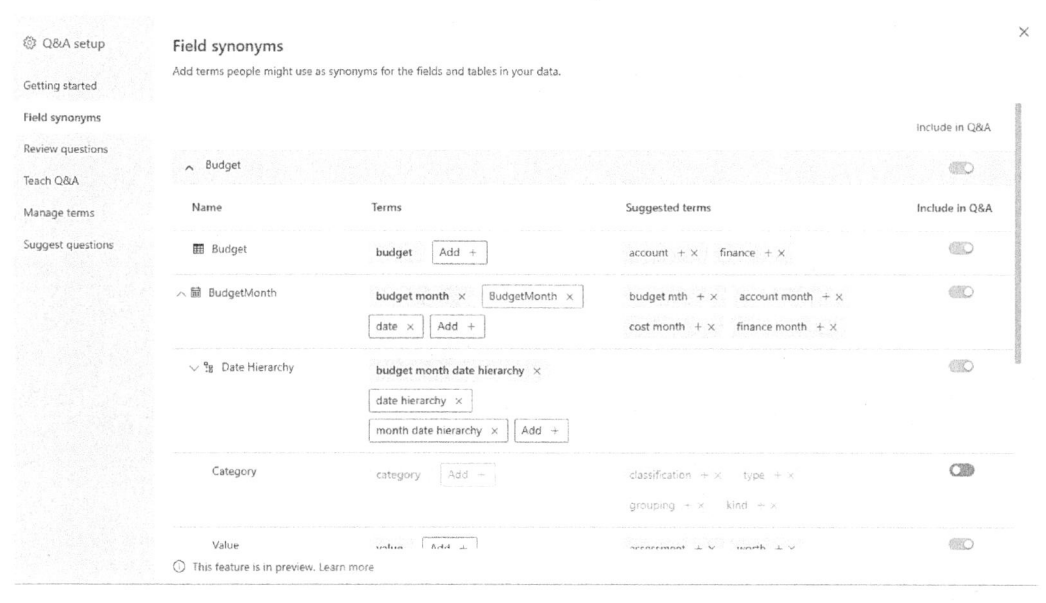

Figure 13.9: Configure Field synonyms

The next tab is useful to review the user questions. Once you log into the Power BI from your account, you can see the questions for each data set. You can review it:

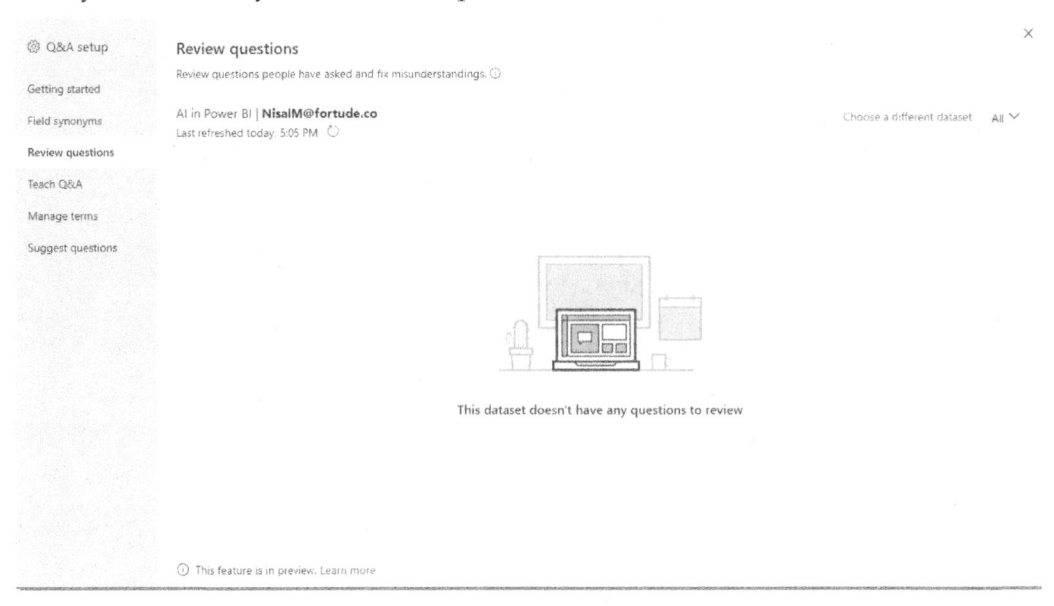

Figure 13.10: Review questions option

The most handy feature is **Teach Q&A**. This is the place where Power BI allows you to train the machine learning model. In order to teach the Q&A, when the user types some questions, and if it is highlighted in red, that means the keyword is unable to recognize:

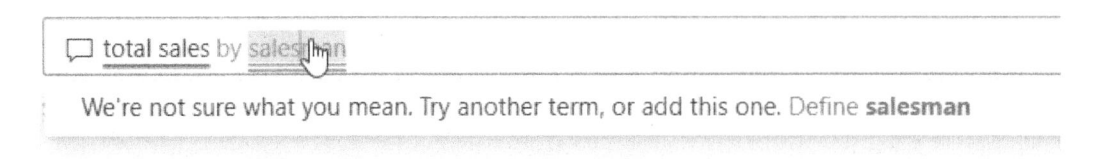

Figure 13.11: Define new keyword option

You can simply click the *blue color text, Define <your new keyword>*. Then it will open a window where you can teach the model to adopt for that keyword:

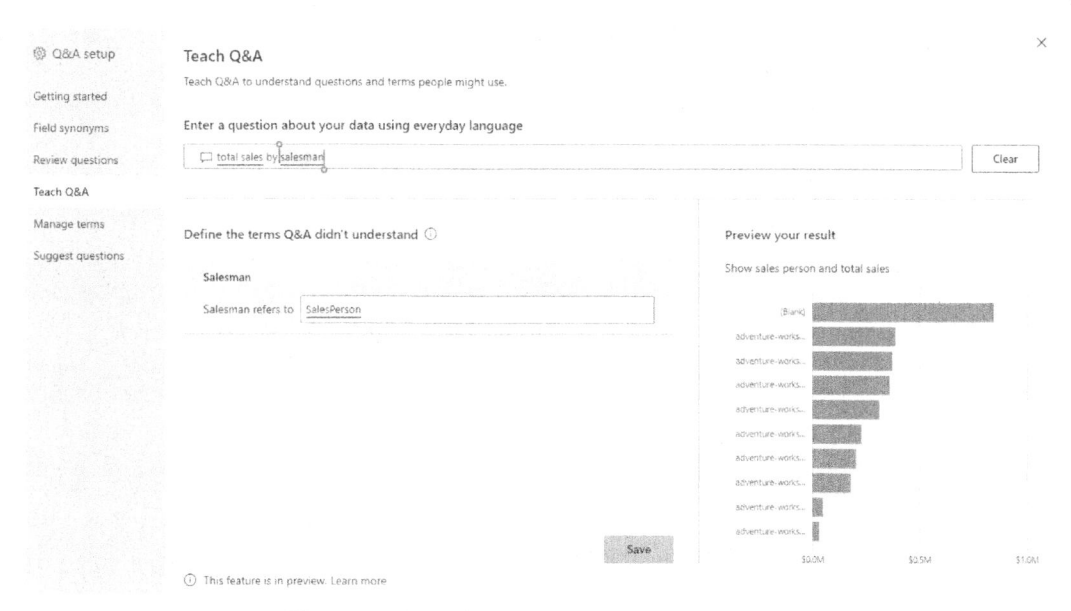

Figure 13.12: Configure new keywords in Teach Q&A

For example, you can define **Salesman** as a similar call for the **SalesPerson** in the model. Then the Q&A will understand the intent accurately and respond accordingly. This will save in the model, and whenever the next time you ask question **total sales by salesman**, it will return the results:

Figure 13.13: Suggest questions

Finally, you can suggest questions as well. You can train the most relevant questions. Then the model can accurately pick and return the right answer next time.

Decomposition tree visual

The **decomposition tree visual** is another AI visual you can find in the Power BI. You can either add this from the `Insert` tab or pick from the `Visual` gallery. You can visualize data across many dimensions in the model. It automatically aggregates data and allows you to drill down accordingly. They consider this AI visual because this has AI features like you can ask to find the next dimension to drill down based on some logic. This visual is capable of analyzing the right information and picking dimensions precisely. So, this is a good chance to run *ad-hoc analysis* against organizational data and perform root cause analysis.

In this visual, you can start off with a measure you want to analyze. You also can add dimension attributes (categorical fields):

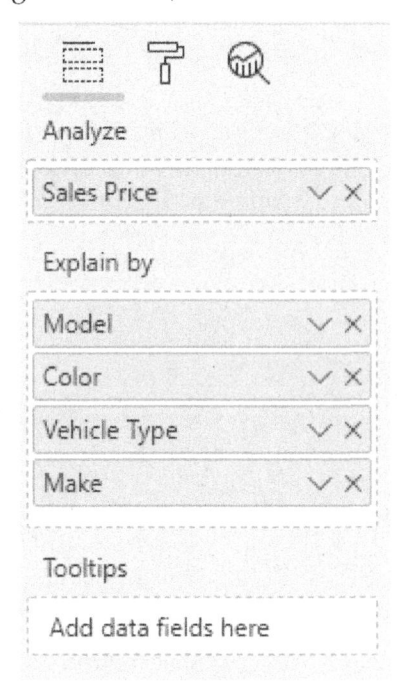

Figure 13.14: Configure decomposition tree

- **Analyze**: For this placeholder, you need to add a metric that you like to be analyzed. It could be a numerical column, calculated column, or calculated measure.

- **Explain by**: You can add dimension attributes from your data set to this placeholder that you wish to analyze by the measure in `Analyze`.

Based on the configuration you do in the visual, you can analyze your data like in the following figure:

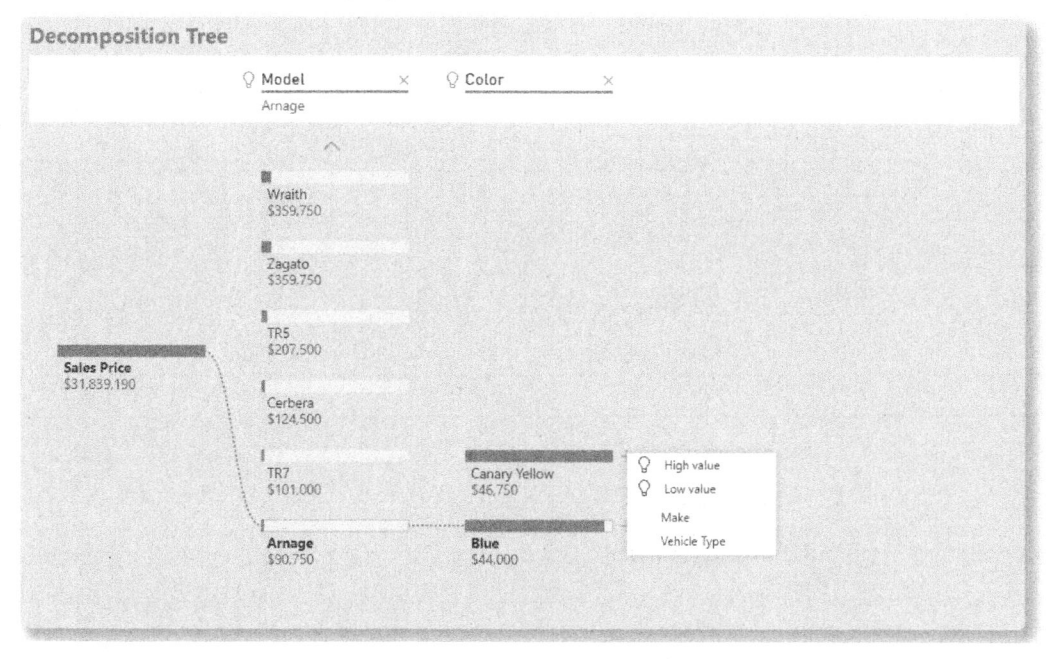

Figure 13.15: Decomposition tree visual

In this example, we want to analyze **Sales Price** and see what impacts lower sales; it instantly gives the few models vehicles are moving slower than others. This priority is selected by the AI program.

> We talked about possible scenarios where we can use the decomposition tree visual. A good example would be root cause analysis for financial accounts. You can find where exceeded the overhead throughout the financial accounts by drilling down without much hassle.

Key influencer

You can use this visual to understand what dimensions make an impact on the growth of a measure. Behind the scene, Power BI runs a *linear regression algorithm* to find the patterns of data.

Add **Sales Price** into **Analyze**, **Color**, and **Vehicle Type** as **Explain by**:

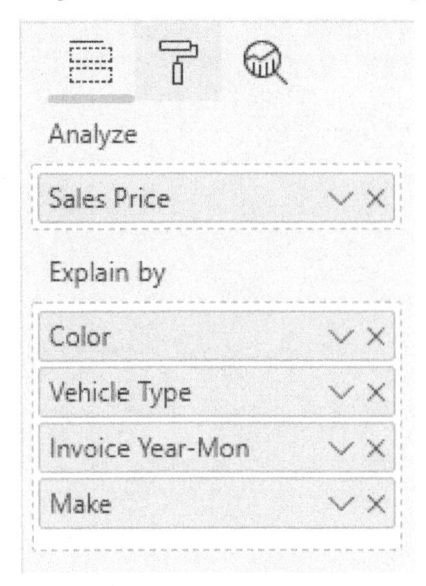

Figure 13.16: Configure key influence visual

It says *No influence found*. In this situation, we can change the visual to *tabular* form and see what is going on inside. You can see the problem here is not enough data points Power BI to run the regression model. For example, if the machine learning model wants to learn

So, we can add a year column, and then the Power BI engine has more and more observations to build the model.

So, we know that when we feed more data to a linear regression ML model, we can obtain better accuracy and results. The same theory will apply here as well. Still, the number of observations is not enough. So, I can add another variable that indicates sales, **Month** and **year**.

The top influencer makes **Triumph**, when sales happened, average sales which cars align to make Triumph **$47.03K** lesser than average sales by others. The average sales are represented in the *red dotted line*. The difference between (*figure 13.17*) scored bar, and the *red dotted line* is the influencer score:

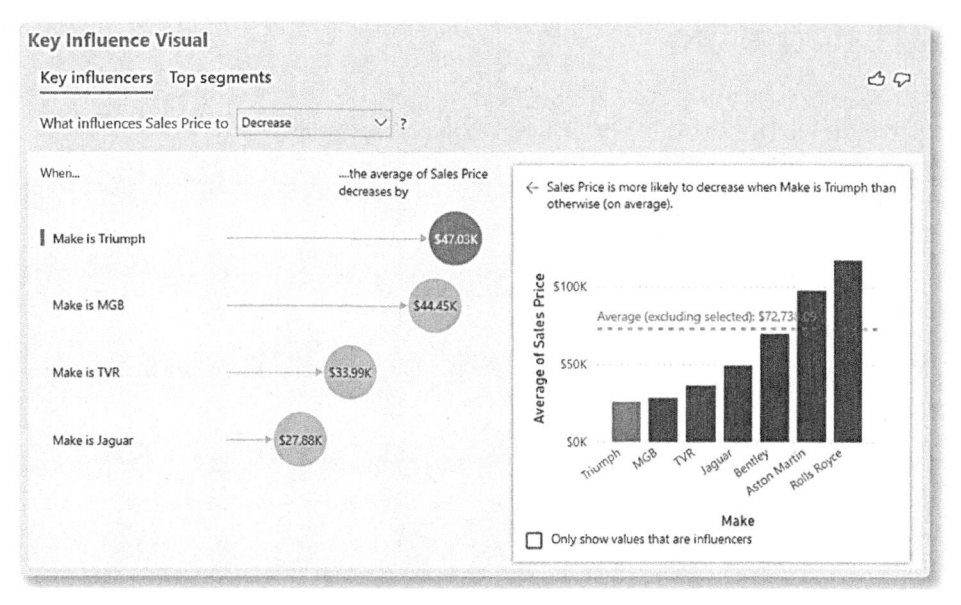

Figure 13.17: Key influences visual

Every time I add a new attribute, Power BI re-run the regression model to factor in the information.

What combination of variables results in high sales, rather treat them individually. Each bubble here represents a *segment*. The *height* of the bubble represents how low the sales were, the size of the bubble represents, the number of observations fallen to that segment:

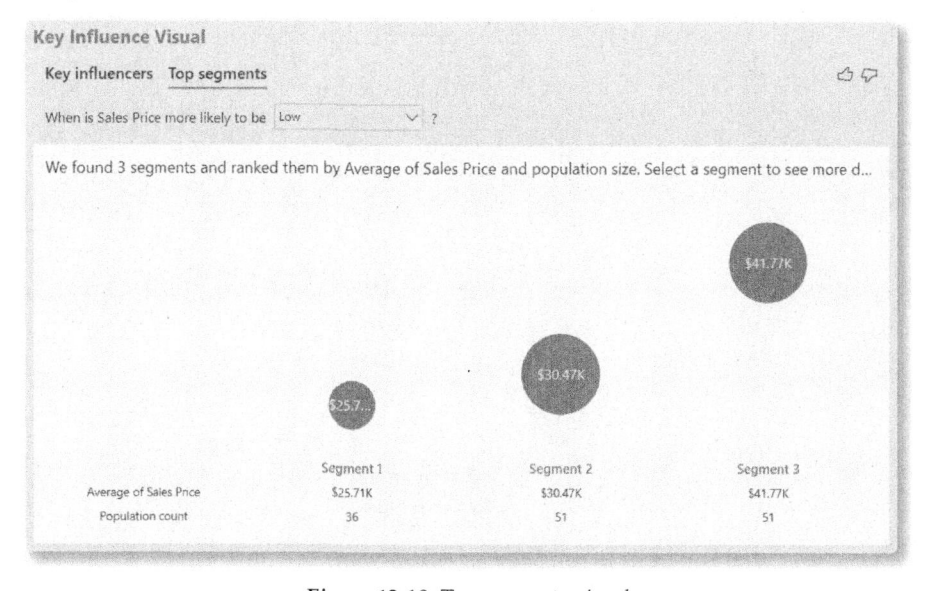

Figure 13.18: Top segments visual

Smart narrative

Smart narrative is another AI visual introduced and freely available to explore. This helps to get the textual summary of what you have visualized:

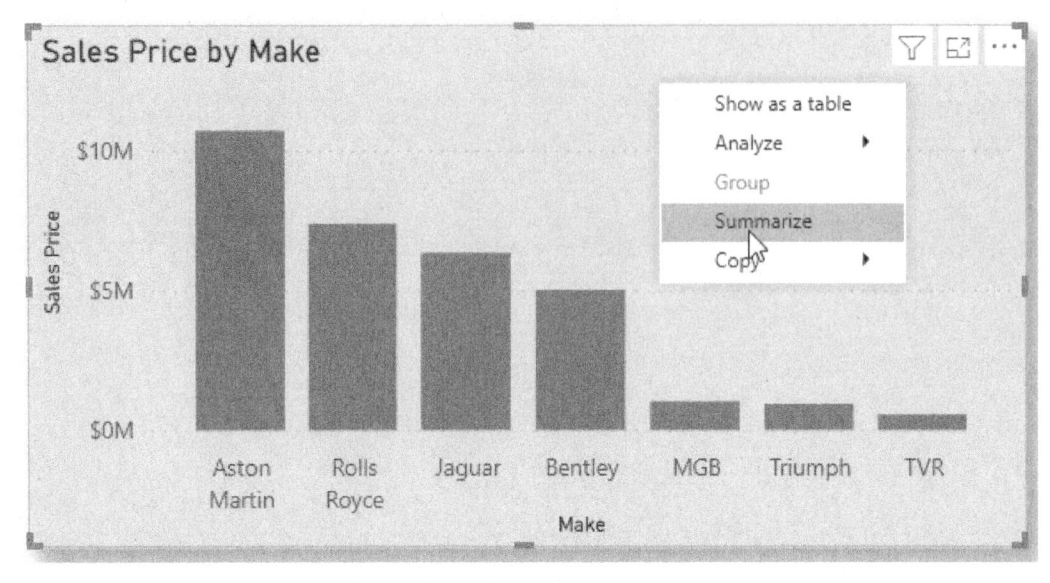

Figure 13.19: Smart narrative option

You can right-click the visual area and select **Summarize** option, which generates a summary view. You can change the format of the summary, use different fonts and colors, and additionally, you can add your own content:

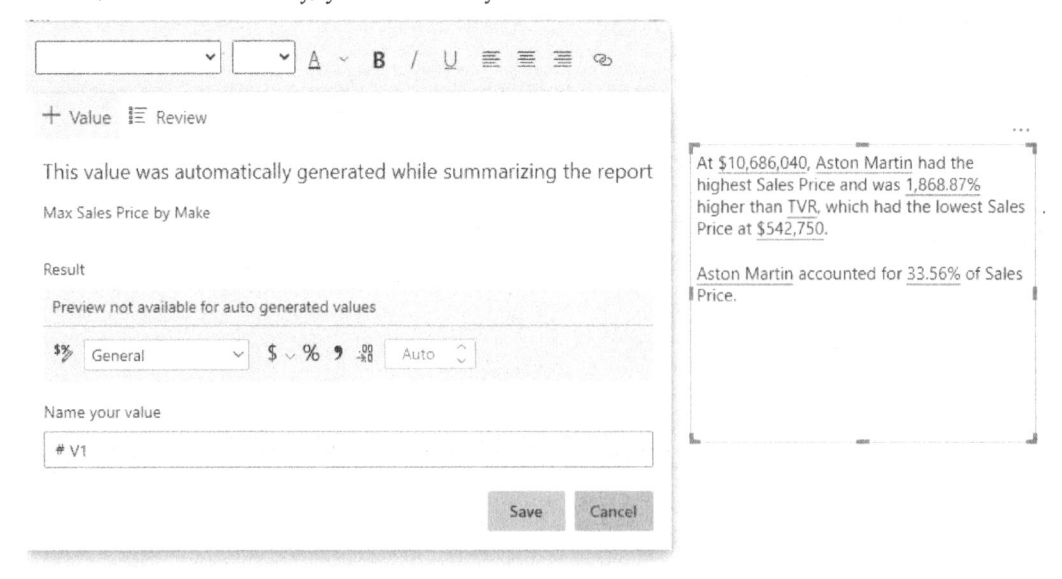

Figure 13.20: Configure the smart narrative summarized view

There is room to review the summary and correct it if something goes wrong. One of the big advantages of this visual is you can add dynamic content.

Perform text analytics, vision, and Azure Machine Learning

There are certain features that are only available for the Power BI Premium license users. If you are a Premium user, you can perform text analytics, able to use vision-related analysis even integrate your data model using Azure Machine Learning:

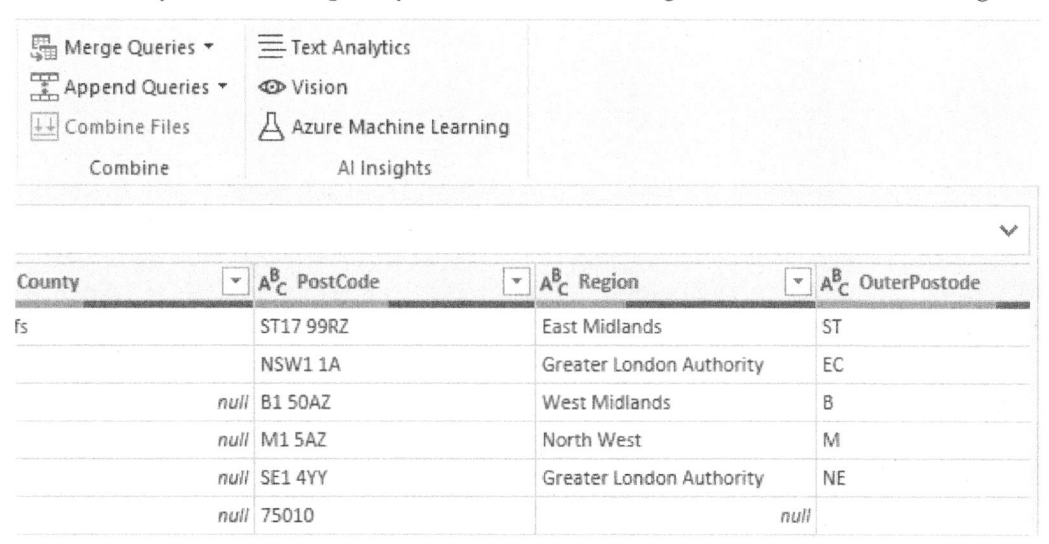

County	PostCode	Region	OuterPostode
fs	ST17 99RZ	East Midlands	ST
	NSW1 1A	Greater London Authority	EC
null	B1 50AZ	West Midlands	B
null	M1 5AZ	North West	M
null	SE1 4YY	Greater London Authority	NE
null	75010		null

Figure 13.21: AI insights

Essentially, you invoke Azure cognitive services here. You can browse more information about how to integrate **Azure Text Analytics** from the official site:

https://docs.microsoft.com/en-us/azure/cognitive-services/text-analytics/tutorials/tutorial-power-bi-key-phrases

R and Python integration

Another biggest innovation in Power BI is to allow more flexibility to data science users. They have integrated **R** and **Python** into the Power BI. Essentially; you can ingest data using an R or Python script, you can transform data, and also visualize it:

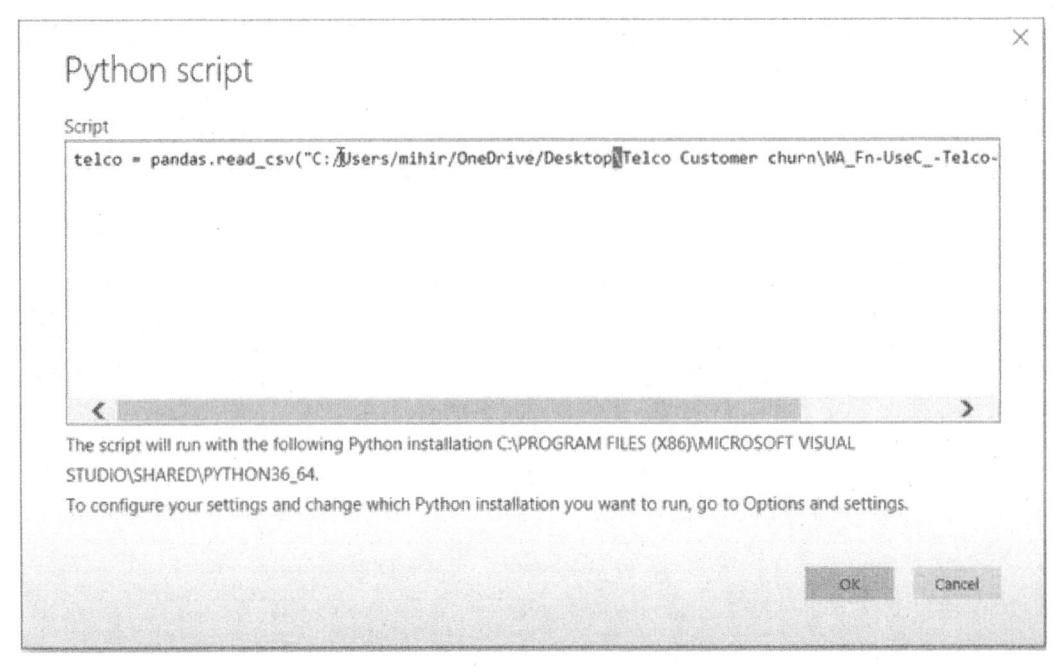

Figure 13.22: Get data using Python script

You can use R or Python to ingest data. In the preceding diagram, it shows that how to import CSV data files into power by using the Pandas library **read_csv** function:

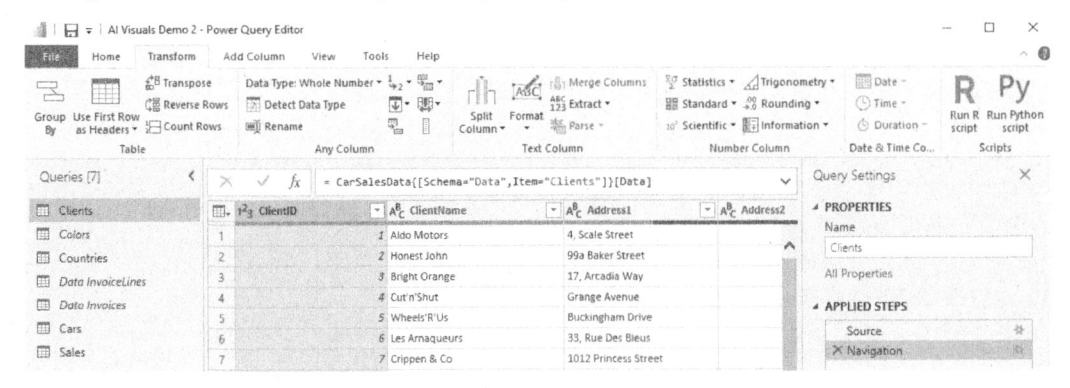

Figure 13.23: Transform data using R or Python script

If you go to **Edit queries**, you can find the **Run R script** and **Run Python script** option in the **Transform** tab (*figure 13.24*):

Figure 13.24: Remove NULL values using Python

This diagram shows how you can remove the **NULL** values using a Python script. You can do a lot more than this by adding more and more transformation scripts.

Conclusion

In this chapter, we focused on various AI offerings in Power BI. Most of them are working as self-service AI, which means they can be used by self-service users without much hassle. Power BI reduces the complexity of advanced machine learning algorithms and offers visual ways to configure AI functionalities to perform easily. In the upcoming chapter, we will discuss a feature called **incremental refresh,** which is vital when you are dealing with large datasets.

Questions

1. Discuss about the usage of self-service AI functionalities and some real-world scenarios, and you can apply this in your working environment.
2. There is an AI functionality that is not covered in this chapter, which is only available for Premium users. Research on it and see how you can use it.

CHAPTER 14
Incremental Refresh for Data Models

Power BI is a versatile BI tool that can handle any amount of data. It is the choice of architectural decision to make when to design the data model and reports that are viable to handle large data sets without performance bottlenecks. However, when you are dealing with large data volumes, it tends to decrease performance, but how to improve the performance of the model will discuss in another chapter. At the same time, this will also impact the time to refresh the tables, mostly the large fact tables, as the data grows. This chapter will focus on how to reduce the time to data refresh through the **incremental refresh** feature.

Structure

The following topics will be covered during this chapter:

- Data refresh requirement
- Incremental data refresh requirement
- Configure the incremental refresh

Objective

The objective of this chapter is to teach you the concept of **incremental refresh** and how to configure it for large data sets to obtain better refresh time.

Data refresh requirement

When you develop Power BI data models, and after you deploy them into the Power BI service, the reports and dashboards need to be up-to-date with the latest data. Therefore, you may need to add a trigger in the service to fetch the latest data in the source and refresh accordingly. This is where the data gateway requirement comes into play. In order to refresh the data, you need to have a component that bridges the gap between the Power BI service and your on-premises source. This is not the case if your source data resides on the server:

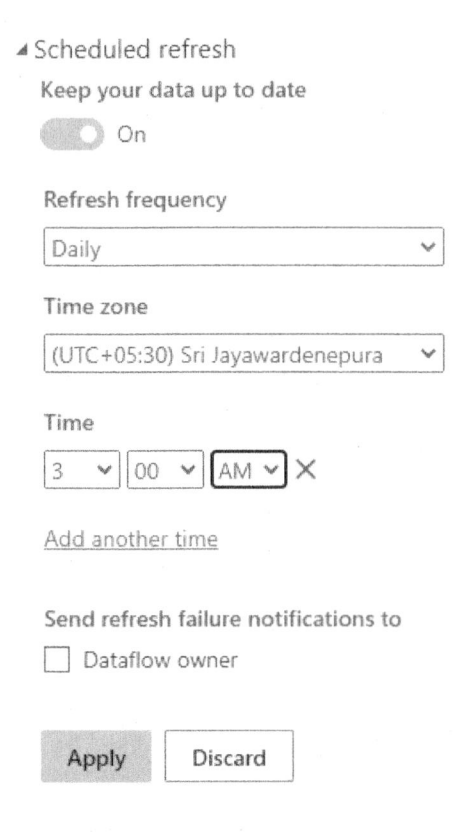

Figure 14.1: Schedule refresh

In the preceding figure, you can see how you can set up the scheduled refresh. Perform the following steps to get into this screen:

1. Log in to the Power BI service.
2. Go to the respective workspace.
3. Open the **Datasets + dataflows** tab.
4. Hover on the data set or dataflow and click the *ellipse* button.

5. Click **Settings**.

6. Go to the **Scheduled refresh** section.

The screen is for a data flow created. This is the same screen you would get for a data set.

This mechanism is fine for average volume data sets. Imagine you have a data set with a large volume of data; maybe you are dealing with billions of records. When refreshing the data refresh, large tables definitely consume a lot of time. This impact to predominantly three issues:

- **Data refresh latency**: The time gets to see the latest data by the end-user increases.

- **Data refreshes are not stable**: When it takes a long time to do a full refresh, it tends to fail due to various factors.

- **High resource consumption**: Not just time taking to refresh, it consumes a lot of CPU and memory.

This is where the concept of **incremental refresh** will be handy.

Incremental data refresh requirement

This feature enables you to refresh a certain subset of data rather than refresh the entire table in your data model. This helps to reduce the data refresh time drastically. There are certain sets of requirements to be fulfilled in order to configure incremental refresh in your Power BI workbook.

Data load mode must be **Import** mode in order to configure incremental refresh. **DirectQuery** means every time is fetching data from the source.

The source must support **query folding**. Many SQL-like data sources support query folding. This is also a must-to-work incremental refresh. In other words, sources such as flat files, blob storage, and internet feeds do not support either query folding or incremental refresh. In such cases, the Power Query engine does apply filters locally. For that, it requires loading the entire data set into the Power BI model. This causes it to take a longer time to do an incremental refresh and slower the process.

Once you have published the report, which enabled incremental refresh, you cannot download it. You will get an error message.

Incremental refresh feature is only available in the Power BI Pro, Power BI Premium, and Premium per user licensing models. That makes sense anyway with the limitations of a free license.

Configuring incremental refresh

The process of configuring incremental refresh is simple and straightforward. You can configure incremental refresh by four steps as follows:

Figure 14.2: Process of implementing the incremental refresh

Defining the filter parameters

First, you need to go to the **Transform** window in the Power Query editor to define the filter parameters. With the previous demos, we have a simple model created atop of the **AdventureWorks** data warehouse database:

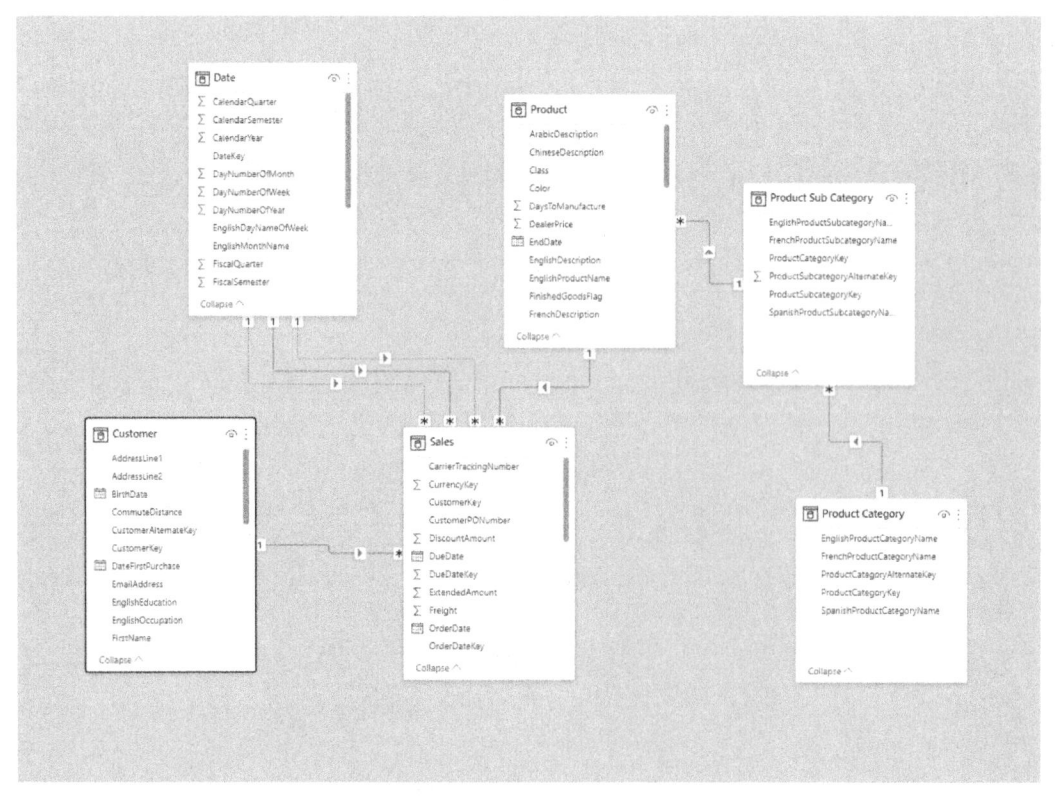

Figure 14.3: Demo data model

Typically, you know that *fact* tables contain more data than *dimension* tables. Because all the transactional events we convert into fact tables. In the model, we have the

Incremental Refresh for Data Models ■ 199

Sales fact table and related dimension tables surrounded. We assume our **Sales** fact table contains billions of rows hypothetically. The idea is we set some parameters to filter data in the sales, in this case, order date, which determines the transactional date for sales. Based on the order date, we are able to do a sort of partition process.

Go to the Power Query window and create parameters. Here, we define range start and range end parameters:

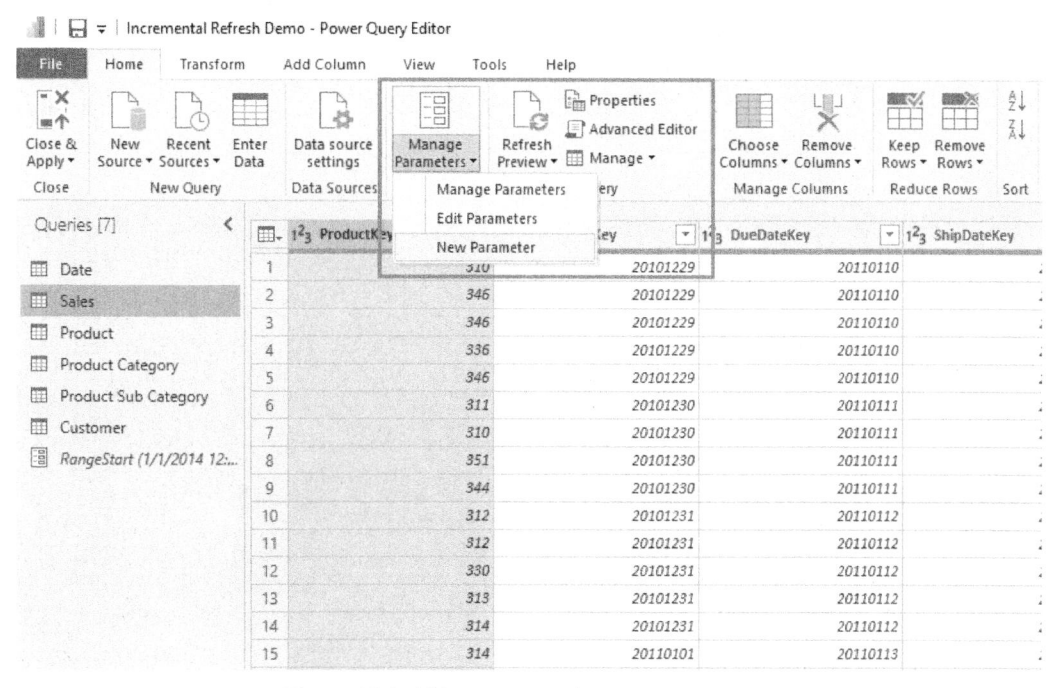

Figure 14.4: Add parameters via manage parameters

To do that, you have to go to the **Home** tab in the Power Query window, then go to **Manage Parameters**, and then click **Manage Parameters**.

In the **Manage Parameters** window, you have to click **New Parameter** and define the parameter. You can give the name for parameter, **RangeStart**, and configure the type as **Date/Time**. Here, I select the default value as **1/1/2014** because the data is pretty old and it contains the records in the range of *2011–2015*:

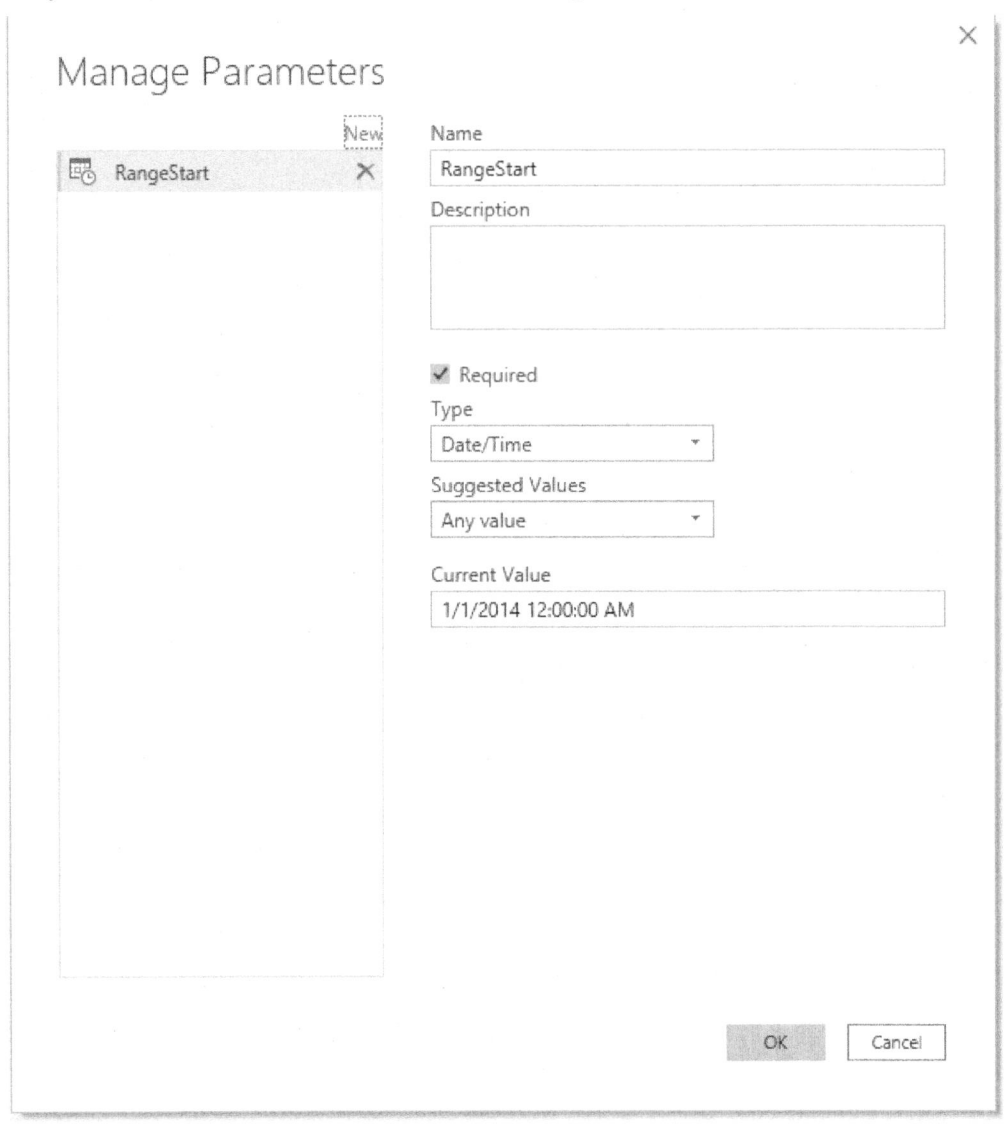

Figure 14.5: *Configure RangeStart parameter*

You must configure another parameter for **RangeEnd**. You can follow a similar step to create the **RangeEnd** parameter with the respective default value, as shown in the following diagram:

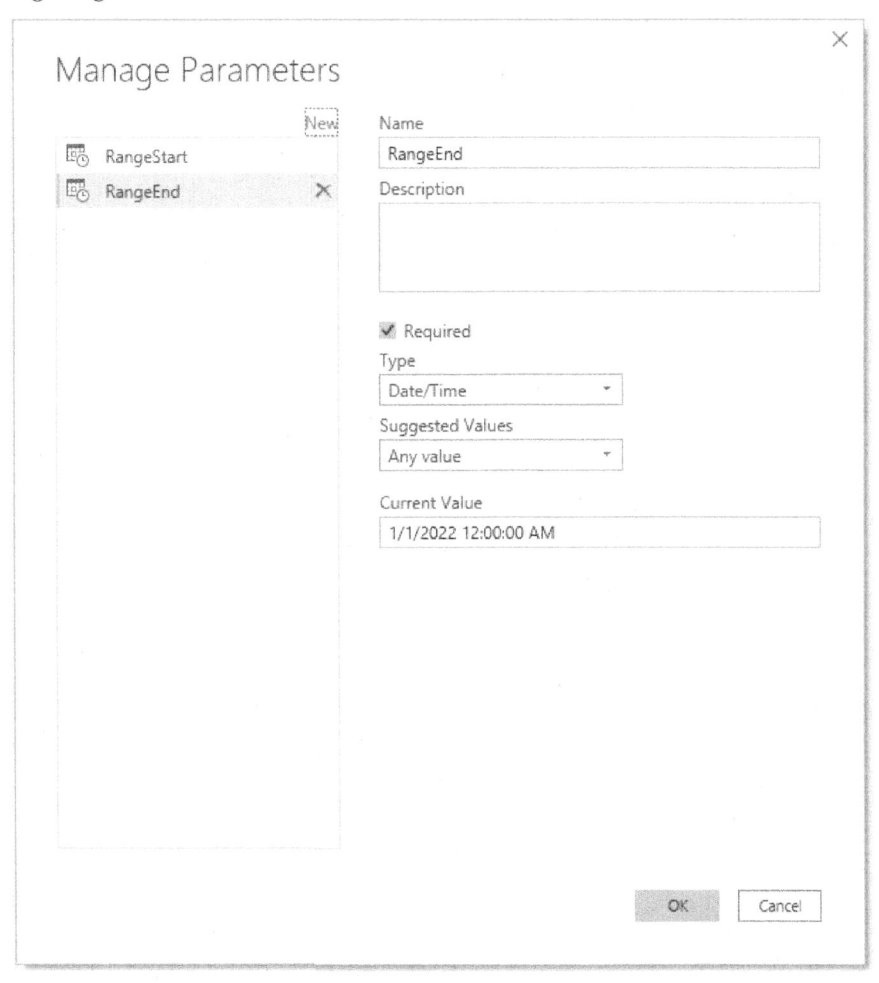

Figure 14.6: Configure range end parameter

Applying filter using parameters

Once you define the parameters, it is time to apply filters. You can apply filters to the **Sales** fact table with the help of the **OrderDate** column. Go to the **Sales** table click the drop-down to apply the filter. Then click **Date/Time Filters**, then click **Custom Filter...**:

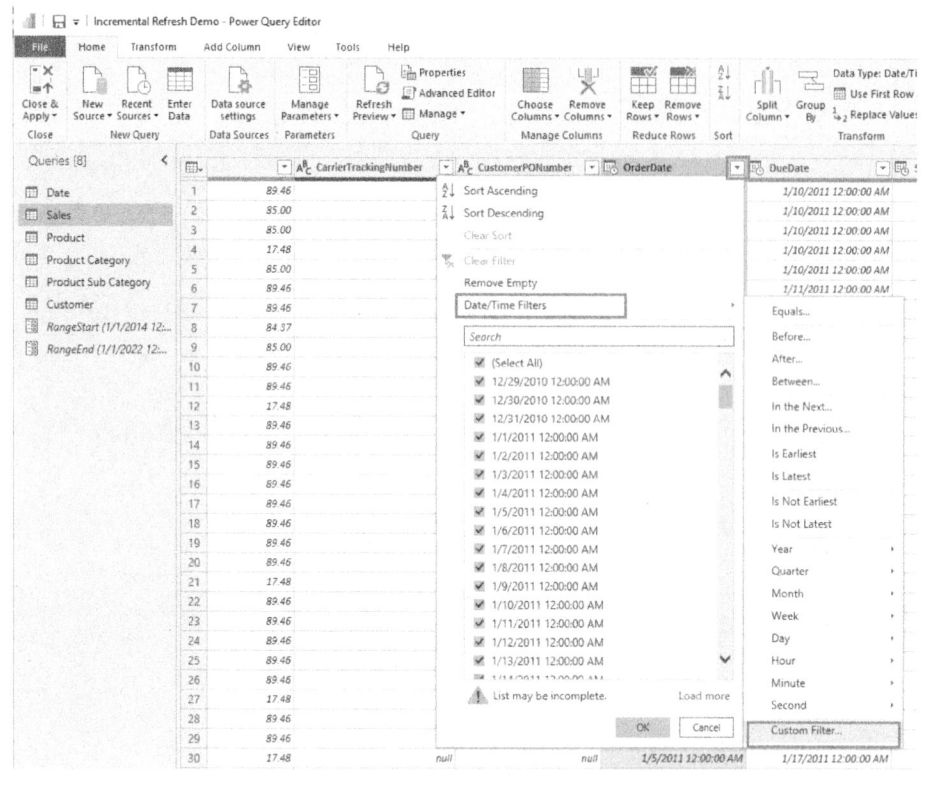

Figure 14.7: Define filters

Once you click **Custom Filter...**, it will open the filter rows dialog box as in the diagram in the next. Here, you need to configure the filter date range. In this scenario, we are not going to key the filter range. Instead of a key, we just select the **Parameter** option and select the parameter:

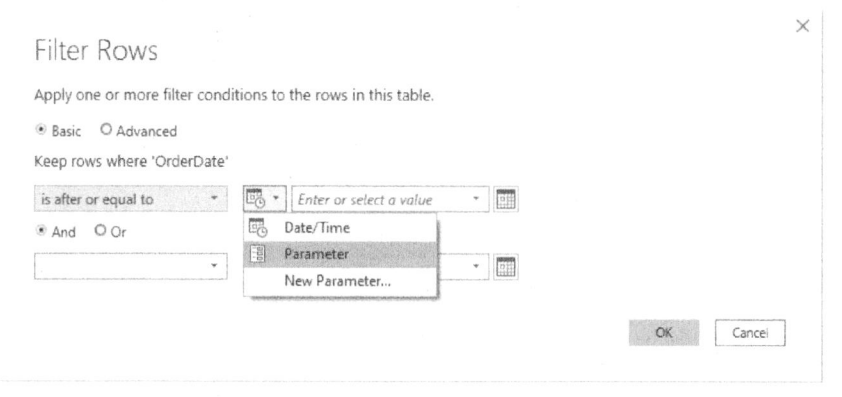

Figure 14.8: Select parameter option

Incremental Refresh for Data Models ■ 203

This is a date range parameter. So, we must set two parameters just like *between* a clause in SQL:

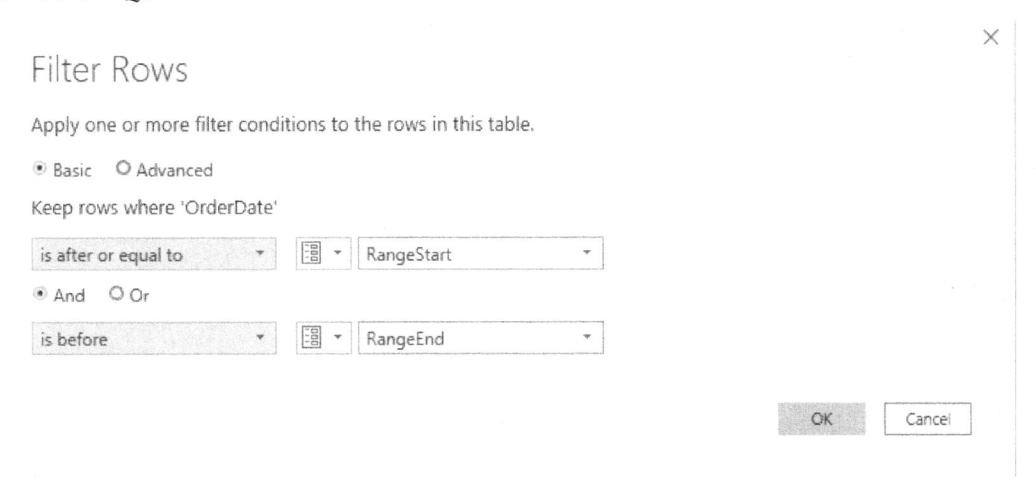

Figure 14.9: Apply date range filter parameter

Like in the preceding diagram, we can set **RangeStart** and **RangeEnd** parameters. After you set the parameters, then go to the table and see whether the parameters have been applied. You can see as per my parameters default values data only can see start from **2014**:

Figure 14.10: Sales table after applying the parameter

Defining incremental refresh policy

Now, we have defined the parameters and applied them to our data model. Its type is to define the incremental refresh policy.

For that, you have to go to the *Report* tab and select the **Sales** query, right-click, and select **Incremental refresh,** as shown in the following figure:

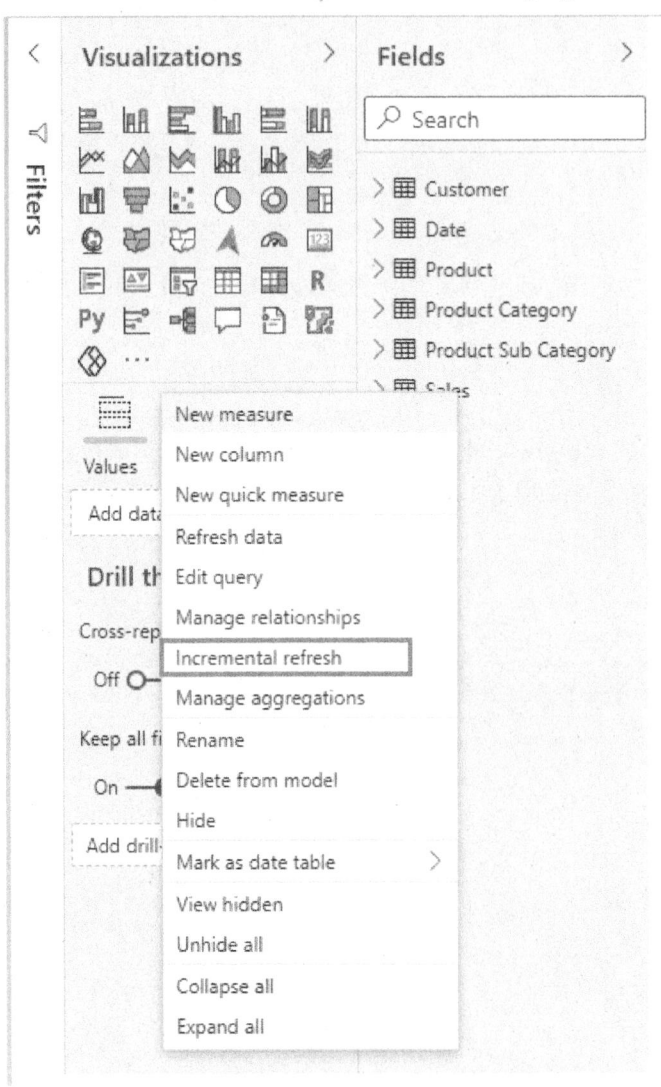

Figure 14.11: Configure incremental refresh policy

Once you click the option, you can see the following screen to configure the incremental refresh policy:

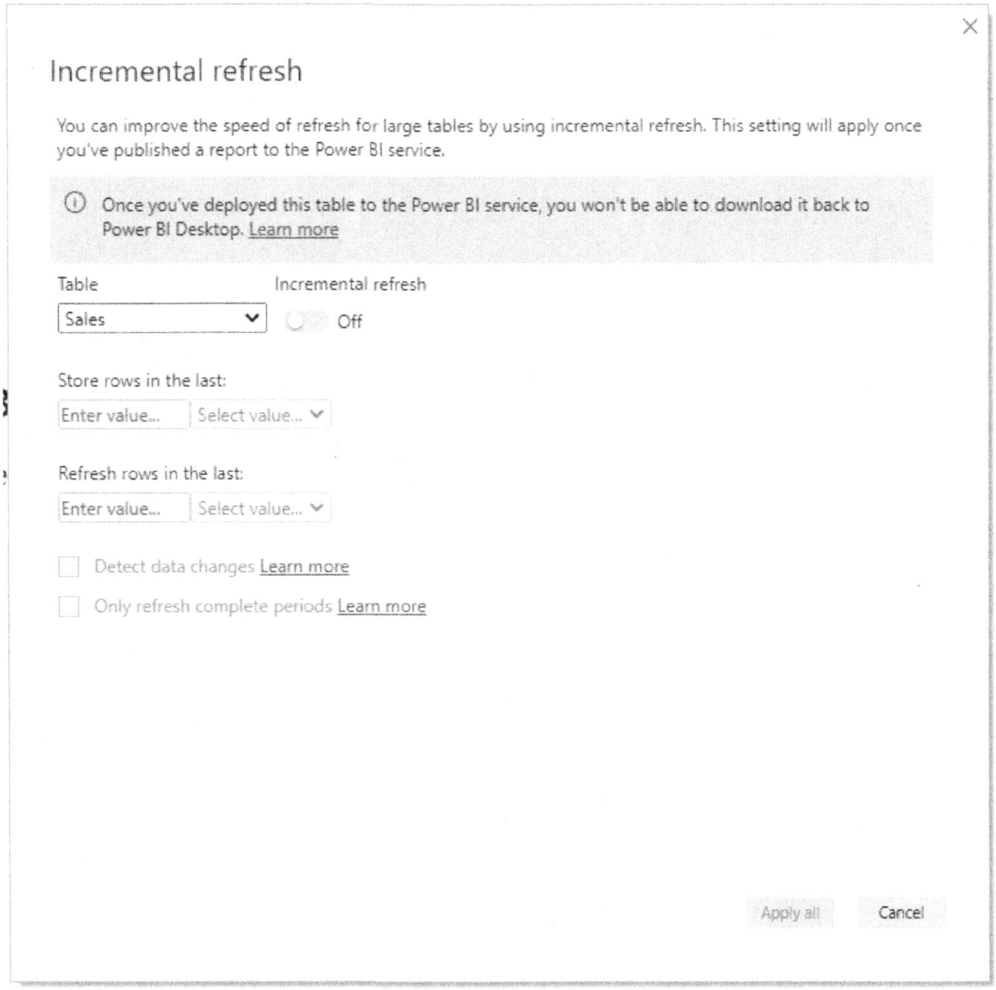

Figure 14.12: Incremental policy configuration window

You can see with the *information* icon; it says that once you deploy to the Power BI service, you will not be able to download it from the Power BI service. Because you open this from the **Sales** table, it is by default selected, and then you have to **On** the `Incremental refresh` radio button:

- **Store rows in the last**: This option allows you to define how much range of data you need to store in the model.

- **Refresh rows in the last**: This is where you can configure the range you want to refresh instead of the entire table.

You have another feature that can find, `Detect data changes`; this is a new feature added that automatically detect changes based on the column defined:

Figure 14.13: Configurations

After you configured the incremental refresh policy, you can publish the report into the Power BI service:

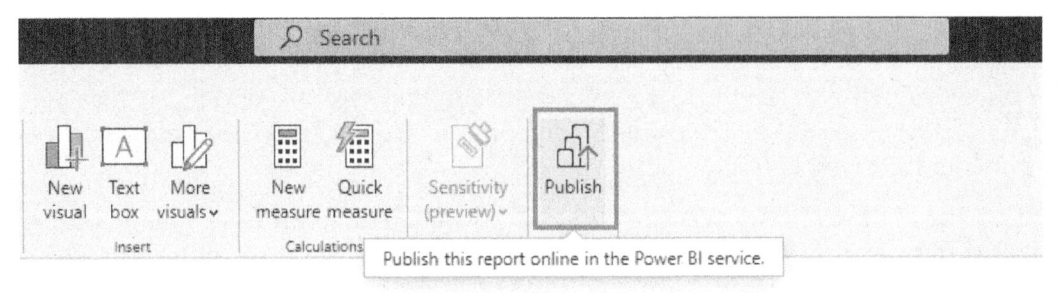

Figure 14.14: Publish the report

Just like a regular Power BI workbook, you can save and publish it to the Power BI service.

> After you publish the Power BI report, which enabled the incremental refresh policy, Power BI does not allow you to download the Power BI report from the service, just like other instances. In this case, you have to keep a copy of your Power BI desktop file, do the changes, and maintain it specifically.

Conclusion

In this chapter, we discussed the requirement of the incremental refresh feature and tried to understand the concept. Then went through how to implement the incremental refresh. Later in this chapter, we discussed how to configure parameters and apply them to a sample fact table. Finally, we discuss how to implement an incremental refresh policy. We will discuss other performance improvement techniques called **aggregations and composite models** feature in the upcoming chapter.

Questions

1. State the limitations for going with an incremental refresh.
2. Explain the concept of query folding in Power BI and its advantages.
3. List down and explain the benefits of an incremental refresh.

CHAPTER 15
Composite Models and Perform Aggregations to Improve Query Performance

In modern days, when it comes to corporate BI, we are not always dealing with a small chunk of data. We may have to work with tables with millions or even billions of records. So, with the growth of the data, it is important to ensure the user experience is consistent. Power BI introduced *architectural techniques* to handle big data with the concept called **aggregations**. In this chapter, we will explain to you step-by-step how to implement aggregations and composite models in order to achieve Big data analytics using Power BI.

Structure

The following topics will be covered during this chapter:

- Connection types recap
- Build aggregations
- Power BI performance analyzer and DAX studio
- Composite models

Objective

The objective of this chapter is to teach you the core concepts of aggregations and how to implement aggregations and make composite models in Power BI.

Prerequisites

Before starting to read this, please download the demo content from the following link. This will contain three files:

https://tinyurl.com/mvj2wm95

- **AggsDemo.bak**: Demo database backup build on SQL Server 2017.
- **Create Aggs Tables.sql** : SQL query to create aggregation tables.
- **AggsDemo.pbix**: Power BI demo file which implemented aggregations in this chapter.

Connection types—recap

Even before we move to aggregations, we think it is important to understand connection types in Power BI. Predominantly, there are two connection types in Power BI: **Import** and **DirectQuery**. You can see the main difference between each connection type, as shown in *figure 15.1*:

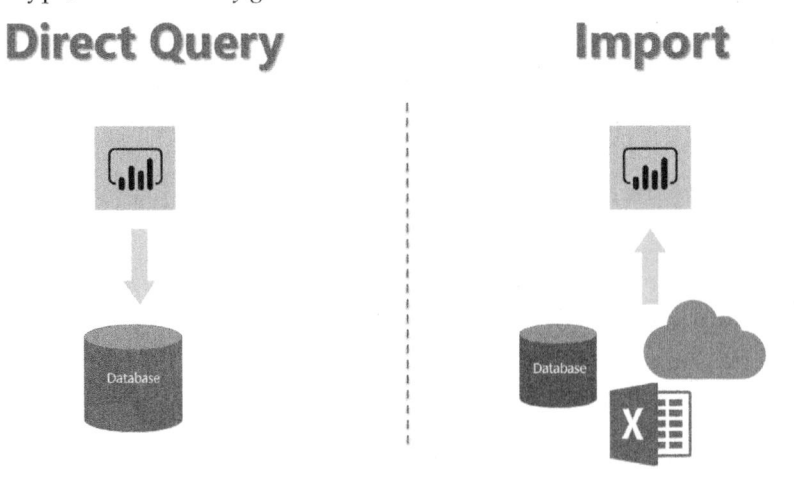

Figure 15.1: Data connectivity types

Import

In the **Import** mode, by the name itself, you import the data into your Power BI file. There are many advantages to this mode like, you can analyze data much faster. Because when you import the data, data will be compressed and stored in an in-memory **VertiPaq** engine, which is the database engine behind the Power BI, analysis services tabular, and power pivot. However, you cannot exceed the upper limit of the import data, which is *1 GB*.

DirectQuery

Oppose to the **Import** mode, in **DirectQuery** mode; you just made the connection with your source. You are not importing data. So, your Power BI file only holds the metadata of your source tables, which means in another way, when you draw a visual to the canvas by consuming your data, in real-time, a DAX query will generate by the Power BI engine and translate to relevant source query, and retrieve the data. For instance, if you connect to SQL Server Data source by DirectQuery when you consume the data, it will translate your DAX query into *T-SQL code*, query the data from SQL Server database and load it into the visuals. In both types, there are pros and cons; for example, **Import** mode data loading to visual is really fast than **DirectQuery**. But you have to refresh the data in the Import mode. Because the data in the model and the source may be different over time. But in **DirectQuery** mode, you do not want to refresh data. Because, in that mode, query the source data in live.

Demo database

Hope, by now, you have downloaded the demo Content. In the demo folder, you will find **AggsDemo.bak** SQL Server database backup. You need to restore it in your SQL Server instance. In the demo database only included four tables: **Product**, **Date**, **Customer**, and **Sales**.

This database, I have made by deriving from **ConsotoDW** database. The reason to use four tables is to make the demo simple and just allow you to learn the concept. But, keep in mind the aggregation concept is *powerful*, and once you learn it, you can apply for Big data sources like data in data bricks (http://nisalbi.blogspot.com/2019/06/azure-databricks-jump-start-series.html) cluster:

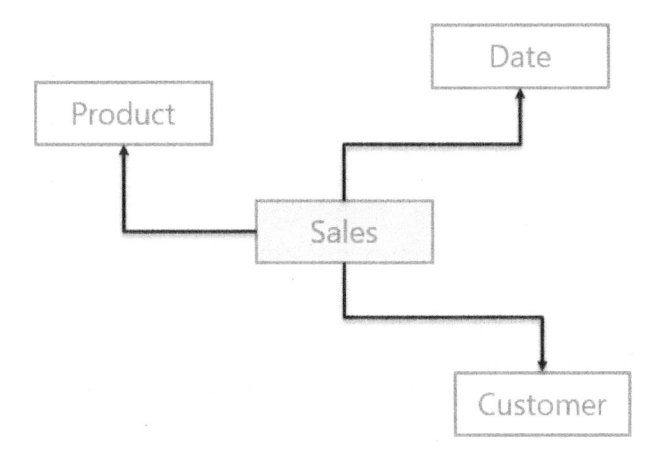

Figure 15.2: Demo data model

This structure is a sample for star schema; `Sales` is a fact table containing *approximately 12M records*:

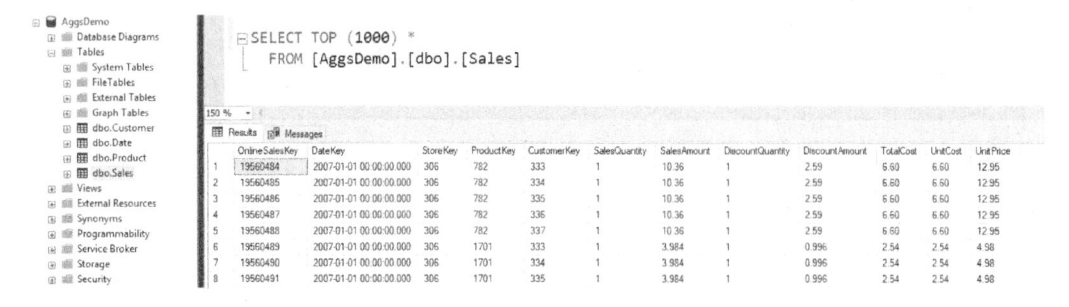

Figure 15.3: Sales table

Let us consume the demo database using Power BI

Follow these steps:

1. Open the Power BI desktop, click `Get Data` to connect to the data source, select SQL Server as source type, select the tables, and make `DirectQuery` to source `AggsDemo` database:

Figure 15.4: Get data from demo SQL Server database

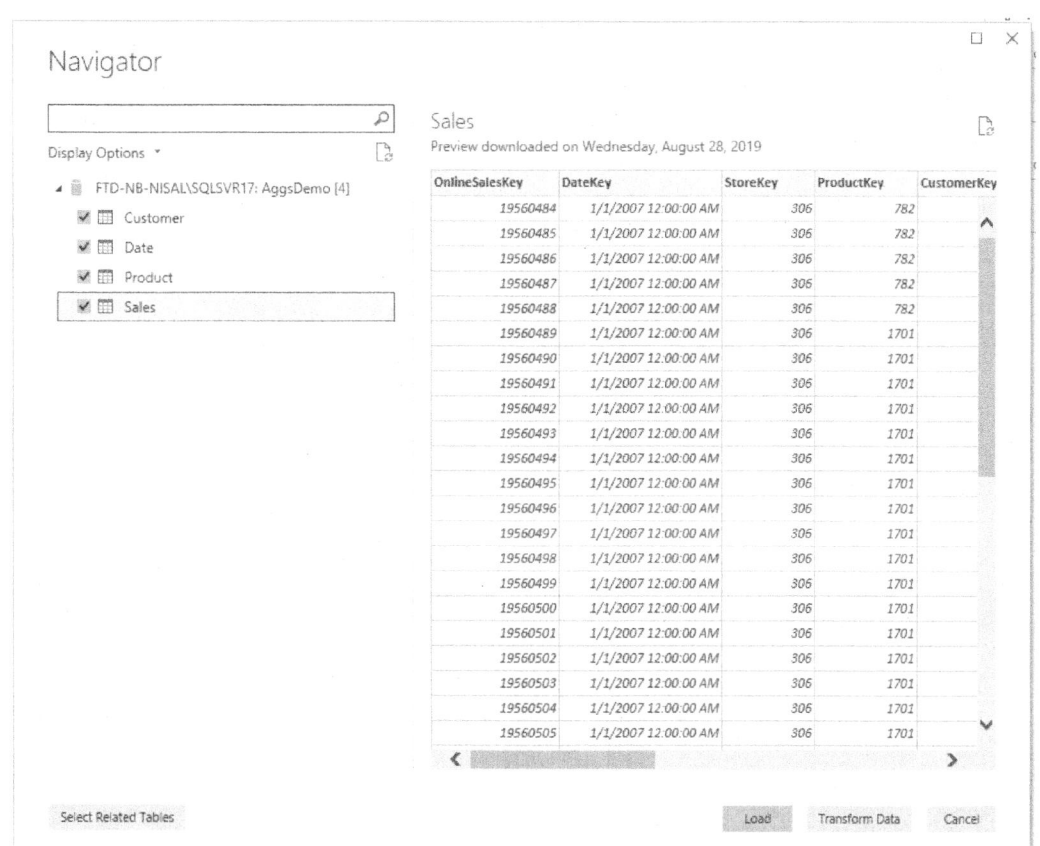

In the next window, select the tables in the database:

Figure 15.5: Select demo tables from Power Query wizard

2. Hence, we chose the **DirectQuery** mode and clicked on the **Load** data; it just made the connection between the Power BI file and the database:

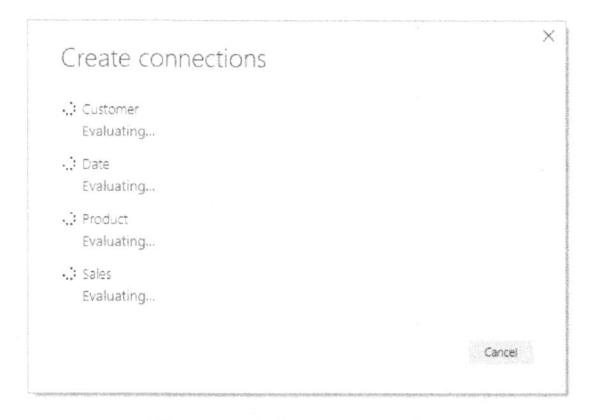

Figure 15.6: Create connections

214 ■ *Power BI Data Modeling*

3. You can ensure that your data set is in DirectQuery storage mode; it is there in the bottom right corner:

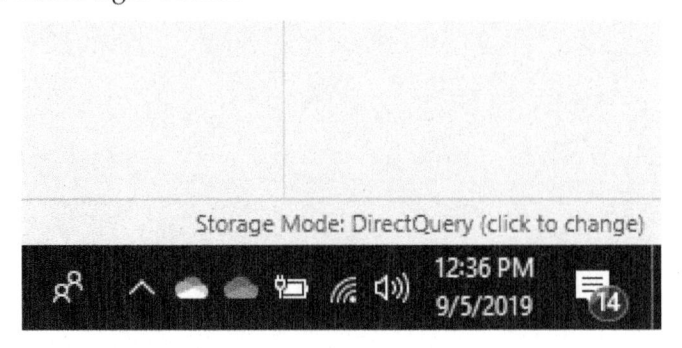

Figure 15.7: Display connection type at the bottom

4. Another indication of you are in DirectQuery mode; in this mode, you will not see a *Data* tab. Only the *Model* tab and *Report* tab will be there:

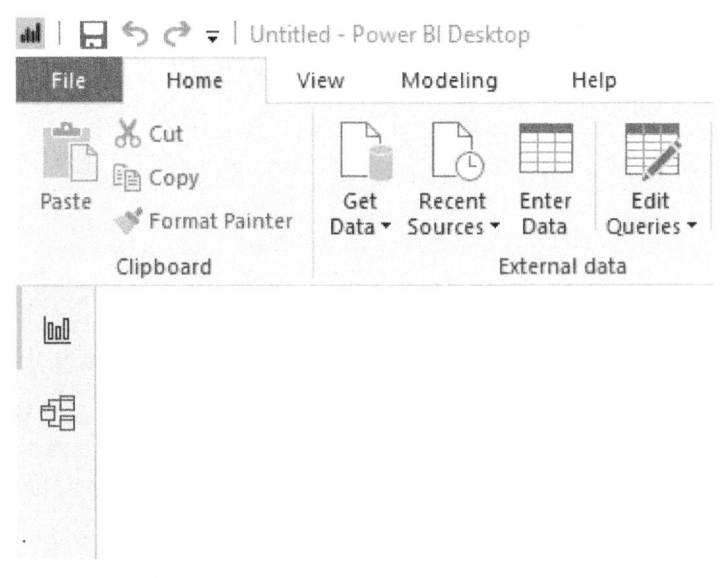

Figure 15.8: DirectQuery mode only two tabs

5. Switch to the *Model* tab, and we are going to create a relationship and build a data model. In the beginning, there are no relationships, and you will see just isolated four tables like as follows:

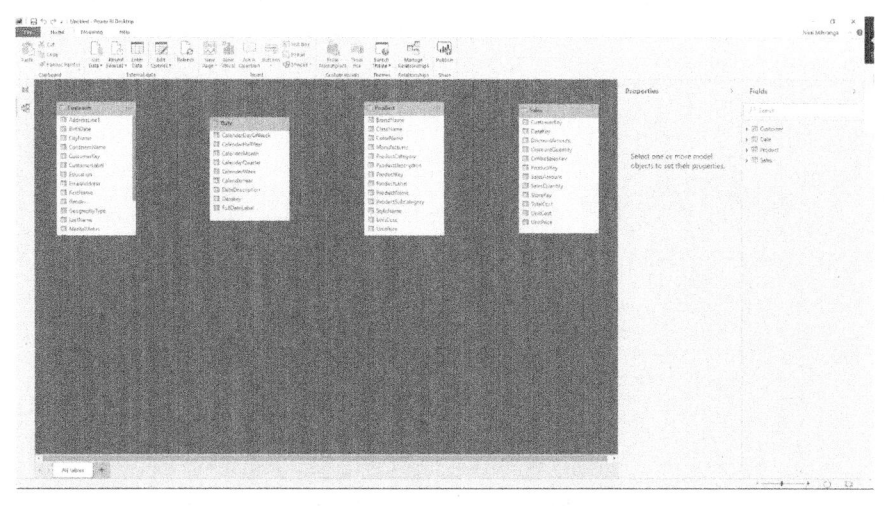

Figure 15.9: Demo tables via DirectQuery mode

6. I am going to connect **ProductKey** in **Sales** connect to **ProductKey** in the **Product** table and create the relationship. **DateKey** in **Sales** table connect to **DateKey** in **Date** table; also, **CustomerKey** in **Sales** table connect to **CustomerKey** in **Customer** table:

   After you have built the relationships, you can see your data model like this:

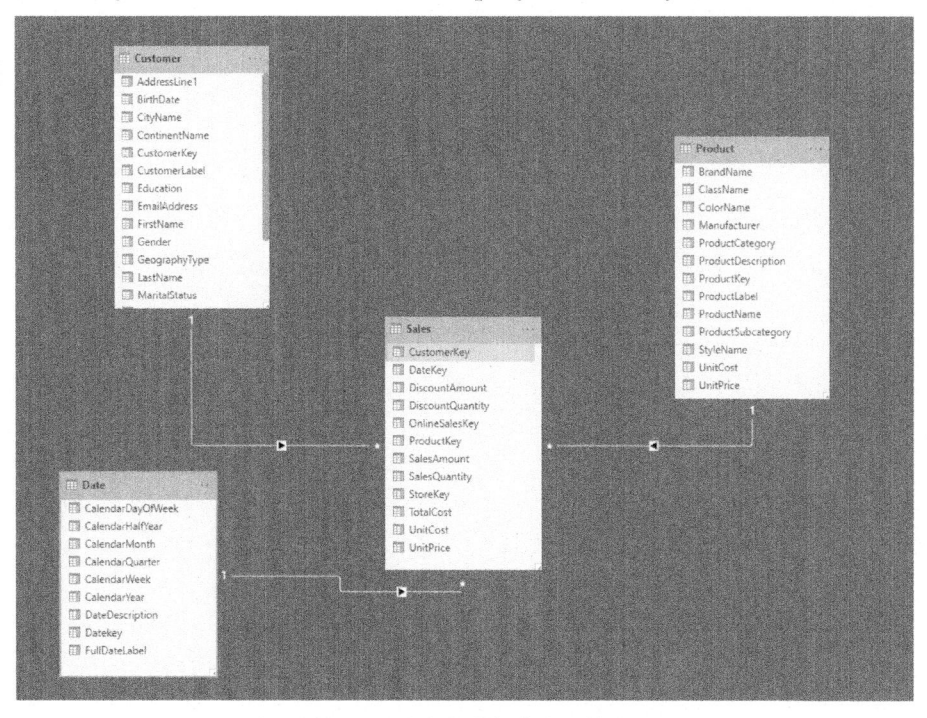

Figure 15.10: Build relationships

216 ■ *Power BI Data Modeling*

7. You can check the relationships you made by clicking the **Manage Relationships** button:

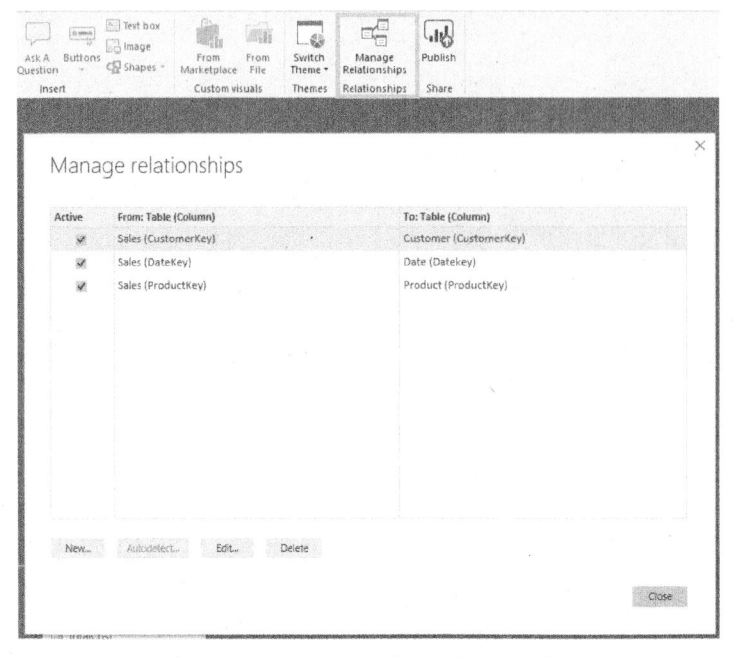

Figure 15.11: *Manage relationships window*

8. Let us draw a visual **Sales by Year**. When you draw, you will notice there is a *small progress icon* to indicate the data loading is in progress. Here, we are scanning the whole *12 M* **Sales** table and joining it with the **Date** table:

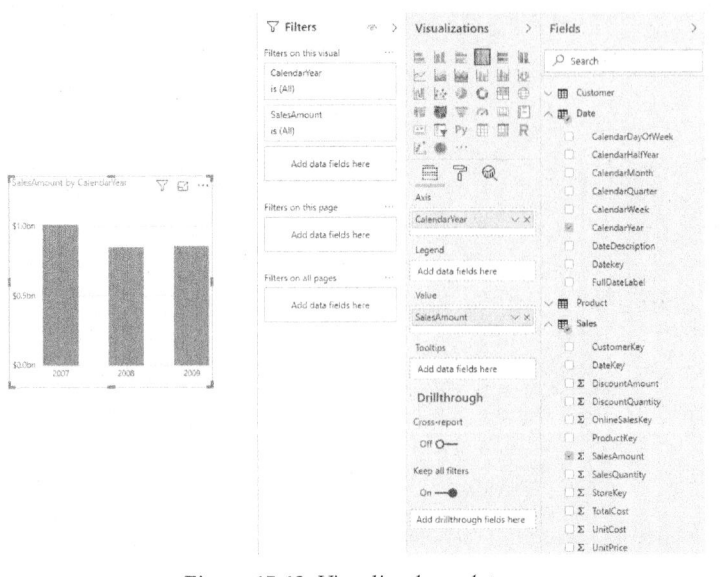

Figure 15.12: *Visualize demo data*

Let us build aggregations

As mentioned earlier in this chapter, we can use **aggregations** to improve query performance. Though we used a relatively small table with *12 M* records, when it comes to billion records, your model defensively takes more time to load data into visuals.

Aggregation is a concept of storing pre-calculated data in tables, especially when you have large tables in your model like billions of records. This helps you to reduce the table scans and improve the query performance.

For example, in order to serve the preceding query, we could have built a table with yearly sales:

Product	Date	Customer	Qty	Amount
PRD01	12/01/2018	CUS01	1	250
PRD12	12/01/2018	CUS10	5	450
PRD41	12/01/2018	CUS01	1	100
PRD22	12/01/2018	CUS01	2	240
PRD29	12/01/2019	CUS05	6	800
PRD41	12/01/2019	CUS10	1	50
PRD41	12/01/2018	CUS01	2	500
PRD22	12/01/2019	CUS105	12	240
PRD12	12/01/2019	CUS80	6	7800
PRD01	12/01/2019	CUS105	12	140

10 M

Aggregation table

Year	Sales Amount
2018	684537001.00
2019	849671203.424

Figure 15.13: How aggregations works

```
-- Aggregated by CalendarYear

SELECT D.CalendarYear, SUM(S.SalesAmount) AS SalesAmount
INTO dbo.SalesByYear
FROM dbo.Sales S
JOIN dbo.Date D ON D.Datekey = S.DateKey
GROUP BY D.CalendarYear
```

218 ■ *Power BI Data Modeling*

Once you run this query, it will create another table called, **SalesByYear.** This table just contains three records. Then we can assume it will take lesser time to load data than earlier:

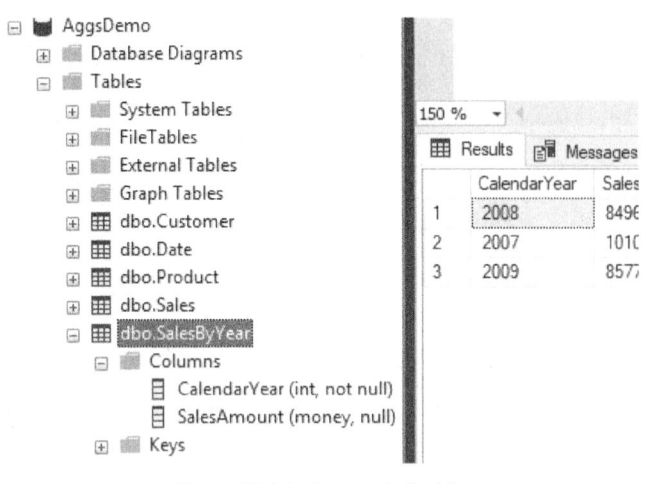

Figure 15.14: Aggregated table

Add newly created aggregated table into model

In this step, we will use a newly created aggregated table in the model. Then, select the **Recent Queries** button, connect to the **AggsDemo** database, and add the **SalesByYear** table into the Power BI file:

Figure 15.15: Aggregated table in Power BI

At this time, also I am using DirectQuery mode and just made the connection.

How to determine whether the aggregation table is used by the Power BI engine or not?

We need to ensure the **VertiPaq** engine uses our aggregation tables. Otherwise, we may just waste our time by creating aggregation tables if the engine does not pick it. Just like we build indexes in SQL Server, we need to ensure our effort. So, *how to detect whether the engine hit the aggregation table or not?*

Power BI performance analyzer

One way of determining that is using **Power BI Performance Analyzer**. You can enable the **Performance analyzer** by going to the **View** tab and checking the **Performance analyzer**. Performance analyzer helps you to analyze the query performance:

Figure 15.16: Enable Power BI performance analyzer

You can start recording; then, it will trace all the queries and execution times in canvas. Here, because the visual is already loaded into canvas, you will not see any query information at the beginning. Then what you must do is click at **Refresh visuals**. Then, it will refresh the visuals again and trace the query information:

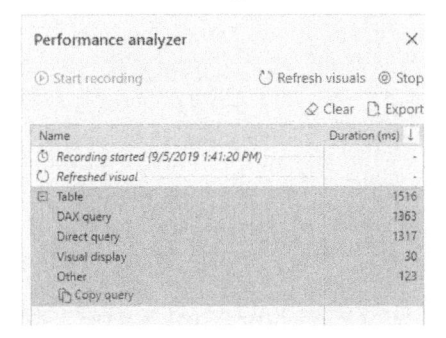

Figure 15.17: Start recording query performance

You can see it has taken **1516** milliseconds to load the data into visual. You can copy the query, paste it into a notepad, and see which tables have been queried. If you look at the following snapshot of my query, you can see there are two query sections. **DAX query** that is generated by **VertiPaq** engine, the second one is the **T-SQL** query, which is translated and executed against my SQL Server **AggsDemo** database:

```
// DAX Query
EVALUATE
  TOPN(
    502,
    SUMMARIZECOLUMNS(
      ROLLUPADDISSUBTOTAL('Date'[CalendarYear], "IsGrandTotalRowTotal"),
      "SumSalesAmount", CALCULATE(SUM('Sales'[SalesAmount]))
    ),
    [IsGrandTotalRowTotal],
    0,
    [SumSalesAmount],
    0,
    'Date'[CalendarYear],
    1
  )

ORDER BY
  [IsGrandTotalRowTotal] DESC, [SumSalesAmount] DESC, 'Date'[CalendarYear]


// SQL Query

SELECT
TOP (1000001) [t1].[CalendarYear],SUM([t3].[SalesAmount])
 AS [a0]
FROM
((select [$Table].[OnlineSalesKey] as [OnlineSalesKey],
    [$Table].[DateKey] as [DateKey],
    [$Table].[StoreKey] as [StoreKey],
    [$Table].[ProductKey] as [ProductKey],
    [$Table].[CustomerKey] as [CustomerKey],
    [$Table].[SalesQuantity] as [SalesQuantity],
    [$Table].[SalesAmount] as [SalesAmount],
    [$Table].[DiscountQuantity] as [DiscountQuantity],
    [$Table].[DiscountAmount] as [DiscountAmount],
    [$Table].[TotalCost] as [TotalCost],
    [$Table].[UnitCost] as [UnitCost],
    [$Table].[UnitPrice] as [UnitPrice]
from [dbo].[Sales] as [$Table]) AS [t3]

  left outer join

(select [$Table].[Datekey] as [Datekey],
    [$Table].[FullDateLabel] as [FullDateLabel],
    [$Table].[DateDescription] as [DateDescription],
    [$Table].[CalendarYear] as [CalendarYear],
    [$Table].[CalendarHalfYear] as [CalendarHalfYear],
    [$Table].[CalendarQuarter] as [CalendarQuarter],
    [$Table].[CalendarMonth] as [CalendarMonth],
    [$Table].[CalendarWeek] as [CalendarWeek],
    [$Table].[CalendarDayOfWeek] as [CalendarDayOfWeek]
from [dbo].[Date] as [$Table]) AS [t1] on
(
```

Figure 15.18: Underline query

If you pay attention to closer on SQL query, you can see the engine has not consumed my aggregated table.

Composite Models and Perform Aggregations to Improve Query Performance ■ 221

The reason for that, just adding your aggregation table is *not enough!* You need to configure the aggregation in order to work.

How to configure aggregations?

Go to the *Model* tab, right-click on **SalesByYear** my aggregation table, and select **Manage aggregations**:

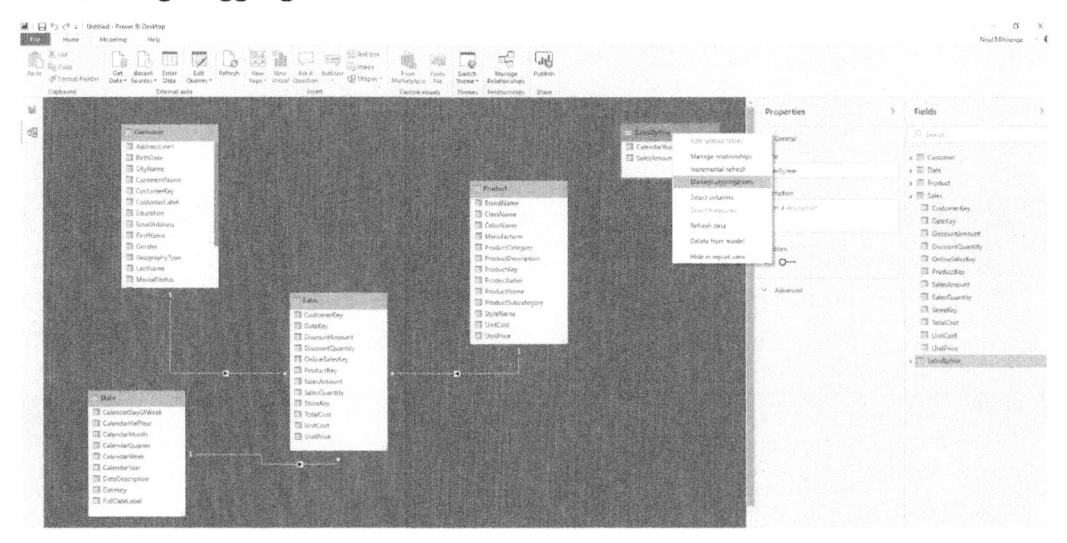

Figure 15.19: How to configure aggregations

In your **Manage aggregations'** window, in the **CalenderYear** row, select **GroupBy** in **SUMMARIZATION**, **Date** in **DETAIL TABLE**, and **CalendarYear** in **DETAIL COLUMN**.

In the **SalesAmount** row, select **Sum in SUMMARIZATION** (if you have used different aggregations like **Count** and **Min**, you can use that as **SUMMARIZATION**), **Sales** in

222 ■ *Power BI Data Modeling*

DETAIL TABLE, and **SalesAmount** in **DETAIL COLUMN**, as shown in the following figure:

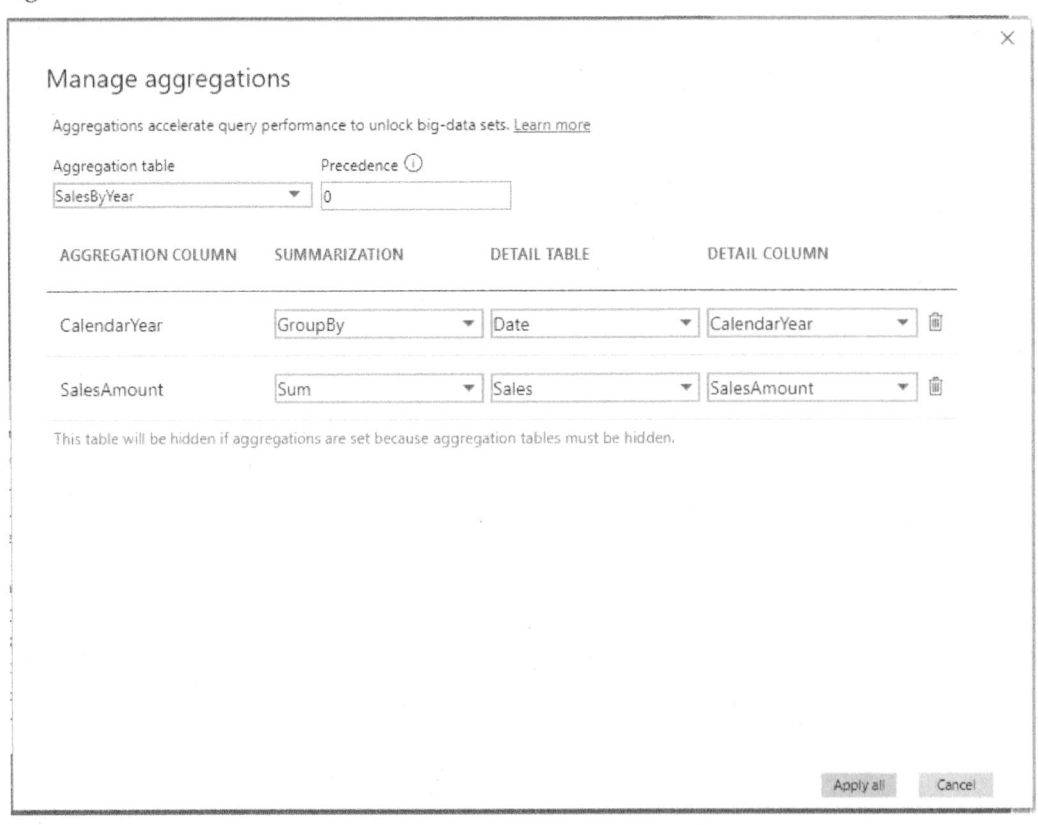

Figure 15.20: Manage aggregations

Once you click the **Apply all** button, this configuration will be applied to your model. As soon as you apply aggregations, the aggregation table will go to the hidden mode, and it is not visible for the end-user:

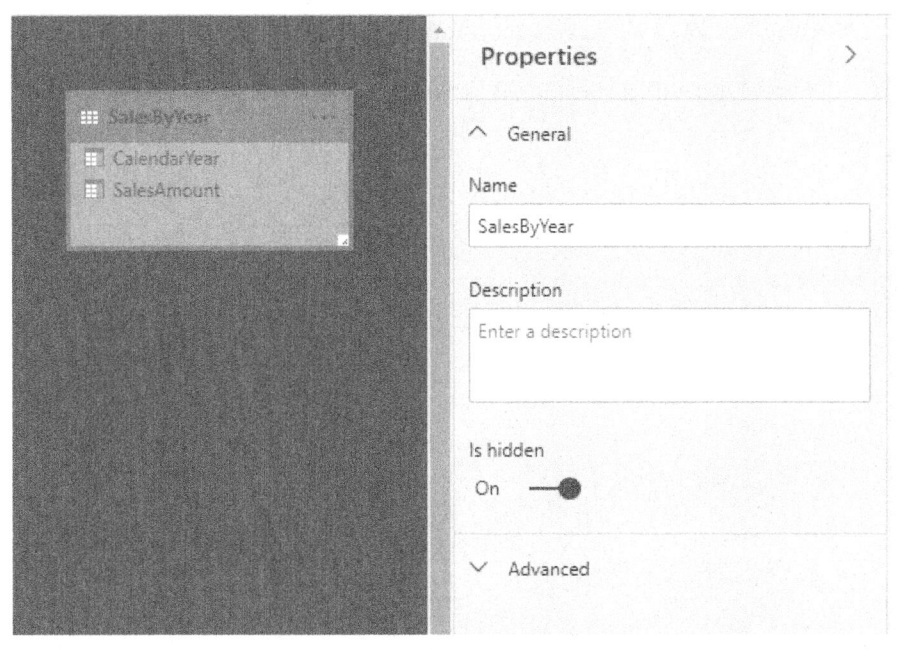

Figure 15.21: Hide the aggregation table

The idea is here, as we understood that you might have many aggregations in your model. After configuring, it goes to *hidden* mode automatically. The end-user does not know there are aggregation tables with duplicate data (if they do, they might get confused). So, the engine is smart enough to switch between your detail table and smaller aggregated table based on the queries you are using. Now once again, I am clearing the performance analyzer stats and refreshing visuals:

Figure 15.22: Record the query performance with aggregation

This time it just took **132** milliseconds to load. *Woohoo!*

Seems like Power BI engine has picked the aggregation table. Let us see the query:

```
// DAX Query
EVALUATE
  TOPN(
    502,
    SUMMARIZECOLUMNS(
      ROLLUPADDISSUBTOTAL('Date'[CalendarYear], "IsGrandTotalRowTotal"),
      "SumSalesAmount", CALCULATE(SUM('Sales'[SalesAmount]))
    ),
    [IsGrandTotalRowTotal],
    0,
    [SumSalesAmount],
    0,
    'Date'[CalendarYear],
    1
  )
ORDER BY
  [IsGrandTotalRowTotal] DESC, [SumSalesAmount] DESC, 'Date'[CalendarYear]


// SQL Query

SELECT
TOP (1000001) [c23],SUM([c58])
 AS [a0]
FROM
(

SELECT [t4].[CalendarYear] AS [c23],[t4].[SalesAmount] AS [c58]
FROM
(
(select [$Table].[CalendarYear] as [CalendarYear],
    [$Table].[SalesAmount] as [SalesAmount]
from [dbo].[SalesByYear] as [$Table])
)
 AS [t4]
)
 AS [t0]
GROUP BY [c23]
```

Figure 15.23: Underline query

You can see this time; it has used the aggregation table **SalesByYear**.

Another way of detecting aggregations

Figure 15.24: DAX studio

Another way of detecting aggregations is using **DAX Studio**. DAX Studio is a free tool you can download from **daxstudio.org** (http://daxstudio.org/), which allows you to perform various tasks like analyzing query performance, browsing model objects, writing DAX queries, tracing and identifying bottlenecks (https://www.youtube.com/watch?v=fAwvJa3Xkso&t=145s), and so on. Using DAX studio, you can connect Power BI models, power pivot, and tabular models:

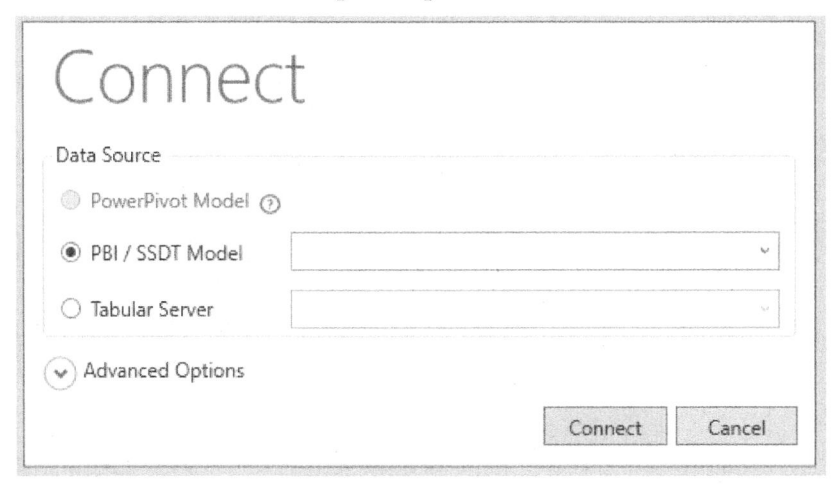

Figure 15.25: Connect to models

226 ■ Power BI Data Modeling

In order to get server execution times, enable **Server Timing** in the menu bar:

Figure 15.26: DAX studio main menu

Let us write a DAX query as follows; this query will return the same information we used in Power BI:

```
EVALUATE
SUMMARIZECOLUMNS('Date'[CalendarYear],
"Sales", SUM(Sales[SalesAmount])
)
```

If you go to the **Server Timing** tab as follows, you can see a lot of information such as **Formula Engine** (**FE**) timing and **Storage Engine** (**SE**) timing. In the result table, there are two records:

- **RewriteA**: **Aggregate Rewrite Attempt**; this indicates whether the engine hits the aggregation table or not. A smart way to identify that.

- **SQL**: The SQL query it generates to query the data:

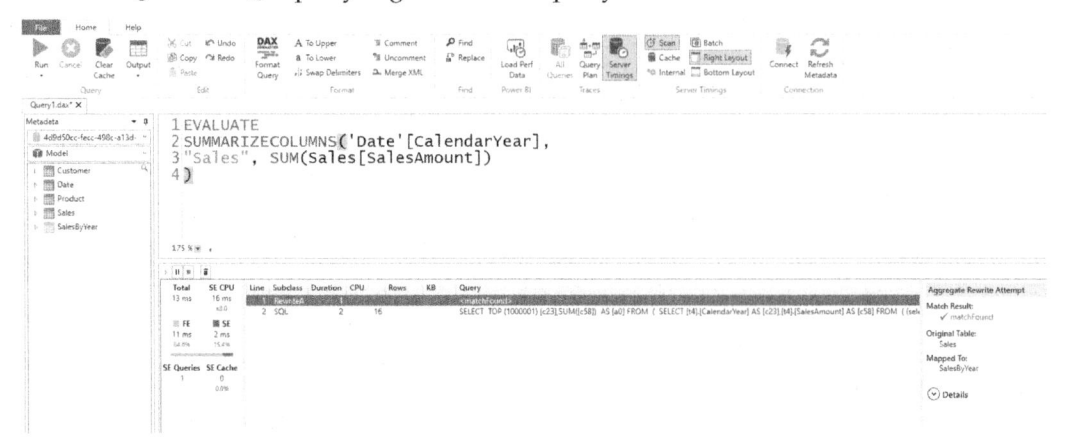

Figure 15.27: Detect aggregations in DAX studio

You can see it says match found in the **Aggregate Rewrite Attempt** section.

Let us try some advanced aggregations

So far in this chapter, we learned the aggregation concept and how to use simple aggregations in your model. Now, let us try to build some advanced aggregations.

We change my DAX query to return **ProductCategory** instead of **CalendarYear**. You can see the aggregation **attemptFailed**:

```
1 EVALUATE
2 SUMMARIZECOLUMNS('Product'[ProductCategory],
3 "Sales", SUM(Sales[SalesAmount])
4 )
```

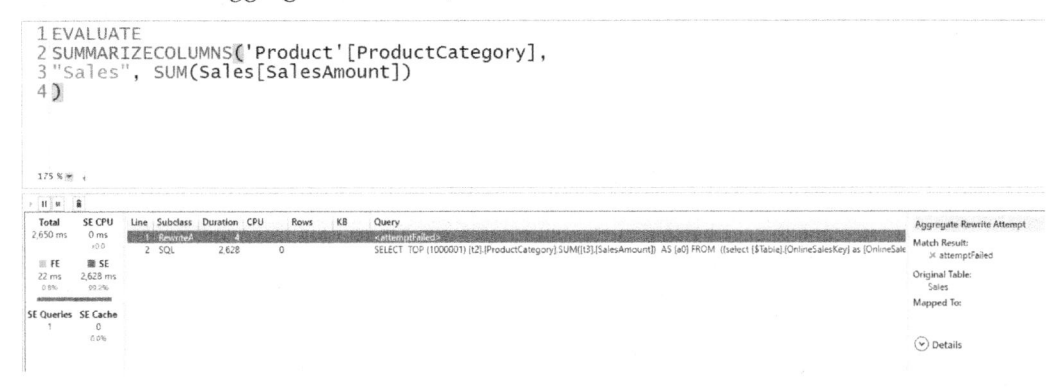

Figure 15.28: Aggregation attempts failed

Not a surprise. Because we have not built any aggregations with the product. Let us create another aggregation table:

```
-- Aggregated by Year and ProductKey
SELECT P.ProductKey,D.CalendarYear, SUM(S.SalesAmount) AS SalesAmount
INTO dbo.SalesByProductYear
FROM dbo.Sales S
JOIN dbo.[Date] D ON S.DateKey = D.Datekey
JOIN dbo.Product P ON S.ProductKey = P.ProductKey
GROUP BY D.CalendarYear, P.ProductKey
```

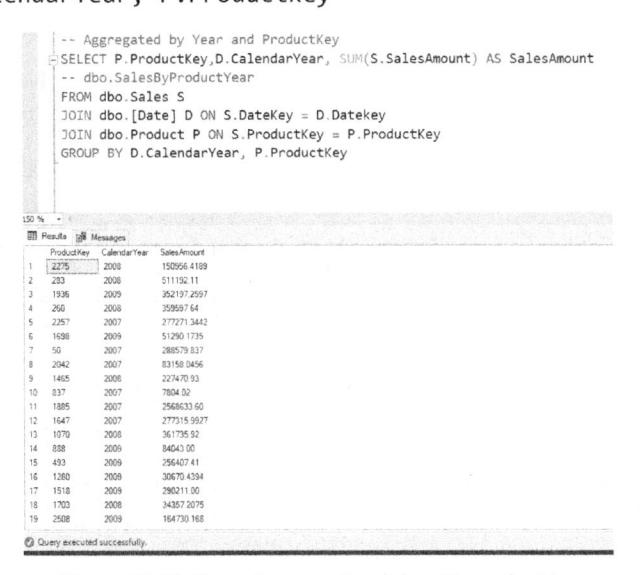

Figure 15.29: Second aggregation tale with product key

Whenever we use product-wise yearly sales, to hit this smaller table rather scan huge sales table. That is my objective by creating this aggregation table.

We are following the same process to add this **SalesByProductYear** table into my Power BI file. Go to **Recent Sources**, select the table, and connection type as **DirectQuery**.

Once again, we need to configure aggregations by selecting **Manage aggregations**:

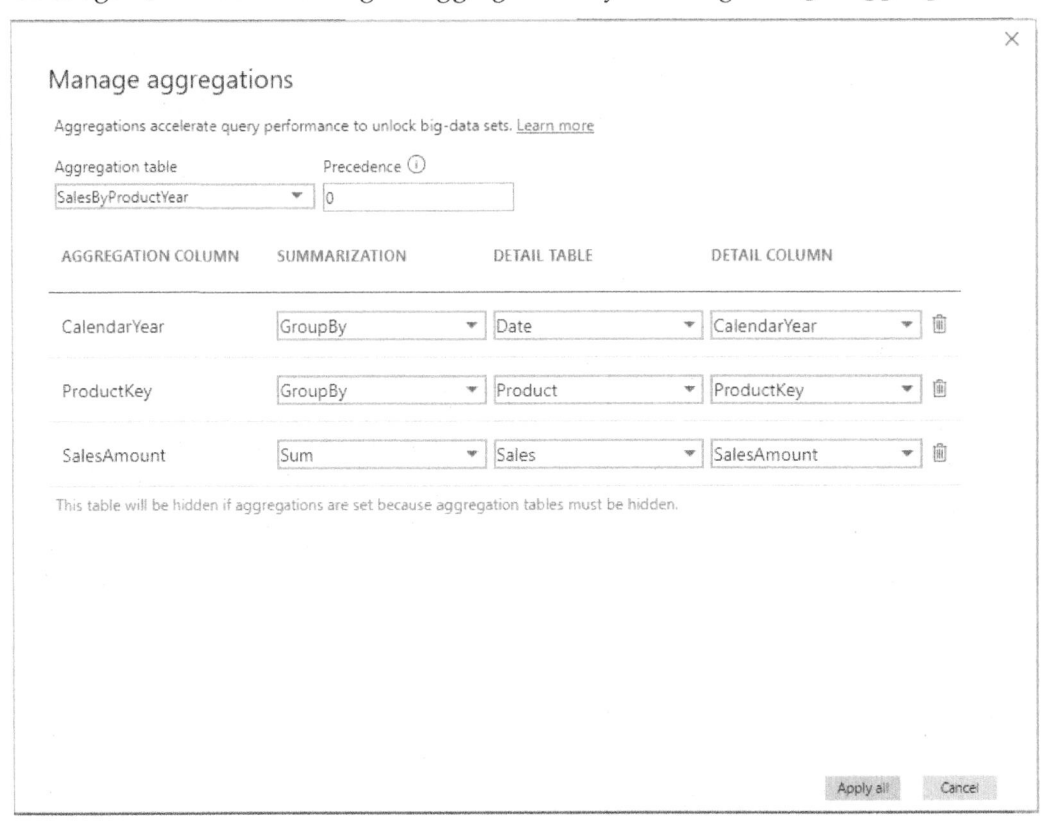

Figure 15.30: Configure aggregations in Power BI

By now, we hope you have understood how to configure this window. So, we are not going to repeat the process. *Leave it to you.*

Now our data model looks like this:

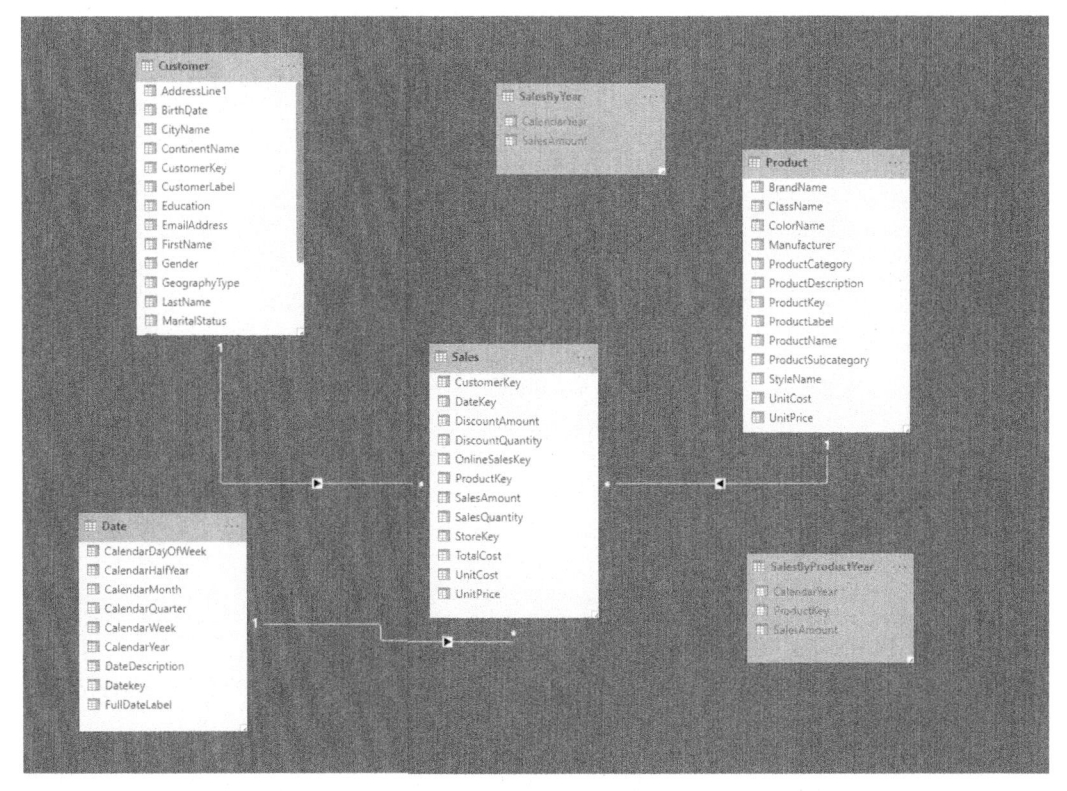

Figure 15.31: Model view

Let us try to run the DAX query again and see whether it picks the **aggregation** table by the engine. It took **1,842** ms, and the aggregate attempt failed:

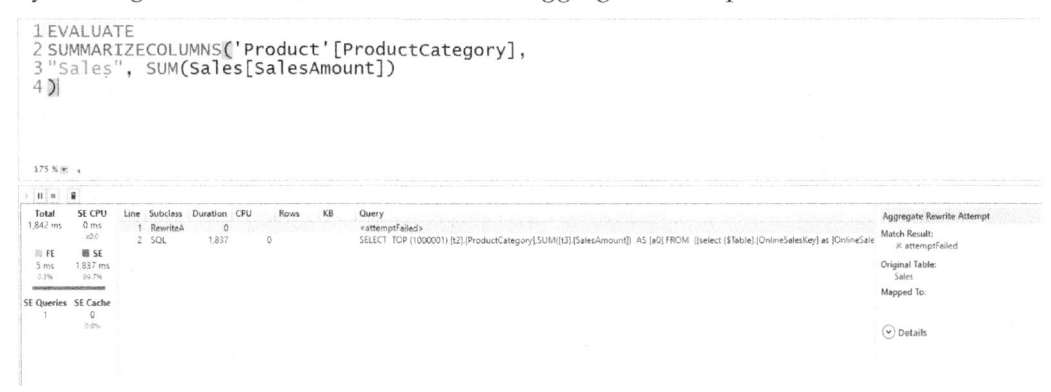

```
1 EVALUATE
2 SUMMARIZECOLUMNS('Product'[ProductCategory],
3 "Sales", SUM(Sales[SalesAmount])
4 )
```

Figure 15.32: Rewrite attempt failed

The reason for this, in our **SalesByProductYear** aggregation table, there is no product category column. So *how to fix this? Should we add another column ProductCategory to* *the aggregation table?* We cannot build aggregations like that. In that case, we may need to add many columns to the aggregation table and end up with useless:

ProductCategory	Sales
TV and Video	412304199.8195
Audio	36856719.4617
Home Appliances	833911778.5433
Computers	601874530.7265
Cell phones	167534502.8816
Games and Toys	33424983.2177
Cameras and camcorders	601950148.8545
Music, Movies and Audio Books	30345766.3034

Figure 15.33: Visualize data

So, till the engine does not know that **Product** table **ProductCategory** has a connection with aggregation table **ProductKey**. In order to tell the engine, we need to build a relationship.

So, I am going to build a relationship between the **SalesByProductYear** aggregation table and the **Product** table by connecting using **ProductKeys**. In that way, we do not require to bring the **ProductCategory** column into the aggregate table. Not only that, we can analyze any attribute in the **Product** table along with an aggregate table.

Just like the normal way, create a relationship with the **SalesByProductYear** table and **Product** table:

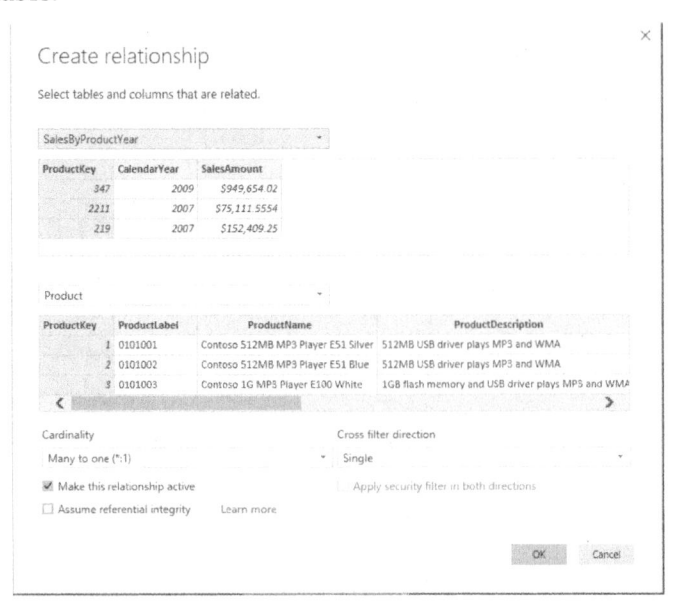

Figure 15:34: Create a relationship with the product table and aggregation table

After creating the relationship, the model will appear like this:

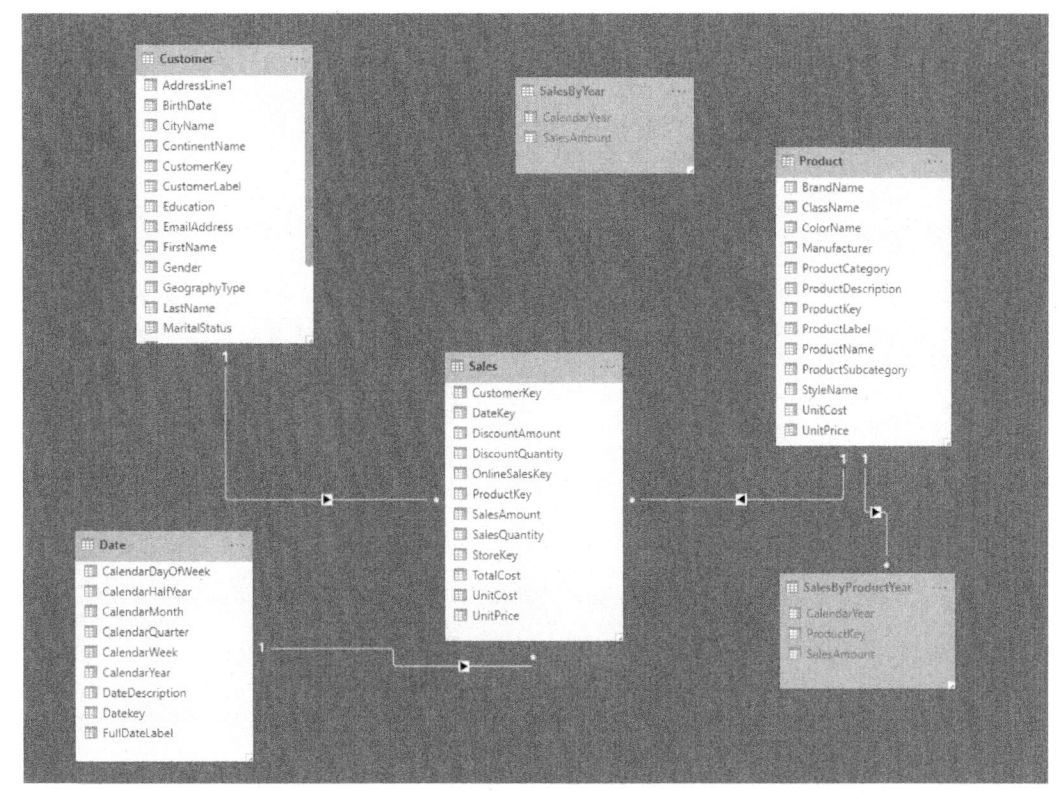

Figure 15.35: Model view

Let us run the query using DAX studio and see the result. Now, it should use the aggregated table:

```
1 EVALUATE
2 SUMMARIZECOLUMNS('Product'[ProductCategory],
3 "Sales", SUM(Sales[SalesAmount])
4 )
```

Figure 15.36: Detect the aggregation

Now, it says, *match found*, it has used the aggregations properly. If you look at the query executed against the SQL Server, you can see it, **JOIN** the `SalesByProductYear` table with `Product` table to produce the result:

```
SELECT
TOP (1000001) [c42],SUM([c62])
 AS [a0]
FROM
(

SELECT [t2].[ProductCategory] AS [c42],[t5].[SalesAmount] AS [c62]
FROM
((select [$Table].[ProductKey] as [ProductKey],
    [$Table].[CalendarYear] as [CalendarYear],
    [$Table].[SalesAmount] as [SalesAmount]
from [dbo].[SalesByProductYear] as [$Table]) AS [t5]

    left outer join

(select [$Table].[ProductKey] as [ProductKey],
    [$Table].[ProductLabel] as [ProductLabel],
    [$Table].[ProductName] as [ProductName],
    [$Table].[ProductDescription] as [ProductDescription],
    [$Table].[Manufacturer] as [Manufacturer],
    [$Table].[BrandName] as [BrandName],
    [$Table].[ClassName] as [ClassName],
    [$Table].[StyleName] as [StyleName],
    [$Table].[ColorName] as [ColorName],
    [$Table].[UnitCost] as [UnitCost],
    [$Table].[UnitPrice] as [UnitPrice],
    [$Table].[ProductSubcategory] as [ProductSubcategory],
    [$Table].[ProductCategory] as [ProductCategory]
from [dbo].[Product] as [$Table]) AS [t2] on
(
[t5].[ProductKey] = [t2].[ProductKey]
)
)

)
 AS [t0]
GROUP BY [c42]
```

Figure 15.37: Query underline

Composite models

Up to now, in this chapter, we have discussed how to create aggregations and detect aggregations hits by using tools such as **performance analyzer** and **DAX Studio**.

Composite Models and Perform Aggregations to Improve Query Performance ■ 233

I assume that you have downloaded the demo content related to the *Aggregations* section. If not, you can download it from the same demo content link:

DirectQuery

Import

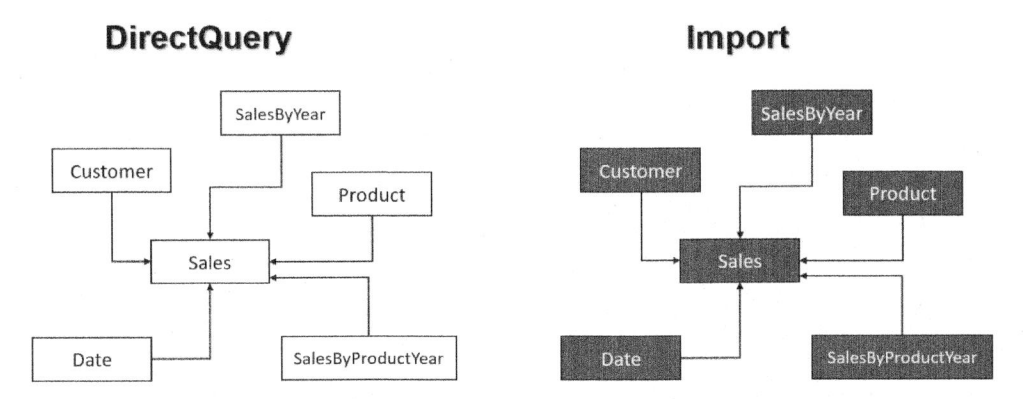

Figure 15.38: Demo model in connectivity modes

Composite models explained

Our data model is in **DirectQuery** mode, where every time we consume the data set, concert the DAX code into SQL code, hit the backend source, and fetch the data. *What if we can bring some of the tables into Import mode while the rest of the data is in DirectQuery mode.* In simple terms, this is the idea of composite models. You can maintain data in both **DirectQuery** and **Import** mode.

Even though we implement aggregations in our data model, still we can do much more to optimize the query performance. In this step, we are going to bring the `SalesByProductYear` table into the Import mode. Once it is brought, the data resides in the in-memory **VertiPaq** database engine. The data retrieval will be faster than now:

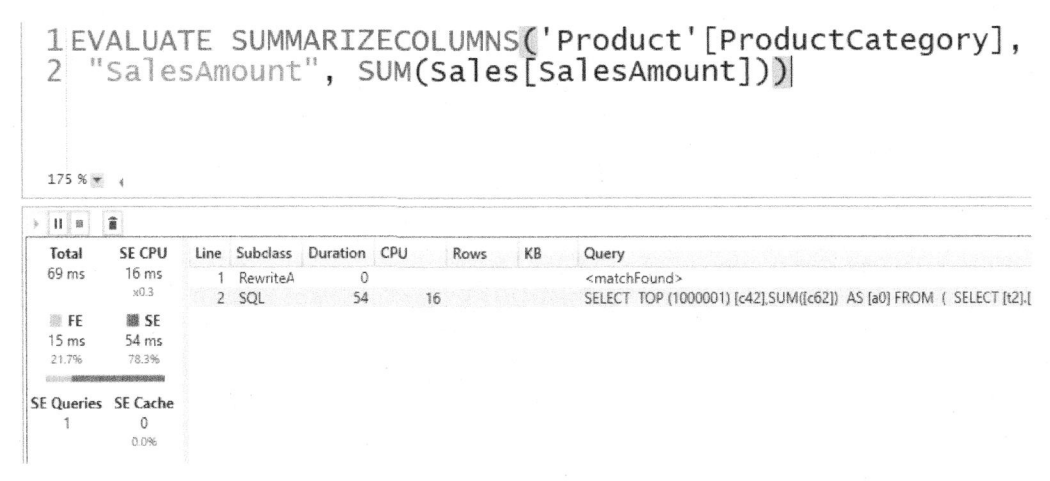

```
1 EVALUATE SUMMARIZECOLUMNS('Product'[ProductCategory],
2 "SalesAmount", SUM(Sales[SalesAmount]))
```

Total	SE CPU	Line	Subclass	Duration	CPU	Rows	KB	Query
69 ms	16 ms x0.3	1	RewriteA	0				<matchFound>
		2	SQL	54	16			SELECT TOP (1000001) [c42],SUM([c62]) AS [a0] FROM (SELECT [t2].[
FE 15 ms 21.7%	SE 54 ms 78.3%							
SE Queries 1	SE Cache 0 0.0%							

Figure 15.39: Sample query executes in DAX studio

Configure storage mode

In order to bring the table into the Import mode, you need to go to the *Model* tab and select the table. In this case, the table is **SalesByProductYear**. Then go to **Properties** and expand the **Advanced** section, then select the **Storage mode** as **Import**:

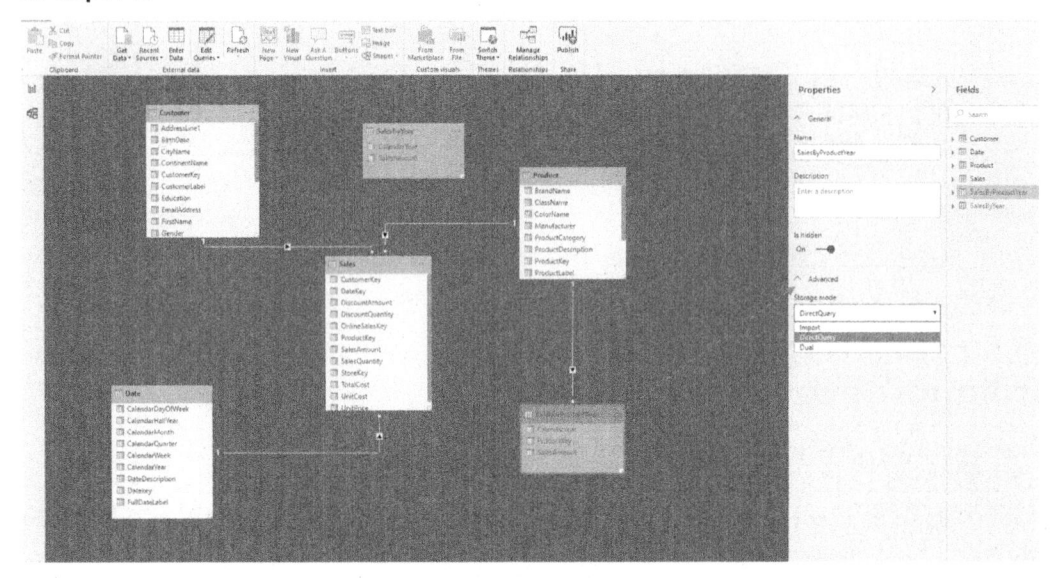

Figure 15.40: Configure storage mode

As soon as you select the **Storage mode** as **Import**, you will get an information dialog as follows:

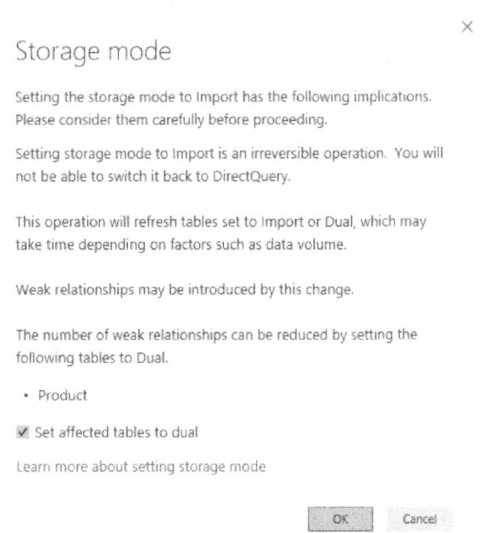

Figure 15.41: Storage mode warning

One of the statements is once you turn into Import mode, you cannot make it back to DirectQuery mode. Unlike DirectQuery, you have to refresh the data portion in VertiPaq because, as you know, data will be updated over time. Hence, part of your data in DirectQuery, and another part in Import, there will be a mismatch of your data unless you refresh the data forcefully.

The next one is because of this change; weak relationships may be introduced. Aggregations will not work with weak relationships. So, you have to do something about that. It says the number of weak relationships can reduce by making it to the **Dual** mode. *OK, here we go*. This make saves our effort of building aggregations.

To read more on strong and weak relationships, read the article from the link: https://www.sqlbi.com/articles/strong-and-weak-relationships-in-power-bi/.

We unchecked the changes and going to click **OK**. We will make tables to dual mode and whatever is required in tables manually.

Now my **SalesByProductYear** table is in **Import** mode. Let us run the query again in DAX studio and see what happens:

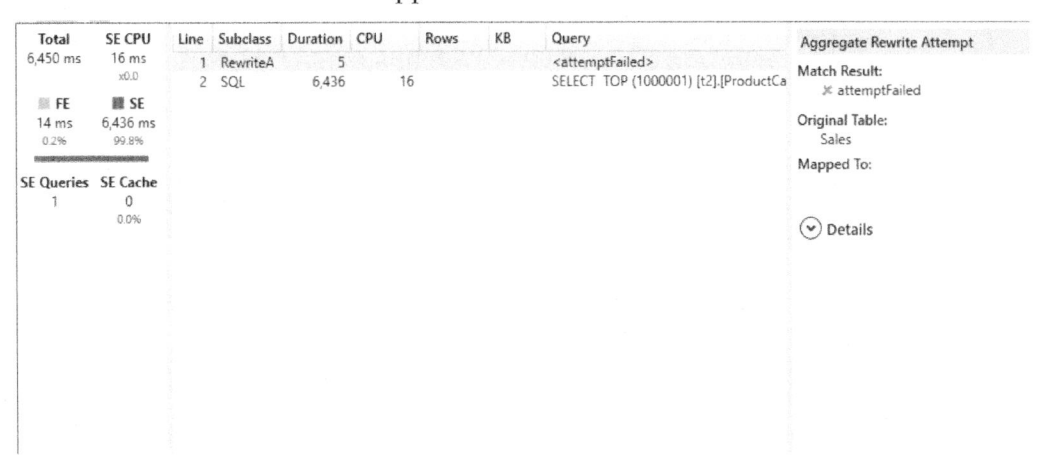

Total	SE CPU	Line	Subclass	Duration	CPU	Rows	KB	Query	Aggregate Rewrite Attempt
6,450 ms	16 ms x0.0	1	RewriteA	5				<attemptFailed>	Match Result: ✗ attemptFailed
		2	SQL	6,436	16			SELECT TOP (1000001) [t2].[ProductCa	
FE 14 ms 0.2%	SE 6,436 ms 99.8%								Original Table: Sales
									Mapped To:
SE Queries 1	SE Cache 0 0.0%								⌄ Details

Figure 15:42: *Aggregation attempt failed*

Why is my aggregation failed?

Because, in theory, the aggregation will not work part by part. This means in aggregation query; one part is in Import mode and the other part in DirectQuery mode. In order to make it work, you need to bring the product table into dual mode.

Let us try to turn **Product** table **Storage mode** as **Dual** and see. You will get a message like this:

Figure 15.43: Storage mode settings

When you click **OK,** an error may be received as follows:

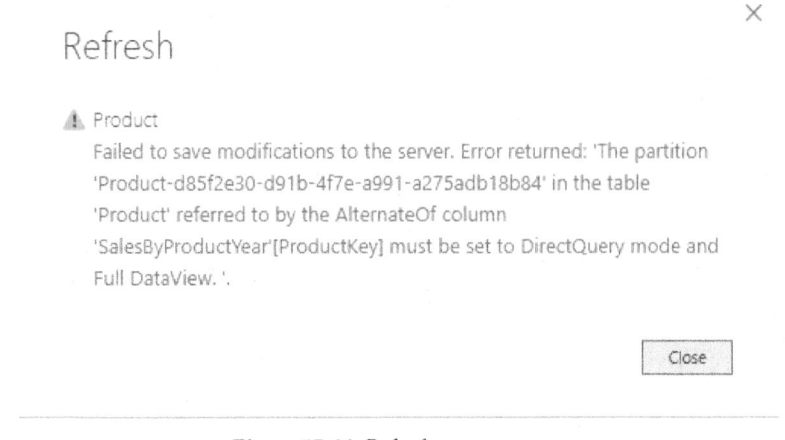

Figure 15.44: Refresh error message

This error (*figure 15.44*) is received because in the aggregation table, **ProductKey** column, we used it from the **Product** table. It is also possible to use it from the **Sales** table. Because you know the **Sales** table is a fact table and it also contains the **ProductKey** column. Just the other side of the relationship.

We reconfigured the aggregation as follows:

Figure 15.45: Reconfigure the aggregation

Let us try again and see to bring the **Product** table into **Dual** mode. This time, we could be brought it into **Dual**-mode successfully:

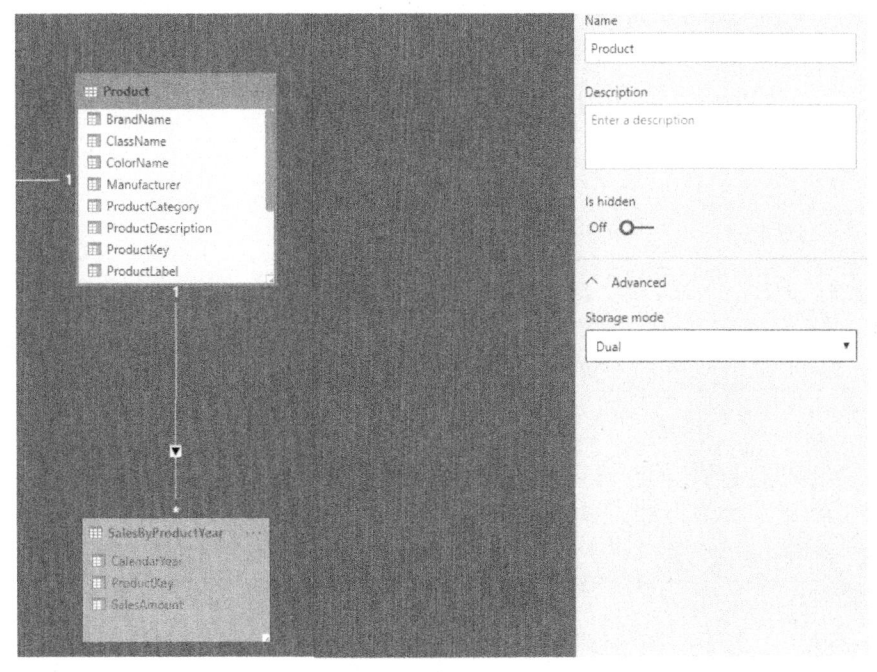

Figure 15.46: Configure the storage mode

Now we were able to implement the composite model successfully. Let us run our DAX query again and see the result:

```
1 EVALUATE SUMMARIZECOLUMNS('Product'[ProductCategory],
2 "SalesAmount", SUM(Sales[SalesAmount]))
```

Figure 15.47: Rewrite attempt succeed

You can see *aggregation re-write attempt succeeded*. Also, if you pay attention closely, you can notice the query generated is different than earlier when we used DirectQuery. This is the query format generated when the data is in VertiPaq storage. And another interesting fact is the query execution time has been reduced from **69** ms to **7** ms. This is the power of the VertiPaq engine.

Let us try to bring another table also into the Import mode. **SalesByYear** table is much smaller. In this step, we brought the table into Import storage mode:

```
1 EVALUATE SUMMARIZECOLUMNS('Date'[CalendarYear],
2 "SalesAmount", SUM(Sales[SalesAmount]))
```

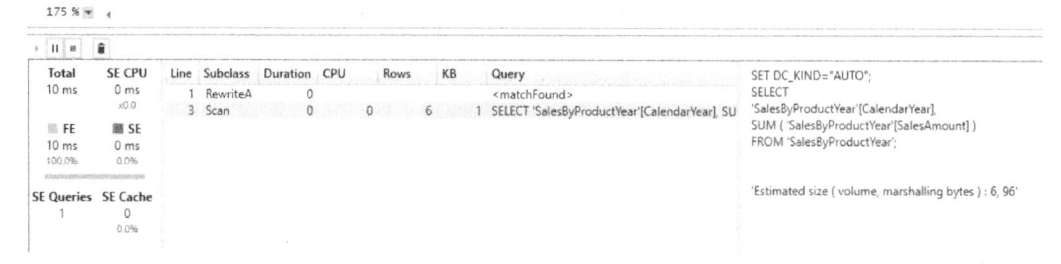

Figure 15.48: Rewrite attempt succeed

Now we have a different problem. I am expecting to retrieve data from the **SalesByYear** table. But actually, when looking at the query result, the data has been retrieved from the **SalesByProductYear** table. We need to force the engine to pick a smaller table when there are **multiple candidates**. We needed to get yearly sales, and there are two aggregation tables that can fulfill the requirement.

Force engine to select right aggregation table

In order to do this, right-click the aggregation table, and go back to **Manage aggregations**. There is a configuration called **precedence**, which is a whole number which you can define the order of selecting aggregation should be considered by query execution. Higher the precedence, the engine will select first. By allowing to configure numeric numbers, Power BI allows defining the order of execution, especially when you have many aggregations in complex models. In that time, you can maintain an Excel document and maintain the sequence properly based on the query audits:

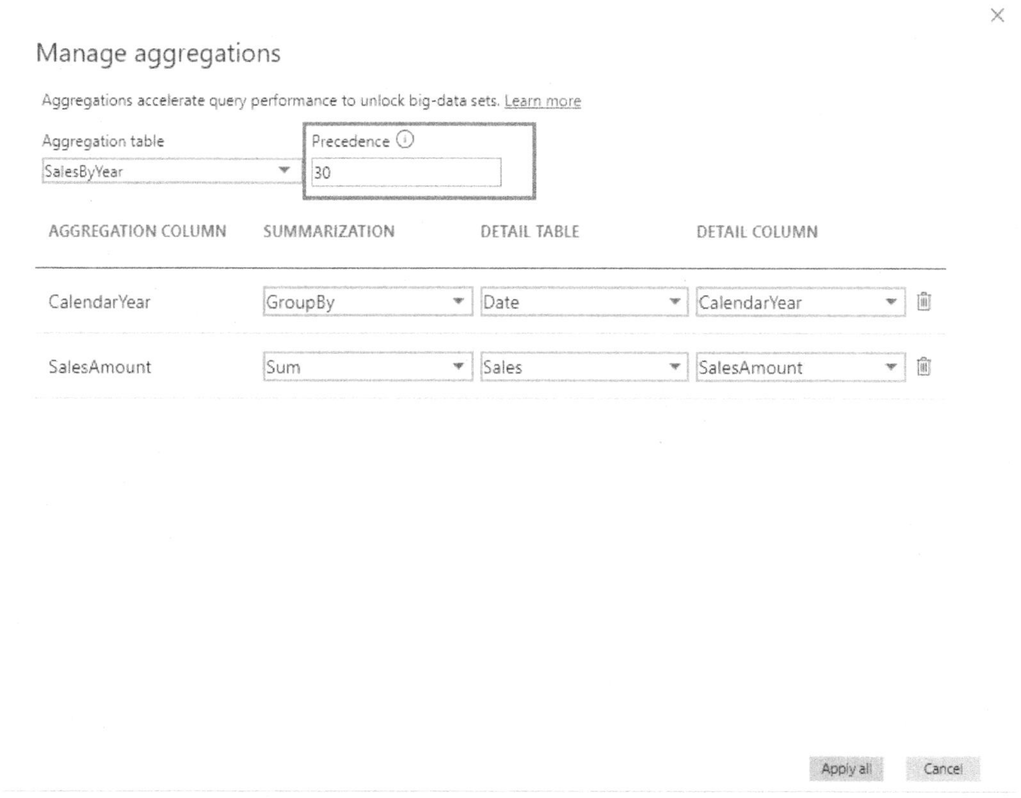

Figure 15.49: Configure the precedence

Now my `SalesByYear` table aggregation precedence is **30,** whereas `SalesByProductYear` remains as **0**. When we execute the same query again, theoretically, the engine should pick the **SalesByYear** table. Let us see as follows:

```
1 EVALUATE SUMMARIZECOLUMNS('Date'[CalendarYear],
2   "SalesAmount", SUM(Sales[SalesAmount]))
```

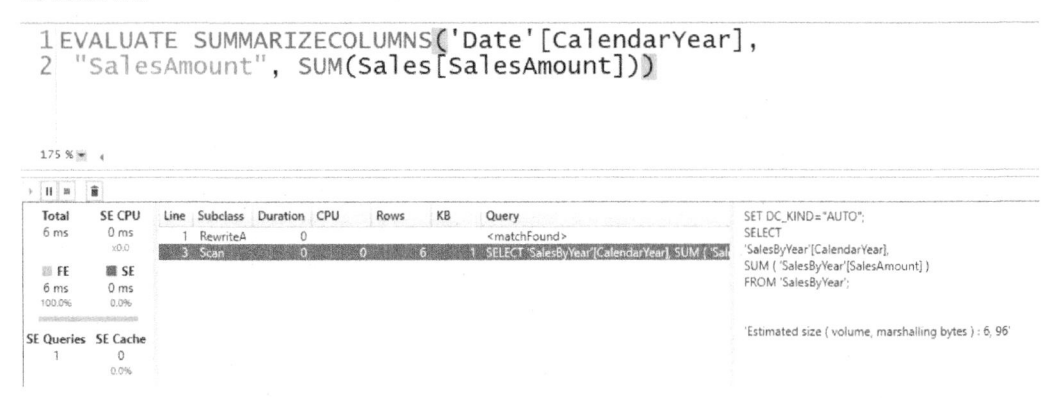

Figure 15.50: *It selects the best aggregation table after configure precedence*

Now you can see the **VertiPaq** engine has picked the **SalesByYear** table by looking at the query.

Composite models allow to achieve balanced architecture

Composite models allow you to have a **balanced architecture** which means you can bring your aggregated tables into the **Import** mode while other large tables are in the **DirectQuery** mode. This feature is a great candidate for **Big data** scenario, where you can leave your transaction fact as DirectQuery, which can never fit into the memory:

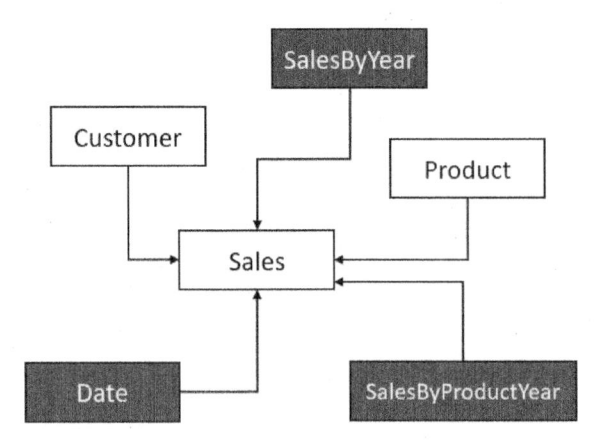

Figure 15.51: *Composite model*

Conclusion

In this chapter, you learned the connection types in Power BI, the concept of aggregations, and how to use aggregations over data mode. Even though we used a relatively smaller data set, yet the concept and the way of implementation are valid for Big data such as data in an **Apache Spark** cluster or a **Data Lake**. Later part of this chapter, we walked through how to detect aggregations using a performance analyzer and DAX studio. Hope, you can learn the concept aggregations in Power BI.

Also, you learned how to use the composite model concept along with the aggregations. The objective is to teach the readers the concept of composite models and how to apply them in real-world scenarios. We recommend you follow the same steps we did in order to achieve better results. The upcoming chapter will focus on how to collaborate data preparation work with Power BI dataflows.

Questions

1. Discuss what aggregation is and how it is useful for modern data implementations.
2. Explain what composite models are and how it is beneficial to improve the model query performance.

CHAPTER 16
Self-service Data Preparation for Any Data

We have previously discussed how to perform data transformations using Power Query in Power BI. If you have noticed, the work you do via Power Query will be scoped to your Power BI workbook. You cannot reuse it for other Power BI development unless tedious copy paste work. In this chapter, we will explain the self-service ETL requirement in the Power BI. *How your self-service ETL workload can collaborate with other users in your organization in order to improve productivity.* Also, later in this chapter, we will discuss how this feature will be a candidate for pre-processing Big data.

Structure

The following topics will be covered during this chapter:

- Introduction to citizen ETLing
- Why self-service data preparation
- How to create dataflows in Power BI
- ETL for large data sets

Objective

The objective of this chapter is to get a high-level understanding of the Power BI connectors offered and the connection types.

Introducing citizen ETLing

By now, you must become familiar with the term **ETL**, which stands for **Extract, Transform, and Load**. During the ETL process, you are connecting to the data in the organization, which is extraction, then perform various transformations such as cleansing data and changing the structure of data in a way the need of the business using Power Query. You learned these in the data transformation and modeling sections of the book. However, the functionalities are depending on the connection method. Also, in your local computer, you have a limited number of hardware resources. Therefore, the amount of data you can process is also limited. In Power BI, you have a *1 GB* of data limit per model. The current process is more suitable if there is one Power BI developer in the organization.

Imagine in your organization having a team of data users. You have built a complex entity, for example, **product** dimension, by spending a certain amount of time that is also useful for their analysis. If you are required to collaborate work on the ETL development, which is not possible right now. Because only one `pbix` file will be generated as an output of your work. If you need to share it with your colleagues, you must share that file. But anyway, it cannot be used for their existing development, like if they already have some data model development and require adding your product dimension to it. This is where Power BI dataflow comes into play.

Power BI dataflow is a feature in Power BI, in which you can do ETL work irrespective of the volume of data, you can share and collaborate with other members of your organization. You can develop dataflow entities using the Power BI service. You can combine multiple sources and create single entities also create calculated columns. Your data will be stored in **Azure Data Lake Storage Gen 2**. Please refer to *figure 16.1* illustration:

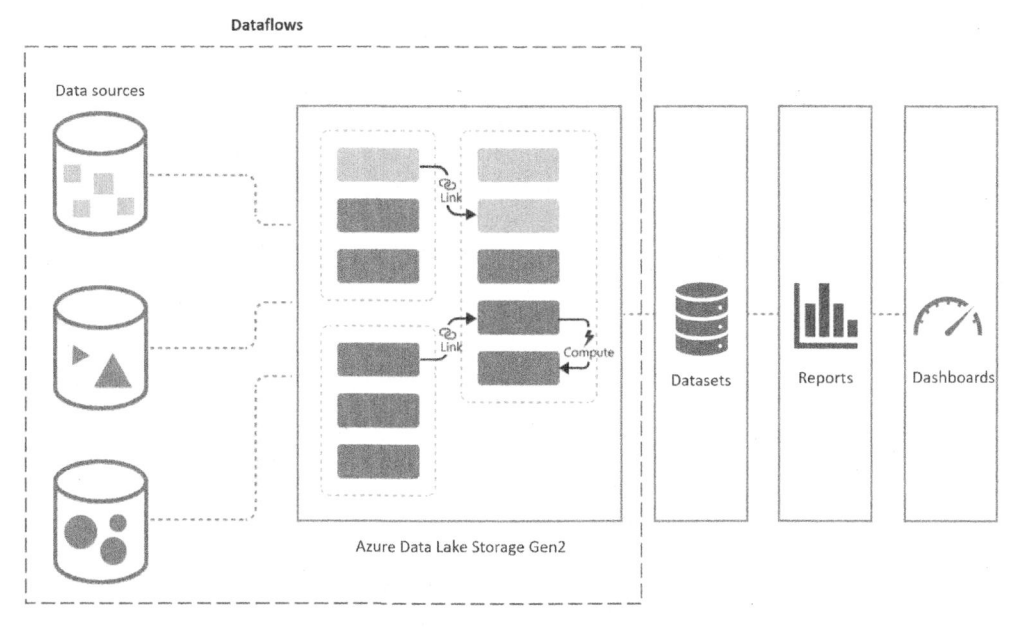

Figure 16.1: Dataflow architecture

Why self-service data preparation?

Collaboration is there in the Power BI for data visualization from the beginning. You can connect to the existing data model and visualize data if you have the right permission. With Power BI dataflows, you can perform ETL work also collaboratively. Either you develop one entity and share it with others, then they can use it for their development, or else multiple developers can develop and do improvements. **Date dimension** is a good classic example of this. The basic date dimension is a very generic one, which contains **Dates**, **Year**, **Quarter**, **Month**, and so on. If your analytics supports multiple languages, then you can maintain month names in different languages accordingly. The finance user knows when the financial year starts and ends. So, they can modify queries according to that. Having fiscals in the same date entity will not overkill the analytics; it just adds more potential into it. In the same manner, the HR department can work together and modify the dataflow by marking holidays, and so on.

In *figure 16.2*, the diagram shows how different departmental users in the organization interact with dataflows to develop common entities:

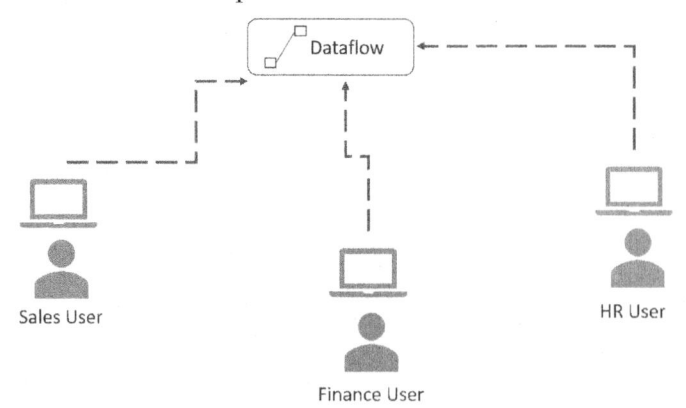

Figure 16.2: *Multiple developers are working on a single dataflow*

By now, hope you got some level of understanding about the dataflows.

Creating dataflows in Power BI

Let us see how to create dataflows in the Power BI service. In order to do that first, you may log in to the Power BI service and select any workspace t you need to create the dataflow. You can create a dataflow from the **+ New** button as shown in *figure 16.3*:

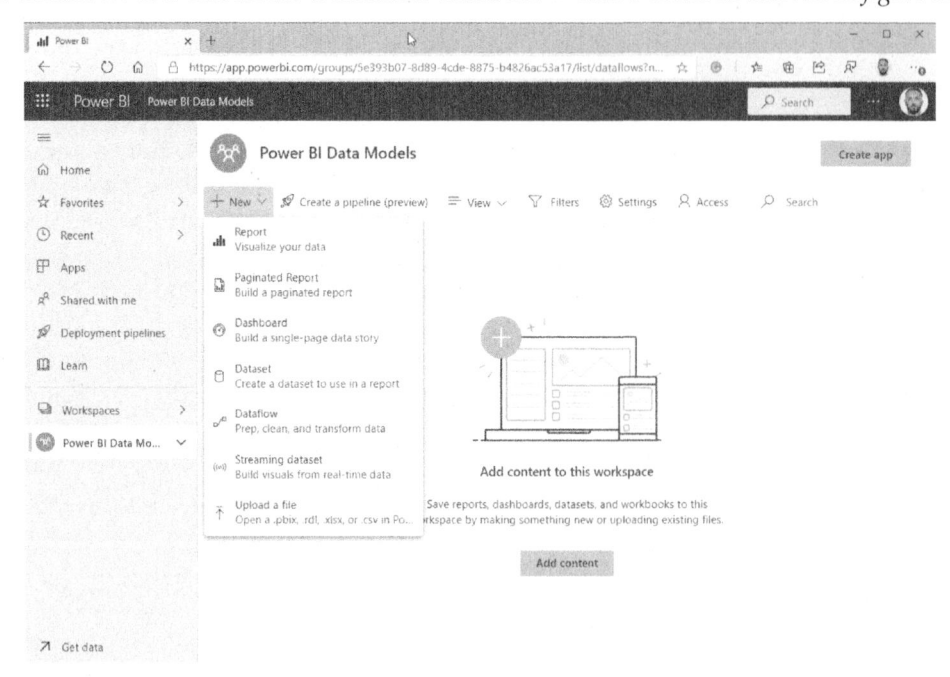

Figure 16.3: *Create dataflow in Power BI*

Once you click the **Dataflow**, it will bring you to the *dataflow startup window*. The startup window has four main areas you can create dataflow related work (refer to *figure 16.4*):

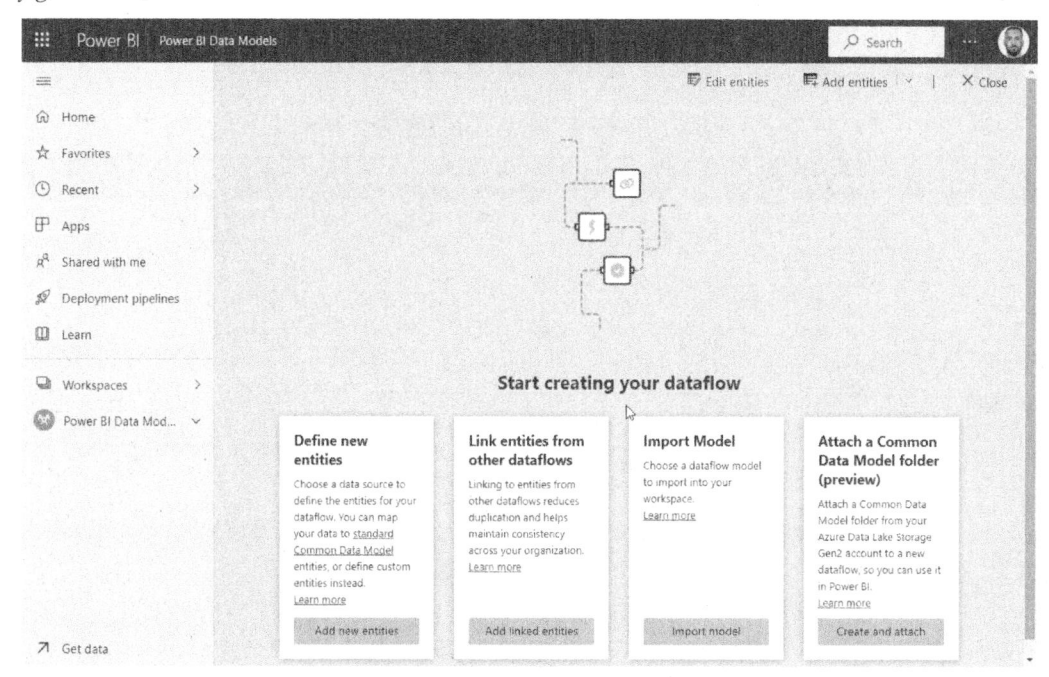

Figure 16.4: Start creating dataflows

There are specific actions to be performed through each button as explained here:

- `Define new entities`: Choose a data source to define the entities for your dataflow. You can map your data to standard **Common Data Model** entities (https://go.microsoft.com/fwlink/?LinkID=2038461) or define custom entities instead.

- `Link entities from other dataflows`: From this option, you can link to an existing entity from other dataflows, reduce duplication, and help maintain consistency across your organization.

- `Import model`: This option for you to choose a dataflow model to import into your workspace.

- `Attach a Common Data Model folder (preview)`: CDM is a storage technology for business applications. Here, you can attach a **Common Data Model** folder from your Azure Data Lake Storage Gen2 account to a new dataflow, so you can use it in Power BI.

Attach a Common Data Model folder feature that is in preview at the time of writing this book. This does not mean that you cannot use this. In this feature, you can add CDM folders stored in organizational Azure Data Lake Gen 2 as dataflows, which can be used in Power BI desktop and service to create data sets, reports, and dashboards based on the data you have in CDM.

In order to create a new entity, you must click the **Define New Entities** button:

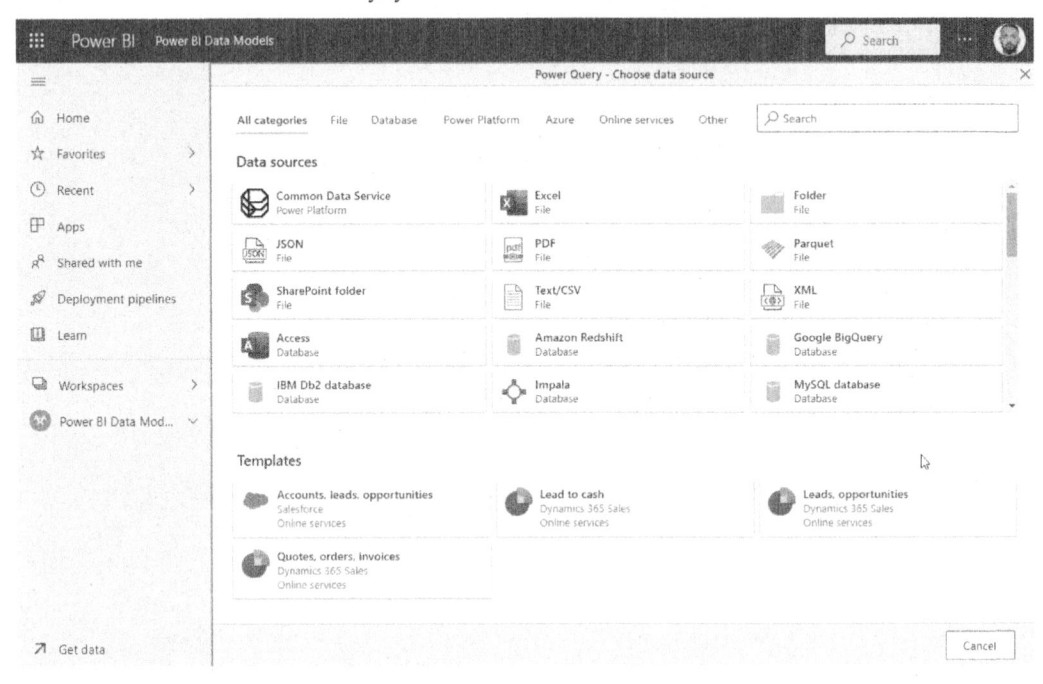

Figure 16.5: Define new entity in dataflow

In the first window, you will find a large number of supported data sources. You can browse through based on the category. Not all the source types are there, which were in the Power BI desktop. However, some data sources exist that are not there on the Power BI desktop. For example, **Parquet**.

Parquet is an Apache-based free and open-source column-based data storage format. It is compatible with most of the Big data processing frameworks. Parquet is quite popular in Azure Data Lake Store Gen 2. As an alternative, you can store data in CSV format. The main difference in Parquet format is that you will be able to store data type as well.

For example, let us connect with SQL Server data source:

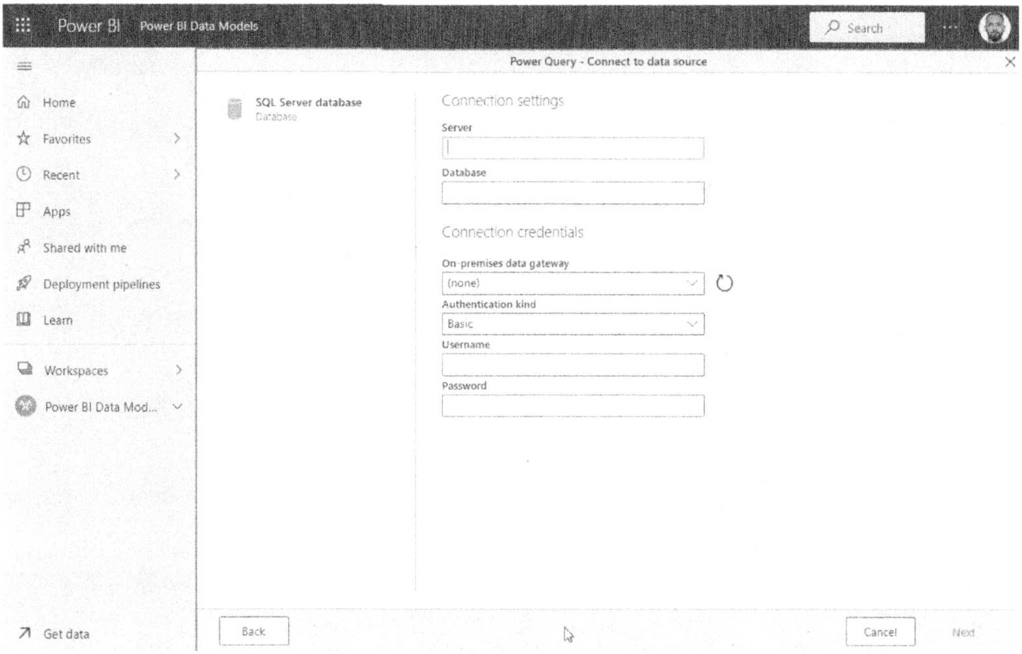

Figure 16.6: Connect to SQL Server database

You must specify the following details in order to make the connection with SQL Server:

- **Server**: Your SQL Server instance name.

- **Database**: The database name you suppose to connect.

- **On-premises data gateway**: You must specify the on-premises data gateway you created with your local computer.

- **Authentication kind**: Authentication method, whether Microsoft account or basic SQL authentication. If you select the **Basic** option, you have to prompt SQL login details.

250 ■ *Power BI Data Modeling*

Once you click **Next**, the wizard will bring you to the next window, which contains a list of database objects and their preview. You can see this in *figure 16.7*:

Figure 16.7: Preview data

Here, we have selected three tables, **Product**, **ProductSubcategory**, and **ProductCategory**. Then click the **Transform data** button. Then it moves to the transform data **Edit queries** window, which is pretty much a familiar view to the Power BI desktop option. There will be some changes between the two versions. You can see how the transform data looks like in Power BI dataflows in *figure 16.8*:

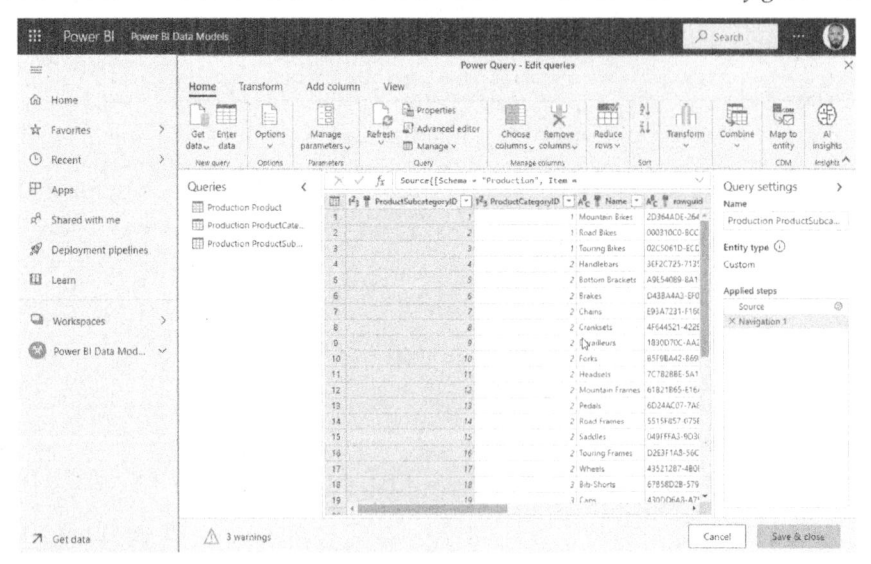

Figure 16.8: Transform data

Self-service Data Preparation for Any Data 251

We are going to create one table called **Product** by combining all three tables. Then, it is easy for analysis, and also, we can create a hierarchy of products if we want later.

You can deselect **Enable load** and create a reference of the product table. Then use the **Combine** option in the *top menu bar* in order to merge two queries:

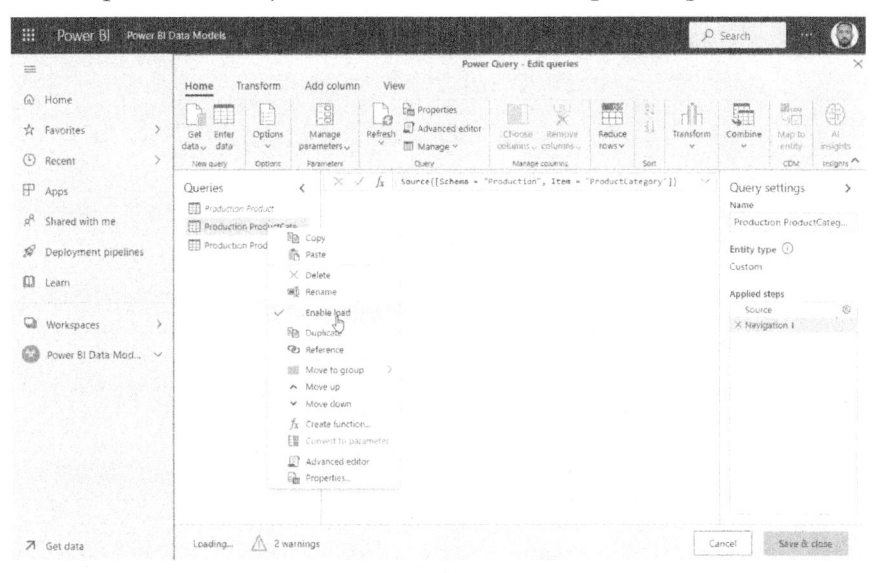

Figure 16.9: Until enable load

In the **Home** tab, select **Combine** and then select **Merge Query**, now you will see a window as follows:

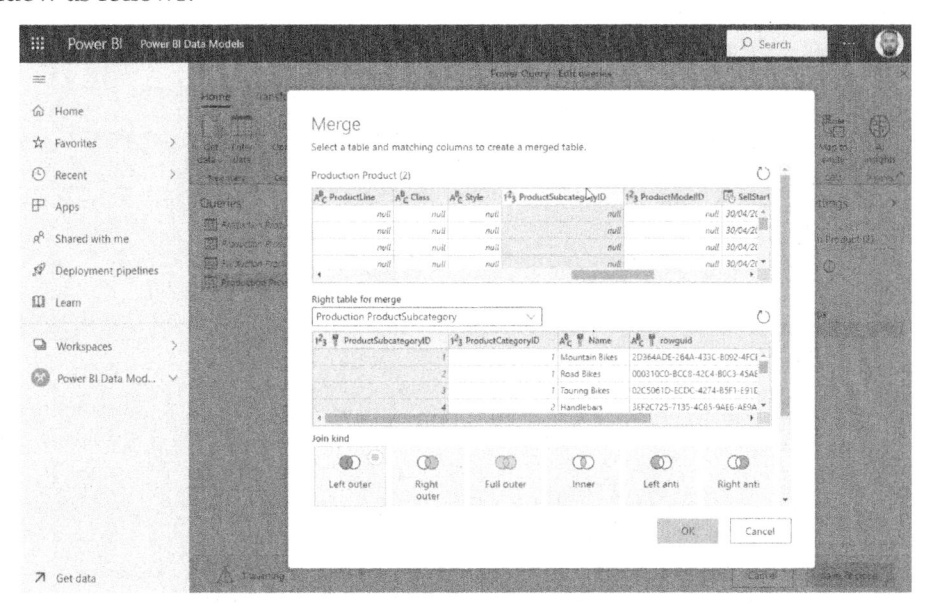

Figure 16.10: Merge query

Then click **OK**. You can click the *Expand* icon and get the new columns in `ProductSubcategory` and `ProductCategoryID,` which will be useful to join with the `ProductCategory` table. Please refer to *figure 16.11*:

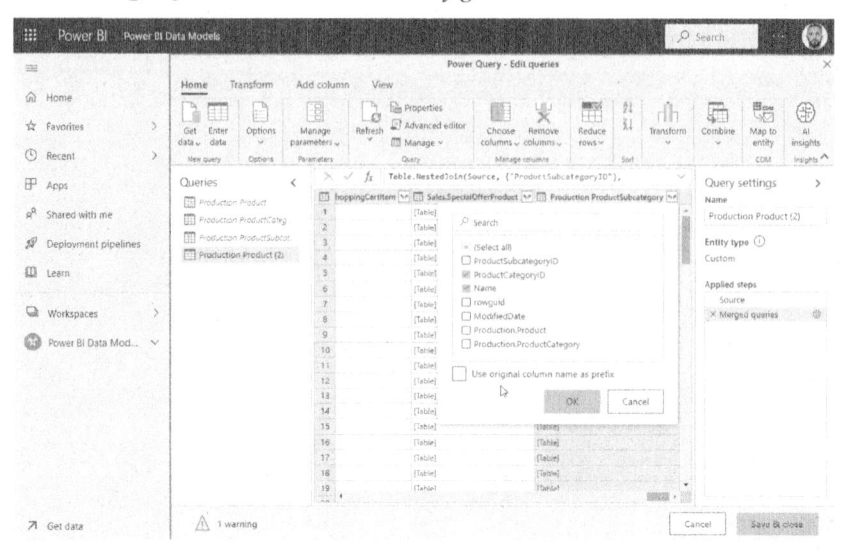

Figure 16.11: Expand the columns

In the same way, you can join the `ProductCategory` table. We just included the product category name. Then rename it as a product category in the column. You can remove unnecessary columns if you want, which are not going to be used in the analysis. Finally, you can click the `Save & Close` button. It will take some amount of time depending on the data size:

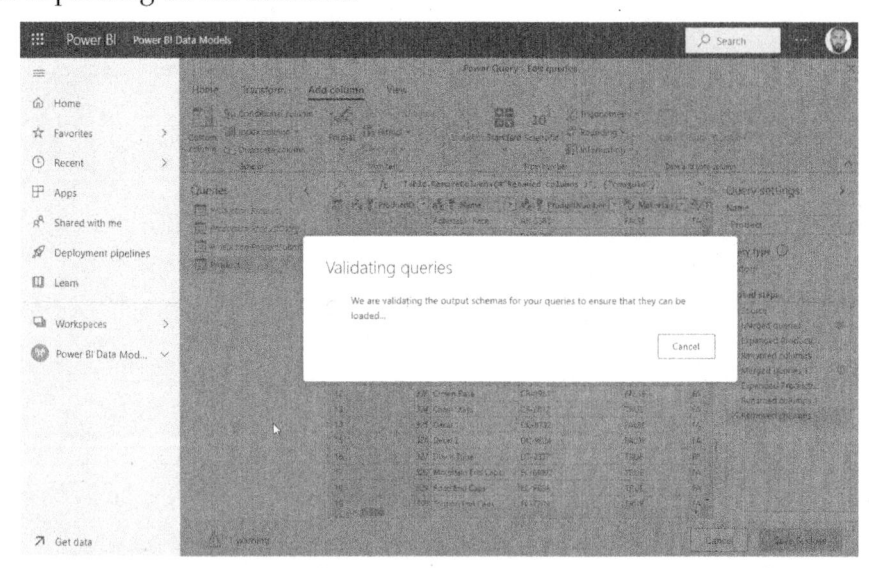

Figure 16.12: Applying the edit queries to actual data

In the end, you have to name your (*figure 16.13*). You have to give some descriptive name because this dataflow is not going to be used by only you:

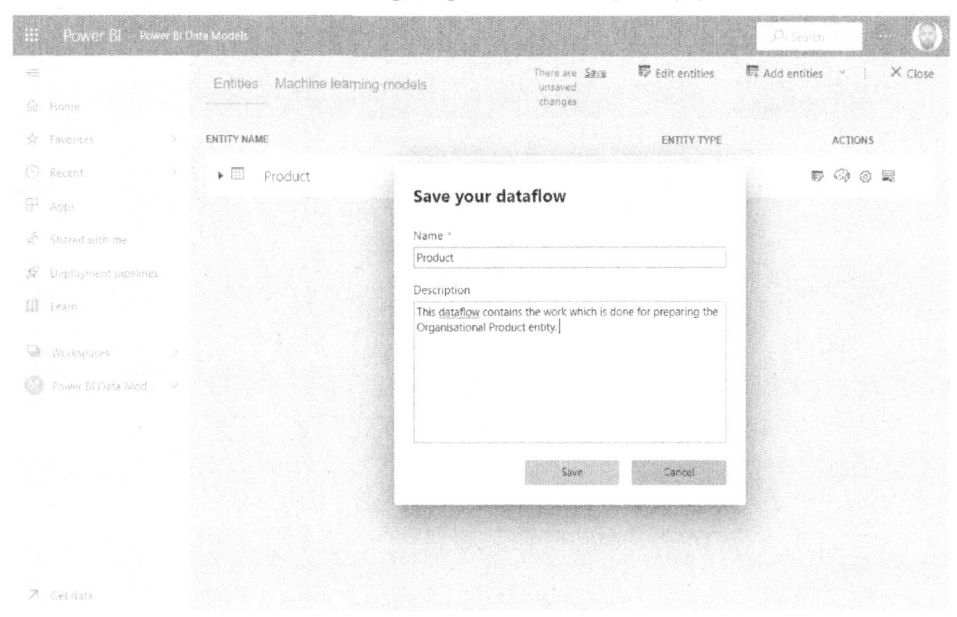

Figure 16.13: Save the dataflow

Once you have created your dataflow successfully, you can view its metadata as follows:

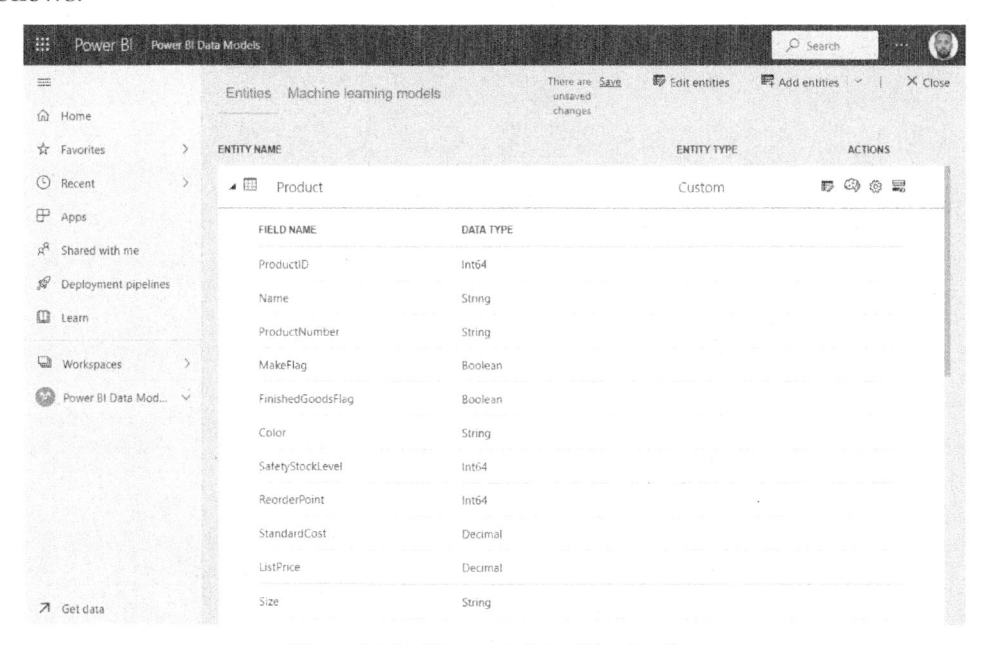

Figure 16.14: View metadata of the dataflow

Power BI Data Modeling

The main idea of having dataflows is the re-usability and cutting the time spent for repeatable work in your organization. Anyone in your organization can access the dataflow with permission and start to use it in their models. *Figure 16.15* shows how to access dataflow:

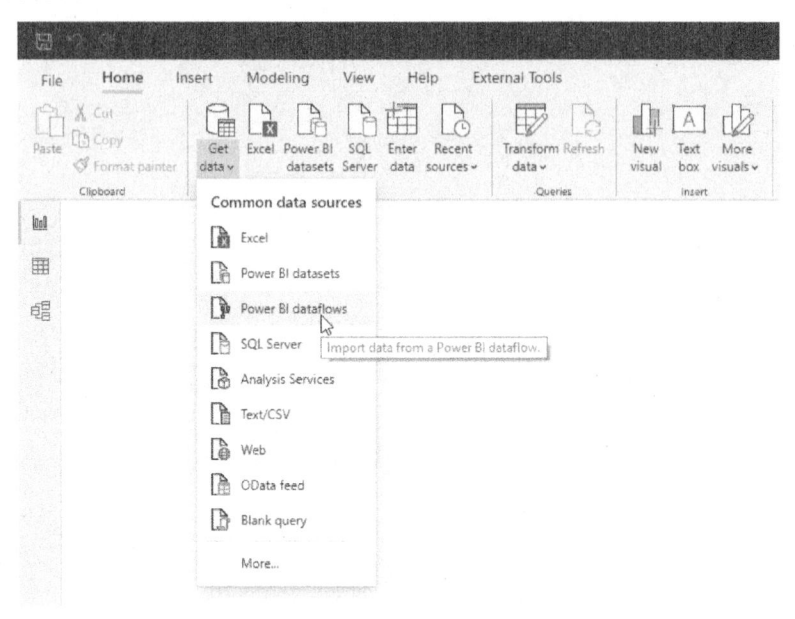

Figure 16.15: Import dataflow

Then you have to select the dataflow you created like in *figure 16.16*:

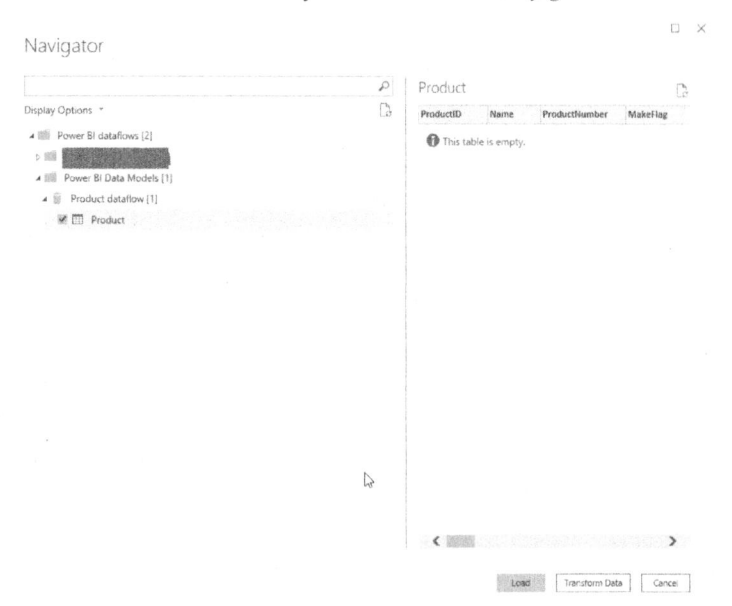

Figure 16.16: Select the dataflow

ETL for large data sets

Usage of dataflows is not just collaborating. You can build dataflows in the same manner for a large amount of data. The data you are transforming resides in the Azure Data Lake Gen 2. There are some extended features for Premium license users, such as **AI features** and **linked entities,** which are out of scope in this chapter.

Conclusion

In this chapter, we discussed the Power BI dataflows, *why it is called citizen ETL,* and *how to get started to create a dataflow in the Power BI service.* Then, we learned about how it has been used to develop entities in the organization, which can be referred for future development, and how this feature is important for large data sets. In the upcoming chapter, we will talk about more into DAX language and how to optimize your code.

Questions

1. Discuss about the usage of the Power BI dataflows and how they can be fitted to the development in your organization.

2. Explain the concept of the Common Data Model and how it is useful for rapid analytical development.

CHAPTER 17
Optimize DAX

We have already introduced **Data Expression Language (DAX)**, the programming language in Power BI, to create calculations and define expressions in *Chapter 9, Introducing DAX, Calculated Columns, Calculated Measures, and Hierarchies*. Although we are working with different sizes of data, it is important to follow best practices when designing and creating objects in order to ensure that we will not encounter any performance bottlenecks in the future with the growth of the data. This chapter will be focused on how to follow a list of best practices to ensure that we are writing optimized DAX code in our Power BI reports.

Structure

The following topics will be covered during this chapter:

- Basic optimization and techniques
- Optimize DAX syntax
- DAX functions optimization

Objective

The objective of this chapter is to discuss and educate best practices follow to write optimized DAX code in your day-to-day Power BI development.

Basic optimization and techniques

Before discussing advanced techniques, let us start with the basics. There are a few basic things you must be aware of when we discuss DAX optimization.

Clear cache

When we develop Power BI reports, it is always necessary to free up the cache. By now, you know that the Power BI database is an in-memory database. Some of the objects are stored in a temporary cache in order to render results fast and give a better end-user experience. However, when we are going to optimize the DAX code, it is important to have accurate performance metrics to have a conclusive answer. Therefore, we must clear the cache before recording any performance metrics.

You can clear the cache by going to **File** > **Options and Settings** > **Options**.

Then, it will open the **Options** window, where you can perform various configurations. In the tabs section, the first tab is for data loading configurations. If it is already selected, you will see a section called **Data Cache Management Options**. Here, you can click the **Clear Cache** button and free up the cache.

You can see the **Options** window in *figure 17.1*:

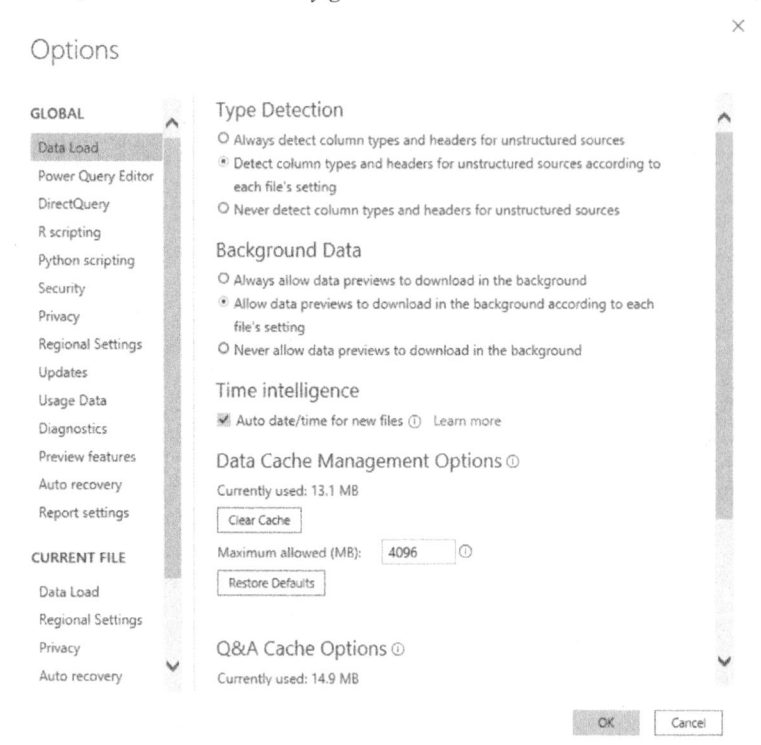

Figure 17.1: Clear cache in Power BI desktop

Measure the performance

There are various techniques we can use to measure the DAX code execution performance. Some of these are already discussed in the previous chapters. However, let us recall them:

- **Performance analyzer**: Power BI desktop has a built-in tool to measure the DAX and visual rendering performance. Here, you can get the DAX query also the duration for query execution in **ms**:

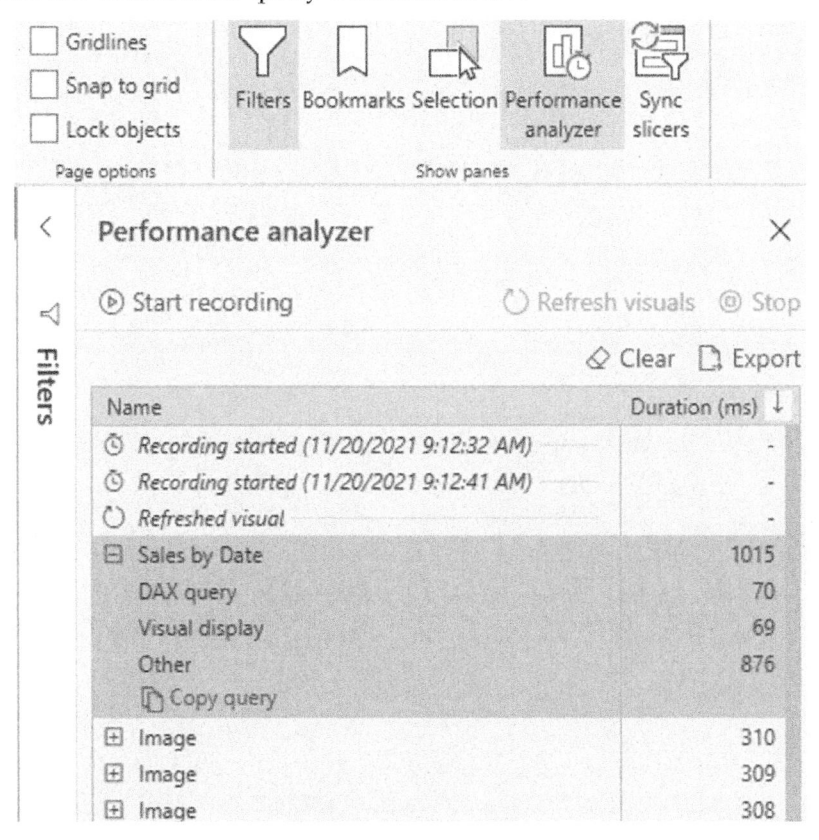

Figure 17.2: Performance analyzer

You can see in this `Performance analyzer` panel each visual has detailed duration time-lapse information. If the visual type is a dynamic (not static one like shape or image), you can find loading time for DAX query execution;

the visual rendering time information also copies query option to extract underneath DAX query. A sample of such query is shown in *figure 17.3*:

```
// DAX Query
EVALUATE
  TOPN(
    502,
    SUMMARIZECOLUMNS(
      ROLLUPADDISSUBTOTAL(
        ROLLUPGROUP('DimClient'[ClientName], 'DimVehicle'[Make], 'DimVehicle'[Model]), "IsGrandTotalRowTotal"
      ),
      "TotalDiscountedSale", 'FactSales'[TotalDiscountedSale],
      "SumSalePrice", CALCULATE(SUM('FactSales'[SalePrice])),
      "SumTotalDiscount", CALCULATE(SUM('FactSales'[TotalDiscount]))
    ),
    [IsGrandTotalRowTotal],
    0,
    'DimClient'[ClientName],
    1,
    'DimVehicle'[Make],
    1,
    'DimVehicle'[Model],
    1
  )
ORDER BY
```

Figure 17.3: Sample extracted query from performance analyzer

- **DAX Studio**: DAX Studio is a free and open-source project you can download and install like an external tool. DAX Studio is a tool you can measure query performance, also very beneficial to write efficient DAX code:

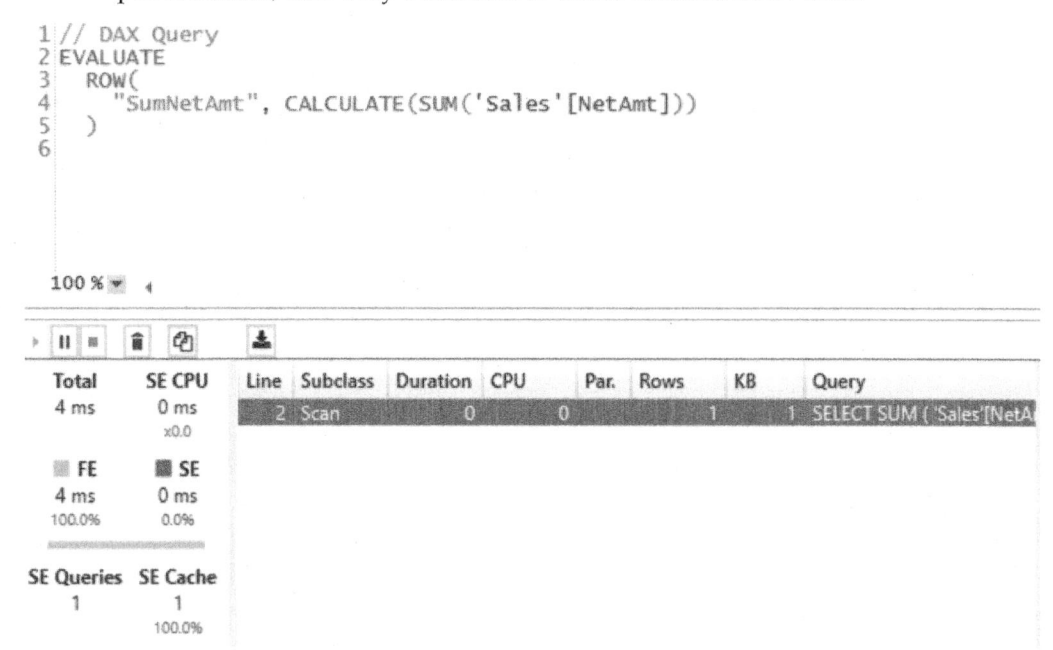

```
1 // DAX Query
2 EVALUATE
3   ROW(
4     "SumNetAmt", CALCULATE(SUM('Sales'[NetAmt]))
5   )
6
```

Total	SE CPU	Line	Subclass	Duration	CPU	Par.	Rows	KB	Query
4 ms	0 ms x0.0	2	Scan	0	0		1	1	SELECT SUM('Sales'[NetA

FE	SE
4 ms	0 ms
100.0%	0.0%

SE Queries	SE Cache
1	1
	100.0%

Figure 17.4: DAX Studio server timing statistics

Optimize DAX syntax

In computer programming, we always discuss methods to write code efficiently. Some of them apply in the DAX world as well. Let us discuss some practices you can follow to improve the readability of your DAX code:

- **Add column reference in your calculations**: When writing calculated measures and columns, always try to add column reference to improve the readability. This helps other developers and users to get a better understanding:

    Sales Gross Profit := Sales[Sales Amount] - Sales[Cost]

- **Use of DISTINCT( ) and VALUES( ) functions when possible**: Power BI by default adds blank values to column results when the referential integrity violation occurs. **DISTINCT ( )** does not return blank values due to integrity violations but **VALUES ( )** function does. So, use them wisely in your code.

- **Format your DAX code**: It is always a good practice to format your DAX code, which helps to improve readability. There will be more tools to format your code. A popular tool is DAX formatter:

    https://www.daxformatter.com/

Figure 17.5: DAX formatter

You can see the DAX formatter Web application preview in *figure 17.5*. It is a self-explanatory and easy-to-use tool. You just have to paste your DAX code in the DAX formatter area and click the **FORMAT** button. All the advanced settings you can see in *figure 17.6* which is as follows:

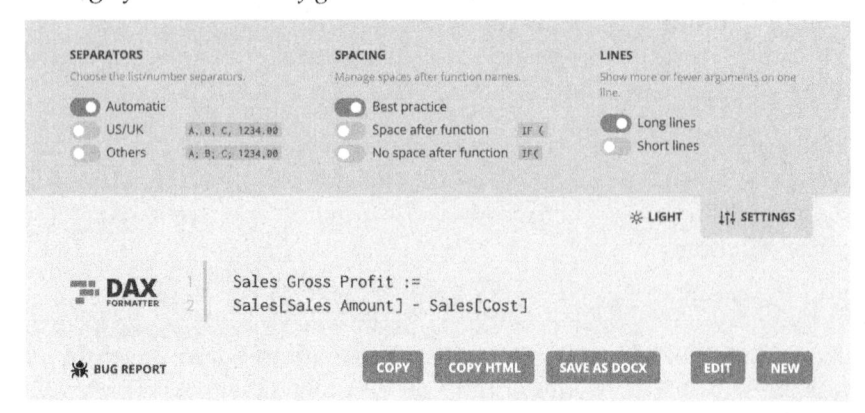

Figure 17.6: DAX formatter advanced configurations

- **Use variables where it is possible**: Variables can help to reduce the code complexity, especially when you have very complex business logic to be implemented. Using variables extensively helps to reduce the complexity and improve the readability:

```
Calendar =
VAR DateStart =
    DATE ( 2000, 1, 1 ) -- Calendar Start Date. Change this as per your requirement.
VAR DateEnd =
    DATE ( 2050, 12, 31 ) -- Calendar End Date.
VAR CalTab =
    ADDCOLUMNS (
        CALENDAR ( DateStart, DateEnd ),
        "DateKey", FORMAT ( [Date], "YYYYMMDD" ),
        "Year", YEAR ( [Date] ),
        "MonthNumber", FORMAT ( [Date], "MM" ),
        "YearMonthNumber", FORMAT ( [Date], "YYYY-MM" ),
        "YearMonthShort", FORMAT ( [Date], "YYYY-mmm" ),
        "MonthNameShort", FORMAT ( [Date], "mmm" ),
        "MonthName", FORMAT ( [Date], "mmmm" ),
        "IsWeekDay", IF ( WEEKDAY ( [Date] ) = 7, "No", IF ( WEEKDAY ( [Date] ) = 1, "No", "Yes" ) ),
        "DayOfWeekNumber", WEEKDAY ( [Date] ),
        "DayOfWeek", FORMAT ( [Date], "dddd" ),
        "DayOfWeekShort", FORMAT ( [Date], "ddd" ),
        "Quarter", "Q" & FORMAT ( [Date], "Q" ),
        "YearQuarter", FORMAT ( [Date], "YYYY" ) & "-Q"
            & FORMAT ( [Date], "Q" )
    )
RETURN
    CalTab
```

Figure 17.7: Variable usage in DAX

You can see the usage of variables in *figure 17.7*. This is a sample code we have used to create a calendar dimension table. Here, two variables are used for the start date and end date to configure.

- **Use calculated measures wisely**: Sometimes, it is a debate when to use calculated columns and measures. It is always recommended to use calculated measures wherever possible.

DAX functions optimization

Apart from optimizing the DAX syntax, we can optimize the DAX functions. Here is the list of best practices of DAX function usage in different use cases:

- Use **SELECTEDVALUE( )** instead of **HASONEVALUE( )**: Sometimes, we are using the **HASONEVALUE( )** function to check whether only one value appears in a column after applying slicers and filters. Along with that, you also have to use the **VALUES( )** function to retrieve the single value. However, if you are using **SELECTEDVALUE( )** instead of that, this function does the job. It internally calls the **VALUES ( )** function, returns a single value, and returns blank if there multiple values for given criteria.

- Use **DIVIDE( ) function instead of '/'**: It is very common you get divided by zero exception in programming. Things are the same in the DAX world also. If you use just to divide two numbers there is a chance your report will get such an exception. As a remedy, you can use the **DIVIDE ( )** function to do the work. It performs an internal check whether the denominator is zero. If the denominator is zero, then it returns the value you specified as the third parameter.

- **Try to use COUNTROWS( )**: When you need to perform **COUNT( )** to get the count of any particular column; a better option would be to use **COUNTROWS( )** instead. Because even though both functions give the same result, **COUNTROWS( )** additionally has more benefits. It works well in terms of performance and is more efficient. Also, it does not consider blank values. So, rather than checking cells, it returns the results much faster.

- Use **ALL( )** instead of **ALLEXCEPT( )**: **ALLEXCEPT( )** and **ALL ( )** functions behave similar manner, **VALUES( )** as long as the exempted columns are columns on the pivot. When it comes to **ALLEXCEPT( )**, which does not include preserver pilot context on columns that are not on the pivot. Therefore, use **ALL( )** instead of **ALLEXCEPT( )** whenever using **VALUES( )**.

Conclusion

In this chapter, we discussed actions we can take to write efficient DAX code. It is important to write optimized code in order to perform well, even the data growth over the period of time. First, we discussed some basics and how to record a performance using built-in and third-party tools. Then slowly, we moved to write DAX and later discussed some best practices when choosing DAX functions. In the upcoming chapter, we will discuss how to collaborate Power BI reports.

Questions

1. Do more research and list more DAX optimization techniques.
2. Mention two reasons to use calculated measures over calculated columns.

CHAPTER 18
Collaborating Your Power BI Workload

This chapter is solely dedicated to discussing sharing options in the Power BI. There are many options introduced. Some features look similar, but definitely, they are for a different purpose. This chapter starts with different ways of sharing content in Power BI and explains details of why they are important to know and their purpose.

Structure

The following topics will be covered during this chapter:

- Power BI workspace 101
- Creating a workspace
- Data gateway configurations
- Sharing Power BI content
- Sharing dashboards
- Power BI app

Objective

The objective of this chapter is to teach you how to understand the business requirement, what sort of questions to pick in order to answer through visuals, and how to transform the data model into insightful visuals using data visualization techniques. Then you can deliver the right information in the right manner.

Power BI Workspace 101

Workspaces are compartments that we can find in the Power BI service where we can store Power BI content and collaborate with colleagues. What special in the workspaces are this can be used to share the content with specific users. This is a good way of managing security. You can see the Power BI workspace button highlighted in *figure 18.1*:

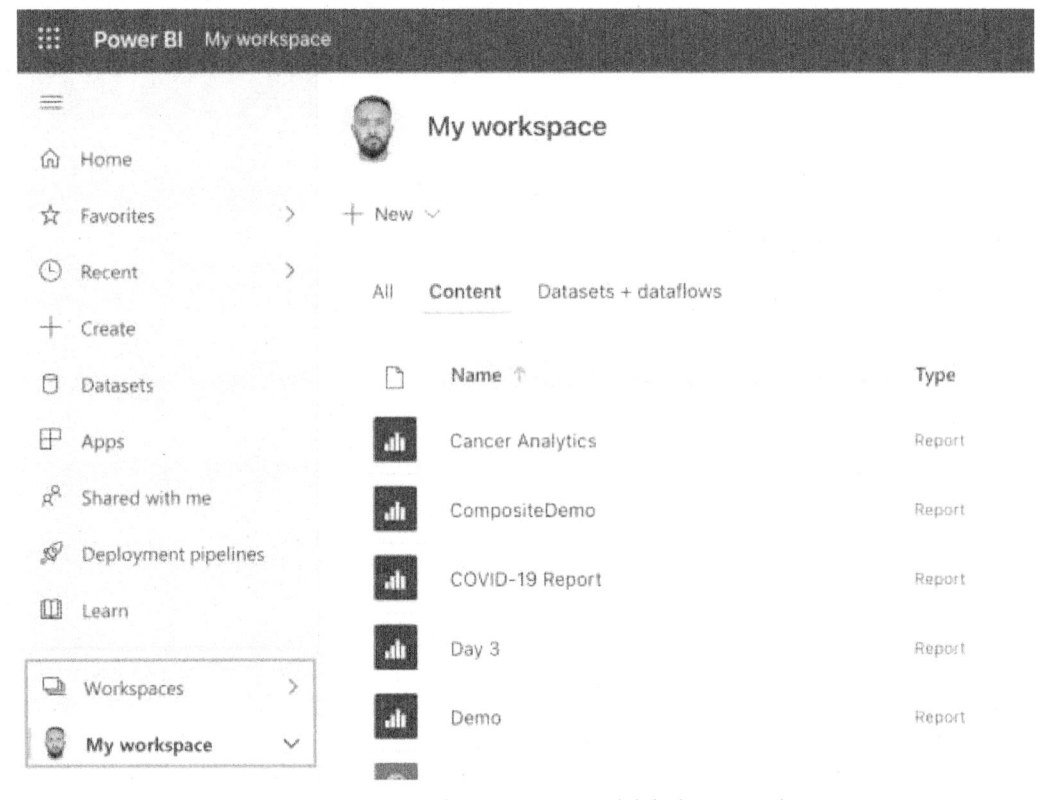

Figure 18.1: In the Workspaces section and default, My workspace

In order to browse the workspaces, you must log in to the Power BI service through the https://powerbi.microsoft.com/en-us/ URL. Then you can see the *sidebar menu* at the left-hand corner, where there is a list of items, which are starting from **Home**. You will find the **Workspaces** menu item, which has an arrowhead. Also, at the same time, the default workspace you were working in is the **My workspace**, which is common for any Power BI user. This is the workspace you can publish and consume the content privately.

> The My workspace is your default workspace, and there is no way of sharing the content with other users in the organization. This is the dedicated workspace for you to maintain the content privately. However, you can publish a Power BI report and share it to the public Web or a site. Your workspace is only visible to you and not for any other user in your organization, and in terms of visibility, this work vice versa too.

Creating a workspace

You can create a new workspace by clicking *ellipse* button in the **Workspaces** menu and then click on the **Create a workspace** button in order to open the new **Create a workspace** window:

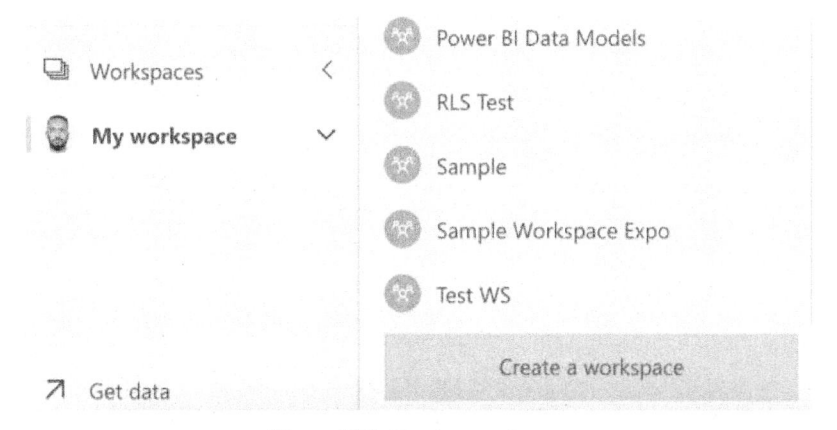

Figure 18.2: Create a workspace

The process of creating a workspace is pretty straightforward. You have to give a name for the workspace, which does not exist currently in your tenant. Then, you can provide some description as well, which helps other users to get a summary of what kind of content comprises the workspace. You can upload a photo as well:

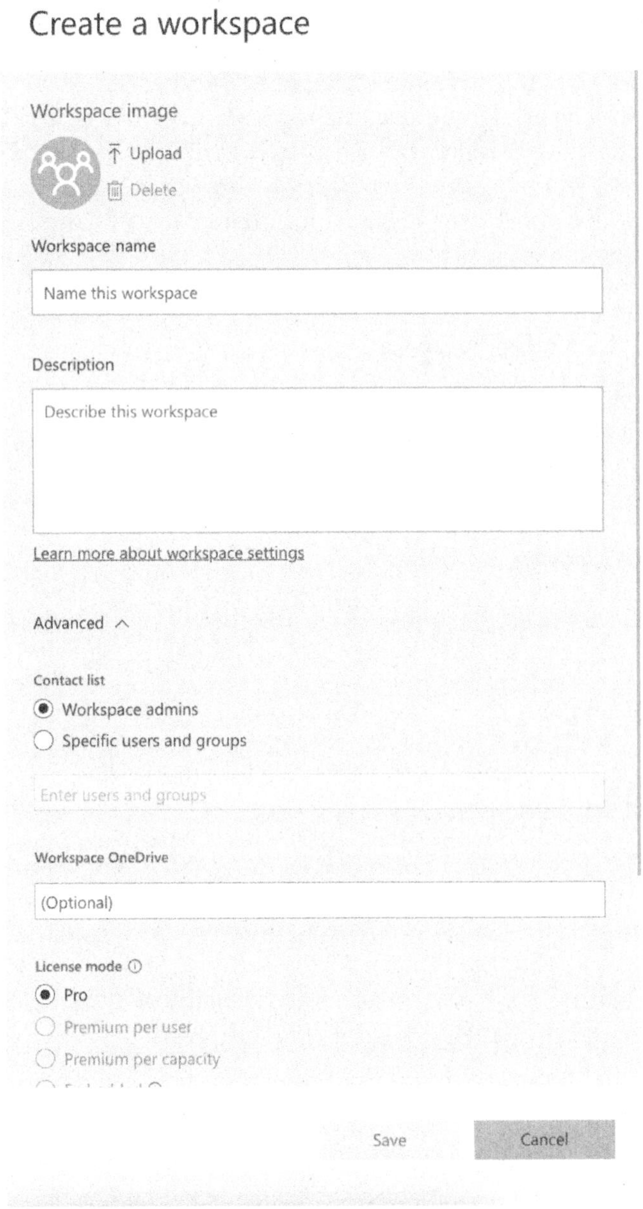

Figure 18.3: Create workspace window

In the **Advanced** section, you have an option to configure the contact list. This is where you can grant access to other users. You can configure them later as well after you created them.

Once you hit the **Save** button, the page will redirect to your workspace:

Figure 18.4: Inside the workspace

Overview of the Power BI service you can see in *figure 18.4*. Each item is explained as follows:

1. **Create a pipeline**: This option allows you to create a deployment pipeline. This feature is only available for the workspaces assigned to a premium capacity.

2. **View**: This is the viewing experience for the Power BI workspace content. By default, you can view the content as a list. However, you can change it to lineage:

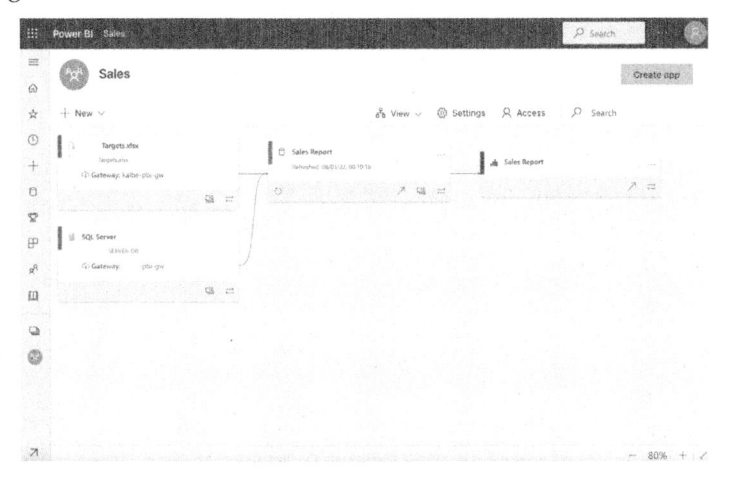

Figure 18.5: Power BI content view

3. **Settings**: This option opens the settings to manage the workspace.
4. **Access**: When you need to add users to the workspace, you have to click the **Access** option. You can add individual members or a group in the organization:

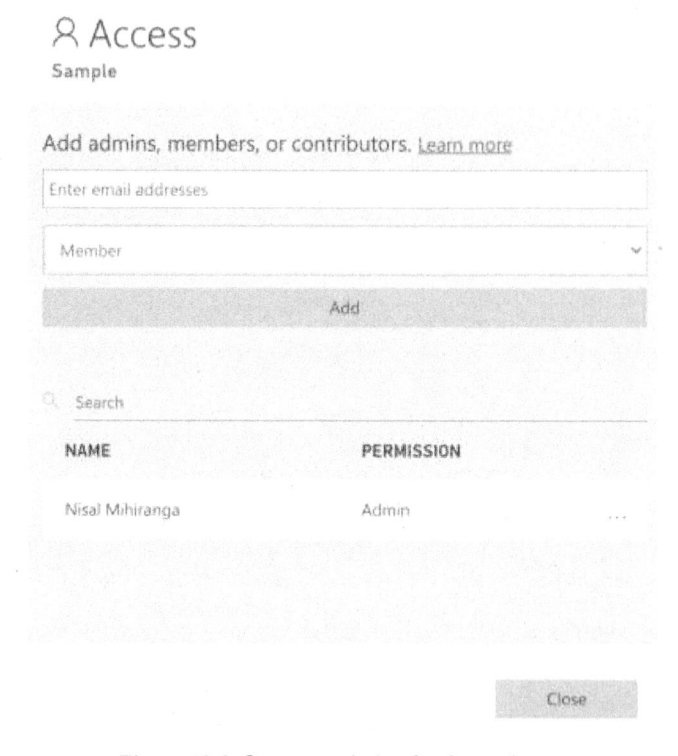

Figure 18.6: Grant permission for the workspace

There are four main roles in the workspace.

- **Viewer**: The users with this role have read-only access to the Power BI content. This means they can interact with the visuals but not change the visuals and modify the reports.
- **Contributor**: This role can access and interact with reports and dashboards. Additionally, you can create, edit, copy, and delete items in a workspace.
- **Member**: The users with member roles have the privilege to do all the preceding tasks. In addition to that, you can publish reports, schedule refresh modifies data gateways, and so on.
- **Admin**: Owner and individuals who have admin permission. The user with the admin role can perform all the preceding tasks and add/remove users, including other admins.

5. **Create app**: An app is another content type you can find in the Power BI, which combines related dashboards and reports into one single place.

6. **Add content**: Because you do not have any content in your Power BI workspace, you will see this, but once you click here, you can see the default view, where you can get organizational content and the option to connect with the app service.

Data gateway configurations

Power BI Data Gateway is an important tool you must configure when you deploy your Power BI content into the Power BI service. It helps to make the connection between the Power BI service and your on-premises node and keep your Power BI content up-to-date (which can be your personal computer or a database server). In this section, we will not explain you how to configure the on-premises data gateway in your computer because it is pretty straightforward.

The person who installs and configures the data gateway is already an administrator who manages the data gateway:

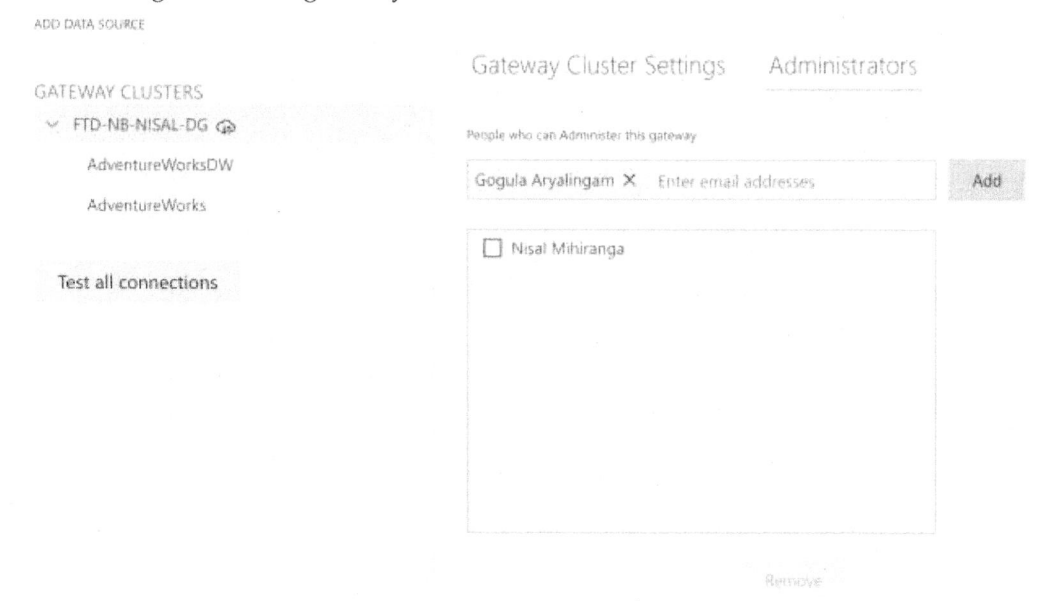

Figure 18.7: Add administrator for the gateway

As the gateway administrator, you can add more users who you think can perform the role of administrator. Then, they are able to manage the gateway. This is a vital role, and you have to consciously decide when you add more users as administrators. Because this is some similar role as **SQL Server database administrator,** which has the authority to add new sources to the gateway and remove it if necessary. More importantly, the information sources that are not supposed to expose to the cloud must not be added to the gateway as a source.

Sharing Power BI content

As mentioned previously, there are multiple ways of sharing the content with organizational users and external users in the Power BI.

Public Web

If you have a public data source, you created an analysis atop of that, which will be an ideal candidate for sharing the report on the public Web. In order to do that, you have to open the Power BI report, then click the **Share** icon at the *top menu bar*, then select **Embed report**:

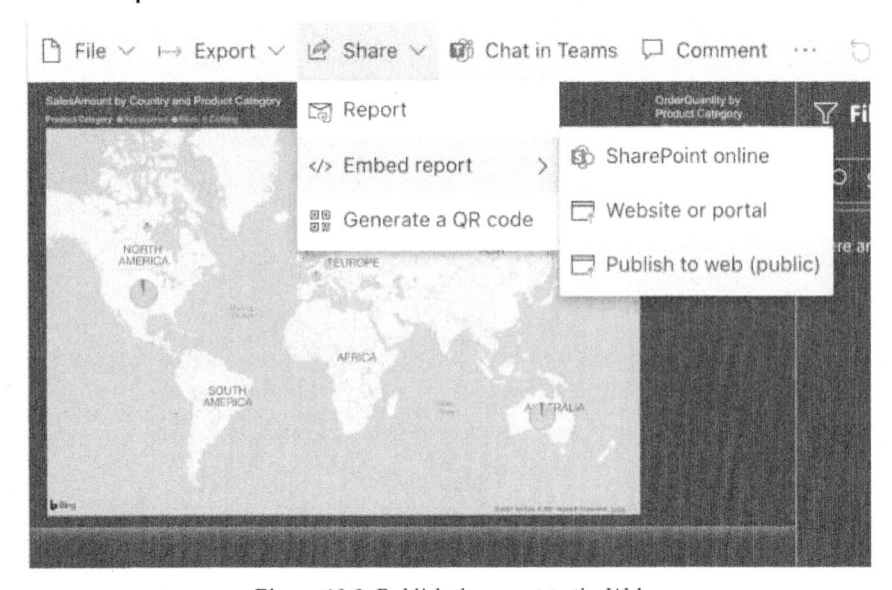

Figure 18.8: Publish the report to the Web

Once you click the `Generate embed code` button, you will get the public URL and an embed code where you can embed to an HTML page. You can set the resolution as well:

Figure 18.9: Embed the report window

Share with a website or portal

You can embed your Power BI report into a website or a portal. Then, you will get a secure URL and embed code which you can put into an iframe.

> When you share your Power BI report into a website or portal, a few things you have to keep in mind. The row-level security you have already been applied with work here without additional configurations. Because the RLS evaluation is based on the AAD account, you log in. RLS always works only if you make the users as viewers.

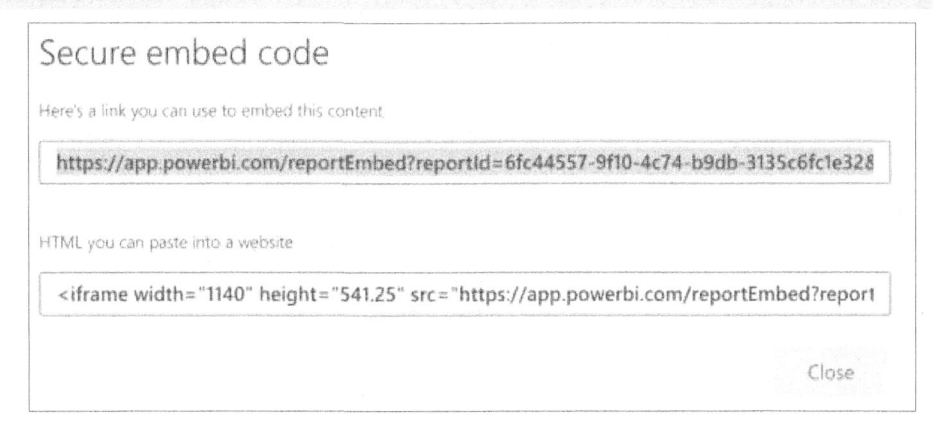

Figure 18.10: Secure embed option for portal or Web

Share dashboards

Another way of sharing content is sharing the dashboards with specific users. By now, you know how to create a dashboard using existing reports or multiple reports. Once you open your dashboard, you can share it with other colleagues by clicking the **Share** button.

It opens a new window with the **Share dashboard** option. You can type names or email addresses of the users in the organization to grant access. In the **Access** tab, you can see the list of users who can access to the dashboard:

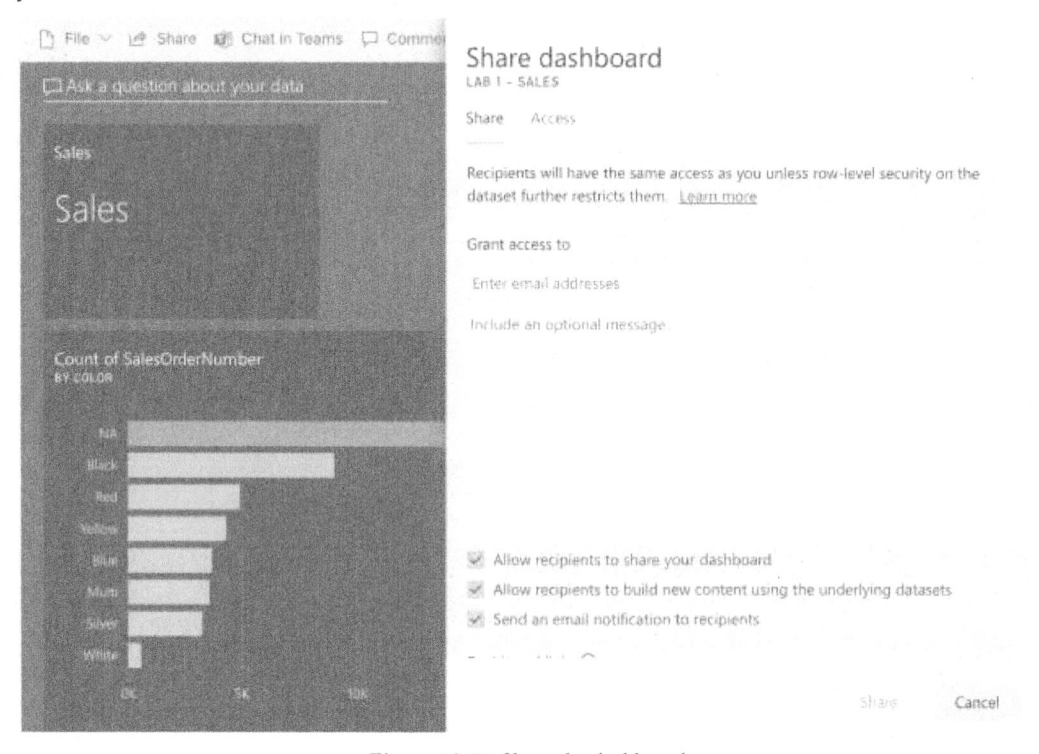

Figure 18.11: Share the dashboard

Power BI app

Power BI app is another content type similar to the workspace, yet this can be found inside the workspace. The app is a smart way of presenting the Power BI reports and dashboards bundled together and shared for viewing. Depending on the privilege, you can create an app. In order to create an app, just go inside the workspace and click the **Create app** button.

The creating process is somewhat similar to the process of creating a workspace. You must give a name for your app and other information:

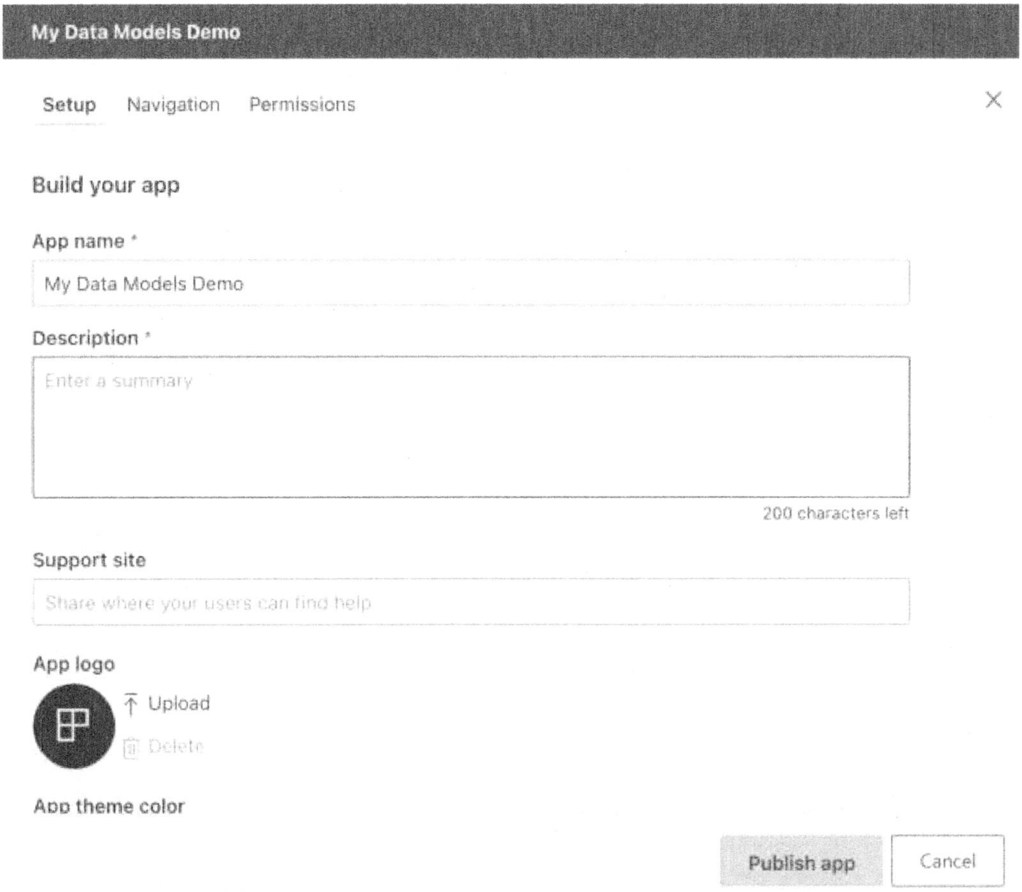

Figure 18.12: Publish an app option

You also can configure a logo for the app and color theme for branding purposes. The next tab is for configuring the navigation experience. You can allow the user to navigate through the pages or else just hide the navigations.

> You can hide the navigation by clicking the `Hide from navigation` option in the `Navigation`
>
> tab. This allows you to improve the user experience by having a custom menu or buttons to navigate through different pages in the report.

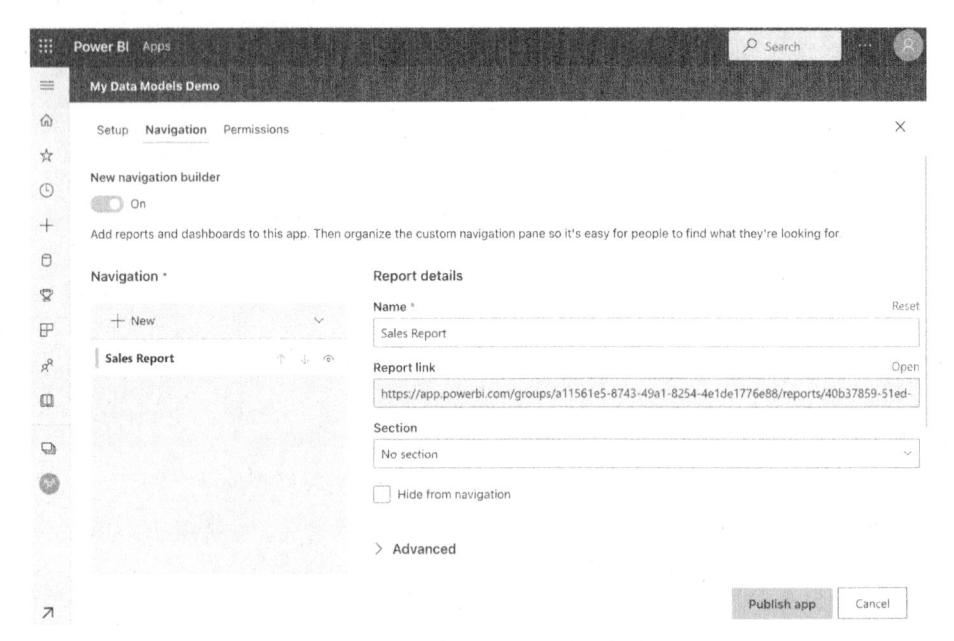

Figure 18.13: Configure navigations in the app

You can add users, either individual users or groups who can access the app after you publish. This can be configured in the **Permissions** tab:

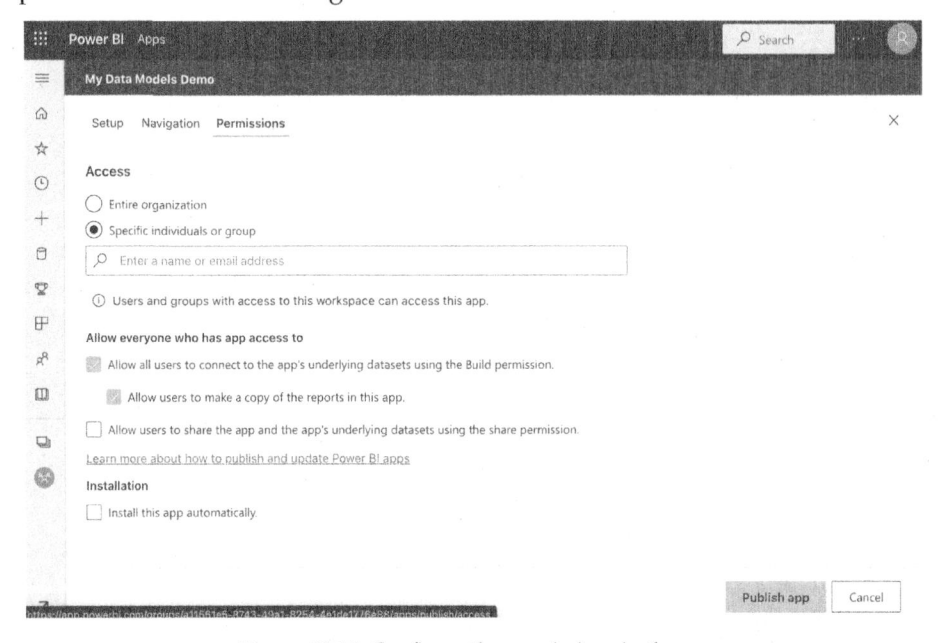

Figure 18.14: Configure the permissions in the app

The app is a great way of collaborating your Power BI content with a large audience.

Conclusion

In this chapter, we discussed about different ways of sharing content with users both within the organization and the public. We started with workspace, and then we went a bit deeper and discussed why it is important to know how to configure and manage the Power BI data gateway. Finally, we discussed how we can create an app and share it with the users. In the upcoming chapter, we will be more focused on performance optimization in storage and memory.

Questions

1. Discuss the different types of methods you can follow to share the content in Power BI.

2. Define the use cases for each sharing option and why it is chosen as opposed to other options to share the content.

CHAPTER 19
Performance Tuning via Optimizing Storage and Memory

Performance is one of the key pillars to the success of any IT solution. This is the same for data analytics and BI solutions. The data models, reports, and dashboards we developed will access by *100+*, even *1000+* users concurrently. This chapter will let you learn several tasks we can perform in order to gain the best performance in the scalable models.

Structure

The following topics will be covered during this chapter:

- Introducing to VertiPaq engine
- Filter only required data for analysis
- Applying correct data types
- Creating custom columns in Power Query
- Using sub-set of data
- Disabling the Power Query load
- Limiting distinct columns as much as possible

Objective

The objective of this chapter is to teach you the concept of incremental refresh and how to implement it for large data sets to obtain better refresh time.

Introducing VertiPaq engine

Performance tuning is an in-depth topic and requires some basics to know about the internals of the Power BI engine. This engine is coded as **VertiPaq,** the same processing engine behind Excel Power pivot and analysis services. This is a very powerful analytics engine, and it does process in-memory.

The internal layout of the Power BI database engine you can see in *figure 19.1*:

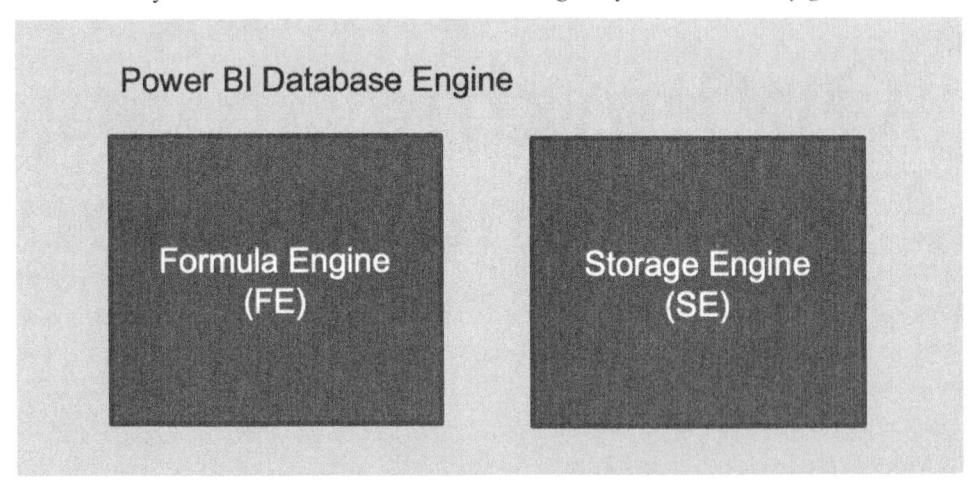

Figure 19.1: Power BI database engine internal structure

The contribution of each engine is specified as follows:

- **Formula engine**: Formula engine rather than calculation engine is responsible for understanding the DAX queries generated by visuals and handling complex expressions.
- **Storage engine**: The storage engine is responsible for handling simple expressions and executing queries against the database.

Though we called the Power BI database engine as VertiPaq engine, you can see in the preceding diagram there are two engines literary for storage and calculation. This database engine is quite different than traditional relational databases.

Let us see the storage and memory optimization tips in the next few sections of the chapter:

Performance Tuning via Optimizing Storage and Memory — 281

Ex: Customer Table

ID	Name	Address	City	State	Amount
1	Jack	....	....	...	3,500
2	Rob	....	....	....	1,000
3	Jane	....	....	....	300
4	Rob	....	....	....	90
5	Dave	....	....	....	2,100
6	Jack	....	....	....	0
7	Dave	....	....	....	1,020
8	Ann	....	....	....	60
9	Rob	....	....	....	1,400

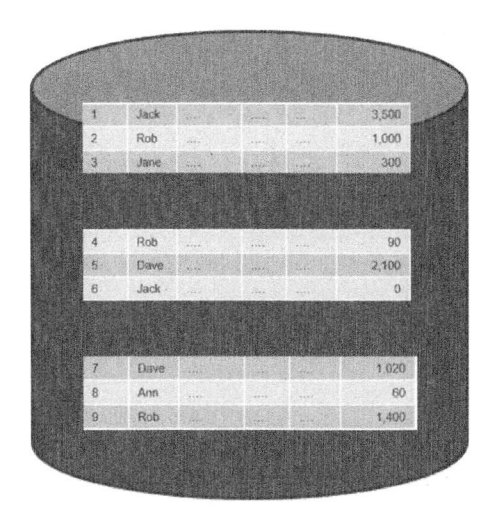

Figure 19.2: Traditional row store database structure

Traditional relational data storage systems store data in row format. In the preceding diagram, it shows how the data is being stored. However, the Power BI database is an analytical columnar database, which means the data is stored in column format. The following diagram illustrates how is the customer table split into individual columns when stored in the database:

Ex: Customer Table

ID	Name	Address	City	State	Amount
1	Jack	....	....	...	3,500
2	Rob	....	....	....	1,000
3	Jane	....	....	....	300
4	Rob	....	...	....	90
5	Dave	....	....	....	2,100
6	Jack	....	....	....	0
7	Dave	....	....	....	1,020
8	Ann	....	....	....	60
9	Rob	....	....	....	1,400

Figure 19.3: Column store database structure

Figure 19.4: Same database technology shares with multiple products

It is important to understand the behavior of storing data in order to optimize it. Usually, each file contains one column. If required to scan, only one file needs to scan there for the less I/O operations. It is a norm; accessing sequential memory manner is faster than random access. So, the structure itself gets the benefit of it.

Single table versus star schema model

We can countlessly argue with the approach, whether we follow a single table or whether do we going with a star schema. When we are creating a star schema, we can split the categorical data into small dimension tables. And keep only numerical values in the fact or transactional tables. This way, we can reduce the storage of the data model. This is what we have already discussed in *Chapter 9, Introduction to DAX and Calculated Columns, Calculated Measures, and Hierarchies*. We can reduce the storage/memory for categorical data by storing much smaller distinct values tables: **dimensions**.

> There are encoding algorithms, run-length encoding, dictionary encoding inside the Power BI database engine, which encode the actual data and compress data into a high compression ratio. That is how the data keep inside the memory. Even the compression is only applied when the size of compressed data is smaller than the original data, which means some fact columns do not follow the same compression algorithm.

Filter only required data for analysis

Sometimes we import the entire table structure from the source. But we may not need all the columns for our analysis; for example, lineage columns and other columns which are not useful for analysis, we can drop them at the beginning of the transformation. This way, we can save a lot of storage and result in a performance-optimized solution:

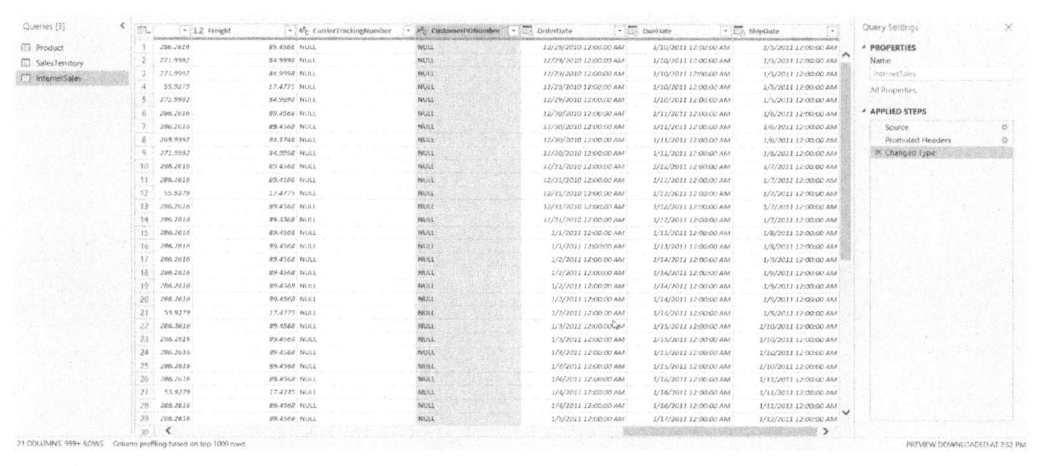

Figure 19.5: Remove unwanted columns for analysis

Applying correct data types

Sometimes you may see data times are not assigned appropriately. Especially when we load data from CSV files. Assigning correct data types also greatly helps to limit the storage taking to hold data and lead to the best performance. We often see Power BI choose **DateTime** if the source data type is also **DateTime** or without having time information. So, you can simply change the data type into a date if that is the case:

Figure 19.6: Creating custom columns using a calculated column

Creating custom columns in Power Query

We frequently create custom columns or derived columns in our Power BI data models based on the requirement. For example, have categorical values based on existing values in another column, or else, you can create a new column by formulating existing numerical columns. We can do this using the DAX formula by creating a calculated column. However, it is recommended to create such columns using Power Query or **M** language:

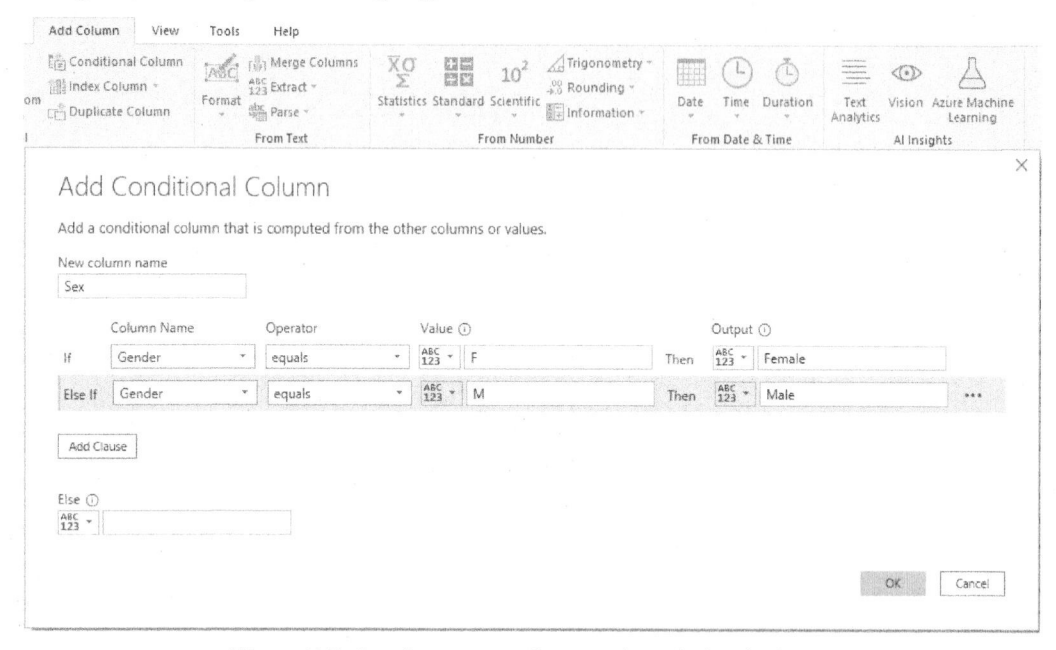

Figure 19.7: Creating custom columns using calculated columns

Using subset of data

We initially discussed about reducing the storage by removing unwanted columns that we can consider as vertical filtering. Sometimes, we just need a subset of data rather entire data set from the source. A good scenario would be to imagine you have *20 years'* worth of data at the source. However, due to the variability and some other reasons, you do not need the entire data set for your analysis. So, you can filter data only for part *10 years* or maybe *5 years'* worth of data:

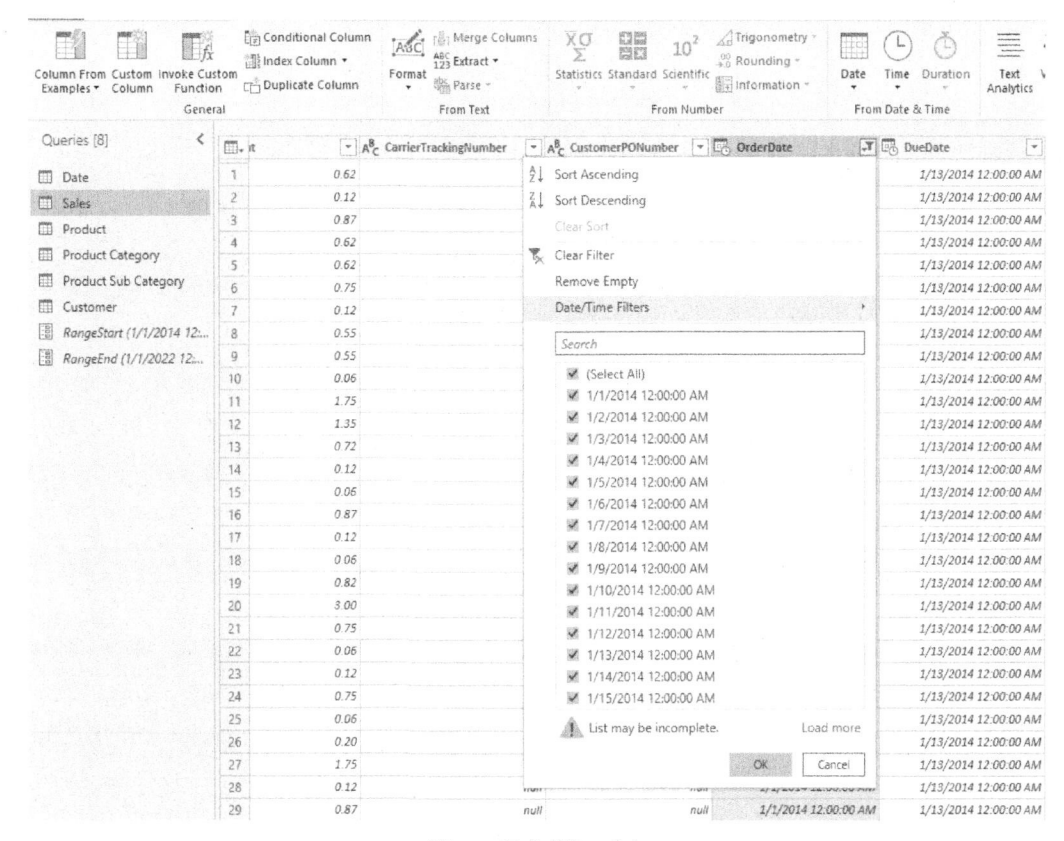

Figure 19.8: Filter data

Usually, if your data set is large, it takes considerable effort and time to process. We can always reduce the time and capacity by taking it by filtering only the wanted data for the analysis.

Disabling the Power Query load

In your data model, every table you load causes memory consumption. When we talk about Power BI performance tuning, we always try our best to reduce memory consumption. Because greater the memory consumption, the chances are high for the negative performance of the model. As a solution, we can tick the disable the load option in the Power Query. This is available for every table in the Power BI model:

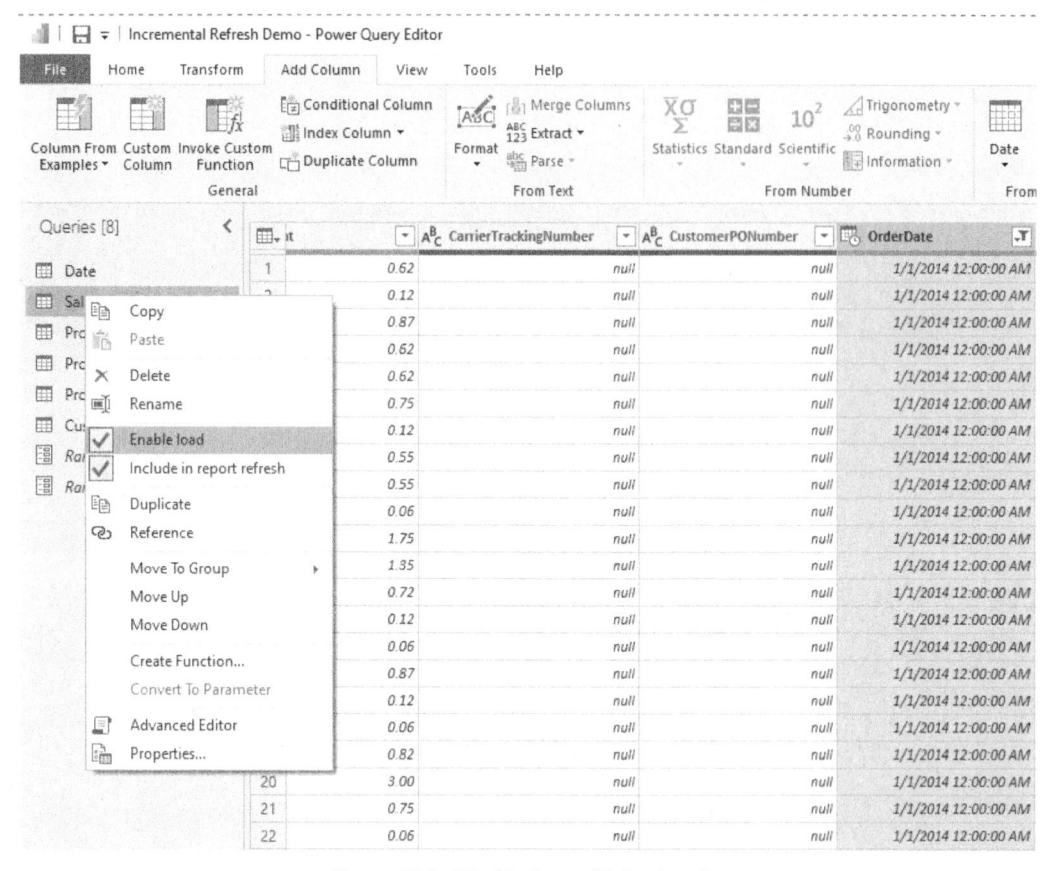

Figure 19.9: Disable the enable load option

Disabling the **Enable load** will stop loading the data into the memory. Once you disable it, you cannot see the table/query in your data model. This option helps to keep some sort of staging layer in your model. You can import data as-is from the source. Then build your model by referencing those initial tables. Disable the **Enable load** after. This method we have already discussed in detail during the data modeling chapter.

Limiting distinct columns as much as possible

If you learn more about data compression algorithms used in the Power BI engine, you will realize it performs well whenever you have.

Conclusion

In the beginning of this chapter, we discussed a little bit about the internals of the Power BI engine. Then moved to best practices and discussed many techniques like how to store data efficiently inside the Power BI, why it is important to select an appropriate data type and some advanced techniques like disabling to Power Query load option to avoid unnecessary load refresh time and compute power. We can follow to optimize the performance of data models in Power BI. Because Power BI is an in-memory database, the data model we develop is always memory concerned one. This is a vast area to follow and expertise with the experience.

Question

1. Research on run-length encoding and dictionary encoding algorithms and how to model to obtain the best performance.

Index

A
Active Directory (AD) 152
active relationship 122
advanced aggregations 226
aggregations 24, 25, 209
  advanced aggregations 226-232
  aggregated table, adding into model 218
  aggregated table usage, ensuring 219
  building 217, 218
  configuring 221
  detecting 225, 226
  managing 222-224
AI capabilities 178
AI features 255
Artificial Intelligence (AI) 177
Attendance fact table 75
Azure Analysis Services 166
Azure Data Factory 96
Azure Data Lake Storage Gen 2 244
Azure Machine Learning
  using 191
Azure Text Analytics 191

B
Big Data analytics 2
Business Intelligence (BI) 2
  characteristics 3
  fundamental components 3
  history 4
  process 4
  self-service BI 5, 6
  traditional BI approach 4, 5
bus matrix architecture 74

C
calculated columns 127

creating 127, 128
calculated engine 131
calculated measures 129-131
calculated tables 131
　creating 132
calculation groups 165
　calculated items, sorting 174
　creating, in Power BI 169-173
　limitations 174
　requirement 166, 167
　working 167, 168
calculations 126
　creating 56
Calendar hierarchy 135
Calendar table 133, 134
cardinality 117
　many to many 118
　many to one 117
　one to many 117
　one to one 117, 118
citizen ETLing 244
classic BI approach 70
　scenarios 71
collaboration 245
components, Power BI 7
composite models 232, 233
　balanced architecture, achieving with 240
connection types, Power BI 210
　connect live connection 39-41
　DirectQuery 35-39, 211
　Import 33-35, 210
connect live connection 39-41
corporate BI 72, 73
cross filtering 64

custom columns
　creating, in Power Query 284

D

data
　data sets 47
　loading, from CSV 44, 45
　loading, into Power BI 44, 45
　obtaining, with SQL Server database 83, 84
　Power query preview 46
Data Analysis Expression (DAX) 18, 126
data cleansing and blending 6, 49
dataflows
　creating, in Power BI 246-253
　importing 254
data gateway configurations 271, 272
data modeling 70, 72
data refresh requirement 196, 197
　filter, applying with parameters 201-203
　filter parameters, defining 198-201
　incremental data refresh requirement 197
　incremental refresh, configuring 198
　incremental refresh policy, defining 204-206
data tab 48
data transformation 49
　appropriate data types, assigning 50, 51
　calculations, creating 56
　column, adding 51, 52
　columns, removing 53, 54
　product hierarchy, creating 54-56
　queries, renaming 49
　values, replacing 52

data type detection 45
data visualizations
  adding 56
  best practices 138, 139
  card visuals, adding 57-60
  clustered column chart, adding 61, 62
  image, adding for branding 57
  map visual, adding 61
  matrix visual, adding 62, 63
  slicer, adding 65, 66
  text box, adding for header 56
data warehouse 73, 74
  dimension tables 75, 76
  fact tables 75
  granularities 76
  structure 74
date dimension 245
Date table 131
DAX functions optimization
  best practices 263
DAX optimization
  cache, clearing 258
  performance, measuring 259, 260
  techniques 258
DAX Studio 225, 260
DAX syntax
  optimizing 261-263
decomposition tree visual 186
  configuring 186, 187
delimiter 45
demo database 211, 212
  consuming 212-216
demo materials
  downloading 44
dimension modeling 70, 72
dimension tables 74, 75
  business key 76
  dimension attributes 76
  surrogate key 75
DirectQuery connection type 35-39
distinct columns
  limiting 286
drill down feature 64
  enabling 65
drow.io 138
dynamic row-level security
  implementing 160-163

E

end-to-end BI 72, 73
Enterprise bus matrix 5
Entity Relational modeling 112
ETL, for large data sets 255
Extract-transform-load (ETL) tools 4

F

fact table 74
  measures 75
  surrogate keys 75
file origin format 45
filter parameters
  applying 201-203
  defining 198-201
formula engine 226, 280

G

granularities 76
  snowflake schema 77, 78
  star schema 76
Graphical User Interface (GUI) 96

H

Hadoop File Systems (HDFS) 32

hierarchies
  creating 134, 135
hierarchy 54

I
Import connection type 33-35
inactive relationship 122
incremental data refresh requirement 197
incremental refresh 195
  configuring 198
incremental refresh policy
  defining 204-206
in-memory database 40

K
key influencer 187
  configuring 188, 189
Key Performance Indicators (KPIs) 3, 4

L
linked entities 255

M
Machine Learning (ML) 177
Microsoft Cortana 8
Microsoft SQL Analysis Services 34
modern self-service BI approach 72
Multidimensional database engine 73

O
Online-Analytical Processing (OLAP) databases 4
Online Transactional Processing (OLTP) systems 70
Order fact table 75

P
performance 279
performance tuning 280

Power BI 6, 7
  AI capabilities 178
  calculations 126
  components 7, 8
  cross filtering 64
  data, loading 44, 45
  drill-down feature 64
  features 9-11
  pricing 11
  Q&A visual 180
  Quick Insights feature 8
  relationships 112
Power BI app 274
  logo, configuring 275
  navigations, configuring 276
Power BI connectors 32, 33
  connection types 33
  reference link 33
Power BI content
  dashboards, sharing 274
  sharing 272
  sharing, on public Web 272
  sharing, with website or portal 273
Power BI database engine 280
  column store database structure 281, 282
  correct data types, applying 283
  required data filtering, for analysis 282
  single table, versus star schema model 282
  traditional relational data storage 281
Power BI dataflow 96, 244
Power BI Data Gateway 271
Power BI desktop 7, 14, 15
  data tab 23, 24
  features 16, 17

Index   293

Get Data button 32
help tab 21, 22
home tab menu items 17, 18
modeling tab 20
model tab 24
model view tab 25
start-up screen 15, 16
view tab 18, 19
Visualizations section 16
Power BI ecosystem 13, 14
  holistic view 14
  Power BI desktop 14
  Power BI mobile 14
  Power BI service 14
Power BI mobile 7, 27
  dashboard sample 28
  menu 28, 29
Power BI performance analyzer 219
  enabling 219, 220
Power BI Premium 11
Power BI Pro license 11
Power BI service 7, 25
  preview 26, 27
  URL 25
Power BI with Excel 8
Power BI Workspace 101 266, 267
Powerful Power Query language 73
PowerPivot 8
Power Query 8, 49, 96
  budget data, working with 106-108
  business scenario 96
  database, connecting 97
  data cleansing 97-106
  tables, extracting 97
Power Query load
  disabling 285, 286

PowerView 8
precedence
  configuring 239, 240
product hierarchy
  creating 54, 55, 56
Project Crescent 8
Proof of Concept (PoC) 36

Q

Q&A visual
  in Power BI 180
  in Power BI desktop 181-185
query folding 197
Quick Insights 8, 178-180

R

R and Python integration 191-193
relational database connectors 82, 83
relationships, Power BI 112
  active relationship 122
  cardinality, selecting 117, 118
  cross filter direction, selecting 119-121
  demystifying 116
  drag and drop from UI 113, 114
  inactive relationship 122
  manage relationships, using 115, 116
  methods, for creating 113
report
  cross-filtering 142
  designing 139
  drill-down visuals 143, 144
  drill-through visuals 145-147
  filters, using 140
  mobile layout 149
  publishing, into Power BI service 66, 67
  slicers, using 141

theming 148, 149
Reporting Services 4
roles, workspace
　admin 270
　contributor 270
　member 270
　viewer 270
row-level security
　dynamic row-level security 160
　static row-level security 152
　testing 156-159

S

security
　overview 152
self-service BI 5, 6
self-service data preparation 245
service period 127
smart narrative
　configuring 190
snowflake structure 24
source data analysis 74
SQL Server Analysis Services Tabular database 40
SQL Server database
　data, obtaining 83
　include relationship columns 86-90
　navigating, with full hierarchy 90
　SQL Server failover support 91-93
SQL Server database settings
　advanced options 84, 85
　configuring 83, 84
SQL Server Integration services 73
SSAS database 39
SSAS Tabular data model 40
star schema structure 24
static row-level security

role-based 152-154
roles, creating 154-156
storage engine 226, 280
storage mode
　configuring 234-238
subset of data
　using 284, 285

T

tabular 126
Tabular database engine 73
Tabular Editor 169
text analytics
　performing 191
traditional report development approach
　calculations, creating 71
　data loading 70
　visuals, creating 71
T-SQL (Transact SQL) 85

V

Vertipaq 34, 39
VertiPaq engine 280
vision
　using 191
Visual Studio 169

W

workspace
　creating 267-269
　roles 270